CRITICAL THEORIES FOR SCHOOL PSYCHOLOGY AND COUNSELING

Critical Theories for School Psychology and Counseling introduces school psychologists and counselors to five critical theories that inform more equitable, inclusive work with marginalized and underserved student populations. Offering accessible conceptualizations of each theory and explicit links to application in practice and supervision, the book speaks to common professional functions and issues such as cognitive assessment, school-based counseling, discipline disproportionality, and more. This innovative collection offers graduate students, university faculty, and practicum and internship supervisors an insightful new direction for serving learners across diverse identities, cultures, and abilities.

Sherrie L. Proctor is Professor in the School Psychology Program at Queens College, City University of New York, USA.

David P. Rivera is Associate Professor in the Counselor Education Program at Queens College, City University of New York, USA.

Consultation, Supervision, and Professional Learning in School Psychology

Series Editor: Daniel S. Newman

Supervision in School Psychology: The Developmental, Ecological, Problem-solving Model
Dennis J. Simon and Mark E. Swerdlik

The School Psychology Supervisor's Toolkit
Meaghan C. Guiney

Technology Applications in School Psychology Consultation, Supervision, and Training
Edited by Aaron J. Fischer, Tai A. Collins, Evan H. Dart, and Keith C. Radley

Problem-solving Parent Conferences in Schools: Ecological-Behavioral Perspectives
Dennis J. Simon

School-Based Consultation and Students with Autism Spectrum Disorder
Elizabeth L. W. McKenney

Handbook of University and Professional Careers in School Psychology
Edited by Randy G. Floyd and Tanya L. Eckert

Critical Theories for School Psychology and Counseling: A Foundation for Equity and Inclusion in School-Based Practice
Edited by Sherrie L. Proctor and David P. Rivera

CRITICAL THEORIES FOR SCHOOL PSYCHOLOGY AND COUNSELING

A Foundation for Equity and Inclusion in School-Based Practice

Edited by Sherrie L. Proctor and David P. Rivera

NEW YORK AND LONDON

First published 2022
by Routledge
605 Third Avenue, New York, NY 10158

and by Routledge
2 Park Square, Milton Park, Abingdon, Oxon, OX14 4RN

Routledge is an imprint of the Taylor & Francis Group, an informa business

Library of Congress Cataloging-in-Publication Data
Names: Proctor, Sherrie L., editor. | Rivera, David P., editor.
Title: Critical theories for school psychology and counseling : a foundation for equity and inclusion in school-based practice / edited by Sherrie L. Proctor and David P. Rivera.
Description: 1st Edition. | New York : Routledge, 2022. | Series: Consultation, Supervision, and Professional Learning in School Psychology Series | Includes bibliographical references and index.
Identifiers: LCCN 2021024218 (print) | LCCN 2021024219 (ebook) | ISBN 9780367405649 (Hardback) | ISBN 9780367415778 (Paperback) | ISBN 9780367815325 (eBook)
Subjects: LCSH: School psychology—Study and teaching. | Educational counseling—Study and teaching. | School psychologists—Training of.
Classification: LCC LB3013.6 .C75 2022 (print) | LCC LB3013.6 (ebook) | DDC 370.15—dc23
LC record available at https://lccn.loc.gov/2021024218
LC ebook record available at https://lccn.loc.gov/2021024219

ISBN: 978-0-367-40564-9 (hbk)
ISBN: 978-0-367-41577-8 (pbk)
ISBN: 978-0-367-81532-5 (ebk)

DOI: 10.4324/9780367815325

Typeset in Bembo
by Apex CoVantage, LLC

This book is dedicated to the three people in my life who are always there for me—Robert Brown, Bria Brown, and Brendan Brown. I am blessed to have you three in my life and also in my corner.
~ Sherrie L. Proctor

This book is dedicated to all the young people in my life who serve as my sources of inspiration, especially Kiera, Luka, and Mila.
~ David P. Rivera

CONTENTS

SECTION 2
Theory to Practice **81**

SECTION 3
Theory to Supervision **159**

ABOUT THE EDITORS

Sherrie L. Proctor, Ph.D. is a professor of school psychology at Queens College, City University of New York (CUNY). She received her doctorate in school psychology from Georgia State University. She also holds degrees in school psychology from the University of South Florida. Prior to becoming a graduate educator, she was a school psychologist in the School District of Philadelphia and in Atlanta Public Schools. Her research is grounded in social justice and critical perspectives and explores issues related to Black students in K-12 and higher education. This work ranges from examining issues of marginalization for Black graduate students in school psychology programs to exploring how school psychologists serve Black children and youth who are exposed to police violence in their communities. She is a past Chair of the National Association of School Psychologists' Social Justice Committee, a 2021 recipient of the American Psychological Association's Division 16 Outstanding Commitment to Anti-Racism Award, a Co-Editor of *Best Practices in School Psychology-7th Edition*, and a member of the Society for the Study of School Psychology.

David P. Rivera, Ph.D. is an associate professor of counselor education at Queens College, City University of New York (CUNY) and founding director of CUNY's LGBTQI+ Student Leadership Program. He received his doctorate in counseling psychology from Teachers College, Columbia University. He also holds degrees in psychology and counseling from Johns Hopkins University and the University of Wyoming. His professional experience includes college counseling, higher education administration, and consultations on diversity, equity, and inclusion. Dr. Rivera has worked at a variety of institutions, including the University of Pennsylvania, Georgetown University, Prince George's Community College, and the Jack Kent Cooke Foundation. His research is guided by critical theories and social justice frameworks, and it explores cultural competency development and issues impacting the marginalization and well-being of people of color and oppressed sexual orientation and gender identity groups, with a focus on microaggressions. He has published journal articles and book chapters in various areas of multicultural psychology and social justice, and his co-edited book, *Microaggression Theory: Influence and Implications*, was released 2019. Dr. Rivera is adviser to The Steve Fund, faculty with the Council for Opportunity in Education, and holds leadership roles in the American Psychological Association. He has received multiple recognitions for his work from the American Psychological Association, the American College Counseling Association, and the American College Personnel Association.

ABOUT THE CONTRIBUTORS

Lisa Aguilar, Ph.D. is an assistant professor at Indiana University.

Jessica Mercado Anazagasty, M.A. is a doctoral student at the University of California, Riverside.

Colleen Boucher is a doctoral student in the School of Education and Human Development at the University of Colorado Denver.

Jeffrey M. Brown, Ph.D. is an assistant professor at San Diego State University.

Robert A. Brown, J.D. is an adjunct professor at Morehouse College.

Amy R. Cannava, Ed.S., NCSP is a school psychologist with Arlington Public Schools in Virginia.

Sydney Carlson, B.A. is a doctoral student at the University of Minnesota-Twin Cities.

Cliff Yung-Chi Chen, Ph.D. is an assistant professor at Queens College, City University of New York.

Adrianna Crossing, M.A. is a doctoral candidate at Michigan State University in East Lansing, Michigan.

Cecile A. Gadson, Ph.D. is a senior staff psychologist, African-American and Black Student Specialist at the University of Oregon.

Pam W. Gershon, Psy.D. is a doctoral lecturer at Queens College, City University of New York.

Sally L. Grapin, Ph.D. is an associate professor at Montclair State University.

Charity Brown Griffin, Ph.D. is an associate professor at Winston-Salem State University.

Meaghan Guiney, Ph.D., NCSP is an assistant professor at Fairleigh Dickinson University.

Jamelia N. Harris, Ph.D. is a postdoctoral fellow at Rutgers University, Newark.

Austin H. Johnson, Ph.D. is an associate professor at the University of California, Riverside.

Jiwon Kim, M.A. is a doctoral student at the University of Minnesota.

Tara Kulkarni, Ph.D. is an assistant professor at California State University, Monterey Bay.

Jioni A. Lewis, Ph.D. is an associate professor of counseling psychology at the University of Maryland, College Park.

Celeste M. Malone, Ph.D. is an associate professor at Howard University.

Angela Mann, Ph.D., BCBA is an associate professor at the University of North Florida.

Carlos Bueno Martinez, M.S. is an M.A. student at the Erasmus Mundus Master's in Educational Policies for Global Development.

Cheryl E. Matias, Ph.D. is a professor in the College of Education at the University of Kentucky.

Shereen C. Naser, Ph.D. is an assistant professor at Cleveland State University.

Thuy Nguyen, B.A. is a doctoral student at the University of Minnesota.

Sherrie L. Proctor, Ph.D. is a professor at Queens College, City University of New York.

David P. Rivera, Ph.D. is an associate professor at Queens College, City University of New York.

Sujay Sabnis, Ph.D. is an assistant professor at Miami University, Ohio.

Amanda L. Sullivan, Ph.D. is a professor at the University of Minnesota.

Desireé Vega, Ph.D. is an associate professor at the University of Arizona.

Rose Vukovic, Ph.D. is a professor at University of Victoria.

Tyler A. Womack, M.A. is a doctoral student at University of California, Riverside.

Justina Yohannan, Ph.D., NCSP is a postdoctoral fellow at Turning Point Associates Inc., in San Antonio, Texas.

PREFACE

Critical Theories for School Psychology and Counseling: A Foundation for Equity and Inclusion in School-Based Practice is the first book in the discipline of school psychology to present critical theory and approaches as a way to conceptualize and engage practice and supervision. Critical theory, a form of cultural criticism, is a theoretical tradition typically associated with the Frankfurt School, a group of philosophers and social scientists in the 1920s who critiqued the social order in Germany after World War I. However, critique of the dominant social paradigm did not solely come from the Frankfurt School; for example, in the United States the scholarship of Black scholars such as W. E. B. Du Bois challenged the dominant white order, and the influence of their work cannot be overlooked. Critical theory has been expanded and changed in response to various social movements. Today, the critique of dominant societal order around which critical theories and approaches center is vitally important given significant social injustices that remain present in American society.

Because critical theories and approaches offer a lens for critical analysis, disruption, and dismantling of social injustices, they are important tools for educators who seek to facilitate equity, social justice, and liberation through education. For school psychologists and counselors, critical theories offer a way to conceptualize and address challenges that marginalized students experience in schools—not as a result of inherent deficits they possess, but because of unfair and oppressive structures and systems that exist within society and are also present in schools. To this end, the first section of *Critical Theories for School Psychology and Counseling* is titled *Theoretical Foundations* and consists of five chapters intended to build readers' foundational knowledge about five critical theories and approaches: Intersectionality Theory, Critical Race Theory, DisCrit Theory, Queer Theory, and Critical Study of Whiteness. The second and third sections of the book link these five critical theories and approaches to key issues in education that are relevant to school psychology and counseling practice and supervision. More specifically, the second section, *Theory to Practice*, explicates how the five critical theories and approaches connect to major job roles and functions of school psychologists and counselors as well as critical issues in elementary and secondary schools. The third section, *Theory to Supervision*, includes five chapters that connect the five critical theories and approaches to critical issues in supervision.

The structure of the book makes it ideal for using each chapter as a standalone or for pairing the theoretical foundational chapters with their corresponding chapters in the practice and supervision sections of the book. Each chapter in the practice and supervision sections offers a brief overview of the relevant theory or approach, while also using case studies and/or experiential activities to enhance understanding of how a specific critical theory or approach connects to practice or supervision issues. The incorporation of case studies and experiential activities in the second and third sections may be particularly useful pedagogical tools for graduate educators and those facilitating professional development and inservices in school districts and other educational institutions. We recommend pairing theoretical foundational chapters with their corresponding chapters in the practice and supervision sections as the *most powerful* use of the book to encourage deep understanding of the critical theory/approach prior to connecting theory with practice and supervision issues.

Before we describe in greater detail the content each chapter contains, we would like to discuss use of language in the book. We are intentional in our use of language as it pertains to sociocultural identities. As a socially just way of emphasizing the pervasiveness of white supremacy and related systemic oppressions, we purposefully lowercase the "w" in *white*, as the capitalized version of *white* is often associated with white power movements. Conversely, we capitalize *Black*, *Indigenous*, *Latinx*, and *Asian* as a way of decentralizing the unquestioned and unproblematized power of whiteness. Given the many ways in which people self-identify and are identified, the authors use a range or sociocultural labels when referring to various groups of people. For example, the authors refer to marginalized sexual orientation and gender identity groups using variations of the commonly used "LGBTQ" acronym. Some will include other letters, such as "I" to include intersex and "A" to include asexuality, and some will include the plus (+) sign to signify that there are many more ways of identifying within these groups that a single acronym cannot fully address. Now, we describe a little more about each chapter's content.

Section 1, *Theoretical Foundations*

- Chapter 1: "Applying Intersectionality to School Psychology: Implications for Research, Practice, and Advocacy" by Jioni A. Lewis and Cecile A. Gadson provides an overview of Intersectionality Theory, including its *herstory* and current applications across fields. The chapter ends with explicit discussion of how Intersectionality Theory connects to key issues in education.

- Chapter 2: "Foundations of Critical Race Theory: Migration From Law to the Social and Applied Sciences" by Robert A. Brown provides an overview of Critical Race Theory, including its history and current applications across fields. The chapter ends with explicit discussion of how Critical Race Theory connects to key issues in education.
- Chapter 3: "DisCrit: Disability Critical Race Theory" by Sujay Sabnis and Carlos Bueno Martinez provides an overview of DisCrit Theory, including its history and current applications across fields. The chapter ends with explicit discussion of how DisCrit Theory connects to key issues in education.
- Chapter 4: "Queering School Psychology: A Queer Theory for School-Based Practice" by David P. Rivera provides an overview of Queer Theory, including its history and current applications across fields. The chapter ends with explicit discussion of how Queer Theory connects to key issues in education.
- Chapter 5: "Toward a Critical Study of Whiteness" by Cheryl E. Matias and Colleen Boucher provides an overview of Critical Study of Whiteness, including critical theories that undergird it. The chapter reviews how a Critical Study of Whiteness approach can be used across fields. The chapter ends with explicit discussion of how Critical Study of Whiteness connects to key issues in education.

Section 2: *Theory to Practice*

- Chapter 6: "When They *Don't* See Us: Using Intersectionality to Examine Black Girls' Discipline Experiences" by Jamelia N. Harris discusses how Intersectionality Theory is applicable to the problem of discipline disparities in U.S. public schools.
- Chapter 7: "Use of Critical Race Theory to Understand Exclusion of Indigenous Students from Gifted Education" by Justina Yohannan, Adrianna Crossing, Lisa Aguilar, and Sherrie L. Proctor uses Critical Race Theory (CRT) as a lens to understand barriers to gifted education programs for students of color, with an emphasis on Indigenous students.
- Chapter 8: "DisCrit Theory: Emotional and Behavioral Disturbance Assessment and Identification" by Amanda L. Sullivan, Rose Vukovic, Thuy Nguyen, Tara Kulkarni, Jiwon Kim, and Sydney Carlson discusses how DisCrit is applicable to Emotional Behavioral Disturbance assessment and identification.
- Chapter 9: "Queer Theory and School-Based Counseling for LGBTQ Students" by David P. Rivera, Sherrie L. Proctor, Cliff Yung-Chi Chen, and Pam W. Gershon discusses how Queer Theory is applicable to school-based counseling and advocacy with LGBTQ students.
- Chapter 10: "Interrogating Cognitive Assessment Using a Critical Study of Whiteness Lens" by Tyler A. Womack, Jessica Mercado Anazagasty, Desireé

Vega, and Austin H. Johnson discusses how a Critical Study of Whiteness approach is applicable to cognitive assessment.

Section 3: *Theory to Supervision*

- Chapter 11: "Infusing Intersectionality Theory Into Multicultural Supervision Practices: A Case Narrative Centering Latinx, LGBT-QIA+, and Undocumented Structural Identities" by Meaghan Guiney and Sherrie L. Proctor describes how Intersectionality Theory can be used by school psychologists who supervise practicum and intern students.
- Chapter 12: "Preparing Supervisees to Support Students Experiencing Microaggressions: Application of Critical Race Theory to Clinical Supervision" by Celeste M. Malone uses Critical Race Theory (CRT) as a framework to better understand the pervasiveness of and harm caused by microaggressions.
- Chapter 13: "DisCrit Theory Applied to Clinical Supervision for Minoritized Students With Social, Emotional, and Behavioral Concerns" by Shereen C. Naser, Sally L. Grapin, Charity Brown Griffin, and Jeffrey M. Brown uses DisCrit Theory as a lens through which to examine the school-based process of identifying and responding to student behavior including student social, emotional, and behavioral challenges.
- Chapter 14: "Queer Theory and Intern Supervision: The Harm of Heteronormative Supervision" by Amy R. Cannava and David P. Rivera presents an application of Queer Theory to school-based supervision, with a focus on supervising school psychology graduate interns.
- Chapter 15: "Critical Study of Whiteness to Dismantle School-to-Incarceration Pathways for Racially Minoritized Students Through Supervision" by Angela Mann discusses dismantling white supremacy especially as it manifests in anti-Black racism by outlining a Critical Study of Whiteness approach to supervision practices related to ending the school-to-prison pipeline.

The chapters in *Critical Theories for School Psychology and Counseling* are authored by leading education and social science experts who articulate the importance of centering our most marginalized students as a way of making educational institutions more equitable and inclusive. The book can be used in graduate programs with preservice school psychologists and counselors, in school districts during inservice and professional development days, and also by school psychologists and counselors who would like to engage in individualized professional reading and development. We hope *Critical Theories for School Psychology and Counseling* is a resource that all educators reach for as we work toward making education and educational spaces more equitable, inclusive, *and* liberatory.

Sherrie L. Proctor and David P. Rivera
Editors

ACKNOWLEDGMENTS

We would like to thank our student editorial assistant, Kathleen Lema, for her excellent work and incredible dedication to this project. We cannot imagine completing this project without Kathleen's help and support. We also appreciate Queens College school psychology students and graduates Nicole Caruana, Natasha Chait, Gary DiFiore, Francheska Grullon, Allison Koenig, Kathrynne Li, Kalyna Melnyk, and Olivia Skowronski for their helpful and thoughtful feedback on the project. We thank Alycia Castillo for her assistance with formatting the tables and figures. We are also thankful for the authors who participated in this project. Their dedication to sharing their knowledge, while also growing and learning with us, is immensely appreciated. Finally, we give thanks to Danny Newman and Daniel Schwartz, whose long-term and sustained engagement with us helped initiate and push this project forward. We are forever grateful for their belief in this project until it became a reality.

SECTION 1
Theoretical Foundations

1

APPLYING INTERSECTIONALITY TO SCHOOL PSYCHOLOGY

Implications for Research, Practice, and Advocacy

Jioni A. Lewis and Cecile A. Gadson

The COVID-19 pandemic has had a disproportionate negative impact on Black, Indigenous, and people of color (BIPOC) in terms of mortality and infection rates (COVID Racial Data Tracker, 2021). In addition, the summer 2020 racial uprisings shined a light on the continued systemic racism, police brutality, and violence that has taken the lives of many BIPOC individuals, particularly Black men and women such as Ahmaud Arbery, Breonna Taylor, George Floyd, and many others. The confluence of these two crises combined to negatively affect BIPOC communities in unique ways. In addition, a majority of K-12 school systems have navigated the pandemic with online instruction, which may exacerbate educational disparities by race, ethnicity, and class. Given these pressing issues in the current sociopolitical climate, it is important to consider the ways that interlocking systems of oppression have a disproportionately negative impact on children, adolescents, adults, and teachers in the educational system.

Intersectionality provides a lens to illuminate the interlocking systems of oppression that shape the lives of marginalized communities. The concept of intersectionality—which considers the ways that simultaneous membership in multiple social categories is linked to interlocking systems of oppression, power, and privilege—has gained increased attention both within academic and activist spaces in the last several years (Bowleg & Bauer, 2016). In the current sociopolitical climate, many social justice movements have embraced intersectional politics in the fight for equity and coalition-building (Hancock, 2016). For example, the co-founders of the Black Lives Matter movement are three Black women who explicitly highlighted the intersections of racism, sexism, classism, heterosexism, transphobia, and xenophobia in their fight for equity, justice, and liberation (Garza, 2020). Given that *intersectionality* as a form of critical social inquiry has traveled across a variety of disciplines, it is important that researchers

DOI: 10.4324/9780367815325-2

and practitioners gain a deeper understanding of the meaning of this concept. As such, it is important to outline the *herstory* of intersectionality, its core theoretical tenets, and how intersectional scholarship has been applied within the field of psychology. In addition, it is important to delineate how intersectionality can be utilized within the field of school psychology to expand our knowledge about the benefits of using an intersectional lens to shape research, practice, and advocacy in working with youth from different backgrounds. This chapter ends with recommendations for how researchers and practitioners can appropriately apply intersectionality to become more culturally responsive school psychology researchers and practitioners.

Historical Underpinnings of Intersectionality Theory: *Herstory* of Intersectionality

Although intersectionality has been articulated in mainstream academic discourse for the last several decades, it is grounded in the *herstory* of Black feminism, which dates back to the mid-19th century when Black women, such as Sojourner Truth, an abolitionist and women's rights activist, highlighted the exclusion of Black women in the suffrage movement (Lewis & Grzanka, 2016). She gave a speech at the 1851 Ohio Women's Rights Convention highlighting the ways that white women tried to exclude Black women from getting the right to vote. Throughout the 20th century, there were numerous women of color scholars, writers, and activists who articulated the unique marginalization of women of color at the intersection of race, class, and gender oppression (Hancock, 2016; Lewis & Grzanka, 2016; May, 2015). In 1977, the Combahee River Collective, a group of Black feminists, many of whom were Black queer women, articulated the struggles of Black women in the 1970s women's movement by stating, "We find it difficult to separate race from class from sex oppression because in our lives they are most often experienced simultaneously" (Combahee River Collective, 1995, p. 234). The Combahee River Collective highlighted the interlocking systems of oppression experienced by people who are marginalized at the center of racism, classism, and sexism. Thus, several Black feminist and women of color feminist scholars paved the way for critical inquiry on intersectionality (Collins, 2000; Hancock, 2016; Lewis & Grzanka, 2016).

During the late 1980s and early 1990s there was a proliferation of scholars who articulated the unique experience of interlocking systems of oppression (Hill-Collins, 2019; Hancock, 2016). In 1989, critical legal scholar Kimberlé Crenshaw introduced the concept of intersectionality in her critique of antidiscrimination law, which often excluded Black women at the intersection of racial and gender discrimination. Crenshaw argued that Black women could experience discrimination that could resemble racism experienced by Black men, sexism experienced by white women, or the additive effects of race and gender oppression (i.e., double jeopardy). However, Crenshaw (1989) argued that Black women often "experience discrimination as Black women—not the sum of race or sex discrimination, but as Black women" (p. 149). Thus, this framework critiques a single-axis analysis of discrimination and pushes a more nuanced investigation of simultaneous interlocking oppressions. In another foundational article, Crenshaw (1991) applied intersectionality to an analysis of violence against women of color in order to illuminate interlocking systems of oppression and point toward solutions for political activism and public policy.

In 1990–2000, sociologist Patricia Hill Collins wrote her foundational book, *Black Feminist Thought*, detailing the ways that African American women's oppression is rooted in a "matrix of domination," which refers to the ways that interlocking systems of oppression are organized by power to produce and sustain inequality. In 1987, Gloria Anzaldua wrote the book *The Borderlands: The New Mestiza*, which focused on the intersections of race, ethnicity, identity, gender, and colonialism in the United States (U.S.). Thus, Anzaldua, Crenshaw, and Collins similarly articulated the importance of centering marginalized people, namely, women of color, in the study of intersectional oppression (Hill Collins, 2019; Hancock, 2016; May, 2015).

Detailed Discussion of Intersectionality Theory

Given the rich interdisciplinary and activist herstory of intersectionality, there has been much debate about the concept of intersectionality. Specifically, there have been debates about intersectionality's origins and genealogy, whether it's a theory or a methodology, and the centrality of social justice activism (Hill Collins, 2019; Hancock, 2016; May, 2015). In their article, "Toward a Field of Intersectionality Studies: Theory, Applications, and Praxis," Cho et al. (2013) highlighted the three primary areas of intersectionality inquiry and theorizing: (1) debates about intersectionality as a theoretical and methodological paradigm, (2) applications of an intersectional framework, and (3) political interventions employing an intersectional lens. They argued that intersectionality is an analytic sensibility that is shaped by the way it is employed. Cho et al. (2013) stated:

> If intersectionality is an analytic disposition, a way of thinking about and conducting analyses, then what makes an analysis intersectional is not its use of the term "intersectionality," nor its being situated in a familiar genealogy, nor its drawing on lists of standard citations. Rather, what makes an analysis intersectional—whatever terms it deploys, whatever its iteration, whatever its field or discipline—is its adoption of an intersectional way of thinking about the problem of sameness and difference and its relation to power. This framing—conceiving of categories not as distinct but as always permeated by other categories, fluid and changing, always in the process of

> creating and being created by dynamics of power—emphasizes what intersectionality does rather than what intersectionality is.
>
> *(p. 795)*

In her book *Intersectionality as Critical Social Theory*, Patricia Hill Collins (2019) articulated four guiding premises (or core tenets) that provide a framework for the theoretical underpinnings of intersectionality's critical social inquiry and praxis. The first core tenet is: "Race, class, gender, and similar systems of power are interdependent and mutually construct one another" (p. 44). Thus, an important contribution to intersectionality is this idea that systems of oppression and privilege are interlocking and constitutive. For example, work that is grounded in Intersectionality Theory understands that systems of oppression and privilege are interlocking and can't be teased apart, such as the experience of Latinx immigrant children who live in a border town in South Texas. An intersectional analytic disposition would necessitate an understanding that those multiple social locations are mutually constitutive and interdependent.

The second core tenet is: "Intersecting power relations produce complex, interdependent social inequalities of race, class, gender, sexuality, nationality, ethnicity, ability, and age" (p. 44). Thus, it is important to acknowledge the ways interlocking systems of power produce and sustain social inequalities. For example, an intersectionality lens would mean that a school psychologist or counselor working with Latinx immigrant youth would have to be aware of the interlocking social inequalities based on race, ethnicity, immigration status, class, and age in working with this multiply marginalized population.

The third core tenet is: "The social location of individuals and groups within intersecting power relations shapes their experiences within and perspectives on the social world" (p. 44). Again, an intersectionality lens requires Intersectionality Theory practitioners to be aware of intersections of power and privilege that shape the experiences of the groups of interest. In addition, social context and complexity are important to an intersectional analysis of the impact on the social world.

The fourth core tenet is: "Solving social problems within a given local, regional, national, or global context requires intersectional analyses" (p. 44). The core purpose of intersectionality is social justice and ensuring that intersectionality is being applied to research and activism for the purpose of solving social problems in the world. In the next section, we explore how intersectionality has been used across fields, with particular attention to its application to psychology broadly.

Current Applications of Intersectionality Theory Across Fields

Although intersectionality emerged from critical legal studies as well as from an activist tradition of critiquing interlocking systems of oppression and advocating for social change and transformation, intersectionality has been increasingly used as a framework across a variety of academic disciplines, ultimately shaping theory building and empirical investigations in law, sociology, education, women and gender studies, public health, and psychology (Cole, 2009; Rosenthal, 2016).

There has been much debate within the social sciences, and within psychology specifically, about how to apply an intersectionality framework to research (see Else-Quest & Hyde, 2016 for a review). In the field of psychology, many of the debates have fallen in the realm of theoretical and methodological implications of intersectionality as a research paradigm. In a majority of the psychology research literature, there are several approaches to considering variables related to multiple social identities and oppression, such as *single-axis* (e.g., exploring a single identity, such as race or gender), *additive* (e.g., measuring race and gender separately and then adding them together), *interactional/multiplicative* (e.g., measuring race and gender separately and then creating a statistical interaction term), or *intersectional* (e.g., measuring the simultaneous experience of interlocking forms of oppression) (Lewis & Grzanka, 2016). Some psychology scholars view the additive or interactional approaches as sufficient approaches to intersectionality (Else-Quest & Hyde, 2016).

However, other intersectionality scholars have categorized additive and interactional approaches as *weak intersectionality* because they are focused on only measuring multiple social identities, whereas analyzing the relationship between multiple social identities and interlocking systems of oppression, inequality, and power is viewed as *strong intersectionality* (Dill & Kohlman, 2012; Lewis & Grzanka, 2016; Moradi & Grzanka, 2017). In addition, *transformative intersectionality* is research that has a focus on the link between multiple social identities, interlocking systems of structural oppression, and social justice activism (Shin et al., 2017). It is also important to note that Crenshaw's (1989) original conceptualization of intersectionality clearly articulated the importance of focusing on illuminating the intersectional vulnerability of multiply marginalized groups, such as Black women, based on their unique experience at the nexus of interlocking systems of oppression, given that their intersectional oppression is greater than the sum of its parts (Bowleg & Bauer, 2016; Lewis & Neville, 2015; Lewis et al., 2017). Thus, we argue that the best approach to *intersectionality* in research is one that measures the simultaneous experience of interlocking systems of oppression, inequality, and power.

In the last 15 years, there has been an increase in intersectionality scholarship in the field of psychology. Many psychology researchers have attempted to apply an intersectionality framework to the study of multiple social identities, stigma, health disparities, discrimination, and interlocking systems of oppression (Lewis & Grzanka, 2016; Rosenthal, 2016). For example, in Cole's (2009) foundational article on intersectionality in psychology, she outlined three questions for psychologists to ask at different stages of the research process to incorporate intersectionality into their research: (1) Who is included within this category?

(challenges psychologists to consider the diversity within a group based on other intersectional identities), (2) What role does inequality play? (challenges psychologists to consider the role of hierarchies and structural inequity and power), and (3) Where are there similarities? (challenges psychologists to consider commonalities within diverse groups, which is beneficial for coalition building and activism). However, much of the current research has not grappled with these fundamental questions articulated by Cole (2009) to push intersectionality in psychology forward. Some intersectionality scholars (e.g., Moradi & Grzanka, 2017; Rosenthal, 2016) have extended Cole's (2009) articulations by suggesting that psychologists need to center social justice activism in the intersectionality work they do within our various roles as psychologists.

Recently, some feminist psychology scholars (Buchanan & Wiklund, 2021; Cole, 2020) have argued that intersectionality research in psychology has become mainstream and strayed from its Black feminist, political, and activist roots. In addition, much of the extant empirical research in psychology is still focused on individual-level identity variables (e.g., race, gender, class, sexual orientation, etc.) and needs to move toward systems-level variables to more effectively capture interlocking systems of oppression (e.g., racism, sexism, classism, heterosexism, etc.). For instance, if a researcher wants to design a quantitative study to explore the impact of racism on health outcomes for Latinx youth, the researcher could try to measure different types of racism that might impact health, such as institutional/structural racism (e.g., laws, policies, and practices of institutions that operate to restrict the rights or access for BIPOC communities) and individual/interpersonal racism (e.g., attitudes, beliefs, and interpersonal behaviors, such as racial microaggressions) (Jones, 1997; Neville et al., 2012). In addition, the researcher could make sure to measure community- or neighborhood-level variables, such as the segregation of the neighborhood, that may also impact the health of Latinx youth. Moreover, although it is important to explore intersections of privilege and oppression, Cole (2020) highlighted that much of the current intersectionality research has focused too much on privileged groups and needs to recenter multiply marginalized groups, namely women of color, and the particular interlocking systems of oppression they face. We are in agreement with Cole's (2020) perspective and assert that although intersectionality is an important framework to incorporate into the field of psychology to illuminate interlocking systems of oppression and privilege, it is particularly important for applied psychologists because it provides an opportunity to center multiply marginalized groups in research, practice, and social justice advocacy.

Relevance of Intersectionality to School Psychology

Intersectionality is essential to incorporate into the field of school psychology because we are at a critical juncture in our educational system. The racial and ethnic diversity of school psychologists does not match the racial and ethnic diversity of students in U.S. schools. Most school psychologists are white women, compared to 50% of students in U.S. public schools who identify as a member of at least one marginalized racial and/or ethnic identity (Proctor et al., 2017; National Center for Educational Statistics, 2017). Given this, it is important that school psychologists fully integrate an intersectionality framework into their research, practice, and advocacy.

Applying Intersectionality to School Psychology Research

The key to applying intersectionality to school psychology research is to understand that research must move beyond a focus on multiple social identities and toward a focus on the role of interlocking systems of oppression and structural inequality in the lives of marginalized youth. This involves grounding research in an intersectional analysis throughout the research process, including in the way research questions are framed, in the types of research methods employed, in the data collection and analysis, and in the interpretation of the findings (Bowleg, 2008; Cho et al., 2013; Lewis & Grzanka, 2016).

Intersectionality scholars highlight the importance of framing research questions in an intersectional way to fully capture interlocking systems of oppression (Bowleg, 2008; Lewis & Grzanka, 2016; Shields, 2008). For example, if a researcher was interested in studying the experiences of Black adolescent girls in schools, research and interview questions should query participants' experiences *as Black adolescent girls*, rather than asking them about their race and gender separately. Additionally, it is important to use research methods that allow researchers to ask complex questions that are grounded in the sociocultural context of the multiply marginalized group of interest. For instance, if a researcher was interested in exploring Black adolescent girls' experiences of intersectional microaggressions in schools, they might utilize qualitative methods if they were interested in the phenomenological experience, especially given that the only current measure to assess gendered racial microaggressions (i.e., everyday gendered racism and subtle racist and sexist slights) is focused on Black adult women (see Lewis & Neville, 2015). It is also crucial for researchers to be mindful about the way interlocking systems of oppression influence the lived experiences of the research participants to appropriately interpret findings grounded in an intersectionality framework.

Gadson and Lewis (2021), for example, utilize a Black feminist and intersectionality framework to extend the taxonomy of gendered racial microaggressions experienced by Black adult women (see Lewis et al., 2016) to Black adolescent girls. They conducted qualitative focus groups with 33 Black adolescent girls between the ages of 13 and 17 and uncovered several themes that highlighted the unique ways that Black girls experience microaggressions based on the intersection of their race, gender, and social class. Specifically, Black girls reported experiencing gendered racial microaggressions that represented *standards of beauty and objectification* (i.e., assumptions and devaluation about beauty, aesthetics, and exoticization of hair), *being silenced and marginalized* (i.e., being silenced, marginalized, and made to feel invisible, over-disciplined, and under-protected in school settings), and *projected stereotypes* (i.e., stereotypes about Black adolescent girls, such as the hypersexual "Jezebel," the "angry Black girl," and the "ghetto Black girl"). These findings highlight the unique intersections of racism, sexism, and classism for Black girls in predominantly white school environments.

In addition, Gadson and Lewis (2021) illuminate the ways that these gendered racial microaggressions of being over-disciplined are connected to the criminalization of Black girls in the school system (Epstein et al., 2017; Morris, 2016). For example, Black girls in their study reported getting over-disciplined for minor infractions, such as dress code violations like wearing leggings, whereas these same infractions often went unnoticed on white girls by school officials. Gadson and Lewis (2021) apply an intersectional analysis to contextualize the findings and highlight the disproportionate negative impact of these school policies on Black girls. In addition, they use findings from the study to provide recommendations to school administrators on how to disrupt the cycle of criminalizing Black girls in the school system, which includes reforming school policies and practices, educating teachers about their gendered racial biases, and creating counter-spaces in schools that are racially and ethnically healing for girls of color (Morris, 2016; Morris, 2019).

Applying Intersectionality to School Psychology Practice

The increased focus on intersectionality in psychology means that it is also important to apply intersectionality to our practice roles as professional psychologists. In 2017, the American Psychological Association (APA) updated its diversity and multicultural practice guidelines, entitled *Multicultural Guidelines: An Ecological Approach to Context, Identity, and Intersectionality* (APA, 2017). These updated guidelines center intersectionality within multicultural practice and encourage psychologists to consider how increasing one's awareness and knowledge of intersecting identities is an important lens for providing multiculturally responsive professional practice with diverse individuals, families, couples, groups, research participants, organizations, and communities. The new multicultural guidelines also include a layered ecological model to highlight the role of the client, student, research participant, and consultee, as well as the role of the clinician, educator, researcher, or consultant. This model has several levels, including the interaction between the clinician and client or educator and student, etc. (level 1); the community, school, and family context (level 2); the institutional level (level 3); the domestic and international level (level 4); and outcomes (level 5). This complex ecological model could be helpful for school psychologists and counselors to situate their practice within an intersectionality framework.

According to cultural-competence scholars, it is important to develop multicultural awareness, knowledge, and skills in working with diverse populations

(Sue & Sue, 2013). Proctor et al. (2017) noted that a first step to applying intersectionality to practice is to develop greater self-awareness of intersecting identities and systems of oppression that reflect the diversity of the students, families, and communities we will encounter in our work. This self-awareness is important for school psychologists and counselors because it is important to develop increased awareness of our privileged and oppressed identities (Carroll, 2009; Proctor et al., 2017; Sue & Sue, 2013). An intersectionality approach to increasing multicultural self-awareness highlights the benefits of developing awareness of one's own privileged and oppressed identities and interlocking systems of oppression that impact our lives based on race, ethnicity, gender, gender identity, sexual orientation, religion, class, and ability, among others.

Another key step to developing multicultural responsiveness that is rooted in an intersectionality framework includes developing knowledge about diverse populations, particularly with a focus on intersecting identities of the multiply marginalized populations (Carroll, 2009; Proctor et al., 2017; Sue & Sue, 2013). It is also important to develop greater awareness about the impact of interlocking systems of oppression students so we can gain a deeper understanding of the systemic and sociocultural issues that impact their daily lives. This can be accomplished by seeking out knowledge and education related to marginalized populations and the role of intersectionality on the lived experiences of students' social, emotional, academic, and behavioral outcomes. It is also beneficial to seek knowledge about the educational policies and practices that have a disproportionate negative effect on students, particularly multiply marginalized students. For example, school psychologists and counselors can read the work of intersectionality scholars and advocates, as well as BIPOC scholars in the field, to gain knowledge about how to best meet the needs of students with multiply marginalized identities and experiences of oppression (e.g., Collins, 2000; Crenshaw, 1989; Morris, 2016).

Furthermore, developing clinical practice skills that are grounded in an intersectionality framework is critical. Building on the multicultural self-awareness and knowledge of intersectional identities, power, privilege, and oppression, school psychologists and counselors should apply these competencies to professional practice when working with students and clients; for example, acknowledging that many interventions and assessments were not developed with marginalized populations in mind and utilizing cultural adaptation of interventions and assessments when working with such populations. School psychologists and counselors must be particularly mindful of the limitations of traditional manualized treatment protocols and assessments that have been developed and normed on white youth.

One example of developing better tools to meet the needs of marginalized students is the work of Monique Morris, education scholar and social justice advocate. She used her extensive research on the criminalization of Black girls in the school system (see Morris, 2016) to help schools create culturally and gender-responsive programs and reimagine their curriculum to better meet the needs of Black and Brown girls. Specifically, Morris (2019) assisted one school with increasing its awareness and knowledge of the disproportionate school discipline policies on Black girls, and this school decided to develop positive interventions that included mentoring, behavioral interventions, and restorative justice rather than exclusionary disciplinary practices. Morris (2019) also highlighted the importance for educators, including school psychologists and counselors, to create in schools empowering and healing spaces for Black and Brown girls to thrive. When counselors and school psychologists better understand the lived experiences of multiply marginalized students and have a sociocultural understanding of the structural systems of oppression negatively affecting them, they are able to apply interventions that heal rather than push out these students (Morris, 2016; Morris, 2019).

Another important skill for practitioners to gain is that of helping BIPOC students develop strategies for radical healing (French et al., 2020; Ginwright, 2010). Radical healing is a process of healing racial trauma that involves becoming whole in the face of identity-based wounds (French et al., 2020). In his book, *Black Youth Rising: Activism and Radical Healing in Urban America*, education scholar Shawn Ginwright (2010) highlighted how educators and school professionals could cultivate hope and healing and create safe spaces for youth of color. French et al. (2020) integrated Ginwright's (2010) conceptualization of radical healing with several foundational psychological theories, including liberation psychology (Martín-Baró, 1994), Black psychology (White, 1970), ethnopolitical psychology (Comas-Díaz, 2007), and intersectionality (Crenshaw, 1989; Cole, 2009) to develop the *Psychological Framework of Radical Healing*. Liberation psychology highlights the importance of psychological liberation from oppression; Black psychology articulates the history of racism in psychology and calls for a strengths-based and culturally centered approach to mental health; ethnopolitical psychology provides a framework for healing from racial trauma; and intersectionality highlights the impact of interlocking systems of oppression on the lives of marginalized groups (French et al., 2020). Together, these theories are integrated to form the foundation of racial healing that centers BIPOC communities and promotes a community and multisystemic approach to healing from racial trauma (French et al., 2020).

There are five core components to radical healing, which include: (1) critical consciousness (i.e., developing a critical understanding of social reality through reflection and action), (2) cultural authenticity and self-knowledge (i.e., connecting with one's ancestral and cultural roots and developing one's own self-definition), (3) radical hope (i.e., fostering hope and envisioning possibilities for a better future), (4) collectivism and social support (i.e., connecting with one's racial/ethnic values and community for support), and (5) strength and resistance (i.e., relying on cultural strength and resisting oppression as a form of healing; French et al., 2020). The psychological framework of radical healing was developed to center the needs of BIPOC communities and honor the ancestral wisdom and resistance strategies that enable these communities to sit in the dialectic between fighting interlocking systems of oppression as well as envisioning possibilities for a socially just future (French et al., 2020).

Applying Intersectionality to School Psychology Advocacy

Given the increasing calls for cultural responsiveness to include a commitment to social justice advocacy (Vera & Speight, 2003; Speight & Vera, 2009), as well as Proctor et al.'s (2017) recommendations for applying intersectionality to practice to focus on encouraging system change and promoting social justice advocacy, we want to reiterate that social justice activism is at the heart of applying intersectionality. Strong social justice advocacy skills allow us to push for equitable policies and practices at the school, district, state, and national levels, particularly for multiply marginalized students. To move toward social justice grounded in an intersectional lens, school psychologists and counselors should have specific training focused on helping them gain self-awareness of power, privilege, and oppression; develop critical consciousness; gain knowledge and education; and develop social justice advocacy skills (see Hage et al., 2020 for an example). This could include training counselors and school psychologists to critically analyze educational policies that have a disproportionate negative effect on marginalized students and to develop skills to advocate on behalf of students and engage in public policy. As counselors and school psychologists apply intersectionality to their research, practice, and social justice advocacy they can develop skills to actively disrupt cycles of oppression ingrained in the school system.

Conclusion

This chapter provided an overview of Intersectionality Theory as well as current applications of intersectionality to research, practice, and advocacy in psychology. Within the chapter, we offer actionable steps that counselors and school psychologists can take to develop their own awareness and knowledge about intersectionality so that they can apply it to their job roles and advocacy. Ultimately, we hope counselors and school psychologists center an intersectionality framework with a commitment to placing social justice at the heart of research, practice, and advocacy.

References

American Psychological Association. (2017). *Multicultural guidelines: An ecological approach to context, identity, and intersectionality*. www.apa.org/about/policy/multicultural-guidelines.pdf

Anzaldua, G. (1987). *The borderlands: The Frontera, the new mestiza*. Aunt Lute Books.

Bowleg, L. (2008). When Black+ lesbian+ woman≠ Black lesbian woman: The methodological challenges of qualitative and quantitative intersectionality research. *Sex Roles*, *59*(5–6), 312–325. https://doi.org/10.1007/s11199-008-9400-z

Bowleg, L., & Bauer, G. (2016). Invited reflection: Quantifying intersectionality. *Psychology of Women Quarterly*, *40*(3), 337–341. https://doi.org/10.1177/0361684316654282

Buchanan, N. T., & Wiklund, L. O. (2021). Intersectionality research in psychological science: Resisting the tendency to disconnect, dilute, and depoliticize. *Research on Child and Adolescent Psychopathology*, *49*, 25–31. https://doi.org/10.1007/s10802-020-00748-y

Carroll, D. W. (2009). Toward multicultural competence: A practice model for implementation in the schools. In J. M. Jones (Ed.), *The psychology of multiculturalism in schools: A primer for practice, training, and research* (pp. 1–16). National Association of School Psychologists.

Cho, S., Crenshaw, K. W., & McCall, L. (2013). Toward a field of intersectionality studies: Theory, applications, and praxis. *Signs: Journal of Women in Culture and Society*, *38*(4), 785–810. https://doi.org/10.1086/669608

Cole, E. R. (2009). Intersectionality and research in psychology. *American Psychologist*, *64*(3), 170–180. https://doi.org/10.1037/a0014564

Cole, E. R. (2020). Demarginalizing women of color in intersectionality scholarship in psychology: A Black feminist critique. *Journal of Social Issues*, *76*(4), 1036–1044. https://doi.org/10.1111/josi.12413

Collins, P. H. (2000). *Black feminist thought: Knowledge, power and the politics of empowerment*. Routledge.

Comas-Díaz, L. (2007). Ethnopolitical psychology: Healing and transformation. In E. Aldarondo (Ed.), *Advancing social justice through clinical practice* (pp. 91–118). Erlbaum.

Combahee River Collective. (1995). Combahee River Collective statement. In B. Guy-Sheftall (Ed.), *Words of fire: An anthology of African American feminist thought* (pp. 232–240). New Press. (Original work published 1977)

Covid Racial Data Tracker. (2021). *The COVID racial data tracker*. https://covidtracking.com/race

Crenshaw, K. (1989). Demarginalizing the intersection of race and sex: A Black feminist critique of antidiscrimination doctrines, feminist theory, and antiracist politics. *University of Chicago Legal Forum*, *8*, 139–167.

Crenshaw, K. (1991). Mapping the Margins: Intersectionality, identity politics, and violence against women of color. *Stanford Law Review*, *43*(6), 1241–1299. https://doi.org/10.2307/1229039

Dill, B. T., & Kohlman, M. H. (2012). Intersectionality: A transformative paradigm in feminist theory and social justice. *Handbook of Feminist Research: Theory and Praxis*, *2*, 154–174.

Else-Quest, N. M., & Hyde, J. S. (2016). Intersectionality in quantitative psychological research: II. Methods and techniques. *Psychology of Women Quarterly*, *40*(3), 319–336. https://doi.org/10.1177/0361684316647953

Epstein, R., Blake, J. J., & Gonzalez, T. (2017). *Girlhood interrupted: The erasure of Black girls' childhood*. Georgetown Law Center.

French, B. H., Lewis, J. A., Mosley, D., Adames, H. Y., Chavez-Dueñas, N. Y., Chen, G. A., & Neville, H. A. (2020). Toward a psychological framework of radical healing in communities of color. *The Counseling Psychologist*, *48*(1), 14–46. https://doi.org/10.1177/0011000019843506

Gadson, C. A., & Lewis, J. A. (2021). Devalued, over disciplined, and stereotyped: A taxonomy of gendered racial microaggressions among Black adolescent girls. *Journal of Counseling Psychology*. https://doi.org/10.1037/cou0000571

Garza, A. (2020). *The purpose of power: How we come together when we fall apart*. One World.

Ginwright, S. A. (2010). *Black youth rising: Activism and radical healing in urban America.* Teachers College Press.

Hage, S. M., Miles, J. R., Lewis, J. A., Grzanka, P. R., & Goodman, L. A. (2020). The social justice practicum in counseling psychology training. *Training and Education in Professional Psychology, 14*(2), 155–166. https://doi.org/10.1037/tep0000299

Hancock, A. M. (2016). *Intersectionality: An intellectual history.* Oxford University Press.

Hill Collins, P. (2019). *Intersectionality as critical theory.* Duke University Press.

Jones, J. M. (1997). *Prejudice and racism* (2nd ed.). McGraw-Hill.

Lewis, J. A., & Grzanka, P. R. (2016). Applying intersectionality theory to research on perceived racism. In A. N. Alvarez, C. T. H. Liang, & H. A. Neville (Eds.), *The cost of racism for people of color: Contextualizing experiences of discrimination* (pp. 31–54). American Psychological Association.

Lewis, J. A., Mendenhall, R., Harwood, S. A., & Huntt, M. B. (2016). "Ain't I a woman?": Perceived gendered racial microaggressions experienced by Black women. *The Counseling Psychologist, 44*(5), 758–780. https://doi.org/10.1177/0011000016641193

Lewis, J. A., & Neville, H. A. (2015). Construction and initial validation of the Gendered Racial Microaggressions Scale for Black women. *Journal of Counseling Psychology, 62*(2), 289–302. https://doi.org/10.1037/cou0000062

Lewis, J. A., Williams, M. G., Peppers, E., & Gadson, C. A. (2017). Applying intersectionality to explore the relations between gendered racism and health among Black women. *Journal of Counseling Psychology, 64*(5), 475–486. http://dx.doi.org/10.1037/cou0000231

Martín-Baró, I. (1994). *Writings for a liberation psychology* (A. Aron & S. Corne, Eds.). Harvard University Press.

May, V. M. (2015). *Pursuing intersectionality, unsettling dominant imaginaries.* Routledge.

Moradi, B., & Grzanka, P. R. (2017). Using intersectionality responsibly: Toward critical epistemology, structural analysis, and social justice activism. *Journal of Counseling Psychology, 64*(5), 500–513. https://doi.org/10.1037/cou0000203

Morris, M. W. (2016). *Pushout: The criminalization of Black girls in school.* The New Press.

Morris, M. W. (2019). *Sing a rhythm, dance a blues: Education for the liberation of Black and Brown girls.* The New Press.

National Center for Educational Statistics. (2017). *Condition of education 2017.* Washington, DC.

Neville, H. A., Spanierman, L. B., & Lewis, J. A. (2012). The expanded psychosocial model of racism: A new model for understanding and disrupting racism and white privilege. In N. A. Fouad, J. A. Carter, & L. M. Subich (Eds.), *APA handbook of counseling psychology: Vol. 2 practice, interventions, and applications* (pp. 333–360). American Psychological Association.

Proctor, S. L., Williams, B., Scherr, T., & Li, K. (2017). Intersectionality and school psychology: Implications for practice. *Communiqué, 46*(4), 1, 19–22.

Rosenthal, L. (2016). Incorporating intersectionality into psychology: An opportunity to promote social justice and equity. *American Psychologist, 71*(6), 474–485. https://doi.org/10.1037/a0040323

Shields, S. A. (2008). Gender: An intersectionality perspective. *Sex Roles, 59*(5–6), 301–311.

Shin, R. Q., Welch, J. C., Kaya, A. E., Yeung, J. G., Obana, C., Sharma, R., Vernay, C. N., & Yee, S. (2017). The intersectionality framework and identity intersections in the Journal of Counseling Psychology and The Counseling Psychologist: A content analysis. *Journal of Counseling Psychology*, *64*(5), 458–474. https://doi.org/10.1037/cou0000204

Speight, S. L., & Vera, E. M. (2009). The challenge of social justice for school psychology. *Journal of Educational and Psychological Consultation*, *19*, 82–92. https://doi.org/10.1080/10474410802463338

Sue, D. W., & Sue, D. (2013). *Counseling the culturally diverse* (6th ed.). John Wiley and Sons.

Vera, E. M., & Speight, S. L. (2003). Multicultural competence, social justice, and counseling psychology: Expanding our roles. *The Counseling Psychologist*, *31*, 253–272.

White, J. L. (1970). Toward a Black psychology. *Ebony Magazine*, *25*(11), 44–52.

2

FOUNDATIONS OF CRITICAL RACE THEORY

Migration From Law to the Social and Applied Sciences

Robert A. Brown

The Black Lives Matter movement prompted a new public examination of the persistence of racism in the United States (U.S.) (Lebron, 2017). In response, some political commentators and elected officials have focused their ire on Critical Race Theory (CRT) as the intellectual framework for Black Lives Matter (Dixson, 2018). Many of the attacks of CRT conflate other anti-racist theories or political theories such as Marxism with CRT (Cole, 2012). However, the history of racism in the U.S. has shown that backlash to anti-racist efforts in the U.S. is not new. Focusing on the arc of racism's effects in the field of education alone, almost immediately after a score of historic legal victories that ostensibly stopped desegregation in public education, there was an active and violent resistance to busing to desegregate schools, the institution of a system of discipline that more severely punished Black children as compared to white ones, and a massive exodus of whites to suburban schools away from Black families (Delmont, 2016). Unsurprisingly, the trajectory of that racialized response continues to this very day.

In the immediate aftermath of the limited gains of the Civil Rights Movement, scholars of color, lawyers, and activists began to interrogate the persistence of racism in societal institutions (Tate, 1997). CRT emerged early in this post-Civil Rights era as a response to two insufficient strategies of solving white supremacy's persistence. One strategy argued that making society's legal architecture color-blind and banning overt egregious acts of racism will produce a just society (DeCuir & Dixson, 2004). The other strategy contended that racism's most pernicious effects are simply symptoms of a larger societal preference for groups with power and wealth (Stovall, 2006). CRT argues both are insufficient because both overlook the permanent and often hidden nature of racism through biases in systemic institutions (Bell, 1992).

DOI: 10.4324/9780367815325-3

Nearly half a century after the initial formulations of CRT, this now mature body of scholarship spans fields as diverse as law, education, medicine, social work, and the social sciences and is referenced by scholars worldwide. Owing in part to its uneven and asynchronous development, CRT (and its related spinoff theoretical frameworks such as LatCrit and DisCrit) can be a field that is broad and difficult to summarize. However, CRT has several key tenets: (1) Racism is normal, not aberrant; it is a normal part of the landscape such that race-neutral obligations will not stand out (Bell, 1992), (2) Dismantling racist systems requires a focus on marginalized voices and outsider narratives to reveal the unique perspective and voice of racialized and minoritized groups (Delgado & Stefancic, 2000), and (3) White elites will only care about advancing anti-racism to the extent that it advances their own self-interest because of the privileged status that whiteness creates (Bell, 1992).

This chapter seeks to document the migration of CRT from law to education and provide a framework for understanding its existence. I describe the historical underpinnings of CRT, highlighting theoretical beginnings in the academic legal literature. I then detail its inner workings, assumptions, and impacts and the current application of the theory across fields. Finally, I describe the relevance of CRT to school psychology.

Historical Underpinnings of Critical Race Theory

The earliest history of CRT is often framed as a series of publications or events associated with a group of academic legal scholars. However, as Crenshaw (2011) noted in her 20-year history of the Movement in 2010, the genealogy of CRT is not merely the names of anti-racist scholars collectively, nor their bodies of work. What distinguishes CRT from the broader field of anti-racism is that CRT is a cohesive body of research dedicated to knowledge production around naming, defining, describing, and ultimately deconstructing how racism creates systems that harm racialized and minoritized individuals and communities. In particular, CRT examines the often hidden (or layered) ways in which systems impose power upon racialized people.

Given that CRT emerged as a response to dominant legal theories, next I detail four major movements in U.S. legal thought that set the context for CRT's growth: (1) the end of the Civil War and the rise of the Industrial Age and the associated 'scientification' of legal analysis from the 1920s, (2) the Great Depression and the associated rise of Realism until the 1960s, (3) the Civil Rights Movement and the concomitant start of the Critical Legal Studies Movement, and (4) the rise of neo-conservatism in the post-Civil Rights era and CRT's birth.

Post–Civil War Era and the Rise of Legal Formalism

While current popular thinking about the law envisions judicial decision-making as precise, from the end of the Civil War until the 1890s, judge-made law and legal commentary in the U.S. was a hodge-podge with no clear doctrinal framework (Patterson, 1995). Legal scholars began to advocate that judges should decide cases strictly based on precedents set by prior courts, mechanistically apply the law, prioritize objectives, and rely on a singular (cohesive) theory without considering the societal effects of their decision-making. This approach to legal analysis soon came to be the dominant and unifying theory of legal thought, termed "Legal Formalism" (Gilmore, 1979).

Legal Formalism has made a recent comeback as neo-conservatives have argued that the U.S. Constitution should be strictly construed to limit the discretion of judges to interpret the Constitution in a way that expands rights, particularly to oppressed groups (Sunstein, 1997). This same neo-conservative approach, which advocates a systemic and formalistic application of race-neutral rules using science to eliminate racism, runs across social science research and societal institutions (Sniderman et al., 1996).

The 1920s to the 1960s and Legal Realism

In the 1920s a group of legal scholars disrupted the dominant hold that Legal Formalism had on the academic legal literature. Their doctrine, which later came to be known as Legal Realism, contended that courts should have a broader discretion to consider the larger societal practices. Legal Realists argued that the mechanistic readings of prior court rulings or statutes to make legal decisions, as required by Legal Formalism, too severely limited judges from making the best legal decisions for society (Gilmore, 1979).

Today, the theories of Legal Formalism and Legal Realism form a hybrid theory that is the dominant theory of legal decision-making, which requires a formalistic focus on consistency with prior decisions, with limited exceptions for changes in response to scientific evidence or overwhelming public support (Posner, 1986). This framework mirrors much of societal thinking about race to which CRT responds: that systems would eliminate racism if they simply removed any racial preferences for any group (a formalism approach that promotes color blindness in the law) and the occasional sanction for egregious acts of racism (a realism approach).

The Civil Rights Movement and Critical Legal Studies

By the 1960s, legal scholars, informed by the social change throughout society of the Civil Rights Movement and the Vietnam War, began to interrogate formalism and realism doctrines in the law (Brown & Jackson, 2013). Those scholars, in a field they named Critical Legal Studies, noted that this 'scientific' and ostensibly 'objective' approach to the law had the consistent and predictable outcome of favoring those in power, and supposedly well-settled legal rules were not applied universally (Tushnet, 1991; Unger, 1983).

Critical Legal Studies advocates pushed back in two principled ways from this dominant thinking in legal scholarship and practice. First, they argued that society's social ordering was a function of the preferences of those in power and those with the greatest economic resources (Cole, 2012). Interrogating expressions of economic power, in their view, required a theoretical framework that looked beyond traditional legal analysis to uncover the power dynamics based on class and economic power (Standen, 1986). Second, they argued that even the purportedly objective long-standing legal rules could not be used to reach a consistent set of outcomes (Delgado & Stefancic, 2000).

Initially, many of the earliest Critical Race Theorists embraced this interrogation in Critical Legal Studies that looked for the hidden drivers of public policy and legal decision-making. However, they soon became frustrated with an argument that there was indeterminacy in legal decision-making. Critical Race Theorists found that this indeterminacy was a function of the normalcy of a society's racism: the creation of categories to advance a white supremacy that protected white bodies at the expense of Black ones.

The Rise of Neoconservatism and Neoliberalism (1990–Present)

The image of these three interlocking theories (formalism, realism, and Critical Legal Studies) created a doctrine that many academic and law practitioners follow in their thinking about the legal rules that govern and create societal institutions: that there should be a relatively static and unitary theory (formalism) that has flexibility for well-known exceptions (realism) and that any large systemic biases the system has against groups are largely a function of class (Critical Legal Studies).

These dominant doctrines have been the impetus for legal rules that only sanction individual actors for overt acts of racism and have overlooked the non-obvious ways that racism (and systems of subordination) hurts racialized groups. As a result, unlike traditional civil rights scholarship, which stresses incrementalism and step-by-step progress, CRT questions the very foundations of the liberal order, including equality theory and legal reasoning (Delgado & Stefancic, 2000).

In sum, CRT developed after the resurgence of color blindness in the law. Starting in the late 1970s and over the next 20 years, law professors and activists developed a body of literature that later inspired scholars in other fields with nomenclature and theoretical framework to engage racism's persistence, the failure of color-blind strategies to remove its effects (in many ways perpetuating those effects), and a theoretical framework to fight systemic racialized bias.

Detailed Discussion of Critical Race Theory

The genealogy of CRT offers important insights in interrogating and evaluating systems that purport to address the effects of racism, even as racism persists. CRT has as its central organizing feature a belief that racism, through the vehicle of white supremacy, is a permanent, normal, and organizing feature of the U.S. In the following section, I outline how CRT and its practitioners use CRT to interrogate and do social justice by answering three crystallizing questions: (1) What does CRT address?, (2) How does CRT create knowledge?, and (3) How do you 'do' CRT?

What Does Critical Race Theory Address?

> *Racism locates the dominant explanation for the depressed socioeconomic, health, and educational condition of people of color in their character and "culture," rather than the structures of power that create the conditions of their lives.*
>
> *(Guinier & Torres, 2002, p. 292)*

Critical Race Theory, as its name suggests, is a theory of race and racism that is critical. The use of 'Critical' is both a reference to critical theories that critique and resolve social inequality through conscious action and a nod to the Critical Legal Studies movement that it was an immediate reaction to. The term 'Race Theory' implies a systematic explanation of the underlying phenomenon or behavior of race. Aggregated together, Critical Race Theory names a social justice and activist theory that focuses on dismantling societal systems based on race, whose core principle is that races have been created by racists to maintain power for white bodies, in ways that are often hidden from plain view.

Racism Is Normal and Permanent

> *Critical race theorists . . . hold that color blindness will allow us to redress only extremely egregious racial harms, ones that everyone would notice and condemn. But if racism is embedded in our thought processes and social structures as deeply as many crits believe, then the "ordinary business" of society—the routines, practices, and institutions that we rely on to effect the world's work—will keep minorities in subordinate positions.*
>
> *(Delgado & Stefancic, 2000, p. 22)*

CRT asserts that racism is a permanent feature of U.S. life (Bell, 1992). This assertion comes in the face of the 1980s argument for color blindness across institutions, or the idea that the best way to remove inequities in society based on race is to remove race as a factor in societal rulemaking. This formalistic thinking about U.S. institutions frames racism as being wrong because people are treated differently based upon their race, an immutable biological characteristic, which they cannot change and is preassigned. This popular view continues noting that because race is merely color, racism's irrational reliance on this characteristic will go away over time, either by education or a focus on the power drivers of race (Bell, 1995).

However, Critical Race Theorists assert that race is not a biological construction, it is a social construction (Pulliam, 2017). Race is not merely a collection of biological characteristics, but rather a marker for whom will feel the brunt of societal power to oppress. While Critical Race Theorists would agree that racial status is ascribed, based in part on biological characteristics (Bonilla-Silva, 1999), they also note that it is pervasive and normal across societal institutions (Ladson-Billings, 2009). As a result, Critical Race Theorists' conceptualization of race as an omnipresent force active in social ordering requires them not to interrogate biology, but how systems use power to socially order groups of people into races (Delgado, & Stefancic, 2000).

Race Is Socially Constructed

The biological determinism position is part of long-standing mythology of white supremacy that is often accompanied by racial essentialism and eugenics. This argument that physical characteristics (predominate amongst them skin color) are associated with character, mental ability, or emotional awareness has been consistently rejected by the scientific community. The belief system associated with this mythology persists in the face of science. Critical Race Theorists argue that it is racism that creates races, and other classes of people, based on sometimes-inconsistent views of skin color, hair texture, and ethnicity. Racism, then, is a belief system that justifies the subordination of racialized bodies for the benefit of white ones.

How Does Critical Race Theory Create Knowledge?

My mother told me, "Baby, doesn't she know that our stories are our theories?"
(Brayboy, 2005, p. 426)

CRT's knowledge-production modality starts with a post-modern embrace that rejects positivism—or the philosophy that all rational assertions can also be scientifically verified—as the sole means of knowledge production. Positivism is a dominant research ideology that attempts to import the consistency of the natural sciences to the social sciences, with a focus on data and measurement of observed phenomena. Critical Race Theorists found that positivism produced legal rules and systems that replicate, but did not interrogate, the status quo. This reification of data without context had the predictable effect of centering traditional research and silencing voices from the margins of our society. As a result, CRT has at its core a knowledge-production posture that positivism reinforces the status quo and silences marginalized voices and that knowledge production should focus on those who have experienced discrimination because they speak with a special voice (Matsuda, 1987).

Rejection of Positivism

> *As CRT scholars, we strive to deconstruct and expose the research paradigms that ignore the role of the observer in the construction of social reality and thereby fail to consider the historical and social conditions that distort and ignore the experiences of People of Color.*
>
> *(Malagon et al., 2009, p. 260)*

Critical Race Theorists found that the very methods of data collection and scholarship themselves created biases that obscured the voices of racialized people and supported the status quo. For example, researchers have noted that "knowledge generation in the social sciences follows a scientifically based, empirical approach of isolating variables and hypothesizing their relationship using a sampling procedure that is believed to increase the probability of the representation of all known characteristics" (Ortiz & Jani, 2010, p. 182). This positivist approach would require researchers to ignore voices at the margin or voices that may fit one of the sampling requirements but not all if they believed that those voices were not 'representative of the population.' Critical Race Theorists argue that this initial choice of research method, where representativeness is prized without context, is one that contains a bias against marginalized voices. Worse yet, the choice of isolating variables to operationalize a hypothesis reduces the complex phenomenon of racism to sometimes-binary choices of chosen variables. For example, studies that evaluate academic achievement by comparing groups by racial identification or the income of their parents, without noting the effects of white supremacy or other confounding variables, may draw conclusions that underweight the impact of racism. As a result, CRT requires researchers and practitioners alike to interrogate their use of statistics, binary formulations, and reductions. This interrogation does not stop at the choice of data but the literature base from which research and practice are done as well.

Relatedly, CRT draws broadly across disciplines to analyze racism in both historical and contemporary contexts (Solorzano, 1998). Its scholarship and practice require fundamentally centering the voices of the marginalized, particularly those outside of the privileged spaces of the Academia. This is done not merely as an additional check to 'confirm' the conclusions of quantitative sources but to determine how those voices inform and add to the literature (Ladson-Billings, 2009).

Focus on Voice and Narrative

> *Critical race theory insists on recognition of the experiential knowledge of people of color and . . . knowledge . . . gained from critical reflection on the lived experience of racism and from . . . active political practice toward the elimination of racism.*
>
> *(Lawrence et al., 1993, p. 6)*

Consistent with a rejection of positivism as the sole method of scientific inquiry, Critical Race Theorists posit that a quantitative-data-focused approach to knowledge production and problem-solving, without other context or the lived experience of those who experienced racism, will replicate the very biases at the heart of racism. As a result, since the very inception of CRT, the centrality of experiential knowledge linked to racism and a connection to historical context and interdisciplinary perspectives have been fundamental principles (Montoya, 2000).

Derrick Bell and Richard Delgado, in their earliest CRT works, argued that narratives, which they termed "counter-stories," were an important method of knowledge production to disrupt the dominant narrative (Jones, 2002). Delgado (1989) noted, "And I don't just mean writing about stories or narrative theory, important as those are. I mean actual stories, as in 'once-upon-a-time' type stories" (p. 2411). The importance of these narratives and counter-stories is to make visible the often-invisible dominant narratives that frame legal and political discourse (Delgado, 1989).

Critical Race Theorists argue that an important method for interrogating race-neutrality or color blindness is hearing stories from racialized and marginalized people. This focus on voice is a critical part of the knowledge-production praxis of CRT because of the hidden and normal operation of racism and white supremacy. Positivist approaches to research suggest that research can be done about systems of power in the U.S. without focusing on race. However, even that very choice is one that relies on a narrative of the normalness of silence—and by design, those silenced voices come from racialized and marginalized bodies.

Scholars have noted that these counter-stories can serve at least four theoretical, methodological, and pedagogical functions: (1) They can build community among those at the margins of society, (2) They can challenge the perceived wisdom of those at society's center, (3) They can open new windows into the reality of those at the margins of society, and (4) They can teach others that by combining elements from both the story and the current reality, one can construct another world that is richer (Yosso & Solórzano, 2005).

Ladson-Billings, the leading scholar to import CRT to education, also cautioned aspiring CRT scholars to be careful with the "lure" of CRT's counter-storytelling as a technique. She noted that there is a danger in the uncritical use of narrative or storytelling that can overlook the importance of advancing the voices of marginalized people "without providing the larger social contexts that can be used to exploit one person or group while simultaneously advantaging another" (Ladson-Billings, 2016, p. ix). Scholars have noted that much of the literature on CRT in education has focused on storytelling as a modality (Ladson-Billings, 2009).

However, Ladson-Billing's admonition is an important reminder that stories of the lived experiences of racialized and marginalized people themselves are theories of existence, theories that may offer more truth and explanatory value toward solving racism than quantitative studies on similar topics. As Matsuda (1987) noted, the "technique of imagining oneself [B]lack and poor in some hypothetical world is less effective than studying the actual experience of [B]lack poverty and listening to those who have done so" (p. 325).

How Do You 'Do' Critical Race Theory Work?

> *Some struggles between old and new ideas, some battles between ways of seeing have only victors.*
>
> *(Bambara, 1980, p. 219)*

The work of CRT is identifying, naming, and dismantling systems that create a social order based upon race. In so doing, other related subordinations will also be uncovered, e.g., subordinations based on gender, sexual orientation, gender expression, or ability.

Delgado and Stefancic (2000) in their classic book, *Critical Race Theory*, noted that there are three categories of CRT scholars and practitioners: Idealists, who work to change discourse and rhetoric that privileges whites and disparages racialized bodies; Economic Realists, who work to change the status that grants whites first and exclusive access to societal resources; and Materialists, who want to change the relationship between economic power and racial subordination (Delgado & Stefancic, 2000). Here, I use that framework to describe the three different activist approaches to dismantling racist systems.

Idealists—Discourse Can Matter

> *Preach, church, tabernacle, Tallahassee sunshine*
> *Southern is my bloodline, we know it'll come time . . . to go*
> *And though I leave like alumni*
> *I'm lying like a lullaby and quiet like my tongue tied . . . alone.*
>
> *(Warner & Wilder, 2016, track 10)*

Delgado and Stefancic (2000) described Idealists as a group of Critical Race Theorists who focus on the social construction of race and related discrimination through images and discourse of racialized bodies. Scholars have noted that markers of difference from whiteness are frequently used as tools to promote racialized agendas and outcomes (Yosso & Solórzano, 2005). As a result, to curb the power of this racialization, these Critical Race Theorists argue for hate speech codes and greater representation of Black images in public discourse (Delgado & Stefancic, 2000).

One of the critical ways that this movement has made an impact on images and discourse is in disputing the discourse around merit. In the color-blind world articulated by neo-conservatives, there is often an argument that society's social ordering is not a function of race but a function of a meritocracy that rewards those who are simply most talented. Critical Race Theorists in the idealist tradition disrupt this framing in two important ways. First, they critique the very notion of a meritocracy, noting the key examples where it does not apply and the idea of a meritocracy as a social construction that favors a certain sort of credentials obtained by white candidates and overlooks those by people of color (Bernal, 2002). Second, they point out the narrative images of Black excellence that are overlooked. This disruptive framing is one of the ways Critical Race Theorists can challenge dominant narratives that cast racialized bodies as less-than and white ones as consistently superior.

Realists or Economic Determinists—Whiteness as Property

> *Whiteness as property has taken on more subtle forms but retains its core characteristic—the legal legitimation of expectations of power and control that enshrine the status quo as a neutral baseline, while masking the maintenance of white privilege and domination.*
>
> *(Harris, 1993, p. 1714–15)*

Economic Determinists argue that racism is a method by which society allocated status to protect the power position of whites at the expense of racialized bodies. It is this status that allocates whites superior and gives them first access to resources.

Cheryl Harris's formulation of Whiteness as Property is perhaps the most influential of the CRT tenets that discusses the status of whiteness and its nature as property and first-priority interest on the resources of society. Professor Harris argued that whiteness is far from just a racial category, but rather an investment in power. In so doing, her formulation pushes the analysis of race not merely as a formulation of anti-discrimination, but rather an exploration into the power of whiteness (Harris, 1993). She noted that the legal status of whiteness grants to whites the power to use societal resources first, including education, and to exclude non-whites, particularly Black people from access to societal resources.

Two years after Harris published her groundbreaking article, Ladson-Billings and Tate (1995) used her framework to argue that access to a high-quality, rigorous curriculum is part of how the status of whiteness has allowed white students unique access to tracking, honors, and/or gifted programs and advanced placement courses. Adrienne Dixson extended this analysis to interrogate the myriad of systems in which whiteness is not merely the absence of oppression but is central to resources being protected (DeCuir & Dixson, 2004).

These scholars have collectively argued that the status of whiteness creates a social ordering where societal benefits can go. Critical Race Theorists in this tradition name and disrupt how purportedly color-blind practices reaffirm a system that grants status and special privileges to white bodies at the expense of Black ones.

Materialists—Interest Group Convergence

> *The interest of [B]lacks in achieving racial equality will be accommodated only when it converges with the interests of whites. . . . The Fourteenth Amendment, standing alone, will not authorize a judicial remedy providing effective racial equality for [B]lacks where the remedy sought threatens the superior societal status of middle- and upper-class whites.*
>
> *(Bell, 1980, p. 523)*

Critical race materialism signifies an approach to interpreting law and society by reading the past to examine the relations between racial status and economic group power (Valdes & Cho, 2011). The Materialists note that history has shown that those with power tend to economically exploit those groups who are not. As a result, Materialists focus on economic power as the primary means of dismantling racism.

Materialism provides a cautionary note: Because racial status is tied to economic positioning, groups at the top of the economic strata have created racism and racial categories to define their position. Derrick Bell's Interest Group Convergence thesis extended this analysis by postulating that white elites will only be motivated to help Black people and other people of color when it is in their economic interest to do so (Bell, 1980).

As an example of this thesis, Bell (1980) noted that even the vaunted *Brown v. Board of Education* decision, which is often noted as a highlight of progress for racial justice, was not done out of an altruistic desire to help Black children obtain a better education—there had been lawsuits for decades making that claim—but rather to help white elites by improving the United States' standing in the international community (Bell, 1980).

Critical Race scholars and activists in this tradition have worked to expand intersections with other marginalized groups to change the power dynamic. Others, noting racism's permanence, have suggested that disruption requires a focus on improving the economic standing of racialized groups to give them access to the resources that white elites have been unwilling to give up (Milner, 2008). Naturally, Critical Race Theorists can work in both traditions simultaneously.

Current Applications of Critical Race Theory Across Fields

Although CRT has its earliest and deepest roots in the academic legal literature base, one of its largest and most robust bodies of literature exists in the field of education. However, given the interdisciplinary nature of CRT, the social sciences have long played a major role in its canon.

Education

Many of the legal scholars that began the tradition of CRT focused on the desegregation of public education in the U.S. As a result, it is not surprising that the field of education would feature a robust amount of CRT literature.

The most well-known foray into CRT was Ladson-Billings' (1998) article entitled "Just what is Critical Race Theory and what's it doing in a *nice* field like education?" Her initial description of CRT was the beginning in a host of other articles by her and William Tate describing how racism and the theory of color blindness had infected education scholarship. Later, scholars like Marvin Lynn and Adrienne Dixson in their books on CRT in education expanded CRT's application to examine the persistence of racial inequities in the educational system in the U.S. (Lynn & Dixson, 2013).

What ties together this sample of work, and the CRT work in the social sciences more broadly, is the extension of anti-racist work to an activist agenda that looks to unmask the hidden manifestations of racism, in both theory and praxis.

Relevance of Critical Race Theory to School Psychology

School psychology educators, practitioners, and policymakers have grappled with the question of racial disproportionality in identifying students for special education (Sullivan & Proctor, 2016) on a parallel track with the 50-year trajectory of legal scholars grappling with similar questions in the advancement of CRT. While in the school psychology literature base there have been calls for more robust use of critical theory (Proctor, 2018), articles that discuss the potential application of CRT (Vega et al., 2015), and other articles that address CRT with passing references to the roles of school psychologists (Anyon et al., 2018), there is only one chapter to date that discusses the application of CRT to the field of school psychology (Newell & Kratochwill, 2007). Taken as a whole, there has not emerged in the extant literature base school psychology-specific CRT. However, CRT's central tenets offer a great toolset to help to name and dismantle school psychologists' role in maintaining an educational system ordered by race.

The academic literature base of school psychology includes a history of studies that improperly assert correlation between racial groups and intelligence because of failures of study design (Pendergrast et al., 2017). Yet there is no shortage of studies in the school psychology literature base—and beyond—which assert *biological* conclusions about *social* categories. As an example, one article, in describing how racial differences in mean scores on psychological and educational assessments may not necessarily be examples of racial bias in testing, draws the comparison to a bathroom scale that shows differences in the mean weight of men and women, with men, on average, weighing more than women and notes that would not show the scale's bias (Pendergrast et al., 2017).

However, CRT (and radical feminists) would note that this example overlooks the fact that gender is a social construct in the same way that race is. Using the CRT modality of employing an outsider narrative, the perspective of gender minorities in this case (e.g., trans men and women, intersex, gender nonconforming, and nonbinary individuals) makes plain that it is the social construction of the concept of gender that determines the weight of men and women, not biological measurement. (The example assumes that men and women only fit traditional gender categories; the conclusion of the example makes no sense when the category of gender is interrogated using CRT's modality of centering outsider narratives.)

This modality would help to unmask and dismantle racism in school psychology more broadly. For example, communities where school psychologist scholars research and where practitioners work must also center narratives from those communities (and outsider narratives specific to those communities) to unmask and name racialized biases that have become normalized. For academic research, that can mean interrogating concepts by centering outsider narratives to uncover bias. It can also mean the intentional inclusion of individuals from racialized groups in all aspects of knowledge production: from conceptualization, research, publication, and discussion within the academic community. For practitioner work, it can mean centering outsider narratives in reports and other works about students, teachers, administrators, and staff members.

Finally, CRT informs us that racial justice will often be fought by white elites who may only act when it is in their perceived self-interest. The important work of changing the narratives around Black children away from deficit-centered narratives (or essentialized views that assume characteristics about all Black children without ever centering their lived experiences), for example, will face opposition from even those who may nominally say that they are allies. Similarly, the work to dismantle a set of preferences that give whiteness a first claim on societal resources will also be fought by those who benefit from the system of white supremacy. As a result, the work of dismantling race-based preferences, be it locally or systemically, is one that will undoubtedly be met with opposition, even by those who ostensibly would be most willing to be allies in the struggle.

Conclusion

In conclusion, since the inception of CRT in the academic legal literature base nearly five decades ago, this powerful lens into the often-hidden ways in which racism has stymied racial justice in the U.S. has migrated across the social sciences. The principal conclusions that racism is permanent, socially constructed, and requires a set of broad tools beyond color-blind applications of positivist methods of knowledge production has had a great effect throughout many fields. The system of white supremacy that has given white citizens priority over societal resources in all aspects of U.S. life is pervasive and often normalized. As a result, if the quest for racial justice is to be successful, we must work to center the experiences of those who experience racism or face a world where your race still determines your place in society.

References

Anyon, Y., Lechuga, C., Ortega, D., Downing, B., Greer, E., & Simmons, J. (2018). An exploration of the relationships between student racial background and the school sub-contexts of office discipline referrals: A critical race theory analysis. *Race Ethnicity and Education, 21*(3), 390–406. http://dx.doi.org/10.1080/13613324.2017.1328594

Bambara, T. C. (1980). *The salt eaters*. Random House.

Bell, D. A. (1980). Brown v. Board of Education and the interest-convergence dilemma. *Harvard Law Review, 93*(3), 518–533. https://doi.org/10.2307/1340546

Bell, D. A. (1992). *Faces at the bottom of the well: The permanence of racism*. Hachette UK.

Bell, D. A. (1995). Who's afraid of critical race theory. *University of Illinois Law Review, 1995*(4), 893–910.

Bernal, D. D. (2002). Critical race theory, Latino critical theory, and critical raced-gendered epistemologies: Recognizing students of color as holders and creators of knowledge. *Qualitative Inquiry, 8*(1), 105–126. https://doi.org/10.1177/107780040200800107

Bonilla-Silva, E. (1999). The essential social fact of race. *American Sociological Review, 64*(6), 899–906. https://doi.org/10.2307/2657410

Brayboy, B. M. J. (2005). Toward a tribal critical race theory in education. *Urban Review, 37*(5), 425–446. http://doi.org/10.1007/s11256-005-0018-y

Brown, K., & Jackson, D. (2013). The history and conceptual elements of critical race theory. In M. Lynn & A. D. Dixson (Eds.). *Handbook of critical race theory in education* (pp. 29–42). Routledge. https://doi.org/10.4324/9780203155721

Cole, M. (2012). Critical race theory in education, Marxism and abstract racial domination. *British Journal of Sociology of Education, 33*(2), 167–183. https://doi.org/10.1080/01425692.2011.649830

Crenshaw, K. W. (2011). Twenty years of critical race theory: Looking back to move forward. *Connecticut Law Review, 43*(5), 1253–1352.

Decuir, J. T., & Dixson, A. D. (2004). "So when it comes out, they aren't that surprised that it is there": Using critical race theory as a tool of analysis of race and racism in education. *Educational Researcher, 33*(5), 26–31. https://doi.org/10.3102/0013189X033005026

Delgado, R. (1989). Storytelling for oppositionists and others: A plea for narrative. *Michigan Law Review, 87*(8), 2411–2441. https://doi.org/10.2307/1289308

Delgado, R., & Stefancic, J. (Eds.). (2000). *Critical Race theory: The cutting edge* (3rd ed.). Temple University Press.

Delmont, M. F. (2016). *Why busing failed: Race, media, and the national resistance to school desegregation*. University of California Press.

Dixson, A. D. (2018). "What's going on?": A critical race theory perspective on Black Lives Matter and activism in education. *Urban Education, 53*(2), 231–247. https://doi.org/10.1177/0042085917747115

Gilmore, G. (1979). Formalism and the law of negotiable instruments. *Creighton Law Review, 13*(2), 441–461.

Guinier, L., & Torres, G. (2002). *The miner's canary: Enlisting race, resisting power, transforming democracy*. Harvard University Press.

Harris, C. I. (1993). Whiteness as property. *Harvard Law Review, 106*(8), 1707–1791. https://doi.org/10.2307/1341787

Jones, B. D. (2002). Critical race theory: New strategies for civil rights in the new millennium. *Harvard Black Letter Law Journal, 18*(1), 1–90.

Ladson-Billings, G. (1998). Just what is critical race theory and what's it doing in a nice field like education? *International Journal of Qualitative Studies in Education, 11*(1), 7–24. https://doi.org/10.1080/095183998236863

Ladson-Billings, G. (2009). Race still matters: Critical race theory in education. In M. W. Apple, W. Au, & L. A. Gandin (Eds.), *The Routledge international handbook of critical education* (pp. 110–122). Routledge.

Ladson-Billings, G. (2016). Forward: The evolving role of critical race theory in educational scholarship. In J. K. Donnor & C. K. Rousseau Anderson (Eds.), *Critical race theory in education: All god's children got a song* (p. ix). Taylor & Francis.

Ladson-Billings, G., & Tate IV, W. F. (1995). Toward a critical race theory of education. *Teachers College Record, 97*(1), 47–68.

Lawrence, C. R., III, Matsuda, M. J., Delgado, R., & Crenshaw, K. W. (1993). Introduction. In M. J. Matsuda, C. R. Lawrence III, R. Delgado, & K. W. Crenshaw (Eds.), *Words that wound: Critical race theory, assaultive speech, and the First Amendment* (pp. 1–16). Westview Press. https://doi.org/10.4324/9780429502941

Lebron, C. J. (2017). *The making of Black lives matter: A brief history of an idea.* Oxford University Press.

Lynn, M., & Dixson, A. D. (2013). *Handbook of critical race theory in education.* Routledge.

Malagon, M. C., Huber, L. P., & Velez, V. N. (2009). Our experiences, our methods: Using grounded theory to inform a critical race theory methodology. *Seattle Journal for Social Justice, 8*, 253–269.

Matsuda, M. J. (1987). Looking to the bottom: Critical legal studies and reparations. *Harvard Civil Rights-Civil Liberties Law Review, 22*(2), 323–399.

Milner, H. R., IV, (2008). Critical race theory and interest convergence as analytic tools in teacher education policies and practices. *Journal of Teacher Education, 59*(4), 332–346. https://doi.org/10.1177/0022487108321884

Montoya, M. E. (2000). Silence and silencing: Their centripetal and centrifugal forces in legal communication, pedagogy and discourse. *University of Michigan Journal of Law Reform, 33*(3), 263–327.

Newell, M., & Kratochwill, T. R. (2007). The integration of response to intervention and critical race theory-disability studies: A robust approach to reducing racial discrimination in evaluation decisions. In S. R. Jimerson, M. K. Burns, & A. M. VanDerHeyden (Eds.), *Handbook of response to intervention: The science and practice of assessment and intervention* (pp. 65–79). Springer. https://doi.org/10.1007/978-0-387-49053-3_5

Ortiz, L., & Jani, J. (2010). Critical race theory: A transformational model for teaching diversity. *Journal of Social Work Education, 46*(2), 175–193. https://doi.org/10.5175/JSWE.2010.200900070

Patterson, D. (1995). Langdell's legacy. *Northwestern University Law Review, 90*(1), 196–203.

Pendergast, L. L., von der Embse, N. P., Kilgus, S. P., & Eklund, K. R. (2017). Measurement equivalence: A non-technical primer on categorical multigroup confirmatory factor analysis in school psychology. *Journal of School Psychology, 60*, 65–82. https://doi.org/10.1016/j.jsp.2016.11.002

Posner, R. A. (1986). Legal formalism, legal realism, and the interpretation of statutes and the constitution. *Case Western Reserve Law Review, 37*(2), 179–217.

Proctor, S. L., Kyle, J., Fefer, K., & Lau, Q. C. (2018). Examining racial microaggressions, race/ethnicity, gender, and bilingual status with school psychology students: The role of intersectionality. *Contemporary School Psychology*, *22*(3), 355–368. https://doi.org/10.1007/s40688-017-0156-8

Pulliam, R. M. (2017). Practical application of critical race theory: A social justice course design. *Journal of Social Work Education*, *53*(3), 414–423. https://doi.org/10.1080/10437797.2016.1275896

Sniderman, P. M., Carmines, E. G., Layman, G. C., & Carter, M. (1996). Beyond race: Social justice as a race neutral ideal. *American Journal of Political Science*, *40*(1), 33–55. https://doi.org/10.2307/2111693

Solorzano, D. G. (1998). Critical race theory, race and gender microaggressions, and the experience of Chicana and Chicano scholars. *International Journal of Qualitative Studies in Education*, *11*(1), 121–136. https://doi.org/10.1080/095183998236926

Standen, J. A. (1986). Critical legal studies as an anti-positivist phenomenon. *Virginia Law Review*, *72*(5), 983–998. https://doi.org/10.2307/1072930

Stovall, D. (2006). Forging community in race and class: Critical race theory and the quest for social justice in education. *Race Ethnicity and Education*, *9*(3), 243–259. https://doi.org/10.1080/13613320600807550

Sullivan, A. L., & Proctor, S. L. (2016). The shield or the sword? Revisiting the debate on racial disproportionality in special education and implications for school psychologists. *School Psychology Forum*, *10*(3), 278–288.

Sunstein, C. R. (1997). Justice Scalia's democratic formalism. *Yale Law Journal*, *107*, 529–567.

Tate, W. F., IV, (1997). Chapter 4: Critical race theory and education: History, theory, and implications. *Review of Research in Education*, *22*(1), 195–247. https://doi.org/10.3102/0091732X022001195

Tushnet, M. (1991). Critical legal studies: A political history. *Yale Law Journal*, *100*(5), 1515–1544.

Unger, R. M. (1983). The critical legal studies movement. *Harvard Law Review*, *96*(3), 561–675. https://doi.org/10.2307/1341032

Valdes, F., & Cho, S. (2011). Critical race materialism: Theorizing justice in the wake of global neoliberalism. *Connecticut Law Review*, *43*(5), 1513–1572.

Vega, D., Moore, J. L., III, & Miranda, A. H. (2015). Who really cares? Urban youths' perceptions of parental and programmatic support. *School Community Journal*, *25*(1), 53–72.

Warner, F. N., & Wilder, Z. (2016). Shadow Man [Recorded by Noname featuring theMIND, Cam O'bi, Saba, Smino, & Phoelix]. On Telefone [MP3 file]. Chicago, IL.

Yosso, T. J., & Solórzano, D. G. (2005). Conceptualizing a critical race theory in sociology. In M. Romero & E. Margolis (Eds.), *The Blackwell companion to social inequalities* (pp. 117–146). Blackwell. https://doi.org/ 10.1002/9780470996973

3

DISCRIT

Disability Critical Race Theory

Sujay Sabnis and Carlos Bueno Martinez

Disability Critical Race Theory (also called DisCrit) carves out a specific space in the field of education where the intersection of race and disability is front and center, rather than an afterthought. Critics within the transdisciplinary field of Disability Studies have noted the exclusion of race from the matter of disability in a way that centered the white disabled body. Bell (2006) labeled the field as "white disability studies" while criticizing its evasion of race. In addition, critical race studies were also criticized for not engaging adequately with disability (Stienstra & Nyerere, 2016), allowing it to center the racial traumas and experiences of nondisabled people of color. As a result, educational researchers Annamma et al. (2013) coined DisCrit to occupy the in-between spaces and build on Crenshaw's agenda of intentionally centering those who fall at the crossroads of multiple axes of oppression.

This chapter will provide a brief historical overview into the theoretical streams that have influenced DisCrit, mainly Disability Studies, Critical Race Theory, and Intersectionality Theory, followed by a discussion of some of the significant tenets of DisCrit as highlighted by Annamma et al. (2013). We want to briefly discuss the question of language. The American Psychological Association advocates for person-first language use when referring to people with disabilities as a way to counter negative bias (Dunn & Andrews, 2015). However, many Disability Studies scholars and disability rights activists self-identify as "disabled people" over "people with disabilities" as a way to "foreground disability as a political category" (Erevelles, 2002, p. 22). They also argue that identity-first language fosters a sense of belongingness and shared purpose toward the disability culture (Dunn & Andrews, 2015). An individual's decision to self-identify using person-first language or identity-first language may depend on many factors, including the stage of their disability identity development (Dunn & Andrews, 2015). In

DOI: 10.4324/9780367815325-4

this chapter, we use both depending on the context. Also note that while disability rights activism has a global presence and regional histories, we specifically discuss it in the context of the U.S.

Historical Underpinnings of DisCrit

Brief History of Disability Rights Activism in the U.S.

Although the construct of disability has long existed, its characteristic as a deficit evoked two common responses. The religious response to disability foregrounded pity and charity (Barton, 2017). The biomedical response to disability (i.e., medical model) utilized "the medical language of symptoms and diagnostic categories" (Linton, 1998, p. 8) to justify various exclusionary practices in the name of treatment or remediation (Erevelles, 2002). In the1970s in the U.S., a newer approach to disability began to take shape among disability rights activities in the light of the Civil Rights Movement—one that treated disability not as a problem to be pitied or solved but as a social group to be respected, represented, and materially empowered *on their own terms*. Disability rights activists argued that while biomedical impairments may exist, the "disability" arises from society's inability or outright refusal to consider the specific needs of disabled people (Amundson, 2005). Social arrangements (architecture, curriculum, communication) privilege the needs of non-disabled people, putting disabled people at a disadvantage, thereby creating disability. This new approach to disability came to be known as the social model of disability because it treated disability as "a social problem that involves discriminatory barriers that bar some people but not others from the goods that society has to offer" (Amundson, 2005, p. 101).

Davis (2013) discussed the first wave of the disability rights movement in which activists organized to put up a united front of people united around their common identity as Persons with Disabilities (PWD). As with most first-wave movements (feminist, Black, queer, etc.), the first wave of disability rights was engaged in shifting the construct of disability into a positive social category and community rather than an individual malady. It also worked to organize and unite People with Disabilities behind a common purpose of demanding a set of basic rights and fighting against discrimination. This organizing bore results in the form of the passage of the Americans with Disabilities Act in 1990—federal legislation that recognized People with Disabilities as a social class with a right to equal treatment (Silvers, 1995).

The second wave of the Disability Rights Movement in the U.S. began to rise in the 1990s. As with many other movements, Davis (2013) discussed how a second wave of the disability movement sought to complicate and add nuance to that which the first wave had successfully stabilized. Having grown up into a relatively stable community of disability rights activists, the newer activists began to introspect the nuances of disability and ethics of liberation (Davis, 2013; Goodley, 2013). They began to address the tensions and the fault lines that had existed within the disability groups along racialized, gendered, and classed lines. In the past, these tensions had been either neglected or deliberately overlooked in the interest of maintaining a unified basis for intragroup unity (Davis, 2013).

Disability Studies

The social model of disability utilized by disability rights activists provided significant impetus to the field of Disability Studies (Erevelles, 2002), a transdisciplinary academic discipline that "challenge[d] the naturalness of these constructions in the curriculum, in popular culture, and in politics" (Erevelles, 2002, p. 8). According to Erevelles (2002), Disability Studies works "in concert with [the] Disability Rights Movement to support the interests of disabled people as a social class" (p. 8). Academic and theoretical work during the early period of Disability Studies heavily involved establishing the various factors that led to the cultural, material, and political exclusion of People with Disabilities (Goodley, 2013, p. 631). Some scholars also began to push back against the presumed universality of the Western-centric theories and analytical tools used in Disability Studies (Meekosha, 2011). They began to engage with the existing pieces of knowledge of and responses to disability in the Global South. The edited volume by Rao and Kalyanpur (2014) exemplified one such attempt to bring these insights into conversation with the Disability Studies in the West. These developments reflected an attempt at decentering the West as the default reference point for analysis. Changes in other cultural spheres also impacted this stage.

By the end of the first decade of the 21st century, Disability Studies began to transform into Critical Disability Studies (Meekosha & Shuttleworth, 2009). Whereas Disability Studies was more or less a modernist project grounded in a structural materialist analysis of the society (Goodley, 2013), Critical Disability Studies reflected the postmodern shift characterized by a crisis of representation, challenges to unified theories of liberation, and complex debates about the ethics of care (Goodley, 2013). Following post-structural critiques of humanism, identity began to be formulated in much less essentialized terms (Erevelles, 2002). Identity began to be understood as a discursive formation that was constantly shifting along with cultural, social, and material conditions. Recently, more specific communities have emerged within the academic community of Critical Disability Studies. For instance, the emerging field of Critical Autism Studies challenges dominant assumptions about autism as a neurological deficit and instead theorizes "autistic" as a social identity "that is materially and discursively produced within specific sociocultural contexts" (O'Dell et al., 2016, p. 2).

Critical Race Theory

CRT emerged in the field of legal studies as a reaction to the liberal approaches to legal theory (Erevelles, 2002). Legal scholars of color such as Crenshaw (1995) questioned the fundamental premise of existing legal scholarship. They challenged many of its assumptions such as courts and legislatures as neutral institutions with no race or class interests and the U.S. as a fundamentally just meritocratic system where racial injustice was merely an occasional aberration. They also worked against narrow definitions of racism as individual acts committed with intention. They broadened the scope of racism to include institutional racism and unintentional acts by individuals. Finally, they pushed to define racism not just in terms of a process but also an outcome (see Crenshaw, 1995). In sum, CRT legal scholars sought to rescue the construct of "racism" from the constraining framework of liberal humanist ideology. See Chapter 2 for a detailed discussion on CRT.

Intersectionality

Kimberle Crenshaw's (1989) theorization of intersectionality provided Annamma et al. (2013) the impetus for DisCrit. An intersectional perspective enables us to consider "the ways in which [structures] of power inextricably connect with and shape each other to create a system of interlocking oppressions" (Roberts & Jesudason, 2013, p. 314). For a more detailed discussion of intersectionality, see Chapter 1.

Detailed Discussion of DisCrit

DisCrit draws on Intersectionality Theory, CRT, and Disability Studies to "investigate how patterns of oppression uniquely intersect to target students at the margins of Whiteness and ability" (Annamma et al., 2018b, p. 46). Annamma et al. (2018a) discussed the case of Natasha McKenna, a 37-year-old Black woman with schizophrenia who was killed in police custody. The justification for excessive force by six deputies involved in her murder was that she had "super human strength" (p. 235) during a confrontation. Annamma et al. (2018a) pointed to how this excuse of superhuman strength is frequently deployed by state representatives when protecting officers involved in extrajudicial killings of Black people due to excessive force. A social psychological experiment conducted by Waytz et al. (2015) found that white people, in general, tend to perceive Black people as having "superhuman" strength. This conflation of Blackness and physical strength then justifies the use of surveillance, police brutality, and incarceration, and even executions. The biased physical appraisal of Black people also leads white people to see Black children as older and less innocent. The material impacts of this are that officers are more likely to use physical force against Black minors than white minors, and schools and the criminal justice system to take more punitive actions against them than against white peers (Epstein et al., 2017).

Medical research also found that doctors tend to view Black people as having a higher tolerance for pain than white people. This construction of Black people as being physically strong, having a thicker skin, and therefore being more resistant to pain often leads physicians to prescribe lower dosages of analgesics or other pain relief medications than they would for a white patient with a similar level of self-reported pain (Hoffman et al., 2016). In K-12 education, there is ample research demonstrating the disproportionate placement of students of color in specific disability categories such as "Learning Disability," "Intellectual Disability," and "Emotional Disturbance or Behavior Disorders" (Harry & Klingner, 2006). These examples demonstrate how race and ability are inextricably entangled. In other words, they come to mutually constitute each other, where Blackness becomes imbued with certain abilities or dis/abilities. Further, these examples also illustrate the *material* impact of the race-disability intersection. Although both race and dis/ability are social constructions, they have real and *material* impacts in the social world, in terms of increased mortality, incarceration, surveillance, and/or the State's neglect of Black people.

The dis/abling of Blackness also involves imbuing it with certain intellectual deficits. In 1920, W. E. B. Du Bois documented the efforts of white eugenicists and phrenologists to tie racial classification to intellectual capacities (see Du Bois, 1920). Valencia (1997) reviewed the history of education policy in the U.S. to show how Black children were constructed as intellectually inferior to white children. This disabling became a common justification for segregated schooling, and it underfunded schools in predominantly Black neighborhoods. Following *Brown v. Board*, newer strategies of segregation came into the picture. Educational practices such as tracking and educational structures such as special education became means for carrying out *de facto* segregation. The social construction of Black students as intellectually inferior compared to white students is frequently cited as one of the reasons for the disproportionate concentration of Black students in special education (Vallas, 2009) as well as lower tracks (Mickelson, 2002).

Tenets of DisCrit

Theorists operating from a DisCrit vantage point theorize ways in which disability and race intersect, often in conjunction with gender, class, and sexuality. Annamma et al. (2013) identified some of the important tenets of DisCrit.

First tenet: Racism and ableism as mutually constitutive. Racism and ableism are ontologically separate but mutually constitutive forces. "Ontologically separate" means that racism is not just a form of ableism, nor is ableism a kind of racism. They are both separate constructs. Nevertheless, they are mutually constitutive as "racism validates and reinforces ableism, and ableism validates and reinforces racism" (Annamma et al., 2013, p. 6). Gillborn (2016) illustrated the mutual constitution of race and dis/ability by analyzing the discourse of racial genism (the idea that race, genes, and abilities are interrelated) in contemporary media and electoral politics to illustrate how racism and ableism are intertwined whereby Black bodies are assigned certain physical or intellectual deficits compared to white bodies.

Annamma et al.'s (2013) framing of racism and ableism as forces may draw partially on a Foucauldian understanding of power; power is not a *specific structure* (e.g., a group of people, a specific institution) as was the way traditional critical theories understood it. Rather, power is actualized in the dominant discourses that circulate everywhere, acting upon everything, and creating oppressive notions of normalcy that form the backdrop against which everyday injustices become socially acceptable. The discourses may operate innocuously in everyday life but come together to generate large-scale outcomes such as disproportionality that may not be easy to attribute to any specific event of explicit discrimination.

Second tenet: Identities as multidimensional. Oppressive ideologies intersect to create interlocking systems of oppression. People live in these interlocking systems at the intersection of various oppressions and privileges. As a result, we cannot talk about people in unidimensional terms (e.g., identifying someone as only Black or gay or disabled) but need to recognize the multiple identities they inhabit simultaneously. This point has special salience for movements and activist or advocacy groups. Often, a justice movement will cohere around a specific axis of oppression (race, gender, class, dis/ability) while backgrounding the other axes. However, as Leonardo and Broderick (2011) stated:

> Historically and materially, these ideologies have operated not in isolation from one another, but as inextricably intertwined systems of oppression and exclusion. Theoretical and political efforts to address one system of oppression without simultaneously addressing the other . . . are incomplete at best and actively (however unwittingly) oppressive to others at worst.
>
> *(p. 2226)*

Thus, for example, a movement by disability rights activists that ignores the role of class may primarily benefit those who have class privilege within that community (Erevelles, 2002). Similarly, a racial justice movement that ignores ableism will predominantly benefit nondisabled people of color in that movement. In sum, this tenet urges scholars and activists to recognize identities as multidimensional and to constantly scan the spaces they inhabit to recognize who is being left behind in a movement.

Third tenet: Materiality. Although DisCrit's ontological and epistemic foundations are in social constructionism, it also attends to the material aspects of race and disability. DisCrit scholarship acknowledges race and disability as social constructs. In other words, "race" and "disability" are not essential pre-existing concepts that people discovered. Rather these constructs were created and imbued with meaning through complex historical social processes. However, DisCrit scholarship acknowledges that these social constructions have material consequences. For instance, even though race is not a biological concept, it still has concrete observable bodily consequences on those who are racialized as Black, such as higher maternal mortality rates in Black women (Flanders-Stepans, 2000).

Fourth tenet: Voice. DisCrit scholarship privileges the voices of those who have been marginalized by or within traditional research. This tenet acknowledges the role of research in perpetuating the marginalization and exclusion of disabled people of color and urges a commitment to do better. It explicitly rejects the patronizing idea of non-disabled researchers "giving voice" to disabled people of color. Instead, researchers who are nondisabled people of color are urged to "listen carefully and respectfully to counter-narratives" and "use [counter-narratives] as a form of academic activism to explicitly 'talk back' to master-narratives" (Annamma et al., 2013, p. 14). Counter-narratives are readings of the world emerging from historically oppressed people that challenge or disrupt dominant narratives about the social world. DisCrit seeks to use creative methods to access the voices that may not be represented using traditional research methods. This methodological tenet is directly influenced by CRT scholars who used parables, composite stories, revisionist retellings of history, poetry, as well as fiction to challenge the orthodoxies of existing scholarship (Ladson-Billings & Tate, 1995).

Fifth tenet: Historicity. DisCrit is interested in excavating the historical processes underlying the contemporary iterations of race and dis/ability and their intersections. They are interested in how institutions with legislative authorities have deployed laws and policies to oppress some people. Valencia (1997) specifically explored the role of the scientific community in legitimizing racist thinking about ability differences in the 20th century. The scientific knowledge was then used in making policies that continue to impact disabled people of color to this day. In addition, DisCrit scholars also attend to the historic processes through which the construct of race came into being, and how the boundaries of what constitutes whiteness have shifted over the ages (Omi & Winant, 1994; Roediger, 1991). This tenet works against ahistoricism, a tendency in many academic disciplines to present sanitized versions of history (if at all) that minimize the responsibility of dominant groups in perpetuating oppression or obstructing progress. By failing to account for oppressive practices, ahistoricism reinforces the perspective that marginalized people are responsible for their own oppression (Fitzgerald, 2012).

Sixth tenet: Whiteness and ability as property. Another tenet of DisCrit is recognizing both whiteness and ability as forms of properties that confer privileges on those who possess them. The thesis of whiteness as property was developed by Harris (1993), a prominent CRT legal scholar. According to Harris (1993), whiteness is *functionally* similar to the legal definition of property. Something can be considered a property of a person if: (1) that person has the exclusive rights to use it, enjoy it, and reap its benefits (e.g., being preferred for a job over another equally qualified non-white applicant), (2) the person gets to exclude others from using it or enjoying its benefits, and (3) the property is recognized socially as conferring social value upon the holder (e.g., in form of increased social status compared to non-owners). Annamma et al. (2013) built on this thesis by adding ability as a form of property too. Disabled people of color lack both, and therefore they can experience acute marginalization.

Seventh tenet: Activism. Finally, DisCrit recognizes that there is no one form of resistance; it can look different for different people in different situations (Annamma et al., 2013). Traditional understandings of resistances rooted in emancipatory theories have often construed true resistance as taking the form of marches, sit-ins, protests, or civil disobedience. Annamma et al. (2013) noted the corporeal or psychological demands associated with these forms of resistance that may make them inaccessible to people with disabilities. As a result, the definition of what constitutes "true" activism should be expanded in order to become accessible to people with disabilities. This can include academic activism (Annamma, 2018b), which we understand as activism geared toward interrupting and re-imagining normative ways of thinking, discussing, or researching in academic spaces such as classrooms, journals, and conferences. Garland-Thomson (2002) made a similar case about the necessity of expanding the meaning of activism and gave the example of academic activism that can take the form of "building an archive through historical and textual retrieval, canon reformation, role modeling, mentoring, curricular reform, and course and program development" (p. 27). Similarly, the cultural work of disabled self-advocates on social media in the form of blog posts, photography, and videos also counts as activism.

These tenets provide a framework to guide future work. Ignoring the mutually constitutive nature of race and disability can lead to complicity in its perpetuation. DisCrit thus creates an intellectual space to foreground that intersection in the field of education and works intentionally to interrupt it. DisCrit centers on the lived experiences of those who live at the race-disability intersection.

Current Applications of DisCrit Across Fields

Scholars in the field of special education have used DisCrit to problematize the institution of special education itself, given the overrepresentation of students of color. Leonard and Broderick (2011) argued that the rhetoric of overrepresentation ignores the macrosystem in which overrepresentation occurs. They asserted that the problem may not be overrepresentation but the institution of special education itself and the ableist and racist ideologies that have historically undergirded its function. Ferri and Connor (2005) analyzed archival data related to debates in special education concerning Black students and/or disabled students to problematize the institution of special education as a covert segregationist mechanism of the State after formal racial segregation had been outlawed. Reid and Knight (2006) similarly argued that the institution of special education provides the State with the justification it needs to exclude students of color. The disciplinary critique undertaken by special education scholars forces the field to reckon with its history and re-evaluate its priorities.

Migliarini and Annamma (2019) demonstrated the implications of DisCrit for the field of teacher education. They argued that the curriculum of teacher education programs is steeped in behavioral technologies of controlling "difficult" students and rewarding "good" ones. Unaccompanied by race-conscious critical thought, this approach to discipline ends up reproducing racist and ableist hierarchies within a classroom (Broderick & Leonardo, 2016). Given this, Migliarini and Annamma (2019) proposed a DisCrit-inspired classroom management course curriculum for pre-service teachers that prepares them to "understand the ways students are systemically oppressed, how those oppressions are (re)produced in classrooms, and what they can do to resist those oppressions" (p. 1). This curriculum also redefines the teacher-student relationship as one characterized by solidarity rather than management.

Relevance of DisCrit to School Psychology

In this section, we contemplate the role of DisCrit in the field of school psychology. We believe DisCrit, along with other forms of critically oriented scholarships (e.g., CRT), can play a salient role in re-shaping the landscape of school psychology.

Relevance of DisCrit to Research

Researchers in special education, such as Ferri and Connor (2005), used the critical scholarship to problematize the field of special education. Although this form of disciplinary critique can be seen as "divisive," it plays an invaluable role in disrupting established ways of doing things in an academic field. Critically oriented scholarship enters a field with the agenda of radical transformation—it catalyzes "a sense of self-appraisal; reassessing where we have come from, where we are at and where we might be going" (Goodley, 2013, p. 632). Through sustained provocative scrutiny of existing conventions and assumptions, it helps to create space for alternative aspirations and agendas of action to emerge. A similar move should be made in school psychology.

A school psychology research agenda influenced by DisCrit values the voices of those who exist at the intersection of race and disability. School psychology researchers driven by DisCrit might use research methodologies that provide ample representational space to the voices of disabled students of color. Participatory research (PR) is a particularly good methodology for conducting such research. PR recognizes the oppressive uneven power dynamics within traditional research processes as well as the exploitative and oppressive history of research. It seeks to democratize the research by dissolving the boundaries between researchers and the "researched." Participants can play important roles in the research questions, development of data collection procedures, as well as data analysis, and dissemination of findings. Fine and Torre (2019) offered an excellent example of the ways in which a core team of researchers actively involved LGBTQIA+ youth in all phases of the research. Gilbert (2004) provided useful tips to make PR accessible for people with disabilities so that they can fully participate in it.

Researchers can use traditional qualitative data collection methods such as semi-structured interviews and focus groups to elicit participant "voices." Newer methods such as photovoice (Palibroda et al., 2009), participatory mapping (Annamma, 2016; Kane & Trochim, 2007), and digital storytelling (Gubrium, 2009) are also becoming common. Researchers must pay special attention to issues of accessibility during data collection. Common ways of planning interviews or focus groups can carry ableist assumptions about participants' vision, speech, hearing, and so forth, which can exclude people with disabilities who might otherwise be interested in participating in that research study. This can lead to research findings that do not adequately reflect the concerns or priorities of people with disabilities. Social policies based on such research are bound to perpetuate the marginalization of people with disabilities. Nind (2008) offered some ways in which researchers can make the data collection process accessible.

DisCrit-influenced research in school psychology can begin to look at the topics that reflect DisCrit's emphasis on race and disability intersection. An example of this could be participatory action research on Black youth with autism. The emphasis on Black youth with autism works against the representation of autistic persons as mostly white (and almost always male) in movies, TV shows, and awareness campaigns (Heilker, 2012).

Relevance of DisCrit to Pedagogy

What implications does DisCrit have for pedagogy and curriculum used in the preparation of future school psychologists? Although policy-based movements such as Response to Intervention have made a move toward pulling the field of school psychology away from the medical model of specific learning disabilities, the medical model of disability continues to be influential in school psychology. There is a popular demand (and funding) for developing behavioral interventions to manage or regulate child behavior deemed as socially inappropriate or undesirable. For disability rights activists, the majority of these interventions serve as technologies of normalization—social strategies that use surveillance (e.g., behavioral monitoring), re-education, and incentives to "catch" and curb behavior that violates ableist social norms (Gruson-Wood, 2016). Autistic self-advocates and scholars have been especially critical of Applied Behavior Analysis, given its historic use of electric shocks and the more recent turn toward "benevolent" interventions for autistic children (Bagatell, 2010; Dawson, 2004). They have also criticized prominent autism advocacy organizations for being led by non-autistic parents and "allies" of autistic children.

School psychology graduate programs should incorporate the voices of disability rights activists and autistic self-advocates in the curriculum. The burgeoning literature from DisCrit, Critical Disability Studies, and Critical Autism Studies should be reflected in the readings and lectures for courses in assessment, interventions, and consultation. Over the last few years, disability rights activists and autism self-advocates have used social media (Tumblr, Twitter, etc.) to document their experiences, connect with other similar activists, and call out problematic policies and practices. School psychology instructors should acknowledge these cultural products as valid forms of knowledge (in accordance with the fourth tenet) and work to incorporate them into the curriculum. Such a diversified curriculum can help foster a sociopolitical analysis of disability and teach non-disabled school psychologists to view people with disabilities as political actors rather than passive objects of psychology's beneficence.

Relevance of DisCrit to Practice

DisCrit could offer important insights for the practice of psychometric testing which enjoys a great deal of salience in the field of school psychology. Graduate programs have multiple courses dedicated to cognitive, intellectual, and behavioral testing. Conferences of school psychology may receive financial sponsorships from companies that develop these tests. School psychologists may make IQ tests and behavioral teacher rating scales a perpetual component of their evaluation repertoire even in cases where such instruments may not be warranted. Given this scenario, it is important to engage with the problematic history of IQ testing and the role of the eugenics movement in the popularization of IQ tests in the 20th century (Valencia, 1997). It is also important to be mindful of how oppressive ideologies shape what is seen as a behavioral problem and how that construction influences a student's scores on behavioral rating scales and other behavioral instruments.

Graduate programs in school psychology must necessarily engage with this history given DisCrit's tenet of anti-ahistoricism. Readings or class discussions can specifically discuss the role of the ideology of whiteness in operationalizing and radically reimagining what counts as intelligent (see Hayman, 1998; Kincheloe et al., 1999). Other scholars such as Leonardo and Broderick (2011) have called into question the possibility of rehabilitating the constructs of intelligence and smartness because, even at their most inclusive, they exclude those marked with severe/cognitive disabilities. They contemplated the possibility of abolishing the constructs of smartness and intelligence from educational rhetoric altogether in the same way that Ignatiev and Garvey (2014) made the case for abolishing the social construction we call "whiteness." These debates should be presented in school psychology classes.

Apart from testing, school psychologists are also engaged in administrative and planning duties. School psychologists may be called to consult on developing a student's interventions. In keeping with the rallying slogan from the Disability Rights Movement—Nothing About Us Without Us—school psychologists should work to include students with disabilities as much as possible in planning the interventions or services they will receive.

The literature on intersectionality teaches us about the importance of being attentive to the power dynamics *within* groups that are otherwise committed to securing justice for everyone. Imagine you (a school personnel) conduct a weekly group for five autistic students in a middle school. If there are four white students and one Black student in that group, make a conscious effort to make the Black student feel valued and fully included. When you are planning your activities for an upcoming group, design them with that student's needs consciously in your mind. If you are introducing materials (e.g., worksheets or social stories), make sure they are culturally relevant to the student. Similar recommendations can be made in regard to handling your administrative caseload of referred students. If you have ten students, hold the one that lives at the crossroads of various oppressions consciously in your mind so that you do not unintentionally skim over their needs in order to attend to more "important" cases.

Conclusion

Foster (1989) described critical scholarship as a "sustained and formal attempt to analyze social relations and the impact of class, power, and ideology on these, with the ultimate, if the utopian, goal of freeing people from the conditions that they identify as being repressive" (p. 10). DisCrit is a relatively new theoretical phenomenon in the field of education although the tenets that undergird it have deep roots in various forms of critical scholarship, most prominently CRT, Intersectionality Theory, and Disability Studies. It is important to note that researchers associated with the transdisciplinary field of Critical Disability Studies publish articles about race-disability interplay without specifically identifying that work as DisCrit. The defining feature of DisCrit appears to be its explicit commitment to disabled people of color in line with the theory of intersectionality. DisCrit might also be understood as an attempt at constructing a bridge between Critical Race Theory and Disability Studies to bring these two knowledge communities in conversation with each other within the discipline of education.

In this chapter, we contemplated several ways in which DisCrit could be relevant to school psychology. It should be noted that as critical writings on disability (DisCrit, Disability Studies, Critical Autism Studies, etc.) have expanded in recent years, some scholars such as Meekosha and Shuttleworth (2009) have criticized their co-option into traditionally medical model-oriented fields such as special education or rehabilitation programs. They criticized these programs for borrowing superficially from the language of critical writings to give a false sense of progress even as the disciplines remain materially invested in the medical model. As we move forward, we should be vigilant about the potential of superficial adoption of DisCrit into school psychology.

References

Amundson, R. (2005). Disability, ideology, and quality of life: A bias in biomedical ethics. In D. Wasserman, J. Bickenbach, & R. Wachbroit (Eds.), *Quality of life and human difference: Genetic testing, health care, and disability* (pp. 101–124). Cambridge University Press. https://doi.org/10.1017/CBO9780511614590.005

Annamma, S. A. (2016). Disrupting the carceral state through education journey mapping. *International Journal of Qualitative Studies in Education, 29*(9), 1210–1230. https://doi.org/10.1080/09518398.2016.1214297

Annamma, S. A., Connor, D., & Ferri, B. (2013). Dis/ability critical race studies (DisCrit): Theorizing at the intersections of race and dis/ability. *Race Ethnicity and Education, 16*(1), 1–31. https://doi.org/10.1080/13613324.2012.730511

Annamma, S. A., Ferri, B. A., & Connor, D. J. (2018a). Cultivating and expanding disability critical race theory (DisCrit). In K. Ellis, R. Garland-Thomson, M. Kent, & R. Robertson (Eds.), *Manifestos for the future of critical disability studies* (Vol. 1, pp. 230–239). Routledge.

Annamma, S. A., Ferri, B. A., & Connor, D. J. (2018b). Disability critical race theory: Exploring the intersectional lineage, emergence, and potential futures of DisCrit in education. *Review of Research in Education, 42*(1), 46–71. https://doi.org/10.3102/0091732X18759041

Bagatell, N. (2010). From cure to community: Transforming notions of autism. *Ethos, 38*(1), 33–55. https://doi.org/10.1111/j.1548-1352.2009.01080.x

Barton, L. (2017). Disability, empowerment and physical education. In J. Evans (Ed.), *Equality, education, and physical education* (pp. 43–54). Routledge.

Bell, C. (2006). A modest proposal. In L. J. Davis (Ed.), *The disability studies reader* (pp. 275–282). Routledge.

Broderick, A., & Leonardo, Z. (2016). What a good boy: The deployment and distribution of "goodness" as ideological property in schools. In S. Annamma, D. Connor, & B. Ferri (Eds.), *DisCrit: Disability studies and critical race theory in education* (pp. 55–67). Teachers College Press.

Crenshaw, K. W. (1989). Demarginalizing the intersection of race and sex: Black feminist critique of antidiscrimination doctrine, feminist theory and antiracist politics. *University of Chicago Legal Forum, 1989*, 139–168.

Crenshaw, K. W. (1995). Mapping the margins: Intersectionality, identity politics, and violence against women of color. In K. Crenshaw, N. Gotanda, G. Peller, & K. Thomas (Eds.), *Critical race theory: The key writings that formed the movement* (pp. 357–383). The New Press.

Davis, L. J. (2013). The end of identity politics: On disability as an unstable category. In L. J. Davis (Ed.), *The disability studies reader* (pp. 265–277). Taylor & Francis.

Dawson, M. (2004, January 18). *The misbehavior of behaviourists: Ethical challenges to the autism-ABA industry*. www.sentex.ca/~nexus23/naa_aba.html

Du Bois, W. E. B. (1920). Race intelligence. *The Crisis, 20*(3), 118–119.

Dunn, D. S., & Andrews, E. E. (2015). Person-first and identity-first language: Developing psychologists' cultural competence using disability language. *American Psychologist, 70*(3), 255–264. https://doi.org/10.1037/a0038636

Epstein, R., Blake, J., & González, T. (2017). *Girlhood interrupted: The erasure of Black girls' childhood*. Center on Poverty and Inequality. www.law.georgetown.edu/academics/centers-institutes/poverty-inequality/upload/girlhood-interrupted.pdf

Erevelles, N. (2002). Material citizens: Cognitive disability, race, and the politics of citizenship. *Disability, Culture, and Education, 1*(1), 5–25.

Ferri, B. A., & Connor, D. J. (2005). Tools of exclusion: Race, disability, and (re)segregated education. *Teachers College Record, 107*(3), 453–474.

Fine, M., & Torre, M. E. (2019). Critical participatory action research: A feminist project for validity and solidarity. *Psychology of Women Quarterly, 43*(4), 433–444. https://doi.org/10.1177/0361684319865255

Fitzgerald, K. J. (2012). A sociology of race/ethnicity textbooks: Avoiding white privilege, ahistoricism, and use of the passive voice. *Sociological Focus, 45*(4), 338–357. https://doi.org/10.1080/00380237.2012.712866

Flanders-Stepans, M. B. (2000). Alarming racial differences in maternal mortality. *The Journal of Perinatal Education, 9*(2), 50–51. https://doi.org/10.1624/105812400X87653

Foster, W. (1989). Toward a critical practice of leadership. In J. Smith (Ed.), *Critical perspectives on educational leadership* (pp. 39–62). Routledge, Falmer.

Garland-Thomson, R. (2002). Integrating disability, transforming feminist theory. *NWSA Journal, 14*(3), 1–32. http://www.jstor.org/stable/4316922

Gilbert, T. (2004). Involving people with learning disabilities in research: Issues and possibilities. *Health and Social Care, 12*(4), 298–308. https://doi.org/10.1111/j.1365-2524.2004.00499.x

Gillborn, D. (2016). Softly, softly: Genetics, intelligence and the hidden racism of the new geneism. *Journal of Education Policy, 31*(4), 365–388. https://doi.org/10.1080/02680939.2016.1139189

Goodley, D. (2013). Dis/entangling critical disability studies. *Disability & Society, 28*(5), 631–644. https://doi.org/10.1080/09687599.2012.717884

Gruson-Wood, J. F. (2016). Autism, expert discourses, and subjectification: A critical examination of applied behavioural therapies. *Studies in Social Justice, 10*(1), 38–58. https://doi.org/10.26522/ssj.v10i1.1331

Gubrium, A. (2009). Digital storytelling: An emergent method for health promotion research and practice. *Health Promotion Practice, 10*(2), 186–191. https://doi.org/10.1177/1524839909332600

Harris, C. (1993). Whiteness as property. *Harvard Law Review, 106*(8), 1709–1791. https://doi.org/10.2307/1341787

Harry, B., & Klingner, J. (2006). *Why are so many minority students in special education?* Teachers College.

Hayman, R. L., Jr. (1998). *The smart culture: Society, intelligence and law*. New York University Press.

Heilker, P. (2012). Autism, rhetoric, and whiteness. *Disability Studies Quarterly, 32*(4). http://dsq-sds.org/article/view/1756.

Hoffman, K. M., Trawalter, S., Axt, J. R., & Oliver, M. N. (2016). Racial bias in pain assessment and treatment recommendations, and false beliefs about biological differences between blacks and whites. *Proceedings of the National Academy of Sciences, 113*(16), 4296–4301. https://doi.org/10.1073/pnas.1516047113

Ignatiev, N., & Garvey, J. (2014). Abolish the White race: By any means necessary. In N. Ignatiev & J. Garvey (Eds.), *Race traitor* (pp. 9–14). Routledge.

Kane, M., & Trochim, W. M. K. (2007). *Concept mapping for planning and evaluation*. Sage.

Kincheloe, J. L., Steinberg, S. R., & Villaverde, L. (Eds.). (1999). *Rethinking intelligence: Confronting psychological assumptions about teaching and learning*. Routledge.

Ladson-Billings, G., & Tate, W. (1995). Toward a critical race theory of education. *Teachers College Record, 97*(1), 47–68.

Leonardo, Z., & Broderick, A. (2011). Smartness as property: A critical exploration of intersections between whiteness and disability studies. *Teachers College Record, 113*(10), 2206–2232.

Linton, S. (1998). Reassigning meaning. In S. Linton (Ed.), *Claiming disability: Knowledge and identity* (p. 8). New York University Press.

Meekosha, H. (2011). Decolonising disability: Thinking and acting globally. *Disability & Society, 26*(6), 667–682. https://doi.org/10.1080/09687599.2011.602860

Meekosha, H., & Shuttleworth, R. (2009). What's so 'critical' about critical disability studies? *Australian Journal of Human Rights, 15*(1), 47–75. https://doi.org/10.1080/1323238X.2009.11910861

Mickelson, R. (2002). The academic consequences of desegregation and segregation: Evidence from the Charlotte-Mecklenburg schools. *North Carolina Law Review, 81*(4), 1513–1562.

Migliarini, V., & Annamma, S. (2019). Applying disability critical race theory in the practice of teacher education in the United States. *Oxford Research Encyclopedia of Education.* https://doi.org/10.1093/acrefore/9780190264093.013.783

Nind, M. (2008). *Conducting qualitative research with people with learning, communication and other disabilities: Methodological challenges.* University of Southampton.

O'Dell, L., Bertilsdotter Rosqvist, H., Ortega, F., Brownlow, C., & Orsini, M. (2016). Critical autism studies: Exploring epistemic dialogues and intersections, challenging dominant understandings of autism. *Disability & Society, 31*(2), 166–179.

Omi, M., & Winant, H. (1994). *Racial Formation in the United States: From the 1960s to the 1990s* (2nd ed.). Routledge.

Palibroda, B., Krieg, B., Murdock, L., & Havelock, J. (2009). *A practical guide to photovoice: Sharing pictures, telling stories and changing communities.* Prairie Women's Health Network.

Rao, S., & Kalyanpur, M. (Eds.). (2014). *South Asia and Disability Studies: Redefining boundaries and extending horizons.* Peter Lang Inc.

Reid, D. K., & Knight, M. G. (2006). Disability justifies exclusion of minority students: A critical history grounded in disability studies. *Educational Researcher, 35*(6), 18–23. https://doi.org/10.3102/0013189X035006018

Roberts, D., & Jesudason, S. (2013). Movement intersectionality: The case of race, gender, disability, and genetic technologies. *Du Bois Review: Social Science Research on Race, 10*(2), 313–328. https://doi.org/10.1017/S1742058X13000210

Roediger, D. R. (1991). *The wages of Whiteness: Race and the making of American working class.* Verso.

Silvers, A. (1995). Reconciling equality to difference: Caring (F)or justice for people with disabilities. *Hypatia, 10*(1), 30–55. https://doi.org/10.1111/j.1527-2001.1995.tb01352.x

Stienstra, D., & Nyerere, L. (2016). Race, ethnicity and disability: Charting complex and intersectional terrains. In S. Grech & K. Soldatic (Eds.), *Disability in the global South* (pp. 255–268). Springer.

Valencia, R. R. (1997). *The evolution of deficit thinking: Educational thought and practice.* Routledge.

Vallas, R. (2009). The disproportionality problem: The overrepresentation of black students in special education and recommendations for reform. *Virginia Journal of Social Policy & the Law, 17*(1), 181–208.

Waytz, A., Hoffman, K. M., & Trawalter, S. (2015). A superhumanization bias in Whites' perceptions of Blacks. *Social Psychological and Personality Science, 6*(3), 352–359. https://doi.org/10.1177/1948550614553642

4

QUEERING SCHOOL PSYCHOLOGY

A Queer Theory for School-Based Practice

David P. Rivera

The etymology of the term *queer* is complex concerning its use regarding sexuality and gender. Initially, the term was used as an adjective to describe something that deviated from the norm as odd or weird. First accounts of the use of *queer* as a label relating to sexuality and gender date back to the late 1800s when it was primarily directed toward men who were accused of engaging in same-sex relationships and sexual activity or expressed femininity in their gender presentation (Halperin, 2003). *Queer* was primarily used in this fashion for almost a century. Although used as an identity term during the 1900s by some men with same-sex attractions and behaviors, it wasn't until later that century that *queer* was more widely used as an identity term. Prominent queer theorists, such as Judith Butler (1993) and Heather Love (2007), suggested that *queer* was purposefully reclaimed in part because of its painful history. "Queer was reclaimed by the LGBTIQ community as an umbrella term to designate resistant and non-normative sexuality" (McCann & Monaghan, 2020, p. 1).

An understanding of *queer*'s history and definitions is foundational to grasping the development of "Queer Theory," which was coined by Teresa de Lauretis in 1990 (de Lauretis, 1991). Embedded in the current queer paradigm is radical resistance to mainstream ideas and norms, including widespread beliefs in normalcy, stability, and absolute truths. *Queer* is a "deliberately ambiguous term" (Monaghan, 2016, p. 7). It is used in many ways to describe how people identify and are identified, but almost more importantly, especially as it relates to Queer Theory, the *processes* by which people are conceptualized, labeled, and positioned in society. It is purposefully an ambiguous term in that it serves to challenge and interrogate normality, stability, universality, and absolutes. Similarly, *Queer Theory* is purposefully ambiguous, and as one queer scholar noted, it "is as elusive to nail down as mercury" (Dilley, 1999). In this fashion, there is a multiplicity of

DOI: 10.4324/9780367815325-5

truths and definitions embedded in how the term *queer* is understood and how the field of Queer Theory originated and continues to evolve (Dilley, 1999). This chronicling of the term *queer* is also an example of one of Queer Theory's many related concepts, this being a genealogical approach to understanding a current conception or perception, which will be explained in more detail later in the chapter. For the purposes of this chapter, the term *queer* will be used as a less-than-perfect umbrella term in reference to people who have marginalized sexualities and gender identities. Similarly, the term *LGBTQ+* will be used as a less-than-perfect way to reference lesbian, gay, bisexual, transgender, and queer people, with the plus sign denoting the many and increasing ways people self-identify sexuality and gender identity. This chapter will elaborate on the multiple ways queer and queerness operate, the theoretical and conceptual underpinnings of Queer Theory, and how Queer Theory can be used to advance school-based practice in equitable, ethical, and inclusive ways.

Historical Underpinnings of Queer Theory and Queer Advocacy

As with many critical theories, Queer Theory has its roots in poststructuralism as articulated by Michel Foucault (1978). Foucault's groundbreaking text, *History of Sexuality, Volume 1*, is often credited as providing many of the key conceptualizations that influenced the advent of Queer Theory. In re-historicizing sexuality, Foucault debunks the myth of what he terms the *repressive hypothesis*. The repressive hypothesis was the commonly held belief that sexuality was suppressed in the Victorian age, and Foucault's re-historicizing, or putting into environmental and social context, sexuality helped debunk this myth. In doing so, Foucault was able to render a potentially more accurate depiction of sexuality as it was experienced and understood in recent history and also articulated tools that are foundational to Queer Theory, such as highlighting the role of *discourse* in shaping meaning and a *genealogical* approach to understanding the history of ideas. A major tenet of Queer Theory, which will be elaborated upon, is the questioning of dominant conceptualizations of sexualities, genders, and other phenomena, and Foucault's process of unearthing the buried truths of sexualities provided a template for queer theorists to follow in their work of building and advancing the field of queer studies.

In Foucault's (1978) genealogical approach to re-storying sexuality's history, he revealed the social, political, and economic motivations for controlling and regulating sexuality. Foucault offered the idea of *bio-power* to help explain how power shaped discourse around sexuality to create the social norms and laws that supported modern capitalism. A capitalistic society benefits from norms regarding social and governmental control of human bodies that favor heterosexuality vis-a-vis sexual reproduction. As such, sexual behaviors and expressions that deviate from heterosexuality are systematically deemed disordered and criminal, and they are regulated by medical and legal institutions as well as via social pressures to conform. An example is homosexuality's inclusion in the *Diagnostic and Statistical Manual of Mental Disorders* (DSM) as a disorder until 1973 (Drescher, 2015). In this way, non-heterosexual sexuality was pathologized and thus controlled via the medical institution.

As discourses regarding sexuality were developed to classify people and behaviors as either normal (heterosexual) or abnormal (homosexual), discourses regarding race created stark distinctions between Black and white in a very similar fashion (Somerville, 2000). As such, the histories of racism and (hetero)sexism share common threads and are inextricably linked. So, just as racial categories emerged to become part of how humanness is "naturally" understood, so also was sexuality. Primary to the emergence of these discourses is power. Categorizing people into normal and abnormal groups based on gender, race, sexuality, and other groupings ensured and upheld hegemonic power. This concept is foundational to Queer Theory, in that "natural" and "essential" states of being, developed and supported by discourses and regulated by social institutions, are challenged and resisted by queer theorists.

As power was realized by those who were subjugated by these "newly" created identity categories and hence rendered as abnormal, criminal, ill, and perverse, the fight for a reversal of this subjugation commenced (Foucault, 1978). One of the earliest examples of activism for "homosexual" rights occurred in the late 1800s by Karl Maria Benkert who was concerned with the anti-sodomy laws targeted toward men with same-sex behaviors (Steakley, 1975). This act of defiance to political efforts to criminalize same-sex behaviors was followed by a series of others, including the German neurologist Magnus Hirshfeld who founded the Scientific Humanitarian Committee, Benedict Friedlander who founded the Community of the Special, and Ellis and Edward Carpenter who founded the British Society for the Study of Sex Psychology (Lauritsen & Thorstad, 1995). These acts of social defiance progressed from reacting to political and legal discriminatory practices to an actual study of sexuality as a way to use science to defend the sexually subjugated. As such, activism and scholarship regarding Queer Theory became intertwined, and the line between activist and scholar blurred and nearly vanished (Altman, 2018).

These efforts were eventually imported to the United States (U.S.), and Alfred Kinsey's extensive studies of human sexualities were published in the mid-1900s (Kinsey et al., 1948; Kinsey et al., 1998). Although Kinsey's studies were limited to white women and men, they challenged widely held beliefs regarding human sexuality, such as attempts at breaking the sexual binary via the use of the Kinsey Scale that plotted sexual desire and behavior on a range from 0 (exclusively heterosexual) to 6 (exclusively homosexual). This method, while not perfect since it relied on a polarized and limited scale, helped reveal that significant numbers of women and men had sexual desires and behaviors that were not limited to either exclusive end of the binary. Kinsey even included a categorization of "X" to denote no sexual behavior, which is a precursor to current understandings of *asexuality*. This scientific evidence challenged the idea of sexual binaries and supports Queer Theory's rejection of these binaries as normal and essential to sexual experience and categorization.

During this same time in the U.S., Harry Hay and Chuck Rowland founded the Mattachine Society (D'Emilio, 2012). Shortly after, Del Martin and Phyllis Lyon founded Daughters of Bilitis (DOB) in response to the Mattachine Society's almost exclusive focus on the experiences and needs of men (Churchill, 2009). While these groups were not particularly concerned as much with science as they were with political and social liberation, they provided meaningful mechanisms for organized social activism for those concerned with the increasing threats against those with same-sex attractions and behaviors exacerbated by McCarthyism. "Homosexuals" were considered a threat to national security, or so it was disguised, and were being systematically eradicated from public service positions, better known as the "Lavender Scare" (Johnson, 2009). However, these organizations and movements were criticized for being too assimilationist and not truly liberatory (McCann & Monaghan, 2020).

The idea of "Gay Liberation" was more fully developed by following frameworks borrowed from the Black Power and Women's Liberation movements in the 1960s and 1970s (McCann & Monaghan, 2020). Rather than trying to assimilate to the then present-day society, the Gay Liberation movement was concerned with demanding civil rights and full participation in a democratic society as their queer selves. Embedded in this movement were pride and a demand to be fully seen (Altman, 1972). This new call for liberation challenged oppressive sexual and gender roles and binaries and resisted police violence, as marked by public demonstrations, the advent of pride marches and parades, and coalition-building with other liberation movements. Intersectionality was interwoven into the fight for liberation and thus influenced the inclusion of an intersectional approach to Queer Theory. One of the earliest and most forthright declarations of intersectionality was developed by the Combahee River Collective (1977), a collective of Black feminists. In the Combahee River Collective Statement (1977), this group of scholar activists was among the first to name race, sexuality, and class oppressions as functioning together to demonstrate the interlocking nature of these systems of oppression.

One of the most iconic and visible enactments of this style of liberatory resistance occurred in the early morning hours of June 28, 1969, at the Stonewall Inn, which was deemed the first National Monument for LGBTQ Rights in 2016 (Varga et al., 2019). There are several defining characteristics of the Stonewall Riots that influenced the progressive development of Queer Theory. This was an overt act of resistance to institutionalized oppression in that the "rioters" were resisting police control over their spaces and overall self-determination. These queer resisters were reacting to a history of police violence and raids of their queer spaces and bodies, one being the Stonewall Inn. What ensued over the days and nights to come was an outpour of resistance from queer-identified people and their allies. This resistance to state-sanctioned policing and violence helped to weaken the perceived power of the police and served as an example of how the system can be challenged by public demonstration and coalition building. In this way, the Stonewall Riots were less about assimilating into the mainstream and more about being visibly seen as queer and trans people with lived experiences and needs that differed from mainstream society.

Detailed Discussion of Queer Theory

Queer Theory is a purposefully ambiguous field of study. Unlike other critical theories, such as Critical Race Theory and DisCrit (see Chapters 2 and 3 this volume), Queer Theory does not have a standard, agreed-upon set of tenets. Among queer theorists there often exist contradictions and disagreements, and some believe that should *queer* and Queer Theory reach a place of standardization and universality in terms of how they are understood, this would be the demise of the concept of queer and a contradiction to how Queer Theory came to be and persists (Jagose, 1996; McCann & Monaghan, 2020). In order to maintain fidelity to the purposefully ambiguous nature of Queer Theory, I offer the following "fundamentals" of Queer Theory as potential lenses that can be used to increase understanding about the concepts of sexuality and gender, as well as the development of interventions to support student social and academic development.

The Problem of Heteronormativity

Historicizing the concepts of sexualities and queerness contextualizes some of the major issues and events that both uphold and challenge Queer Theory's main problem, that of heteronormativity. *Heteronormativity* describes the dominance of heterosexual ways of being, thinking, and feeling that pervade every societal institution, including education, health care, and criminal justice (Goodrich et al., 2017). Warner (1991), who coined the concept of heteronormativity, posited that heterosexuality has become normalized in society, which explains heteronormativity's pervasive and often invisible nature. For example, the concept of the "nuclear family" is commonly and simply defined as two parents and their children who make up the "typical" household. However, the implicit understanding of the nuclear family automatically attaches the sexuality and gender heteronormative assumptions of the parents being in a heterosexual relationship and all members of the family being cisgender and heterosexual. Assumptions about the nature of this heterosexual relationship can also include ideas about monogamy, child-rearing, and other related concepts as "essential" to the creation and maintenance of the nuclear family. Society signals, and even dictates, heteronormative ways of being via laws and discourses that favor heterosexuality and cisgender identities and penalizes all other sexual and gender identities. Examples of the myriad penalties encountered that uphold heteronormativity include laws and policies that prevent queer people from accessing rights and social services to the daily microaggressions that serve as regular reminders to queer people that they live in a heterosexist society (Rivera et al., 2013; Hatzenbuehler, 2014). As such, Queer Theory centers heteronormativity as a primary lens to view, understand, and critique the world around us.

Genealogical Approach to Interrogating Discourses

How did we arrive at our current understanding of sexuality, sexual orientation, gender, and gender identity? Textbook definitions of these concepts are often static and void of context and etymology, which leave us with underdeveloped understandings of these phenomena including their originations. As previously indicated, two concepts fundamental to Queer Theory are the *genealogical approach* to historicizing ideas and events, and *discourses*, which are the ways we communicate that shape how we think about and understand these ideas and events (Foucault, 1972). The genealogical approach to historicizing sexualities and genders and the resulting discourses is a common methodology used by queer theorists to more dynamically and accurately understand and critique the manifestation of heteronormativity across the human experience. Exploring the genealogy of any basic unit of understanding brings forth a historicization of this understanding by rendering an explanation inclusive of how the historical social environments shape contemporary understandings. The process of historicizing is used to interrogate how the idea's social environment over history may have shaped the development of the idea, especially in terms of how our current conceptualizations have come to be. Historicizing concepts, such as gender, gender identity, sexuality, and sexual orientation, through the lens of heteronormativity, gives a more accurate and complex understanding that helps explain how these concepts were constructed and how static and binary definitions uphold heteronormativity in society. Queer Theory forces us to interrogate and challenge concepts, especially mainstream concepts. This interrogation can reveal how a current, mainstream practice is supported by a concept that evolved from an origin in oppression.

Deconstruction of Finite Categorization

"The condition of being **male, female,** or neuter. In a human context, the distinction between gender and sex reflects the usage of these terms: Sex usually refers to the biological aspects of **maleness or femaleness**, whereas gender implies the psychological, behavioral, social, and cultural aspects of being **male or female** (i.e., **masculinity or femininity**; APA, n.d. b)." This definition of *gender*, taken from the *American Psychological Association's Dictionary of Psychology*, serves to replicate the binaried way of conceptualizing gender and sex, leaving us with only two options for understanding and communicating gender and sex. This conceptualization of gender has pervaded psychological research ever since the profession's beginning in the 1800s with the persistent and consistent emphasis on binaried gender as a commonly collected demographic and means of understanding differences in research results (Hyde et al., 2019). This "gender problem" in psychological research stems from the binaried dominant conceptualization of research that positions the researcher as "expert" and the subject of research ("the researched") as the "studied" (Dilley, 1999). Queer Theory calls us to interrogate and deconstruct binaried ways of being, thinking, and feeling that only serve to limit and control the ways gender and sexuality operate in intrapersonal, interpersonal, and systemic ways.

The binaries that constrict and restrict conceptualizations of gender and sexuality are not only found in the various definitions found in dictionaries, encyclopedias, and online, but rather they live and are reinforced in everyday social interactions (e.g., asking someone the gender of their fetus or baby), environments (e.g., binaried bathrooms), and laws and policies (e.g., birth certificates, Title IX), for example. Categorization, especially into binaries that are shaded by "good/bad," create hierarchies that often form the basis for the creation of the social control mechanisms of rules, laws, procedures, and practices that govern how sexuality and gender are to be understood and expressed. The definitions and discourses regarding gender and sexuality and the myriad ways society supports these definitions and discourses create endless binds that limit human development from a self-determination perspective. Binaries and finite categories are limiting and often static, in that they presume to be untouched by context and time. The field of cultural psychology teaches us that context matters, debunks many psychological processes as universal, and maintains a cultural relativist stance in understanding humankind (Heine, 2010).

Resistance to Essentialism and Essential States of Being

The reliance on binaried categorizations of gender (man-woman) and sexuality (heterosexual-homosexual) supports essentialist thinking regarding these identities. *Essentialism*, or more precisely for the purposes of this chapter, *psychological essentialism*, refers to the classification schemes humans use to make sense of the world around us by assigning "essential" and "natural" characteristics, both observable and unobservable, to create finite categories (Prentice & Miller, 2007). There are a few features of psychological essentialism, such as "naturalness, stability, discreteness of category boundaries, immutability of category membership, and necessity of category features or characteristics" (Prentice & Miller, 2007, p. 202). These features create what is considered "the essence" of what is being observed.

However, the meaning behind the essential features does not have to be understood in order for it to become an essential state. The "placeholder" notion suggests that it is possible for humans to believe a certain category possesses an essence without having a full understanding of what the essence means or from where it developed (Medin & Ortony, 1989). For example, gender has been rated highest in essentialism as compared to other common social identities, such as ethnicity, race, disability, and age (Haslam et al., 2000). Many unknowns undergird notions of gender, especially for children who seem to adopt an essentialist view of gender from a very early age without fully knowing the meaning of gender (Meyer & Gelman, 2016). The essence placeholders that we use for many of the categories humans have created to distinguish each other, such as gender, lead to underdeveloped conceptualizations of gender that encourage people to believe that there are underlying realities common for all women and all men. These presumed underlying realities create the basis for stereotyping, which is a consequence associated with strong essentialist beliefs (Bastian & Haslam, 2006).

Realities Are Socially Constructed/Constricted

In line with resisting essentialism and the trappings of heteronormativity, queer theorists understand that gender and sexuality categorizations are socially created and maintained. Race is often conceptualized as a socially constructed identity category; however in practice race is still thought of as an essential state (Morning, 2007). While some understand the social construction of gender in similar ways, as previously suggested, gender is by and large considered an essential state of being. Judith Butler's (2011) ground-breaking work on *gender performativity* is a significant contribution to Queer Theory and provides a framework for understanding the performative element connected to the social construction and maintenance of gender. Butler's theory of gender performativity seeks to uproot the essentialist features of gender that creates the idea that gender is an innate and static state of being. Through a performative lens, Butler suggested that gender is not inherently innate, but rather it is "manufactured" through repetitive, ritualized actions that start with the vocal and written announcement of an infant's gender and is maintained via the gender social norms that dictate gendered-behaviors, thinkings, and feelings from the cradle to the grave. This performativity of gender is what induces the internal sense of gender that is manufactured and sustained over time by binaried gender norms.

Challenges to Empiricism

"Empirical research" is commonly thought of as the gold standard for how to approach the study of any given phenomenon. Discourses regarding scientific inquiry often include a centering of empiricism, a paradigm that mandates the use of observable data to support the theoretical underpinnings of the phenomenon in question (APA, n.d. a). Empiricism has been a subject of debate in psychology; however, these debates have primarily focused on the study of specific phenomena and theoretical frameworks, such as positive psychology (Wong,

2011) and evolutionary and moral theories (Indick, 2002). These debates rarely, if ever, include the appropriateness of empirical methods for marginalized social groups. Given Queer Theory's focus on understanding the development of discourses, many queer theorists challenge mainstream notions of empiricism that originated and are grounded in Western European philosophies spanning back to the 17th century. This multi-century reliance on this methodological research tenet has rendered empiricism largely unchallenged across disciplines, including in psychology. For example, the scientific method, especially the preference for experimental designs in psychology, upholds this strong preference (if not mandate) for not only observable data, but a certain kind of observable data. Statistical procedures that establish statistical significance, for example, rely on the premise that the phenomenon in question is indeed observable and attainable. While this method of scientific inquiry may work for any phenomenon that relates to the experiences of those privileged enough in society to live their truths openly, queer theorists argue that mainstream scientific empiricism will not capture the experiences of the socially marginalized who encounter threats to living their truths openly (Muñoz, 1996; Rivera & Nadal, 2019).

José Esteban Muñoz (1996), the late performance-studies scholar and queer theorist, was concerned with the nature of observable material data for queer people. Muñoz asserted that the ways phenomena manifest for queer people, and all marginalized people for that matter, are neither experienced nor observed in the same way as the experiences of the privileged (e.g., the white heterosexual man). Given the many historical and contemporary threats that exist for the sexually marginalized (e.g., hostile laws and policies, daily microaggressions, gross lack of representation, etc.), these experiences are often socially rendered invisible and relegated to "the closet." As such, queer manifestations are often fleeting and may not materialize in "solid," visible forms capturable by traditional empirical methodologies. Muñoz gifted Queer Theory with the concept of "ephemera material" as a unit of observable data that may be more appropriate as a methodological conceptualization when studying the experiences of queer people. This is an example of how Queer Theory challenges the very nature of empirical methodologies and offers more flexibility in how the concept of "observable data" is conceptualized and captured from queer participants. Queer challenges to empiricism support the interrogation of the entire process of scientific inquiry, including the binaried hierarchy that often exists between the "researcher" and the "researched."

Current Application of Queer Theory Across Fields

Queer Theory has its roots in the humanities, and that is where the bulk of historical and current thought and work utilizing a queer theoretical framework resides (McCann & Monaghan, 2020). The initial luminaries of Queer Theory, whose work is often cited, include Michel Foucault (philosophy), Teresa de Laurentis (modern languages and literature), Gloria Anzaldúa (English), Judith Butler (philosophy), José Esteban Muñoz (performance studies), Eve Kosofsky Sedgwick (literature), Adrienne Rich (poetry), David Halperin (classics and humanities), and Michael Warner (English), for example. Given these academic roots of Queer Theory, it's not surprising that the bulk of thought and application reside in the humanities. These queer scholars have applied a queer theoretical lens to analyzing texts, media, and the arts, as well as advancing philosophical thought, which have led the way in understanding the insidious and pernicious dynamics of heteronormativity and essentialism in society.

Although the work of Queer Theory has yet to reach a critical mass in fields outside of the humanities, there are examples in education and psychology that indicate an growing interest in expanding the disciplinary reach of Queer Theory (e.g., Abes et al., 2019; Carroll & Gilroy, 2001; Hegarty, 2011; Minton, 1997; Riggs & Treharne, 2017; Rodriguez & Pinar, 2007). In education, Queer Theory has been used as a lens to understand the experiences of students and learners in both K-12 education (Rodriguez & Pinar, 2007) and higher education (Abes et al., 2019), as well as in the development of pedagogies and interventions to support identity, social, and academic development. In psychology, there have been calls for the field to adopt a Queer Theoretical framework to advance psychological/philosophical paradigms (Hegarty, 2011; Minton, 1997). While a few psychologists have taken up the call to incorporate Queer Theory as an overt framework, many have incorporated Queer Theory implicitly. For example, the American Psychological Association's Guidelines for Psychological Practice with Sexual Minority Persons (2021) and Guidelines for Psychological Practice with Transgender and Gender Nonconforming People (2015) were developed with the foundational understanding that queer and trans people are often mistreated in the field of psychology and are forced into socially normed and essentialized identities that may not reflect their truths. While not naming Queer Theory as a guiding theoretical framework, these practice guidelines reflect much of what Queer Theory is about.

Relevance of Queer Theory to School Psychology

Although Queer Theory has yet to be fully applied to the field of school psychology, queer issues have been the topic of inquiry for school psychologists, especially in relation to bullying (e.g., Espelage, 2014; Robinson & Espelage, 2011). Despite this attention on revealing the severity of bullying toward LGBTQ+ students, as well as related well-being and educational consequences, these issues have not yet received adequate attention by researchers and school-support personnel journals that have a large influence on shaping research agendas (Espelage, 2016; Graybill & Proctor, 2016). Additionally, there have been efforts to develop interventions to reduce the occurrence and harmful impacts of bullying in schools; however, many of these efforts take a unidimensional approach to conceptualizing bullying that is void of demographic and identity context (e.g., Craig, 2007; Hymel & Swearer, 2015; Merrell et al., 2008). One way Queer Theory can help advance the school psychology bullying scholarship and development of interventions is to contextualize these efforts in the dynamics of heteronormativity. This type of analysis can help reveal the systemic and interpersonal sources of bullying, which can better inform where to direct proactive intervention efforts, as opposed to reactive, remedial interventions.

While the issue of bullying and aggression toward LGBTQ+ students is significant given the related harmful consequences, including suicide, the focus of analyzing the school-going experiences for LGBTQ+ students cannot solely reside in *what results from* pervasive heteronormativity and cissexism in school environments. Queer Theory and the resulting queer analyses can provide a re-imagining of LGBTQ+ students, as well as the school systems and structures in which they are embedded. Using the *genealogical approach* to understand phenomena such as bullying based on sexual orientation and gender identity can help put these issues into historical context. This historicization of bullying specific to the experiences of LGBTQ+ students can help reveal the structures and policies schools use to essentialize binaried gender (e.g., girl/boy, woman/man) via the history and various forms of gender segregation in schools (Wiseman, 2008). Gender segregation ranges from the extreme end of not allowing girls and women to attend school to the development of separate schools for girls and boys to the prevalence of gendered bathrooms and gendered sports. Gender segregation only serves to promote heteronormativity and the essentialism of binaried gender and sexuality, and contextualizing LGBTQ+ bullying in this way can help reveal the structural sources of bullying as opposed to a focus on the interpersonal and intrapersonal dimensions of bullying's consequences.

Inclusive excellence is a common framework utilized by those who work toward making educational institutions more equitable and inclusive contexts for all (Williams, 2013). This framework focuses on institutional and structural changes that can lead to long-lasting change toward equity and inclusion. This work is primarily found in higher-education contexts (e.g., Bleich et al., 2015; Posselt, 2014), however, this focus on institutional change can provide a helpful framework for K-12 education. Common to the family of critical theories (e.g., Critical Race Theory, DisCrit, Intersectionality Theory, Critical Study of Whiteness) is an emphasis on systemic and structural change as means of addressing disparities caused by oppression. Combining the frameworks of inclusive excellence and Queer Theory to address the issues that negatively impact LGBTQ+ students helps to maintain a proactive stance in the creation of affirming school climates for LGBTQ+ students. Again, the focus of intervention should not only be on remediating the bullied and the bully, but it should also include a focus on the institutional structures that allow for bullying to exist. This is crucial in the battle to create a sense of safety for LGBTQ+ students so that they can reach their fullest academic potentials.

Conclusion

Queer Theory, although an ambiguous field of study, provides tools that can be applied to school psychology to help create school contexts that are more affirming and validating of the lived experiences of LGBTQ+ students. Queer Theory helps to reveal the histories and discourses regarding the prevalence and impact of heteronormativity and cissexism on school structures and policies that create the harmful school environments that LGBTQ+ students navigate on a daily basis. Queering school psychology can help the field become truly transformational in part by shifting the focus from remediation of the issues that negatively impact LGBTQ+ students to creating school structures and climates that promote, uplift, and bear witness to the vast strengths of LGBTQ+ students that have been rendered invisible via oppression and marginalization. We are losing too many LGBTQ+ youth to suicide; now is the time for action.

References

Abes, E. S., Jones, S. R., & Stewart, D. L. (Eds.). (2019). *Rethinking college student development theory using critical frameworks*. Stylus Publishing, LLC.

Altman, D. (1972). *Homosexual: Oppression and liberation*. Angus and Robertson.

Altman, D. (2018). The growing gap between academia and activism? *Sexualities*, *21*(8), 1251–1255. https://doi.org/10.1177/1363460718771489

American Psychological Association. (n.d. a). *Empiricism*. APA Dictionary of Psychology. https://dictionary.apa.org/empiricism

American Psychological Association. (n.d. b). *Gender*. APA Dictionary of Psychology. https://dictionary.apa.org/gender

American Psychological Association. (2015). Guidelines for psychological practice with transgender and gender nonconforming people. *American Psychologist*, *70*(9), 832–864. https://doi.org/10.1037/a0039906

American Psychological Association, APA Task Force on Psychological Practice with Sexual Minority Persons. (2021). *Guidelines for psychological practice with sexual minority persons*. www.apa.org/about/policy/psychological-practice-sexual-minority-persons.pdf

Bastian, B., & Haslam, N. (2006). Psychological essentialism and stereotype endorsement. *Journal of Experimental Social Psychology*, *42*, 228–235. https://doi.org/10.1016/j.jesp.2005.03.003

Bleich, M. R., MacWilliams, B. R., & Schmidt, B. J. (2015). Advancing diversity through inclusive excellence in nursing education. *Journal of Professional Nursing*, *31*(2), 89–94. https://doi.org/ 10.1016/j.profnurs.2014.09.003

Butler, J. (1993). Critically queer. *GLQ: A journal of Lesbian and Gay Studies*, *1*(1), 17–32. https://doi.org/10.1215/10642684-1-1-17

Butler, J. (2011). *Gender trouble: Feminism and the subversion of identity*. Routledge.

Carroll, L., & Gilroy, P. J. (2001). Teaching "outside the box": Incorporating queer theory in counselor education. *The Journal of Humanistic Counseling, Education and Development*, *40*(1), 49–57. https://doi.org/10.1002/j.2164-490X.2001.tb00101.x

Churchill, D. S. (2009). Transnationalism and homophile political culture in the postwar decades. *GLQ: A Journal of Lesbian and Gay Studies*, *15*(1), 31–66. www.muse.jhu.edu/article/255286

Combahee River Collective. (2007). A Black feminist statement. In E. B. Freedman (Ed.), *The essential feminist reader* (pp. 325–330). Modern Library. (Original work published 1977).

Craig, W., Pepler, D., & Blais, J. (2007). Responding to bullying: What works? *School Psychology International, 28*(4), 465–477. https://doi.org/10.1177/0143034307084136

de Lauretis, T. (1991). Queer theory: Lesbian and gay sexualities, differences. *Journal of Feminist Cultural Studies, 3*(2), iii–xviii.

D'emilio, J. (2012). *Sexual politics, sexual communities*. University of Chicago Press.

Dilley, P. (1999). Queer theory: Under construction. *International Journal of Qualitative Studies in Education, 12*(5), 457–472. https://doi.org/10.1080/095183999235890

Drescher, J. (2015). Out of DSM: Depathologizing homosexuality. *Behavioral Sciences, 5*(4), 565–575. https://doi.org/10.3390/bs5040565

Espelage, D. L. (2014). White House conference on bullying prevention: Bullying and the lesbian, gay, bisexual, transgender, questioning (LGBTQ) community. In *Student bullying: Federal perspectives and reference materials* (pp. 158–168). Nova Science Publishers, Inc.

Espelage, D. L. (2016). Sexual orientation and gender identity in schools: A call for more research in school psychology—No more excuses. *Journal of School Psychology, 54*, 5–8. https://doi.org/ 10.1016/j.jsp.2015.11.002.

Foucault, M. (1972). *The archaeology of knowledge and the discourse on language*. Translated from the French by A. M. Sheridan Smith. Pantheon Books.

Foucault, M. (1978). *The history of sexuality: Volume 1*. Translated by Robert Hurley. Penguin (originally published in 1976).

Goodrich, K. M., Luke, M., & Kassirer, S. (2017). Heteronormativity. In K. L. Nadal (Ed.), *The Sage encyclopedia of psychology and gender* (pp. 841–844). Sage Publications.

Graybill, E. C., & Proctor, S. L. (2016). Lesbian, gay, bisexual, and transgender youth: Limited representation in school support personnel journals. *Journal of School Psychology, 54*, 9–16. https://doi.org/10.1016/j.jsp.2015.11.001

Halperin, D. M. (2003). The normalization of queer theory. *Journal of Homosexuality, 45*(2–4), 339–343. https://doi.org/10.1300/J082v45n02_17

Haslam, N., Rothschild, L., & Ernst, D. (2000). Essentialist beliefs about social categories. *British Journal of Social Psychology, 39*, 113–127. https://doi.org/10.1348/0144666000164363

Hatzenbuehler, M. L. (2014). Structural stigma and the health of lesbian, gay, and bisexual populations. *Current Directions in Psychological Science, 23*(2), 127–132. https://doi.org/10.1177/0963721414523775

Hegarty, P. (2011). Becoming curious: An invitation to the special issue on queer theory and psychology. *Psychology & Sexuality, 2*(1), 1–3. https://doi.org/10.1080/19419899.2011.536308

Heine, S. J. (2010). *Cultural psychology*. John Wiley & Sons.

Hyde, J. S., Bigler, R. S., Joel, D., Tate, C. C., & van Anders, S. M. (2019). The future of sex and gender in psychology: Five challenges to the gender binary. *American Psychologist, 74*(2), 171. https://doi.org/10.1037/amp0000307

Hymel, S., & Swearer, S. M. (2015). Four decades of research on school bullying: An introduction. *American Psychologist, 70*(4), 293. https://doi.org/10.1037/a0038928

Indick, W. (2002). Fight the power: The limits of empiricism and the costs of positivistic rigor. *The Journal of Psychology, 136*(1), 21–36. https://doi.org/10.1080/00223980209604135

Jagose, A. (1996). *Queer theory: An introduction*. New York University Press.

Johnson, D. K. (2009). *The lavender scare: The cold war persecution of gays and lesbians in the federal government*. University of Chicago Press.

Kinsey, A. C., Pomeroy, W. B., & Martin, C. E. (1948). *Sexual behavior in the human male*. Sanders.

Kinsey, A. C., Pomeroy, W. B., Martin, C. E., & Gebhard, P. H. (1998). *Sexual behavior in the human female*. Indiana University Press.

Lauritsen, J., & Thorstad, D. (1995). *The early homosexual rights movement (1864–1935)*. Times Change Press.

Love, H. (2007). *Feeling backward: Loss and the politics of queer history*. Harvard University Press.

McCann, H., & Monaghan, W. (2020). *Queer theory now: From foundations to futures*. Red Globe Press.

Medin, D. L., & Ortony, A. (1989). Psychological essentialism. In S. Vosnaidou & A. Ortony (Eds.), *Similarity and analogical reasoning* (pp. 179–195). Cambridge University Press.

Merrell, K. W., Gueldner, B. A., Ross, S. W., & Isava, D. M. (2008). How effective are school bullying intervention programs? A meta-analysis of intervention research. *School Psychology Quarterly*, *23*(1), 26–42. https://doi.org/10.1037/1045-3830.23.1.26

Meyer, M., & Gelman, S. A. (2016). Gender essentialism in children and parents: Implications for the development of gender stereotyping and gender-typed preferences. *Sex Roles*, *75*(9), 409–421. https://doi.org/10.1007/s11199-016-0646-6

Minton, H. L. (1997). Queer theory: Historical roots and implications for psychology. *Theory & Psychology*, 7(3), 337–353. https://doi.org/10.1177/0959354397073003

Monaghan, W. (2016). *Queer girls, temporality and screen media: Not "just a phase."* Palgrave Macmillan.

Morning, A. (2007). "Everyone knows it's a social construct": Contemporary science and the nature of race. *Sociological Focus*, *40*(4), 436–454. https://doi.org/10.1080/00302237.2007.105713

Muñoz, J. E. (1996). Ephemera as evidence: Introductory notes to queer acts. *Women & Performance*, *8*(2), 5–16. https://doi.org/10.1080/07407709608571228

Posselt, J. R. (2014). Toward inclusive excellence in graduate education: Constructing merit and diversity in PhD admissions. *American Journal of Education*, *120*(4), 481–514. https://doi.org/10.1086/676910

Prentice, D. A., & Miller, D. T. (2007). Psychological essentialism of human categories. *Current Directions in Psychological Science*, *16*(4), 202–206. https://doi.org/10.1111/j.1467-8721.2007.00504.xh

Riggs, D. W., & Treharne, G. J. (2017). Queer theory. In *The Palgrave handbook of critical social psychology* (pp. 101–121). Palgrave Macmillan.

Rivera, D. P., & Nadal, K. L. (2019). The intersection of queer theory and empirical methods. In M. Brim & A. Ghaziani (Eds.), *Queer methods* (pp. 191–206). New York University Press.

Rivera, D. P., Nadal, K. L., Fisher, L. D., & Skolnik, A. A. (2013). Sexual orientation and gender identity microaggressions in the workplace. In M. Paludi (Ed.), *Psychology for business success, volume 2: Institutional equity and compliance* (pp. 81–100). Praeger.

Robinson, J. P., & Espelage, D. L. (2011). Inequities in educational and psychological outcomes between LGBTQ and straight students in middle and high school. *Educational Researcher*, *40*(7), 315–330. https://doi.org/10.3102/0013189X11422112h

Rodriguez, N. M., & Pinar, W. F. (Eds.). (2007). *Queering straight teachers: Discourse and identity in education* (Vol. 22). Peter Lang.

Somerville, S. B. (2000). *Queering the color line: Race and the invention of homosexuality in American culture*. Duke University Press.

Steakley, James D. (1975). *The homosexual emancipation movement in Germany*. Arno Press.

Varga, B. A., Beck, T. A., & Thornton, S. J. (2019). Celebrating Stonewall at 50: A culturally geographic approach to introducing LGBT themes. *The Social Studies*, *110*(1), 33–42. https://doi.org/10.1080/00377996.2018.1536643

Warner, M. (1991). Introduction: Fear of a queer planet. *Social Text*, *29*, 3–17. www.jstor.org/stable/pdf/466295

Williams, D. A. (2013). *Strategic diversity leadership: Activating change and transformation in higher education*. Stylus Publishing, LLC.

Wiseman, A. W. (2008). A culture of (in) equality? A cross-national study of gender parity and gender segregation in national school systems. *Research in Comparative and International Education*, *3*(2), 179–201. https://doi.org/10.2304/rcie.2008.3.2.179

Wong, P. T. (2011). Reclaiming positive psychology: A meaning-centered approach to sustainable growth and radical empiricism. *Journal of Humanistic Psychology*, *51*(4), 408–412. https://doi.org/10.1177/0022167811408729

5

TOWARD A CRITICAL STUDY OF WHITENESS

Cheryl E. Matias and Colleen Boucher

Leading scholar Zeus Leonardo claimed that whiteness studies have reached a fork in the road whereby one path leads us down white whiteness studies, the other down Black whiteness studies (personal communication, 2012). Meaning, the evolution of whiteness studies has brought the field to an interesting epistemological fulcrum: one that either presumes racial innocence or ignorance amongst white educators, which then can be simply rectified by re-educating for awareness, and the other which does not presume racial ignorance naturally exists. The latter honors historical, ideological, and political maneuvers white people partake in to operationally feign racial ignorance. Meaning, ignorance is a deliberate strategy used to maintain whiteness ideology and cannot be so simply rectified. Therefore, Black whiteness studies steer clear from the narcissism of whiteness that attempts to recenter whiteness (and its presumed innocence) yet again (see Matias, 2016).

Sullivan and Tuana (2007) asserted that although there exists an ignorance that can easily be remedied by the introduction of knowledge, the oft trope is that racial ignorance can, at times, be "consciously produced" (p. 1). They contended that white ignorance "support[s] a delusion of white racial superiority that can afflict white and nonwhite people alike" (p. 3). As such, Black whiteness studies ideologically rest upon the epistemological stance that white people are not racially ignorant and thus in need of simple remedies such as anti-bias education. Instead, such an approach is more critical of race in that it does not quickly pardon those who racially benefit from hegemonic whiteness. If racism is a nuanced, complex, and entrenched practice and ideology, then simple remedies are not the answer. Therefore, if the roots of racism and white supremacy are deeply embedded in every fabric of society, as suggested by Gillborn (2005), then presumptions of racial ignorance cannot explain why we still have racism without racists (see Bonilla-Silva,

DOI: 10.4324/9780367815325-6

2010). Clearly, folks *do* know about race and how it operates *and* strategically use it to feign innocence when engaging in racially micro-aggressive ways as to not be held accountable. As such, we, the authors, opt for a Black whiteness study, or as we so offer, a *Critical Study of Whiteness*. We know Critical Whiteness Studies (CWS) has become a burgeoning interdisciplinary field of study in education. We admit we too have claimed CWS in our own scholarship. With that said, we contend that simply placing the term *critical* in front of *whiteness studies* does not make it critical. Furthermore, though we label ourselves as critical whiteness scholars we do not presume CWS is in and of itself a theory; more so it is a critical approach to a field of study that draws from transdisciplinary theoretical perspectives. Insomuch as CWS is not a racial theory unto itself, it is nonetheless vital in studies that inch toward racial justice. This importance is due in part because CWS delves directly to the root cause of racism (white supremacy) by investigating how whiteness embeds ideologically, emotionally, rhetorically, epistemologically, and behaviorally. And, since one of the earmarks of whiteness is how it hegemonically manifests in its presumed naturalness, normalcy, and invisibility, critical scholarship that takes whiteness to task by making the normal abnormal or estranged—to borrow from Said (2000)—can more effectively reveal racial power and privilege.

As such, although CWS has become the more popularized terminology, we strategically opt for the term *Critical Study of Whiteness* because of the following:

1. Though presumed to be critical by virtue of word placement, CWS has also been used to theoretically undergird educational studies that still stem from a white epistemological standpoint (that of racial ignorance in simple need of racial awareness);
2. Oftentimes white scholars doing work in CWS do not cite or give any credence to scholars of color who originally investigated operations of whiteness; and
3. CWS scholarship that too narrowly focuses on "helping" white people become so self-absorbed in white racial epiphanies that it overlooks the connection of whiteness to racist practices like anti-Blackness. Meaning, this shifted focus makes critical whiteness studies all about one's whiteness and not about the interpellation between one's whiteness and its damaging impact on people of color (see Yancy, 2008). In doing so, whiteness studies become as Matias (2016) suggested, narcissistic.

We acknowledge that CWS can both break down whiteness and inadvertently uphold it. To avoid upholding whiteness and to better honor racial justice, we opt for a *Critical Study of Whiteness* that forever acknowledges the place, space, and sacrifice of scholars of color and does not too heavily rely on white scholars to define the field. Essentially, we seek to put criticality back into Critical Whiteness Studies by offering a perspective that does not center whiteness and instead focuses on the *critical studies* that dismantle it.

Historical Underpinnings of Critical Study of Whiteness

Like Dewey's philosophical ruminations on democratic education (1923) or more critical scholarship like McLaren's (2015) critical pedagogy, CWS draws from a variety of theoretical and philosophical standpoints. And, more poignantly, with respect to *Critical Study of Whiteness*, we ensure these theoretical points of departure are not always from white scholars who make the popularity of whiteness studies so known. In the next section, we theorize the phenomenological manifestation of whiteness before delving into a more nuanced understanding of the theories that undergird *Critical Study of Whiteness*.

How Is Whiteness Conceptualized?: Historical Evolutions of Whiteness and CWS

Whiteness, though socially constructed, continues to structure "the overall organization of society" based on skin pigmentation and physical phenotypes (Leonardo, 2009, p. 92). Meaning, whiteness reaps real material benefits, or as Harris (1993) offered, being white "meant gaining access to a whole set of public and private privileges that materially and permanently guaranteed basic subsistence needs and, therefore, survival" (p. 1713). This valorization of what it means to be white becomes an embodied politics that one must actively invest in to reap material, institutional, and societal benefits—oftentimes at the expense of equity for people of color (Liptsitz, 2006). Therefore, "Whiteness is a social construction that embraces white culture, ideology, racialization, expressions and experiences, epistemology, emotions, and behaviors" (Matias et al., 2014, p. 290), but because global white supremacy (see Allen, 2001) elevates whiteness as the prevailing, normalized condition for which racial others are denied, whiteness becomes much more. The intricacies of racial analyses should always consider the power structures of whiteness and how it intersects with racism. As such, we draw from Matias (2016, p. 186) to offer a visual representation of how we conceptualize whiteness (see Figure 5.1).

As seen in Figure 5.1, white supremacy is the overarching institution of race manifesting in two ways: racism and whiteness. Inasmuch as racism has various dynamics enacted on people of color, so too does whiteness enact various elements of whiteness on white people. Though not an exhaustive list, some elements of whiteness include the following: white privilege, whiteness as property, whiteness as natural/normal, color or race evasiveness, post-racialism, white racialization, and white identity. Although there are many theoretical frameworks from which to study these elements of whiteness, the most notable is Critical Whiteness Studies (CWS).

The farthest-reaching roots of CWS in education can be found in African American traditions (Doane, 2003; Jupp et al., 2019) such as writings from Du Bois (1935), who observed racial disparities in education and the power of

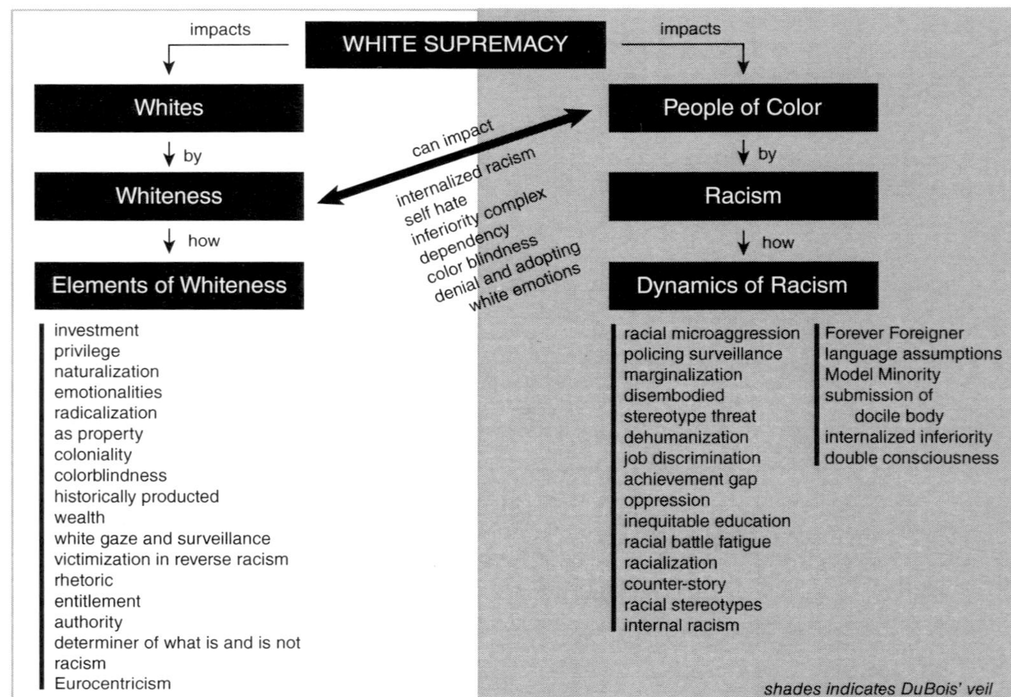

FIGURE 5.1 Operations of Power in Institutionalized White Supremacy

Note: Not an exhaustive list.

whiteness, protesting that whiteness was the exact reason that Black people in America suffered inequities in education and beyond. Later African American scholars continued the work of Du Bois by outlining ways whiteness dehumanizes people of color (see Baldwin, 1963; Bell, 1992; Morrison, 1992) especially with respect to race and property rights that lead to social (i.e., school) inequity (Ladson-Billings & Tate, 1995).

Whiteness has some cunning operations especially with respect to color-blind racism (Bonilla-Silva, 2003, 2010). Used to strategically feign racial reality, color-blind racism wrongly presumes that society is "post-racial" or beyond race when it is not. As such, and in the case of education, upholding color-blind racism harms students of color. Rhetorically, if "race doesn't matter" then educators do not have to address the racial inequities in school districts qua redlining policies, English-only movements, or segregation practices. Further, if education is to look beyond race as color-blind racism so offers, then racist policies such as school choice, racial opportunities gaps, and discrepancies in punitive discipline policies on Black and Brown students are explained as cultural deficits, removing the dynamics of white supremacy altogether. In light of this, scholars Annamma et al. (2017) opted for the term *color-evasiveness* (p. 147). Evading color or race is making a conscious choice to look the other way when confronted with racial injustice, and similarly if CWS scholarship evades the impact on whiteness on people of color, it too chooses to look the other way on the impacts of racial injustice.

Another cunning operation of whiteness is how white identity is conceptualized as both a cultural phenomenon and as not. Meaning, as Roediger (2005) demonstrated, subscribing into the white race means losing one's ethnic identity, resulting in some form of identity crisis for white people. That is, when one becomes white, they are no longer Irish, German, or Jewish. Yet, oddly enough, when whiteness is upheld, sometimes society will opt-in as a white cultural polity (see Roediger, 2005). Thus, "White ethnicity is reconstructed as the social equivalent of being [B]lack or Asian . . . [which] allows whites simultaneously to be victims and not to be held accountable for the past and present social arrangements that maintain white racial privilege" (Gallagher, 2003, p. 146). Whiteness then becomes a cultural fallacy pretending to have a common culture based on fictitious stories of Horatio Alger ("'We' pulled up from our bootstraps.") while also playing victim of a loss of cultural identity politics ("Why don't we have a white cultural club?"). As stated by Bonilla-Silva (2003), "Whiteness, then, in all of its manifestations, is embodied racial power" (p. 271). Having the ability to vacillate between group identity politics only further proves its power.

Detailed Discussion of Theories Undergirding Critical Study of Whiteness

To employ a *Critical Study of Whiteness*, we begin with the Frankfurt School's Critical Theory. Informed by Marxist thought—capitalism will implode due to its inherent discrepancies and maldistribution of wealth and power between the Haves and the Have Nots—Critical Theory critiques capitalism and class stratification found in societies and their institutions, like schools, through the lens of *Conflict Theory* (see Tables 5.1 and 5.2). Unlike functionalism that perceives schools as social reproducers that merely prepare students for the society in which they live, "conflict theorists believe the driving force in complex societies is the unending struggle between different groups to hold power and status" (Feinberg & Soltis, 1998, p. 43). Despite the fact that schools, as an institution of a given society, advocate democracy, they are nonetheless "destined not merely to perpetuate social differences but to crystallise them" (Gramsci, 2012, p. 40). Or, as Bowles and Gintis (2011) argued, schools serve "to reproduce economic inequality and to distort personal development" (p. 48). In this sense, critiques are made of a society under the presumption that there are conflicting groups constantly in competition for power and that such power is not benign.

With this lens, the process and purpose of schooling is viewed differently. On one hand, functionalists presume that society is inherently good and that schools simply reproduce the existing social, economic, and racial stratifications that already exist in a given society. On the other hand, conflict theorists believe:

> that schools serve the dominant privileged class by providing for the social reproduction of the economic and political status quo in a way that gives the illusion of objectivity, neutrality, and opportunity. They believe that schools reproduce the attitudes and dispositions that are required for the continuance of the present system of domination by the privileged class.
>
> *(Feinberg & Soltis, 1998, p. 43)*

As such, approaching a *Critical Study of Whiteness* never overlooks how racial power operates in a white supremacist system. That white supremacy is in and of itself an ideological aberration is not what conflict theory would contest. What conflict theory does contest is how schools, within a white supremacist society, serve to uphold white interests at the expense of students of color, particularly of Black students.

Upholding white interests so that the racially dominant class continues to retain its power produces the following results: the persistence of racial gaps in achievement; racially biased standardized exams and curricula; overrepresentation of Black and Brown students in special education and detentions; underrepresentation of Black and Brown students in gifted education; and the lack of diversity amongst teachers, administrators, and other school personnel. All of which, when viewed in relation to a white supremacist society, continue to relegate students of color, particularly Black and Brown students, to the lower socio-economic echelons of said society. Thus, one theory that undergirds CWS, or as we prefer to call it here, *Critical Study of Whiteness*, is the use of conflict theory that acknowledges the constant toiling for racial power; one in which it is not benign but

TABLE 5.1

Theories Undergirding Critical Study of Whiteness

Critical Theory/Pedagogy • Frankfurt School • Antonio Gramsci • Karl Marx • Erich Fromm • Henry Giroux • Paulo Freire						
Conflict Theory Competing powers						
Philosophies of Race	Sociology of Race	Psychology of Race	Humanities of Race	CRT	Postcolonial Theories	Women and Ethnic Studies
Racial Contract (Charles Mills) Phenomenology of Race (George Yancy)	Color-blind Racism (Eduardo Bonilla-Silva) Culture and Truth (Renato Rosaldo)	Racial Psychosocial Analysis (Franz Fanon) Racial microaggressions (Derald Sue)	White literary imagination (Toni Morrison) Racial Haunting (Lamar Johnson) Racial Psychoanalysis (Annie Cheng)	Permanence of race (Derrick Bell) Intersectionality (Kimberle Crenshaw) Counterstories and Ethnic Studies (Daniel Solorzano) White Supremacy (David Gillborn)	Portraiture of Colonization (Albert Memrni) Orientalism (Edward Said)	Black Feminism (Patricia Hills Collins) white supremacist patriarchy (bell hooks) Pinayism (Allyson Tintiangco-Cubales) Borderlands (Gloria Anzaldua)

Note: Not an exhaustive list; just a sample.

TABLE 5.2 Other Underlying Theories for Critical Study of Whiteness

Critical Race Theory	*(Critical) Whiteness Studies*	*Critical Theories of Race*	*Critical Theory*	*Critical Pedagogy*	*Critical Emotion Studies*
Delgado and Stefancic	Ignatiev	Bonilla-Silva	Frankfurt School	Giroux	Boler
Solórzano	Leonardo Allen	Mills	Foucault	McLaren	Ahmed
Taylor, Gillborn, and Ladson-Billings	Lee	Brodkin-Sacks	Fromm	Freire	Zembylas
Bell	Lipsitz	Roediger	Gramsci	Macedo	Fromm
Crenshaw	Thandeka	Oliver and Shapiro	Bowles and Gintis	Boal	
Delgado-Bernal	Fanon	Massey and Denton		Andrade	
Ladson-Billings	Baldwin	Noguera		Darder	
	Morrison	Tatum			
	DuBois				
	Matias				

actively sought after to continue the inequitable racial hierarchy already existing in a white supremacist society.

Since some CWS studies do not articulate a formal racial theory for their analyses, a *Critical Study of Whiteness* draws from transdisciplinary racial theories, such as a philosophy of race. In particular, one such racial theory that seeds a *Critical Study of Whiteness* is its application of Mills' (1997) racial contract. As Mills (1997) offered, the racial contract is a social contract between groups that also informs the political, moral, and epistemological structures of a racialized society. He wrote:

> The Racial Contract is the set of formal and informal agreements or met-agreements, higher-level contract *about* contracts, which set the limits of the contracts' validity between the members of one subset of humans, henceforth designated by (shifting) 'racial' (phenotypical/genealogical/cultural) criteria C1, C2, C3 . . . as 'white,' and coextensive (making due allowance for gender differentiation) with class of full persons, to categorize the remaining subset of humans as 'nonwhite' and of a different and inferior moral status, subpersons, so that they have a subordinate civil standing in the white or white-ruled polities. . . . All whites are *beneficiaries* of the Contract, through some whites are not *signatories* to it.
>
> (*p. 11*)

From this, a *Critical Study of Whiteness* premises upon a racial contract that positions white people as a moral ruling elite. When applying a *Critical Study of Whiteness*, actions, rhetoric, and policies within schooling practices are not exempt from participating in the racial contract. On the contrary, schooling practices continue to purport white people to the apex of the racial hierarchy and do so in supposedly "moral" ways. An example of this is when educators, school psychologists, counselors, and administrators alike (many of whom are white and have not had experiences with communities of color prior to their appointment into urban schools) quickly rely on their idea of "moral" disposition to justify their positions in low-income urban schools rich with students of color. This will be explained in more detail.

Another such racial theory that undergirds a *Critical Study of Whiteness* is the application of Yancy's (2008) racial phenomenology. Fortuitous is Yancy's (2008) work in that his work investigates the racial interpellation between whiteness and Blackness. In particular, his racial analysis on how the white body interacts, surveils (through the operating apparatus of the white gaze), and exacts power over the Black body is noteworthy. Or, as Yancy (2008) described, "Whites 'see' the Black body through the medium of historically structured forms of 'knowledge' that regard it as an object of suspicion" (p. 3). He further contented then, "The meaning of my Blackness is constituted and configured (*relationally*) within a semiotic field of axiological difference, one that is structured vis-a-vis the construction of whiteness as the transcendental norm" (Yancy, 2008, p. 3). Therefore, whiteness is constantly relational in that it is defined only in its juxtaposition: Blackness. In fact, this argument echoes James Baldwin. Baldwin (1963) wrote:

> In order for me to live, I decided very early that some mistake had been made somewhere. I was not a "nigger" even though you called me one. But if I was a "nigger" in your eyes, there was something about you—there was something you needed. . . . I knew enough about life by this time to understand that whatever you invent, whatever you project, is you! . . . Because if I am not what I've been told I am, then it means that you're not what you thought you were either! And that is the crisis.
>
> *(no page)*

Therefore, a juxtapositional approach to a *Critical Study of Whiteness* is ever needed. Meaning, the study of whiteness is not for the sake of whiteness itself, but more so for the sake and humanity of those who are most dehumanized by it. So, if research employs CWS to demonstrate how whiteness is skewed, needing redress *and* solely fixates on the skewness or redress, then it does not get at the crux of who is most hurt by this skewness and why it needs to be fixed. A *Critical Study of Whiteness* must demonstrate the interpellation between the exertion of whiteness to how it dehumanizes people of color.

Just as Yancy's work helps to understand the interconnectedness of racial dynamics, so too does the work of Franz Fanon. Fanon (1967) drew on racial psychoanalytics and claimed that a Black man is not only black; "he must be black in relation to the white man . . . a real dialectic between my body and the world" (pp. 110–111). Echoed again is the epistemological thought that whiteness, as hegemonic racial ideology, is defined by its ontological opposite, and thus a divorce from the expressions of whiteness to how whiteness is received cannot be had. In the same vein, then, studies using CWS cannot allow whiteness to be divorced from its interconnectedness to anti-Blackness, racial oppression, or the racial microaggression of people of color, lest it appear too self-indulgent. To engage in a *Critical Study of Whiteness* that does not recenter whiteness, research must not: (1) rely too heavily on scholarship stemming solely from white scholars, or (2) fixate the study on white people alone. Failing to articulate the hegemonic ideological apparatus of whiteness that, by its very presence, is used as surveillance (see Foucault, 1977) to impose a racial contract onto people of color (Mills, 1997), research ultimately caters to the centrality of whiteness by coddling white emotions and needs above those of people of color.

Furthermore, in this abusive marriage between whiteness and Blackness, Fanon (1967) asserted that the "white man is no more aware of his masochism when he is being titillated by the subtle content of the stereotyped grin than the Negro is aware of his sadism when he transforms the stereotype into a cultural bludgeon" (p. 176). By positing a psychosocial component to the issues of whiteness and Blackness, Fanon opened the door to racial psychoanalysis. Meaning, beyond large-scale sociological, economic, or political analyses on the disparities between Black people, and by extension people of color at varying degrees, and their white counterparts there is a psychosocial component to race and whiteness that necessitates racial psychoanalysis. Inasmuch as the Black man internalizes inferiority within a colonial racist structure, Matias (2016) argued that white people also internalize their sense of superiority under a white supremacist structure. The resulting psychological condition is that of maldevelopment of identity and how those identities interpellate between each other.

Critical Race Theory (CRT) is the leading analytical tool that allows researchers to examine the impacts of white supremacy and racism directly, setting a foundation for employing a critical study of whiteness. This is because as it emerged from legal studies (Bell, 1992; Delgado & Stefancic, 2012; Wing, 2003) it premised on the grounding fact that racism and white supremacy exist. Therefore, unlike other studies that focus on proving the existence of race, racism, and white supremacy, CRT centralizes this as fact and, in doing so, can better concentrate on ferreting out masked elements of race in the everyday rhetoric found in legal doctrine, proceedings, and laws themselves. Later, CRT was adopted into education when Ladson-Billings and Tate (1995) provided an overview of how race and property rights converge to generate social inequities in education. Though CRT grounds itself in the premise that racism exists, more studies were needed to explain whiteness and white supremacy specifically. Legal scholars Delgado and Stefancic (1997) edited a book on critical white studies that focused on "putting whiteness under the lens" (p. xvii) precisely because "whiteness, acknowledged or not, has been the norm against which other races are judged" (p. 1). Later, education scholar Ladson-Billings (1998) asserted, "It is because of the meaning and value imputed to whiteness that CRT becomes an important intellectual and social tool" (p. 9).

Whiteness became a unit of analysis within CRT especially because there exists an overwhelming number of white teachers (NCES, 2018) and whiteness ideology in teacher education (see Sleeter, 2001), many of whom teach in schools predominantly with students of color. In addition, research that is too narrowly focused on multiculturalism (see Sleeter, 2001) or cultural responsivity (see Matias, 2013a) overlooks how whiteness filters that ocular in ways that ultimately reinforce whiteness yet again (Matias et al., 2014). Because of these reasons, CRT undergirds a *Critical Study of Whiteness*. It cannot be divorced. Whereas a *Critical Study of Whiteness* examines how whiteness operates in ways that deleteriously dehumanize both white people and people of color (see Matias & Allen, 2013), CRT provides the tool for demonstrating specifically how whiteness dehumanizes people of color. Though CRT did not give birth to CWS, it is instrumental in how *Critical Study of Whiteness* is conceptualized and applied. As such, a *Critical Study of Whiteness* operates from a CRT basis that: (1) Race, racism, and white supremacy are operating at all times, and (2) The study of whiteness is in and of itself a way through which society can better understand how people of color are racially oppressed. To skew too far from this point makes the research on whiteness more self-indulgent in its.

There are many more transdisciplinary theories that undergird a *Critical Study of Whiteness* like Black, Chicana, and AAPI feminism (e.g., bell hooks, Alma Garcia, Sara Ahmed, Allyson Tintinangco-Cubales), postcolonial theories (e.g., Albert Memmi, Edward Said), and sociological theories of race (e.g., W. E. B. Du Bois, Eduardo Bonilla-Silva). Such theories present an epistemological perspective that never overlooks the interconnectedness and impact that whiteness, white supremacy, or white colonialism have on people of color while simultaneously honoring past scholarship made primarily by critical scholars of color.[1] These theories examine and identify the complexities behind racial dominant ideology *and* demonstrate its impact on people of color. Or, said differently, whether describing the existence of a veil in a racist society that allows one to see (or by virtue of whiteness—not see) the realities of race (Du Bois, 1903) or conceptualizing a portraiture of the colonized and the colonizer under colonial racism (Memmi, 1965), these theories expand what it means to uphold racial domination in the field of race studies while also detailing the psychological, material, and rhetorical impact it has on folks of color. Each theory and scholarship then provide a foundational understanding for a *Critical Study of Whiteness* to arise. Therefore, a *Critical Study of Whiteness* is deliberate in fully immersing the racial analysis with theories made by critical scholars of color.

An example of this immersion is how critical emotion studies conceptualize emotions. According to Ahmed (2004) racism is not exempt to how emotions are felt and produced precisely because racism is a power structure that impresses anti-Black associations to Black people. She wrote:

> A white racist subject who encounters a racial other may experience an intensity of emotions (fear, hate, disgust, pain). That intensification involves moving away from the body of the other, or moving towards that body in an act of violence, and then moving away. The 'moment of contact' is shaped by past histories of contact . . . rehearsing associations that are already in place. I have thus described emotions as performative: they both generate their objects, and repeat past associations. . . . The loop of the performative works powerfully: in reading the other as being disgusting, for example, the subject is filled up with disgust, as a sign of the truth of the reading.
>
> *(p. 194)*

Therefore, emotions that surface via racial interactions are not benign; in fact, they are, at times, performative in ways that elicit or enact racial power. Emotions then are socialized by one's proximity to race, whiteness, and white supremacy in ways that ultimately impact one's psychology: hence, racialized emotions. Depending on one's racial identity, racialized emotions have the power to enforce white supremacy by racially oppressing people of color. Therein lies the hegemonic condition. What is misunderstood is that racialized emotions are a preexisting psychosocial condition in need of racial psychoanalysis, or as Matias (2016) posited, in need of race-based counseling and therapy.

Based on this pre-existing psychosocial condition that happens too often in a white-dominated field like education, Matias (2016) posited the emotionalities of whiteness. She claimed racialized emotions psychoanalytically stem from one's socialization into whiteness, thus creating a condition of white ethnic shame (see Thandeka, 1999). Meaning, since one builds their sense of identity, interactions, and association off their socialization into whiteness they feel defensive anytime they perceive this shame will be exposed. For example, Thandeka (1999) described how white children are socialized into whiteness and are taught to feign color blindness despite actually witnessing racial reality. Meaning, live like "someone who is living a lie" (p. 34). She stated, "The child learns to silence and then deny [their] own resonant feelings toward racially proscribed others, not because [they choose] to become white, but because [they wish] to remain within the community that is quite literally [their] life" (p. 24). In doing so, these children are taught to bear false witness to racial reality that, in turn, produces a "white ethnic shame" (p. 36).

Now grown up, these individuals express unhealthy defense mechanisms (anger, sadness, violence, gaslighting) anytime they perceive their shame might be exposed (see Matias, 2016). And these defense mechanisms are not just innate ways to protect one's inner emotional core. As Matias (2016) suggested, because the emotionalities of whiteness exist within a white supremacist society, their employment becomes power plays used to uphold white emotions above the emotions of people of color. Meaning, one's discomfort at simply having a discussion of race is held above the discomfort of those who are testifying to racial reality. And, this is of grave importance with respect to education and schooling because if the emotionalities of whiteness are too unfettered the learning and teaching about race ceases. Or poignantly applied, schooling processes (dominated by whites and whiteness) can then refuse to engage in any form of antiracism for fear it may unfetter the emotional fragilities of whiteness. And, by kowtowing to the emotionalities of whiteness the resulting manifestation is seen in the misdiagnosis of special needs amongst Black and Brown students or pathologizing of Black and Brown cultures and families as subhuman. Hence, to truly engage in a *Critical Study of Whiteness*, researchers must take heed to how something as seemingly innate as emotions are nonetheless structured by white supremacy and how their mere expressions are racial power plays racially oppressing people of color. Otherwise, within a white supremacists' society white tears trump the real tears of those most impacted by racial oppression.

Current Applications of Critical Study of Whiteness Across Fields

Using a *Critical Study of Whiteness* means that research must remain true to its original intent: debunk whiteness for a greater racial humanity, not just for white humanity. Nowhere is this more applicable than in a field like teacher education, where the majority of K-12 teachers are white (NCES, 2018) and teach in schools that have students who are increasingly racially diverse. Clearly, there are power differentials at play: teacher-student; white teachers and students of color. In delving deeper into the application of a *Critical Study of Whiteness* in teacher education we engage some of the narratives of one of the authors. The first author, for example, openly discusses how her white teacher candidates (teacher trainees) often justify their decision to become an urban school teacher with the phrase, "Because I want to give back." By saying "I want to give back," they are aware enough to know urban students of color have fewer opportunities and access to resources than they, many of whom grew up in white, upper middle-class suburbs. The quandary that the first author poses then is what is it that you have presumably taken from urban communities of color that makes you now feel compelled to give back? In fact, on what moral basis do you feel qualified enough to teach in a community or with people you have no experience in relating to?

In a functionalist perspective, one may argue that these teachers are simply replicating structures that already exist in society and that such society is relatively benign. Meaning, there is no contestation of racial powers and that white people naturally receive the best resources and opportunities whereas students of color do not. Or, with respect to school psychology, a functionalist perspective would suggest that Black and Brown students have more cultural dispositions that make them naturally more susceptible to being diagnosed with learning disabilities, which then overrepresents their groups in special education.

However, within a *Critical Study of Whiteness* framework one sees a different racial analysis. Because white teacher candidates have been indoctrinated into whiteness since childhood (qua Thandeka, 1999) they hold onto a white epistemological stance, one that is not benign but indeed competes for racial power (qua Feinberg & Soltis, 1998). With respect to Critical Race Theory (qua Delgado & Stefancic, 2012; Ladson-Billings, 1998), such ideology embeds the notion that white people are superior to racial others, or as Kendi (2016) suggested, they are *un*stamped from the beginning. This is corroborated with the fact that society and all its institutions like schooling, educational policies, and practices are also structured by white supremacy (qua Gillborn, 2005). If, then, a teacher candidate is raised within whiteness ideology, they build their identity off of it (see Helms, 1990), subconsciously knowing that whiteness is always morally constructed to its imagined opposite (qua Baldwin, 1963; Fanon, 1967). Meaning, whiteness is imagined as a moral standard whereas Blackness is constructed as "a walking dung-heap" (Fanon, 1967, p. 98).

Because whiteness is all moral, those who subscribed to that ideology have no qualms in self-proclaiming themselves as qualified to teach in urban schools despite the fact that they have no experience with communities of color, let alone people of color. In fact, because the emotionalities of whiteness (qua Matias, 2016) have never been challenged, these teacher candidates may be aware of the unequal distribution of wealth and resources between white communities and communities of color but feign racial ignorance (qua Mills, 2007) in understanding how that manifestation came to be through active racist practices like redlining, racial covenants, and housing discriminations (all of which their families directly or indirectly benefited from). And, when learning about the racial legacies of urban schools they hope to teach in, they get emotionally flustered by the discomfort (qua Matias, 2016) such that they engage in emotional tactics (white guilt, emotional frozenness, anger, defensiveness, sadness) to silence issues of race throughout teacher preparation courses and the entirety of the teacher preparation program. These teacher candidates then become urban K-12 teachers, many of whom wrongfully claim they are the ones who are racially micro-aggressed simply because they are the only white person in the urban classroom—refusing to acknowledge that as a teacher they still have power over their students of color, and so racial microaggression does not apply to them (see Matias et al., 2014). Thus, students of color suffer from the racial bias, and inherent whiteness, made by the same teachers who once said they want to give back and love kids. Or, as Matias (2018) eerily reminded us, "Ignoring whiteness, specifically the emotionalities of whiteness, becomes a dangerous game that thickens the fakeness of white masks while burying more deeply a chance for freedom in developing humanizing relationships" (p. 37).

Relevance of Critical Study of Whiteness to School Psychology

The relevance of *Critical Study of Whiteness* to school psychology is equally important in that much like the field of teaching, most school psychologists are also racially deemed white and thus are confronted with dispositions that may align with whiteness. These dispositions impact one's interactions with racial Others and can lead to racially biased diagnoses. Meaning, parallel to teaching, school psychologists and counselors must build trust, understanding, and emotionally invest with their clients: students of color. This is a known fact. Yet, just as Matias (2018) said about therapy and counseling, "What is not so clearly understood is how does privilege, specifically white privilege, influence how one defines, applies, and enacts notions of trust, understanding, and emotional investment?" (p. 21). In fact, there are grave consequences for leaving hegemonic whiteness ideology and emotionality intact that negatively impact students and families of color. Suffice it to say that the educational decisions school psychologists make render too steep a consequence if one is not willing to engage in a critically thoughtful reflection on their racial privileges. For example, to render a Black male student emotionally disturbed without contextualizing the larger anti-Black movement that structures his life is to overlook the negative impacts that racism and white supremacy have on the Black psyche. Additionally, the Black psyche, for a student damaged by the oppression of white supremacy, will be far less likely to seek mental or emotional help from school personnel, who embody the white power structure (Nickerson et al., 1994). Or as Yancy (2008) stated in his racial interpellations between a white woman and his Black self in an elevator, the school psychologist may "not see that her identity is constructed and shaped through her negation of my humanity" (p. 21). Notwithstanding this negation, school psychology must take up a *Critical Study of Whiteness* to forever be committed to racially just practices in its practices inside schooling.

Conclusion

We posit a new approach to researching whiteness, hoping that it better informs future research in the field. Additionally, we offer this approach to be ever critical of how we approach research on whiteness; for overlooking the impact whiteness has on whites *and* people of color makes research on whiteness too narrowly focused, and thus does exactly what it hopes not to: center whiteness. For example, the commonplace practice to cite only white scholars in whiteness studies is equally problematic. In fact, it is tantamount to saying a researcher will engage in a feminist critique by only using scholarship created by male scholars. Such a practice is in and of itself a hypocritical form of socially just research; for how can one claim to be doing research for the betterment of women if they operationally choose to ignore the voices and scholarship of women in such research? Alas, such an approach to research makes it a contradiction in its intent. If, we, as education researchers, claim commitment to racial justice, in any form, then we must be deliberate in our approach to research. This is no different than the challenge posed by bell hooks (1994), who claimed that a professor's syllabus must include scholarship made by scholars of color to be racially equitable, otherwise currently observed as the larger Twitter phenomenon of #CiteBlackWomen. In fact, recent articles (see Malone, 2019) have suggested that whiteness should be studied in teacher education, overlooking the fact that many scholars, mostly female scholars of color like the first author of this chapter, have been doing this work for decades. This becomes not only an issue of analyzing whiteness and racism in society but also an issue of whiteness, racism, and sexism in scholarship and research. Notwithstanding this, we present this critical approach to keep the spirit of racial justice in the work of CWS so that the intent of racial justice embeds itself even in the way we research race. To be clear, the authors are not exempt from this critique; in fact, we implicate ourselves in our studies of whiteness in teacher education alongside others. But in the end, when it comes to race and gender, we strive for a better, more equitable approach to society and research, and thus do not fear pushing our own work to the next level. As such, we take heed to Patel and Price's (2016) theoretical push to articulate what racial justice means in research by articulating what truly undergirds a *Critical Study of Whiteness*. In doing so, we attempt to honor past scholars of color, build upon critical scholarship, and, in the end, hope to put criticality back in Critical Whiteness Studies.

Special Note

To scholars who study whiteness: Be forever diligent, critical, and ever so hopeful for a better society.

Note

1. We strategically include the word "critical" to highlight scholars of color who use critical dispositions like that of conflict theory. We do this to avoid the oft trope that by virtue of being a scholar of color, one believes in criticality. This is not our contention. Instead, we recognize that beyond skin color, ideological and epistemological standpoint matters, and if such standpoint is not critical of the overarching system of white supremacy, we then remove such dispositions from our definition of critical scholars of color. As such, there are white scholars who use a critical disposition of race, but for the purposes of this chapter we focus purposefully on critical scholars of color because they are too often denied recognition for their work. For an example see Morris (2017).

References

Ahmed, S. (2004). *The cultural politics of emotion*. Edinburgh University Press.

Allen, R. L. (2001). The globalization of white supremacy: Toward a critical discourse on the racialization of the world. *Educational Theory*, *51*(4), 467–485. https://doi.org/10.1111/j.1741-5446.2001.00467.x

Annamma, S. A., Jackson, D. D., and Morrison, D. (2017). Conceptualizing color-evasiveness: Using dis/ability critical race theory to expand a color-blind racial ideology in education and society. *Race Ethnicity and Education, 20*(2), 147–162. https://doi.org/10.1080/13613324.2016.1248837

Baldwin, J. (1963). A talk to teachers. *Saturday Review.*

Bell, D. (1992). *Faces at the bottom of the well: The permanence of racism.* Basic Books.

Bonilla-Silva, E. (2003). "New racism," color-blind racism, and the future of whiteness in America. In A. Doane & E. Bonilla-Silva (Eds.), *White out: The continuing significance of racism* (pp. 271–284). Routledge.

Bonilla-Silva, E. (2010). *Racism without racists: Color-blind racism and the persistence of racial inequality in the United States* (3rd ed.). Rowman & Littlefield.

Bowles, S., & Gintis, H. (2011). *Schooling in capitalist America: Educational reform and the contradictions of economic life.* Haymarket Books.

Delgado, R., & Stefancic, J. (1997). *Critical white studies: Looking behind the mirror.* Temple University Press.

Delgado, R., & Stefancic, J. (2012). *Critical race theory.* New York University Press.

Dewey, J. (1923). *Democracy and education: An introduction to the philosophy of education.* Palgrave Macmillan.

Doane, W. (2003). Rethinking whiteness studies. In A. Doane & E. Bonilla-Silva (Eds.), *White out: The continuing significance of racism* (pp. 3–18). Routledge.

Du Bois, W. E. B. (1903). *The souls of Black folks.* University Press.

Du Bois, W. E. B. (1935). Does the negro need separate schools? *The Journal of Negro Education, 4,* 328–335. https://doi.org/10.2307/2291871

Fanon, F. (1967). *Black skin, white masks.* Grove Press.

Feinberg, W., & Soltis, J. F. (1998). *School and society.* Teachers College Press.

Foucault, M. (1977). *Discipline and punish.* Pantheon Books.

Gallagher, C. A. (2003). Playing the white ethnic card: Using ethnic identity to deny contemporary racism. In W. Doane & E. Bonilla-Silva (Eds.), *White out: The continuing significance of racism* (pp. 145–158). Routledge.

Gillborn, D. (2005). Education policy as an act of white supremacy: Whiteness, critical race theory and education reform. *Journal of Education Policy, 20*(4), 485–505. https://doi.org/10.1080/02680930500132346

Gramsci, A. (2012). *Selections from the prison notebooks of Antonio Gramsci.* International Publishers.

Harris, C. I. (1993). Whiteness as property. *Harvard Law Review, 106*(8), 1707–1791. https://doi.org/10.2307/1341787

Helms, J. E. (Ed.). (1990). *Black and white racial identity: Theory, research and practice.* Greenwood Press.

hooks, b. (1994). *Teaching to transgress: Education as the practice of freedom.* Routledge.

Jupp, J. C., Leckie, A., Cabrera, N. L., & Utt, J. (2019). Race-evasive White teacher identity studies 1990–2015: What can we learn from 25 years of research? *Teachers College Record, 121*(1), 1–58.

Kendi, I. X. (2016). *Stamped from the beginning.* Nation Books.

Ladson-Billings, G. (1998). Just what is critical race theory and what's it doing in a nice field like education? *International Journal of Qualitative Studies in Education, 11*(1), 7–24. https://doi.org/10.1080/095183998236863

Ladson-Billings, G., & Tate, W. (1995). Toward a critical race theory of education. *Teachers College Record, 97*(1), 47–68.

Leonardo, Z. (2009). *Race, whiteness, and education.* Routledge.

Liptsitz, G. (2006). *The possessive investment in whiteness*. Temple University Press.

Malone, H. (2019). Teacher education needs to acknowledge 'whiteness'. *Education Week*, *39*(4), 15. www.edweek.org/teaching-learning/opinion-teacher-education-needs-to-acknowledge-whiteness/2019/09

Matias, C. E. (2013a). Check yo'self before you wreck yo'self and our kids: Counterstories from culturally responsive white teachers? . . . to culturally responsive white teachers! *Interdisciplinary Journal of Teaching and Learning*, *3*(2), 68–81.

Matias, C. E. (2016). *Feeling White*. Sense Publishers.

Matias, C. E. (2018). Before cultural competence. In S. S. Poulsen & R. Allan (Eds.), *Cross-cultural responsiveness & systematic therapy* (pp. 21–40). Springer International Publishing, AG.

Matias, C. E., & Allen, R. L. (2013). Loving whiteness to death: Sadomasochism, emotionality, and the possibility of humanizing love. *Berkeley Review of Education*, *4*(2), 285–309.

Matias, C. E., Viesca, K. M., Garrison-Wade, D. F., Tandon, M., & Galindo, R. (2014). What is critical whiteness doing in our nice field like Critical Race Theory? Applying CRT and CWS to understand the white imaginations of white teacher candidates. *Equity & Excellence in Education*, *47*(3), 289–304. https://doi.org/10.1080/10665684.2014.933692

McLaren, P. (2015). *Life in schools*. Routledge.

Memmi, A. (1965). *The colonizer and the colonized*. Beacon Press.

Mills, C. (1997). *The racial contract*. Cornell University Press.

Mills, C. (2007). White ignorance. In S. Sullivan & N. Tuana (Eds.), *Race and epistemologies of ignorance* (pp. 11–38). SUNY Press.

Morris, A. (2017). *The scholar denied*. University of California Press.

Morrison, T. (1992). *Playing in the dark*. Vintage Books.

National Center for Education Statistics (NCES). (2018). *Characteristics of public school teachers*. The Condition of Education. https://nces.ed.gov/programs/coe/indicator_clr.asp

Nickerson, K. J., Helms, J. E., & Terrell, F. (1994). Cultural mistrust, opinions about mental illness, and Black students' attitudes toward seeking psychological help from White counselors. *Journal of Counseling Psychology*, *41*(3), 378–385. https://doi.org/10.1037/0022-0167.41.3.378

Patel, L., & Price, A. (2016). The origins, potentials, and limits of racial justice. *Critical Ethnic Studies*, *2*(2), 61–81. https://doi.org/10.5749/jcritethnstud.2.2.0061

Roediger, D. (2005). What's wrong with these pictures? Race, narratives of admission, and the liberal self-representations of historically white colleges and universities. *Washington University Journal of Law & Policy*, *18*, 203–222.

Said, E. W. (2000). *Reflections on exile and other essays*. Harvard University Press.

Sleeter, C. (2001). Preparing teachers for culturally diverse schools: Research and the overwhelming presence of whiteness. *Journal of Teacher Education*, *52*(2), 94–106. https://doi.org/10.1177/0022487101052002002

Sullivan, S., & Tuana, N. (2007). *Race and epistemologies of ignorance*. SUNY Press.

Thandeka. (1999). *Learning to be White*. Continuum.

Wing, A. K. (2003). *Critical race feminism*. New York University Press.

Yancy, G. (2008). *Black bodies, White gazes*. Rowman & Littlefield Publishers.

SECTION 2

Theory to Practice

6

WHEN THEY *DON'T* SEE US: USING INTERSECTIONALITY TO EXAMINE BLACK GIRLS' DISCIPLINE EXPERIENCES

Jamelia N. Harris

Reigan,[1] a 12th-grade Black girl who experienced multiple forms of exclusionary punishment while attending Desert Rose High School (DRHS), wrote the following list of reasons why she believed Black girls at her high school were suspended at a rate four times higher than all other girls:

1. *The zero-tolerance policy is unjust because obviously it only attacks Black girls.*
2. *No one really takes the time to understand us. Nobody really like . . . understands why we're mad or why we're angry. Instead, they assume we're just being bitter.*
3. *Nobody nowadays, unless they were really bold, nobody's going to be direct with their racism. Racism has evolved because like it's all going to be undercover. But they still look at us differently. They're going to do little things like suspensions, but they're not going to say, "Oh it's because you're a Black girl." They're going to say, "Oh it's because you were disrespecting the teacher."*
4. *It's another form of oppression.*

Through her concise and trenchant analysis, Reigan offers a perceptive insight into the discipline experiences of Black girls that extends far beyond DRHS. She characterizes a decades-long pattern of intersectional oppression that systematically diminishes Black girls within the United States public school system. In her own words, Reigan theorizes about intersectionality (Crenshaw, 1989) and how the convergence of racism and sexism interact with school disciplinary systems, producing inequitable outcomes for Black girls.

Under the guise of policies and practices purported to be race- and gender-neutral, Black girls nationwide are subject to punitive practices and policies that physically, culturally, and socially distance them from their learning environments (Davis, 2020; Evans-Winters, 2018; Joseph et al., 2016). In fact, they are subject

DOI: 10.4324/9780367815325-8

to punishment at rates higher than girls of any other race/ethnicity group and non-Black boys (U.S. Department of Education Office for Civil Rights, 2016). While these statistics help explain the extent of racialized and gendered discipline disparities, there is no way to quantify the harm and suffering Black girls endure in their learning environments (Love, 2019; Morris, 2016; Wun, 2016). Contemporary social media movements, including #BlackGirlsMatter and #SayHerName, are documenting how Black girls as young as five years old are placed in handcuffs, physically thrown across classrooms, and committed to mental health facilities (Smith, 2016). One mind-numbing example of this took place in September of 2019 when Kaia Rolle, a 6-year-old Black girl at a charter school in Orlando, Florida, was arrested and charged with battery for throwing a "temper tantrum" in her kindergarten classroom (Flores & Weisfeldt, 2020). Following the incident, we learned from Kaia's grandmother that Kaia's behavior resulted from a medical condition called sleep apnea, which among other things leads to sleep deprivation. Even though the grandmother told Officer Dennis Turner about the condition, the school officials moved forward with criminalizing the child, placing handcuffs on her tiny wrists and thrusting her body into the back seat of a police car, transporting her to a youth prison. To quote the words of Kaia's grandmother, whose tears streamed down her face as she recounted the emotional suffering and trauma her granddaughter endured: "How do you reverse the fact that a 6-year-old was fingerprinted. . . . Mugshots! Put in the backseat of a patrol car in handcuffs, over a kick during a tantrum?" (NBC, 2019).

While this incident garnered considerable public attention due to Kaia's young age, it is imperative to emphasize that her experience fits within a recurring pattern that remains muted in education and policy reform discourses: how school officials subject Black girls to overly harsh punishments that facilitate their school pushout and criminalization (Annamma, 2018; Morris, 2016). Further, this incident fits within a larger reality in which schools punish students with the greatest social, emotional, and economic needs due to a "fixation with behavior management and social control that outweighs and overrides all other priorities and goals" (Noguera, 2003, p. 342). Racial and gender disparities in school discipline attest to how the intersections of racism and sexism simultaneously perpetuate a widening chasm among Black girls and other racial/ethnic groups as well as an unfulfilled promise of equitable life chances (Ladson-Billings, 2009).

This chapter is written in pursuit of justice for Black girls and is firmly grounded in the moral declaration that *Black girls' lives matter*. Black girls are entitled to humanizing learning environments. Black girls are entitled to have their hard-won knowledge nurtured. Black girls are entitled to be embraced, affirmed, and celebrated (Brown, 2009; Joseph et al., 2016). Yet, in public schools across the nation, the voices of Black girls are often silenced and punished; their talents misrecognized and denied; their bodies surveilled and overpoliced; their most critical needs remain unmet. In this vein, with the support of 14 adolescent Black girls who entrusted me with their testimonies about the harmful consequences of punitive discipline, *we* offer this chapter in hopes that it will benefit the livelihoods of Black girls in public schools across the nation.

This chapter begins with a brief review of Intersectionality Theory and selected literature highlighting what is currently understood about the nature of Black girls' disciplinary experiences. Next, the chapter highlights a case narrative featuring Teiera, one of the 14 Black girls who contributed her story to *The Concrete Rose Project*, which was a participatory research study exploring Black girls' discipline experiences at DRHS. The intent is for the narrative to illustrate how structural forces that emerge at the intersection of racism, sexism, and poverty shape Black girls' worlds in and outside of the school context. As Teiera's narrative will reveal, the hardships and emotional stressors Black girls navigate outside of school are often compounded by a punitive learning environment in which, as the girls repeatedly emphasized, discipline and punishment feel overemphasized, yet relationship building, compassion, and understanding feel non-existent. This chapter underscores the imperative need for school leaders and educators to develop an intersectional awareness regarding Black girls' nuanced identities and the structural forces that shape their daily lives. The chapter concludes with experiential activities that provide educators with practical tools for engaging intersectionality as a social justice praxis toward improving school ecologies for Black girls.

Brief Introduction to Intersectionality Theory

The permanence of discipline disproportionality facing Black girls is rooted in Black girls and women's subjugation throughout the U.S. history of colonialism, imperialism, and chattel slavery. Such patterns necessitate a multifaceted lens that moves beyond siloed thinking about race, class, and gender toward understanding the multiple spectrums of identity and systems of domination as they intersect with one another and produce inequitable outcomes for Black girls (Crenshaw et al., 2015). Thus, in this section, I relay a brief synopsis of Intersectionality Theory as conceptualized by Kimberlé Crenshaw (1989) and many other Black Feminist Scholars (Collins, 1989, 2000; Davis, 1983; hooks, 1984; Richie, 2012).

Black girls occupy a distinct location at the crux of structural inequality, as the only group of girls in the United States with ancestral links to chattel slavery. The critical scholarship of Black Feminist intellectuals—including Patricia Hill Collins, Kimberlé Crenshaw, Audre Lorde, bell hooks, Angela Davis, and the women of the Combahee Collective—articulated the need for analyzing how multiple interlocking systems of power simultaneously shape the experiences of Black girls and women in society, particularly experiences that relate to oppression, domination, and discrimination (Collins, 1989; Crenshaw, 1989; hooks, 1984). At once, Black girls and women face oppression rendered by their Blackness and femaleness, positioning them as socially and structurally vulnerable within systems of racism, patriarchy, and capitalism. As a frame to combat Black women's erasure within feminist, antiracist, and legal discourses, Crenshaw (1989) introduced intersectionality into the field of critical race and legal studies. Central to the intersectionality concept is the assertion that single-axis frameworks, which treat race and gender as mutually exclusive, elide the challenges many Black women face at the intersection of multiple marginalized social identities.

According to Crenshaw (1989), the centrality of race and gender factors into Black women's experiences of discrimination in ways that often "do not fit neatly within the legal categories of either 'racism' or 'sexism'—but as a combination of both racism and sexism" (p. 150). To illustrate the concept, Crenshaw offered the analogy of a traffic intersection:

> Discrimination, like traffic through an intersection, may flow in one direction, it can be caused by cars traveling from any number of directions and, sometimes, from all of them. Similarly, if a Black woman is harmed because she is in the intersection, her injury could result from sex discrimination or racial discrimination.
>
> *(p. 149)*

Furthermore, Crenshaw (1991) argued, these forms of discrimination are not intentionally produced, but rather, they are frequently the "consequence of intersecting oppressions where one level of oppression interacts with pre-existing vulnerabilities to create yet another dimension of disempowerment" (p. 1249). Crenshaw's theorization of intersectionality is not merely a matter of naming markers of identity and diversity but instead intends to extend social justice and human rights to Black girls and women. Thus, intersectionality offers a valuable prism to identify and respond to the contentious interaction between systems of power and Black girls' multiple social locations and how these complex interactions shape their experiences of oppression and marginalization in school.

While intersectionality and other Black Feminist theories provide an invaluable framework for understanding the subordinated position of Black girls in the U.S., there is a need for specific theorizations of intersectional oppression that extend beyond the experiences of adult Black women. As Smith (2019) wrote:

> The goal here is not to eliminate Black Feminism as a theoretical lens for Black girlhood; without its contributions and the necessary language of intersectionality and the exploration of blackness interlocked with gender, class, sexuality, and age, we would lose many narratives of Black women's and girls' various experiences with oppression in this world.
>
> *(p. 8)*

However, as Ruth Nicole Brown (2009) reminded us, Black girls "are not free from injustice and inequality, as they negotiate state structures and agencies that are often hostile to their well-being, Black girls experience politics at an early age" (p. 3). The intersections of race, gender, class, and age oppression sprout unique assaults on Black girls' bodies and livelihoods that are often overlooked outside the field of Black Girlhood studies. Therefore, employing Intersectionality Theory and other Black Feminist theories to analyze Black girls' lived experiences must account for the interstices of race, gender, sexuality, class, and age oppression that simultaneously shape their lived experiences.

Black Girls and School Discipline

In public schools across the nation, Black girls are overwhelmingly subject to punitive discipline practices and policies that deprive them of valuable learning opportunities (Annamma et al., 2019) and facilitate their contact with the youth prison system. These disparities—which continue to exist after years of emphasis on reducing 'racial' discipline disproportionality—cannot be accounted for by differences in socioeconomic status or student behavioral patterns between Black and non-Black girls (Morris & Perry, 2017). Rather these troubling patterns illustrate that complex discrimination emerges at the intersections of race *and* gender, which produce punitive inequities for Black girls that remain absent in the education policy discourses (Evans-Winters, 2018).

When scholars have interrogated the contributing factors of Black girls' experiences with school discipline, the influence of race and gender biases consistently emerge (Blake et al., 2011; Crenshaw et al., 2015; Morris, 2007; Wun, 2016). The most inequitable discipline patterns emerge for behavioral categories that are subjectively interpreted and non-threatening in nature, such as defiance (Blake et al., 2011). For example, Morris and Perry (2017) used an intersectional lens to examine interactions between race and gender on office referrals in a large urban school district and found that Black girls were disciplined primarily for "disruptive behavior, dress code violations, disobedience, and aggressive behavior" (p. 144). Further, these scholars' findings revealed an important intersectional inequality in which "Black girls' behavior was perceived as misbehavior far more often compared to other girls" (Morris & Perry, 2017, p. 144). Decades of research studies buttress these findings, suggesting that the offenses incurred most often by Black girls are largely influenced by school officials' racialized-gendered interpretations of their behaviors (Blake et al., 2011; Crenshaw et al., 2015; Morris, 2007).

Classroom-level empirical research studies further contextualize these quantitative studies by offering critical insight into the processes, practices, and ideologies that reinforce the over-punishing of Black girls. Morris (2007) illustrated how racist and sexist stereotypes about Black femininity govern teacher-student social interactions in the classroom, resulting in punishments stemming from perceptions of Black girls' embodied femininity as defective, coarse, 'loud, and not ladylike' (p. 12). Black girls' disciplinary experiences are often rooted in cultural dissonance. When these girls speak or engage in ways that are culturally unfamiliar to their educators or other staff, the girls' behavior and interactions are often misinterpreted and unjustly problematized. Black girls are then subject to classrooms as sites of social control and correction: their bodies, their tone of voice, and their posture are routinely regulated as deviant, a potential threat to authority (Bae-Dimitriadis & Evans-Winters, 2017; George, 2015).

Epstein et al. (2017) attributed this to a phenomenon called *adultification*. According to their groundbreaking report, these scholars found that adults perceive Black girls to be *less innocent* and less in need of protection than white girls. These findings help explain why Black girls are disciplined more often and more severely across schools and the youth prison system. The perception of Black girls as being overly mature and less innocent leads to differential discipline outcomes that reinforce the racialized school/prison nexus (Annamma, 2018; Morris, 2016). Instead of attempting to understand the underlying circumstances of perceived behavior challenges or granting "Black girls the benefit of the doubt that they are acting like adolescents," educators enforce harsh disciplinary consequences because they perceive these girls as adults and thus more culpable for their actions (Joseph et al., 2019, pp. 134–135).

Murphy and colleagues (2013) extended this research by centering the disciplinary experiences of Black girls in middle schools, from their perspective. These students articulated incidents where they chose not to comply with specific teachers as a deliberate act of resistance against unfair treatment by teachers who denied their requests for social and academic support or "punish[ed] students without listening to their explanations" (Murphy et al., 2013, p. 605). At the same time, Black girls reported fewer discipline issues with teachers who invested time by explaining curriculum, nurturing interpersonal relationships, and supporting these girls in navigating social and emotional challenges. Centering these girls' lived experiences as sources of expertise offers invaluable lessons on the important role of teacher-student relationships in redressing problematic discipline culture and school climate. Echoing the words of Morris (2016), "Black girls desire a safe space in which to learn . . . and where positive student-teacher relationships are reinforced through dialogue and engagement" (p. 188). Thus, improving Black girls' educational experiences requires fostering inclusive and culturally responsive learning environments that affirm their humanity, empower their voices, and make possible the diverse expressions of Black girlhood (Brown, 2013).

Relevance of Intersectionality to Black Girls and School Discipline

As Crenshaw (1991) reminded us, the intersection of racism and sexism factors into Black girls' lives in ways that "cannot be captured wholly by looking at the race or gender dimensions of those experiences separately" (p. 1244). Intersectionality offers an effective lens for educational stakeholders to examine and redress the structural forces that often contribute to Black girls' marginalization in school settings. For instance, the studies described in the literature review broadly suggest that Black girls are punished for behaviors perceived to challenge institutionalized expectations of what it means to be 'appropriately feminine.' The notion that Black girls' ways of being and engaging in the classroom are inadequately feminine alienates these girls by rendering their embodied femininity to an inferior and undesirable status. Deficit thinking and stereotypes can also be enacted in the classroom environment through subtle microaggressions that reproduce hostile and exclusionary learning environments in which Black girls feel they do not belong (Davis, 2020; Joseph et al., 2016; Parks et al., 2016; Wun, 2016). As Collins (2000) noted, white, heterosexual, middle-class femininity is widely constructed as the normative standard, which is imperative to address considering many teachers of Black children are white middle-class women.

Oftentimes, many of the characteristics and personality traits for which Black girls are condemned in school spaces are valorized and embraced in their communities as strengths and vital navigational capital for surviving in a racist, sexist, and classist society (Evans-Winters & Esposito, 2010; Jones, 2010; Yosso, 2005). For example, studies show that Black girls are punished for talking loud or with 'attitude' (Watson, 2016), being outspoken (George, 2015; Wun, 2016), fighting to defend themselves against sexual violence (Crenshaw, 2015), and wearing their natural hair (Morris, 2016). Lindsay-Dennis (2010) attributed such discipline malpractices to a lack of cultural competence among teachers and pre-service teacher education training programs. She argued that when teachers neglect to acknowledge how Black girls' cultural realities and socialization shape their culturally situated adaptive strategies, worldviews, identities, and behaviors, the consequences can be negative and severe for these girls' educational experiences. Intersectionality offers a framework for understanding how these cultural processes shape Black girls' identities. An intersectional competence can also facilitate educators' (including non-white educators) internal processes of interrogating how white supremacist cultural values manifest in the behavioral norms they draw upon when evaluating Black girls.

Further, many Black girls navigate complex lives and structural conditions including poverty, parental incarceration, and foster care that they do not have the luxury to leave outside of the classroom (Ladson-Billings, 2009; Parks et al., 2016; Wun, 2018). These challenging circumstances can create emotional stress for Black girls that affects their behavior and the ways in which they engage in the classroom. Yet, rather than recognizing the social and emotional needs of Black girls, schools often *misrecognize* the hurt they carry with them for an 'attitude problem' and punish them instead (Wun, 2018). School officials can employ intersectionality as a practitioner lens to interrogate how structural and institutional forces (i.e., policies, practices, processes) position Black girls vulnerable to school punishment and further marginalization. Proctor et al. (2017) offered important guidance about ways school psychologists can incorporate an intersectional lens to unpack their own intersectional identities and challenge power/

privilege that can foster imbalanced dynamics with the Black girls they work with. These scholars' recommendations for practice reveal the promise of engaging intersectionality as a pathway to promoting inclusive learning environments in ways that extend educational justice for Black girls.

Case Narrative

The following case illustrates the experience of Teiera, a 12th grade Black girl who contributed to the Concrete Rose Project (CRP). The CRP was a collaborative research study, grounded by the tenets of Black Feminist Thought, which centered the lived experiences, knowledge, and expertise of Black girls to explore the root causes and impact of punitive punishment.

This case illustrates how the pervasive culture of punitive punishment misrecognized the social and emotional needs of a Black girl who navigated intersectional violence in her daily life. Through her own words, Teiera describes the emotional hardship she endured while navigating various interlocking systems of oppression, including racism, sexism, poverty, and the child welfare system. This case narrative does not explicitly detail the circumstances of what led Teiera into the foster care system because these details obscure the influence of structural violence that perpetuates the removal of Black children in resource-poor communities from their mothers. Further, educators and other school officials have an obligation to ensure that the social and emotional needs of all students are addressed regardless of their structural conditions and life circumstances. However, it is necessary to briefly contextualize how the child welfare system directly relates to and is compounded by the interlocking structures of poverty, racism, and sexism.

Black children are the most likely of any group to be systematically removed from their homes by government authorities. Black children make up nearly 50% of the total foster care population, although they constitute less than 20% of children in the U.S. (Roberts, 2002). The overrepresentation of Black children is fundamentally an intersectional violence against Black women. Richie (2012) described the child welfare system as a vestige of the mass incarceration of low-income Black mothers who often are challenged by systemic racism, sexism, and poverty in ways that pose barriers to motherhood. Roberts (2002) forcefully argued that the overrepresentation of Black children in the contemporary child welfare system systematically destroys the Black family structure and is inextricably linked to the denigration of Black womanhood that constructs a perception of Black women as inadequate and unworthy mothers.

As you will read in Teiera's narrative, when girls are removed from their homes, they can suffer from housing instability for years as they move among foster homes. Not surprisingly, these challenges can severely harm their educational pathways as girls in placement often navigate the trauma from their familial separation and often switch schools repeatedly, which requires them to adapt to new home and school environments. Given what we know about the school/prison nexus, namely the criminalization of Black girls with unmet needs, it is also unsurprising that Black girls are significantly overrepresented among youth who 'crossover' from the child welfare system into the prison system (Sherman & Balck, 2015). Black girls are often educated in environments where discipline is emphasized over their social and emotional well-being. Thus, girls who struggle with socioemotional hardships, trauma, and other "unmet needs often only come to the attention of school personnel when their behavior leads to punishable offenses" (Crenshaw et al., 2015, p. 11).

With this context in mind, I now turn the chapter over to Teiera, whose story sheds necessary light on the challenges she and many other Black girls face in classrooms when their intersecting identities and needs are overlooked and disregarded.

Teiera's Story

> *Dear teachers,*
> *I want you to know* ***I'm more than just a Ghetto Black Girl.***
> *I am independent, intelligent, and trustworthy.*
> *I can sometimes get distracted . . . but I am driven.*
> *In my classes, I want to feel equal and included.*

These were the most important things Teiera wanted her teachers to know, which she felt would help them *see* her and support her needs as an adolescent Black girl at Desert Rose High School.

Teiera was a 17-year-old self-identified "quiet, pretty, dark-skinned, Black girl" in her senior year at DRHS. She was "determined to graduate high school on time" despite the obstacles she faced in her personal and school lives. She walked through the hallways with a large cheer duffle bag draped over her shoulders, freshly manicured white nails, and a high curly afro-textured bun with baby hairs laid softly around the perimeter of her face. It was her first year on the cheer team. "I just wanted to be a part of something. It made me feel proud to be a part of something and to do something, because my whole high school experience, I didn't really do stuff [in school] because I had went through foster care," she explained.

Motivated by her aspirations to be the first in her family to attend college and to become a pediatrician, Teiera was known to be a "Straight A" student throughout most of her school years. Her determination to achieve these goals was fueled by her "desire to be truly happy, successful, and to provide a better life for her future kids." Teiera described a situation that took place during her freshman year of high school that disrupted her educational trajectory.

> *I walked to school, and I was late . . . so I made it really to second-period class. It was the end of it, so the security guard was like, "Oh, they want you to go to the*

> *office, you're going home," but I'm like, "I just got here." I know that didn't make sense, my mom doesn't have a car, so I know she's not fixing to just pick me up that quick after I just got to the school. But she wasn't there though. I already knew they were going to probably take us, but I wasn't sure. So, I just went to the office. Then I see my little sister and the social worker, and she was like, "Oh, we came to surprise you." I'm like, "That's not funny to me, why would you say that?" because this is nothing good, to be taken away from our family, this is not good.*

Navigating the emotional trauma caused by her separation from her mother, as well as being placed in homes that felt physically unsafe caused Teiera's grades to decline significantly after her first year in placement. Teiera recalls that foster care negatively affected her educational experiences:

> *I had to protect my little sister; I couldn't sleep at night because she would cry every night because she missed home. I feel like my life and school were just going downhill. . . . I've always been shy all my life, that's no lie, I've always been really cool and talkative to people, but once I was in foster care . . . I started to really isolate myself more than usual. I had a therapist at that time and she helped me realize I was depressed. I didn't even realize I was depressed at the time.*

After spending two years shuffling between three separate foster care placements and five different high schools, Teiera was eventually reunited with her mother. Teiera spent two years recovering credits at Raven High School, a nearby continuation school where she received most of her lessons through an online course. Her yearning to be reconnected with her friends and teachers in her traditional school setting motivated her to persist.

> *My 10th-grade year, that whole year, I'm just trying to catch up, catch up, catch up, because my whole goal to motivate me was like, "Okay, I want to be on track, I want to be in my classes for 11th grade, I want to be with my friends."*

Teiera returned to her traditional high school, Desert Rose High School, for 11th grade and finished the year "on track to graduate" earning nearly a 4.0 GPA.

Desert Rose High School

Located in a low-income and economically marginalized, predominantly Black and Latinx neighborhood, DRHS has a reputation throughout the community as being a "failing school." DRHS serves 1,700 students. The racial composition of its student body is diverse, with 31% of students identifying as Black, 60% of students as Hispanic or Latino, and 4% as white. Of this demographic, 20% of students are classified as special education, 12% are living in foster care placements, and 89% of students are classified as "socioeconomically disadvantaged/eligible for free and reduced lunch." Quite the opposite of the student population represented at Desert Rose High School, 70% of the teaching and administrative staff identify as white, 17% as Hispanic/Latinx, and 20% as Black. Of the ten administrators on the school leadership team, five identify as white men, three as white women, one as a Latinx woman, one as a mixed (Latino/Asian) man, and one as a Black man. There are no Black women on the administrative leadership team.

Staff members would commonly remark on the school's high turnover rates for teachers. As one teacher explained to me, "The reputation among teachers here is that if you can *survive* teaching the kids at DRHS then you can teach anywhere in the world." This reputation was attributed to the deficit perception that students at DRHS were plighted by broader structural conditions in the community, including poverty and violence, that made them particularly difficult to teach.

Last academic year, DRHS was featured in a report that revealed troubling disparities at the intersection of race and gender: Black girls were suspended at a rate higher than all other racial groups of girls and boys, with the exception of their Black boy counterparts. Black girls were five times more likely than white girls to be suspended and three times more likely than Latina girls. Black girls were the only group of girl students who faced expulsion. During the same academic year, Black girls also experienced the lowest school completion rates of all girl students.

In response to the report, DRHS faced tremendous pressure from the school district and state to address the root causes of racial-gender discipline disparities for all Black students. In particular, three discipline categories emerged as the areas where Black girls experienced the most inequitable outcomes: truancy; defiance, insubordination, and disruption (DID); and dress code violations. The school offered several non-mandatory professional development sessions for teachers related to classroom management. These training sessions did not efficiently address how the intersections of race and gender shape Black girls' experiences, nor did they address how racial and gender biases can influence how Black girls' behaviors are interpreted and how discipline policies are enforced in response to said behaviors.

Teiera's Reflection

Reflecting on how being a Black girl at Desert Rose High School shapes her schooling experiences, Teiera explained that the confluence of race and gender shaped the perceptions of her teachers:

> *I just feel like it's a lot of stereotypes, I feel like I'm getting judged. People see me and they assume I'm going to act the way other girls act. Like, "Okay, she's ghetto, she's ratchet, she's probably going to be all loud." I know I shouldn't care as much as what people think, but I just still feel some type of way . . . especially when it's adults.*

Teiera felt that being stereotyped subjected her to biased treatment by both her teachers and cheer coach. As a student in the classroom and as one of the few Black cheerleaders on the school's cheer team, Teiera kept to herself and described her quiet demeanor as a strategy to navigate what she perceived to be a hostile and often unpredictable learning environment. Aware of the stereotypes that surrounded Black girls at her school, Teiera recalled various classroom interactions between teachers, herself, and other Black girls that influenced her decision to silence herself in class.

> *You know how when you just have bad days or something, and you just want to be left alone and you try to tell the teacher you want to be left alone but they just keep picking at you? I just feel like my teacher picks on me, and it's not just me, it's other Black girls in there too who feel the same way. One day we had a paper I had to do in my art class, and I admit I was not doing my work at the time. I tried to tell my teacher that I was having a bad day and would do the assignment later . . . and she kept picking at me asking why I'm not doing my work. She kept asking me and I tried to tell her nicely . . . . She tried to make it seem like I had an attitude when I told her, but I didn't. She knocked points off of my grade for participation and sent me to OCD (On-Campus Detention) because she felt like I was being disrespectful.*

Teiera described 'disrespect' as a discriminatory catch-all discipline infraction that was often used to punish Black girls who were perceived as 'outspoken.' The loosely defined parameters of 'disrespectful behavior' empowered Teiera's teacher to subjectively enforce school discipline policies based on her interpretation of what constitutes respect. This fostered a hostile classroom atmosphere in which Teiera felt her teacher 'abused her power to deduct points' from her overall course grade based on their tenuous relationship. Teiera felt her experience was common among Black girls and boys who were often singled out and excessively policed based on perceptions about their attitudes and tones of voice:

> *There are other races in the classroom and they can curse, be on their phones, wear crop tops. Nothing happens to them. But as soon as a Black person does something, she tells them to get out or deducts their points. It doesn't even make me want to speak up when stuff like this happens, because it happens so much, and it's just like, "Really?" It makes me kind of want to shut myself down like I said, I go in my class and I do it because I know that I actually enjoy art, and she's the only art teacher. I don't have a voice.*

As a Black girl who transitioned between three high schools and five foster care placements during her high school years, Teiera wished adults in her school would "be more understanding that sometimes she has bad days and wants to be left alone." Teiera offered the following advice about ways schools can better support her needs and those of other Black girls just like her.

> *I just feel like we need more personal connections with adults at our school. It doesn't have to be too personal but I feel like they should try to get to know us a little bit more. Communicate and talk to us, and don't just assume that we're acting up, because something might be actually happening and going on in our lives that they don't even know about, and we don't know how to express it, or something like that. I just feel like being more personal would make me more comfortable to speak up . . . and also if I'm having a bad day then maybe my teachers would be more understanding.*

Experiential Activities

1. **Large-group discussion:** Intersectionality refers to the ways social categories such as race, gender, socioeconomic status, and sexuality intersect to create systems of privilege, domination, and oppression. Oftentimes, intersecting identities can interact with structural forces, creating multi-layered dimensions of social inequality (Crenshaw, 1991). Reflecting on Teiera's story, what intersecting identities and structural forces does she describe, and how do these affect her educational experiences?
2. **Large-group discussion:** Teiera began her story with a letter to her teachers in which she declared 'I am not a ghetto Black girl.' How do you think being perceived as a 'ghetto Black girl' relates to intersectional oppression? How might this narrative relate to the challenges she experiences with her teacher? How might this narrative impact her academic development? What strategies, resources, or professional developments might help counteract deficit perspectives about Black girls and nurture their academic development?
3. **Partner activity:** Throughout history, Black women and girls have developed their own self-definitions as a way to resist negative stereotypes and control narratives that render them unseen and dehumanized (Collins, 2000). A self-definition empowers Black girls to evaluate themselves—their values, strengths, intersecting identities, dreams—distinct from how society perceives them. These definitions can provide educators and school officials with important insight into who Black girls are and who they aspire to become (from their own perspectives). With a partner, discuss activities or outlets that you/your school can create/develop to empower Black girls in declaring their own self-definitions.

   One activity that can empower Black girls in communicating their self-definition is an 'I Am' poem (see Tatum, n.d.). While there are many free 'I Am' poem templates available online, these templates can easily be created.

Using a worksheet format, this activity includes the prompt "I am" followed by a blank space with a prompt underneath that allows students to reflect on their personal qualities including but not limited to their identities, their cultures, their values, and their dreams. Figure 6.1 is an example of an 'I Am' poem created by Teiera.

4. **Large-group discussion:** As mentioned, Black girls are often punished for behaviors perceived to challenge authority or defy white-centric gendered norms. Wun (2016) found that Black girls were often subject to informal punishments that were punitively enforced yet fell under the purview of formal school discipline practices (e.g., suspensions and expulsions). In Teiera's case, she described an informal and formal punishment in which her teacher deducted points from her overall grade and referred her to OCD because she perceived her to be 'disrespectful.' What might be the implications of having a broad "defiance, insubordination, and disrespect" discipline policy as they relate to Black girls' discipline experiences? How might you support a student who approached you in navigating a situation in which they felt unfairly treated or punished?
5. **Small-group role play activity:** You are an administrator hosting your weekly all-staff meeting. During your check-ins, Mrs. Porter, a first-year English teacher, mentions for the sixth consecutive week that she is having a 'problem' with her Black girl students' attitudes, who she also describes as 'loud and disrespectful.' Upon reviewing Mrs. Porter's discipline data for the semester, you observe that she disproportionately refers Black girls to on-campus detention for 'disrespect' and 'disruption.' What conversations, targeted interventions, and supports would you implement to support this group of students and Mrs. Porter?

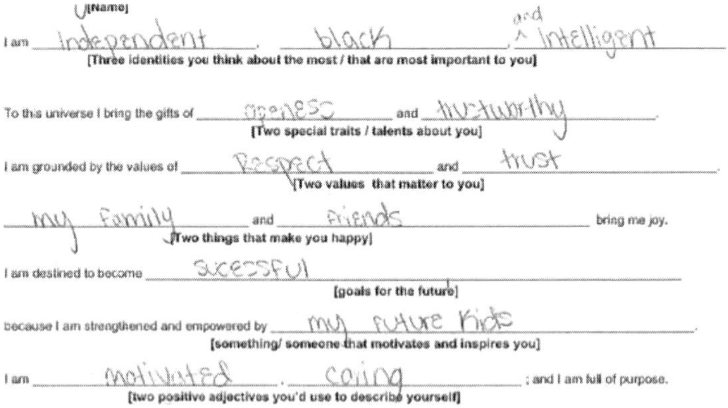

[Name]

I am independent, black, and intelligent

[Three identities you think about the most / that are most important to you]

To this universe I bring the gifts of openess and trustworthy.

[Two special traits / talents about you]

I am grounded by the values of Respect and trust.

[Two values that matter to you]

my Family and friends bring me joy.

[Two things that make you happy]

I am destined to become sucessful

[goals for the future]

because I am strengthened and empowered by my future kids.

[something/ someone that motivates and inspires you]

I am motivated, caring; and I am full of purpose.

[two positive adjectives you'd use to describe yourself]

FIGURE 6.1 Teiera's Self-Definition

6. **Strategic team planning sessions:** Teiera described a need/desire to foster 'personal connections' with her teachers and other adults at her school. In a large group, discuss the significance of interpersonal relationships as it relates to school climate for Black girls. Next, divide into small groups and identify three strategies and practices in response to the following questions:

   - What practices or strategies can we implement to learn more about the social and cultural backgrounds of the Black girl students we serve? How can we learn more about Black girls' intersectional identities?
   - What practices can we implement to foster community and positive relationships with Black girl students in our school/classrooms?
   - What infrastructures or spaces can we develop to ensure the voices, needs, and experiences of Black girl students are centered in our school/classrooms?
   - What infrastructures or spaces can we develop to learn more about Black girls' perspectives on the quality of school climate and their suggestions for improvement? Based on what we currently know, how can our school work as a collective to improve the school climate for Black girls?

Conclusion

Through the many conversations I have shared with Black girls such as Teiera, Reigan, and the remaining 12 contributors of the Concrete Rose Project, I have struggled with the intolerable truth that "quite a few girls, too many to be acceptable, are brilliant yet routinely disciplined into taking up less and less space" (Brown, 2013, p. 2). Outside of school, many girls are navigating complex entanglements of structural injustices shaped by racism, sexism, and poverty that perpetuate hurt and injury in their daily lives even as they continue to thrive, persist, and resist. Dishearteningly, many girls believe that their educators and other adults are unaware and unconcerned about their lives outside of school. When Black girls are rightfully angered and hurt by the challenging circumstances and structural conditions that constrain their livelihoods, their anger is dismissed by controlling narratives that depict them as miniature angry Black women. Without the protections of 'girlhood innocence,' Black girl hurt becomes pathologized as 'Black girl attitude,' and the consequence of being perceived to have 'attitude' in a body that is both Black and female is almost always harsh, exclusionary, and punitive. Teiera and many other Black girls embrace education as the direct pathway to their future dreams; however, the hostile, punitive, and often unpredictable nature of their learning environments has forced them to adopt strategies, such as silencing themselves, in order to survive and persist. Schools have the potential to offer critical spaces of support that embolden Black girls as they negotiate the diverse complexities within Black girlhood and their transition into Black womanhood. As we continue to reimagine school ecologies where the promise of equitable educational opportunity for all students is fulfilled, we must recenter the intersectional needs and identities of Black girls from the public periphery, redirect attention away from punishing and constraining the expressiveness of Black girlhood, and recommit to rendering the humanity and brilliance these girls embody—recognized, affirmed, and *seen*.

References

Annamma, S. A. (2018). *The pedagogy of pathologization: Dis/abled girls of color in the school-prison nexus*. Routledge/Taylor & Francis Group.

Annamma, S. A., Anyon, Y., Joseph, N. M., Farrar, J., Greer, E., Downing, B., & Simmons, J. (2019). Black girls and school discipline: The complexities of being overrepresented and understudied. *Urban Education*, *54*(2), 211–242. https://doi.org/10.1177/0042085916646610

Bae-Dimitriadis, M., & Evans-Winters, V. E. (2017). Flipping the script: The dangerous bodies of girls of color. *Cultural Studies/Critical Methodologies*, *17*(5), 415–423. https://doi.org/10.1177/1532708616684867

Blake, J. J., Butler, B. R., Lewis, C. W., & Darensbourg, A. (2011). Unmasking the inequitable discipline experiences of urban Black girls: Implications for urban educational stakeholders. *Urban Review: Issues and Ideas in Public Education*, *43*(1), 90–106. http://dx.doi.org/10.1007/s11256-009-0148-8

Brown, R. N. (2009). *Black girlhood celebration: Toward a hip-hop feminist pedagogy*. Peter Lang Publishing Inc.

Brown, R. N. (2013). *Hear our truths: The creative potential of black girlhood*. University of Illinois Press.

Collins, P. H. (1989). The social construction of Black feminist thought. *Signs*, *14*(4), 745–773.

Collins, P. H. (2000). *Black feminist thought: Knowledge, consciousness, and the politics of empowerment*. Routledge.

Crenshaw, K. (1989). Demarginalizing the intersection of race and sex: A Black feminist critique of antidiscrimination doctrine, feminist theory and antiracist politics. *University of Chicago Legal Forum*, *1989*(1), 139–167.

Crenshaw, K. (1991). Mapping the margins: Intersectionality, identity politics, and violence against women of color. *Stanford Law Review*, *43*(6), 1241–1299. https://doi.org/10.2307/1229039

Crenshaw, K., Ocen, P., & Nanda, J. (2015). *Black girls matter: Pushed out, overpoliced, and underprotected*. www.atlanticphilanthropies.org/app/uploads/2015/09/BlackGirlsMatter_Report.pdf

Davis, A. Y. (1983). *Women, race, & class*. Black women writers series (1st ed.). Vintage Books/Random House.

Davis, S. (2020). Socially toxic environments: A YPAR project exposes issues affecting urban Black girls' educational pathway to STEM careers and their racial identity development. *Urban Review: Issues and Ideas in Public Education*, *52*(2), 215–237. https://doi.org/10.1007/S11256-019-00525-2

Epstein, R., Blake, J., & González, T. (2017). *Girlhood interrupted: The erasure of Black girls' childhood*. Center on Poverty and Inequality: Georgetown Law. www.law.georgetown.edu/poverty-inequality-center/wp-content/uploads/sites/14/2017/08/girlhood-interrupted.pdf

Evans-Winters, V. (2018). Locating Black girls in educational policy discourse: Implications for every student succeeds act. *Teachers College Record, 120*(13), 1–18.

Evans-Winters, V., & Esposito, J. (2010). Other people's daughters: Critical race feminism and Black girls' education. *Educational Foundations, 24*(1–2), 11–24.

Flores, R., & Weisfeldt, S. (2020, February 26). Body camera videos show 6-year-old sobbing and pleading with officers during arrest. *CNN.* www.cnn.com/2020/02/26/us/body-camera-video-6-year-old-arrested/index.html

George, J. A. (2015). Stereotype and school pushout: Race, gender and discipline disparities. *Arkansas Law Review, 68*(1), 101–129.

hooks, b. (1984). *Feminist theory: From margin to center.* South End Press.

Jones, N. (2010). *Between good and ghetto: African American girls and inner-city violence.* Rutgers University Press.

Joseph, N. M., Hailu, M. F., & Matthews, J. S. (2019). Normalizing Black girls' humanity in mathematics classrooms. *Harvard Educational Review, 89*(1), 132–155. https://doi.org/10.17763/1943-5045-89.1.132

Joseph, N. M., Viesca, K. M., & Bianco, M. (2016). Black female adolescents and racism in schools: Experiences in a colorblind society. *High School Journal, 100*(1), 4–25. http://dx.doi.org/10.1353/hsj.2016.0018

Ladson-Billings, G. (2009). 'Who you callin' nappy-headed?' A critical race theory look at the construction of Black women. *Race Ethnicity and Education, 12*(1), 87–99. https://doi.org/10.1080/13613320802651012

Lindsay-Dennis, L. A. (2010). African American girls' school experience in context: Implications for teacher education. *Journal of the Georgia Association of Teacher Educators, 12*(1), 26–35.

Love, B. L. (2019). *We want to do more than survive: Abolitionist teaching and the pursuit of educational freedom.* Beacon Press.

Morris, E. W. (2007). "Ladies" or "loudies"? Perceptions and experiences of Black girls in classrooms. *Youth & Society, 38*(4), 490–515. https://doi.org/10.1177%2F0044118X06296778

Morris, E. W., & Perry, B. L. (2017). Girls behaving badly? Race, gender, and subjective evaluation in the discipline of African American girls. *Sociology of Education, 90*(2), 127–148. https://doi.org/10.1177%2F0038040717694876

Morris, M. (2016). *Pushout: The criminalization of Black girls in schools.* The New Press.

Murphy, A. S., Acosta, M. A., & Kennedy-Lewis, B. L. (2013). "I'm not running around with my pants sagging, so how am I not acting like a lady?": Intersections of race and gender in the experiences of female middle school troublemakers. *Urban Review, 45*(5), 586–610. https://doi.org/10.1007/s11256-013-0236-7

NBC. (2019, September 22). *School tantrum leads to 6-year-old's arrest; grandmother outraged.* www.nbc12.com/2019/09/22/school-tantrum-leads-year-olds-arrest-grandmother-outraged/

Noguera, P. A. (2003). Schools, prisons, and social implications of punishment: Rethinking disciplinary practices. *Theory Into Practice, 42*(4), 341–350. https://doi.org/10.1207/s15430421tip4204_12

Parks, C., Wallace, B. C., Emdin, C., & Levy, I. P. (2016). An examination of gendered violence and school push-out directed against urban black girls/adolescents: Illustrative data, cases and a call to action. *Journal of Infant, Child, and Adolescent Psychotherapy, 15*(3), 210–219. https://doi.org/10.1080/15289168.2016.1214451

Proctor, S. L., Williams, B., Scherr, T. & Li, K. (2017). Intersectionality and school psychology: Implications for practice. *Communiqué 46*(4), 1, 19–22.

Richie, B. (2012). *Arrested justice: Black women, violence, and America's prison nation*. New York University Press.

Roberts, D. (2002). *Shattered bonds: The color of child welfare*. Civitas Books.

Sherman, F., & Balck, A. (2015). Gender injustice: System-level juvenile justice reforms for girls. *The National Crittenton Foundation and National Women's Law Center*. www.nationalcrittenton.org/wpcontent/uploads/2015/09/GenderInjusticeReport.pd

Smith, A. L. (2016). #BlackWomenMatter: Neo-Capital punishment ideology in the wake of state violence. *Journal of Negro Education, 85*(3), 261–273. https://doi.org/10.7709/jnegroeducation.85.3.0261

Smith, A. L. (2019). Theorizing black girlhood. In A. S. Halliday (Ed.), *The black girlhood studies collection*. Women's Press, Canadian Scholars' Press.

Tatum, B. (n.d.). *The five-minute poem*. https://sites.lsa.umich.edu/inclusive-teaching/sample-activities/the-five-minute-poem/

U.S. Department of Education, Office for Civil Rights. (2016). *2013–2014 civil rights data collection: A first look*. 1–13. http://www2.ed.gov/about/offices/list/ocr/docs/2013-14-first-look.pdf

Watson, T. N. (2016). "Talking back": The perceptions and experiences of Black girls who attend City High School. *The Journal of Negro Education, 85*(3), 239–249. https://doi.org/10.7709/jnegroeducation.85.3.0239

Wun, C. (2016). Unaccounted foundations: Black girls, anti-Black racism, and punishment in schools. *Critical Sociology, 42*(4–5), 737–750. https://doi.org/10.1177/0896920514560444

Wun, C. (2018). Angered: Black and non-Black girls of color at the intersections of violence and school discipline in the United States. *Race Ethnicity and Education, 21*(4), 423–437. https://doi.org/10.1080/13613324.2016.1248829

Yosso, T. J. (2005). Whose culture has capital? A critical race theory discussion of community cultural wealth. *Race Ethnicity and Education, 8*(1), 69–91. https://doi.org/10.1080/1361332052000341006

Note

1. Pseudonyms were used to protect the confidentiality of all participants.

7

USE OF CRITICAL RACE THEORY TO UNDERSTAND EXCLUSION OF INDIGENOUS STUDENTS FROM GIFTED EDUCATION

Justina Yohannan, Adrianna Crossing, Lisa Aguilar, and Sherrie L. Proctor

> "*But the image right here is, 'If you're white, you're in the gifted program.' . . . If you're in there, you can have a good education. If you are in regular, you're right where everybody's at. . . . I think they should have a good education for everybody.*"
>
> ~Jose

Honoring the Critical Race Theory (CRT) tenet of centering the voices of marginalized people when it comes to their experience of racism, we begin with a quote by Jose. Jose is a Mexican American high school senior who was a participant in Staiger's (2004) study that examined the conflation of whiteness and giftedness at a high school magnet program in California. In the quote, Jose's perception of the gifted program at his school is reflective of how many others view gifted education in the United States (U.S.). That is, gifted education serves as vehicle for racial segregation in schools, a protected space of whiteness for white students, a place of exclusion for Black, Latinx, and Indigenous students, and a place that was never intended to allow access and opportunity *for all* (Grissom & Redding, 2016; Staiger, 2004).

According to the U.S. federal government, gifted and talented students are those who evidence "high achievement capability in such areas as intellectual, creative, artistic, or leadership capacity, or in specific academic fields, and who need services or activities not ordinarily provided by the school in order to fully develop those capabilities" (Title 20—Education, 2011). Additionally, the National Association for Gifted Children ([NAGC], 2010) defined giftedness as "an exceptional ability to reason and learn" or "documented performance or achievement in top 10% or rarer" in academics, intellectual functioning, creative or artistic ability, or leadership (p. 1). Of the 50.6 million students who attend

DOI: 10.4324/9780367815325-9

public schools in the U.S., approximately 6.7% receive gifted education (National Center for Education Statistics [NCES], 2019).

Currently, Black, Latinx, and Indigenous students are underrepresented in gifted education in U.S. public schools. Black students make up just 10.33% of students enrolled in gifted and talented programs, despite being 16% of the overall public-school student population. Additionally, Latinx students constitute 18.75% of students enrolled in these programs but make up 27% of students enrolled in public schools. Indigenous/Alaska Native students make up 1% of the total student population and 0.87% of those in gifted education programs (NCES, 2019).

Notably, Asian American students are overrepresented in gifted education. Asian American students make up 9.97% of students enrolled in gifted programs but 5% of the total student population. Yoon and Gentry (2009) explained that Asian American students may not encounter similar challenges as other students of color related to participation in gifted education because of the *model minority myth*, which is the harmful and divisive stereotype that Asian Americans are smarter and more successful than other people of color in America. The stereotype contributes to conflict between groups of color and places undue stress and pressure on Asian American students. However, it is important to note that patterns of Asian American participation in gifted education vary across ethnicities and socio-economic status. Staiger (2004), for instance, hypothesized that Asian American students were underrepresented in gifted programs at the school where she conducted her ethnographic study because the student body had a larger proportion of economically marginalized, recent immigrants from Southeast Asia. Yoon and Gentry (2009) explained that most studies related to gifted education in the U.S. include samples with Asian Americans who were voluntary immigrants who have higher median incomes versus those with lower median incomes who came to the U.S. as refugees.

Underrepresentation of Black, Indigenous, and Latinx students in gifted education is concerning because of the many positive outcomes, such as increased academic performance, motivation, self-efficacy, engagement in learning, self-concept, and stress reduction, associated with attending gifted programs (Grissom & Redding, 2016). Further, gifted education programs have been documented to produce longer-term economic and social benefits for those who participate (Barlow & Dunbar, 2010). These documented benefits and positive outcomes of gifted education require us to question how and why so many Black, Latinx, and Indigenous students are systematically shut out of gifted education.

Thus, the purpose of this chapter is to use CRT as a lens to interrogate how gifted education maintains segregation and white supremacy in schools in the U.S. The chapter begins with a brief introduction to CRT followed by a research review that explicates how gifted education practices and processes normalize racism and maintain white interests and supremacy. We then center Indigenous students' experiences with gifted education given their historical and current exclusion. Through a case narrative, we introduce you to Niibwin (pronounced

Knee-bwin) Spotted Bear, a 5th-grade Indigenous boy who attends school in Bismarck, North Dakota, and who is shut out of his school's gifted program. We conclude the chapter with experiential activities to help connect CRT tenets to Niibwin Spotted Bear's narrative. Using CRT, we aim to elucidate how the normalcy of racism and the perpetuation of white supremacy through gifted education processes are unfair and unjust to Indigenous students and other students of color who are systematically excluded from the academic, social, and longer-term economic benefits associated with participation in gifted education.

Brief Introduction to Critical Race Theory

As noted in Chapter 2, CRT is a theory that names, defines, describes, and ultimately deconstructs how racism creates systems that harm racialized and minoritized individuals and communities. CRT has several key tenets that authors across fields tend to agree on: (1) Race is a social construction, (2) Racism is a normal part of U.S. society, (3) Dismantling racist systems requires a focus on voices and narratives of marginalized populations to reveal their unique perspectives (i.e., counter-narratives), and (4) White people will only advance anti-racism if it advances their own self-interest to maintain their privilege and white supremacy (i.e., whiteness as property and interest group convergence; Brown, this volume). While Brown in Chapter 2 described these four CRT tenets as being commonly discussed across fields, it is important to note that others have articulated additional tenets of CRT, including intersectionality as described in Chapter 1 and anti-essentialism as described in Chapter 4. Although CRT is rarely engaged in school psychology, in broader education research, tenets of CRT have been used to critique school structures such as special education (Connor et al., 2019), school disciplinary systems (Anyon et al., 2018; Fisher et al., 2019; Hines-Datiri & Carter Andrews, 2020), and gifted education (Montoya et al., 2016). In fact, CRT can be used as a theoretical lens for understanding how gifted education serves to marginalize and deny some students of color equal access to enriched educational opportunities in U.S. schools. In the next section, we problematize gifted education and some of its associated processes by describing how it is intricately tied to white supremacy and racism in America.

Gifted Education in the United States

Giftedness as a Construction of White Supremacy

Despite attempts to help educators clarify and quantify what giftedness means, the reality is that giftedness is a construct created by white people in positions of power to maintain societal norms (Ford & Harmon, 2001; Tonemah, 1991). Both historically and currently in the U.S., giftedness has been normalized to reflect behavioral characteristics valued by middle-class, white Americans (Ford & King,

2014; Howard, 2018; Montoya et al., 2016). Resultantly, the associated methods for determining giftedness used today were not designed nor intended to capture giftedness in students of color. In fact, giftedness is a social construction initially designed to exclude students of color as one way to signal white supremacy—the ideology that white people and their ideas, beliefs, and actions are superior to those of other races and thus should dominate them (Dismantling Racism Works [dRworks], 2020). In U.S. society, white supremacy also refers to a political or socio-economic system where white people enjoy structural advantage and rights that other racialized groups do not (dRworks, 2020). As described in the following text, the U.S. education system has been a primary vessel through which giftedness as white supremacy has been asserted.

There is a long history of white supremacy permeating education in the U.S. For example, the U.S. government forcibly removed Indigenous children from their families and reservations in an attempt to commit cultural genocide through involuntary boarding school enrollment in the late 19th century. Indigenous parents who engaged in acts of resistance by refusing to let their children go were punished by the government withholding basic necessities such as clothing and rations (Tonemah, 1991). Another example of steeped white supremacy is the research conducted in support of intelligence testing used to justify the eugenics movement, which started in the 1880s and ended around World War II (Goodwin, 2015). This early intelligence assessment research—much of which excluded Black participants from standardization samples—concluded that Black people were intellectually inferior to white people (Aston & Brown, 2020). These findings were heralded despite evidence of Black children outperforming white children on standardized measures of memory, a less culturally loaded construct (Aston & Brown, 2020). Below, we discuss how racism (i.e., the marginalization and/or oppression of people of color based on a socially constructed racial hierarchy that privileges white people) is pervasive and normal in gifted education, which serves to maintain white supremacy.

Normalizing racism in gifted education to maintain white supremacy. Gifted education has not escaped the impact of racism, with some arguing that the gifted education system itself is racist and that racism is normalized within gifted education processes and practices (Howard, 2018). Lewis Terman, widely known as the father of gifted education in the U.S., was a prominent eugenicist and believed that Black and Latinx students were genetically and intellectually inferior to white students (Cumings Mansfield, 2016). Terman promoted social opportunities for gifted (i.e., white) students, believing them to be naturally endowed with superior intelligence. Terman was not alone in his efforts to advance white students using eugenics as justification for systematically denying educational opportunities to students of color. As noted by Cumings Mansfield (2016), Leta Hollingworth, who studied gifted students, "popularized eugenics to generations of prospective teachers to the point of integrating eugenic content into teacher education courses" (p. 298). This history impacts how gifted education operates in U.S. schools today, including who gets access to gifted education and who does not. For instance, as previously noted, research has shown that white and Asian American students are most likely to be identified as gifted while Black, Indigenous, and Latinx have been historically, and are currently, underrepresented in gifted education programs (Ford et al., 2016; Howard, 2018; Yoon & Gentry, 2009). Such deep-seated, systemic racism is the root cause of racial inequality and disproportionality in gifted education today and a primary upholder of white supremacy in gifted education (Cumings Mansfield, 2016).

Racism as a gatekeeper to gifted education. The historical and sociocultural context of U.S. society steeped in white supremacy and racism continues to influence how educators interact with students of color today and has direct impact on access to and participation in gifted education. One way racial inequalities manifest in gifted education is through educators' schemas, or preexisting notions, about students of color. One deficit paradigm Terman promoted remains prevalent today in education—that is, the belief that intellectual differences between races are inherited and fixed (Tomlinson & Jarvis, 2014). This paradigm permeates gifted education in powerful ways: from influencing educators' view of Black, Indigenous, and Latinx students as intellectually and academically inferior to blaming poorer academic achievement and outcomes on students of color when they have been systematically denied equal educational opportunities (e.g., well-funded schools, experienced teachers, advanced coursework) compared to their white peers (DeMonte & Hanna, 2014; Staiger, 2004).

Research has found, for example, that teachers are not as effective at recognizing and acknowledging giftedness in students of color (Ford & Harmon, 2001). This is likely due to many teachers' expectations that all students should exhibit behaviors that mirror white, middle-class norms along with inherent biases against students' of color ways of being (Staiger, 2004; Tomlinson & Jarvis, 2014). To illustrate, Elhoweris and colleagues (2005) found in their sample of predominantly white teachers that students' racial backgrounds influenced which students teachers referred for gifted eligibility assessment, with Black students being less likely to be referred. Using ethnographic methods, Staiger (2004) studied the ways one school orchestrated "whiteness as giftedness," noting that teachers made stereotyped statements that implied white students belonged in gifted programs because of their academic skills and intellectual abilities while students of color were placed in gifted programs because of factors such as affirmative action for Black students (p. 162). Yet, there is evidence that the racism that permeates gifted education eligibility processes is somewhat countered when teachers of color are involved in the eligibility process. For instance, Grissom and Redding (2016) found that Black and Latinx students are more proportionately represented in gifted programs in schools with more Black and Latinx teachers. This may be because teachers of color are more likely to recognize talent in students of color and less subject to the implicit and explicit racial biases that result in fewer referrals of Black, Latinx, and Indigenous students for gifted education eligibility assessment (Grissom & Redding, 2016). Still, even in schools where students of color actually met criteria for gifted programs, they were less likely than their white peers to be identified by teachers (Ford et al., 2008).

Gifted education as a white space. When Black, Indigenous, and Latinx students do make it beyond systemic barriers that impede referral for gifted education, they are then often subjected to assessment practices that do not capture their intellectual strengths and academic and non-academic talents (Ford et al., 2016). Although best practices in determining gifted eligibility call for use of multiple criteria (e.g., use of qualitative and quantitative data), traditional practices rely heavily on use of Full Scale IQ cut-off scores for qualification (e.g., 130 or above; Silverman & Gilman, 2020). Critiques of current gifted education eligibility assessment practices for students of color focus on IQ tests being culturally embedded (Ford et al., 2016), having linguistic bias (Ford et al., 2008), being normed on middle-class white values and experiences (Montoya et al., 2016), and being less effective for identifying students of color (Ford & Harmon, 2001). Further, as indicated in the federal definition, giftedness extends beyond superior academic achievement and intellectual ability, so the IQ tests traditionally used to determine gifted eligibility do not capture gifts and talents in other domains students might possess (Ford & Harmon, 2001). Thus, the gifted education eligibility process results in inequitable placement in gifted education for students of color, particularly those who attend schools in districts where giftedness is defined more narrowly through the use of IQ cut-off scores. In essence, IQ tests serve as tools to reify whiteness and help maintain gifted education as a space predominantly for white students—or property of whiteness.

Student voice and perspectives. Gifted education as a white space is evident in the narratives of Black, Latinx, and Indigenous students who do gain access to gifted education, particularly their reports of feelings of exclusion and marginalization. For example, research has found that students of color left gifted education programs because of the lack of culturally competent teachers, low teacher expectations of them, and poor academic support (Gentry & Fugate, 2012; Henfield et al., 2008). Prior research (i.e., Ford, 1998) documented that Black students in gifted education were concerned about being isolated from white peers and not wanting to be the sole Black student in the gifted education space. Students of color and white students in Staiger (2004) described gifted classes as consisting of mostly white students—some even believing that gifted programs were only for white students.

In the next section, we explore the research related to gifted education and Indigenous students, whose voices and experiences are rarely centered in educational literature and research. We review what is known about Indigenous students and gifted education and then explain how CRT is relevant to their experiences. Then, we share Niibwin Spotted Bear's narrative.

Gifted Education and Indigenous Students

> *"Education is your most powerful weapon. With it, you're the white man's equal. Without it, you become his victim."*
>
> ~ *Apsaalooke Chief, Plenty Coups*

Missing Voices in Gifted Education and Essentialism in Research

When researchers speak to the exclusion of students of color from gifted education programs, they typically are referencing Black, Latinx, and Indigenous students. There is a dearth of literature focusing exclusively on the state of Indigenous student participation and performance in gifted education programs outside of this broader collective of students (Gentry & Fugate, 2012). Despite stretching back nearly 40 years, the body of scholarship focusing on Indigenous students in gifted programs is sparse and has weaknesses (Gentry et al., 2014). Namely, in approximately one-third of papers Wu (2011) reviewed in a comprehensive review of the extant literature on gifted education for Indigenous students, authors failed to name the tribal affiliations of the Indigenous students involved in the studies. This generic and essentialism approach to studying Indigenous students erases the rich cultural diversity between and within their communities; this flaw is especially problematic given that there are 574 federally recognized tribes in the U.S. (National Congress of American Indians, 2020). Though certain tribes may share some cultural values, there are myriad cultural traditions, ceremonies, and beliefs across the 5 million citizens in this nation who identify as American Indian and Alaska Native (Norris et al., 2012). Thus, empirical work that refers to Indigenous students and their communities as monolithic has limited practical utility for social change (Brayboy, 2005; Ladson-Billings & Donner, 2005). It is clear that *anti-essentialism* and critical frameworks like Tribal Critical Race Theory (TribalCrit) are needed to guide research related to gifted education to ensure that Indigenous students' voices and ways of knowing are honored.

Lack of Access and Opportunity

One theme that occurs consistently in the research that *is* available is that Indigenous students are underrepresented in gifted education programs in U.S. schools, especially in non-reservation schools (Ford, 1998; Yoon & Gentry, 2009). Access is one of the greatest obstacles to the participation of Indigenous students in gifted education programs. More than 20 years ago, Ford (1998) reported the underrepresentation of Black, Latinx, and Indigenous students in gifted education programs, and that problem persists to this day (Connery et al., 2019; U.S. Department of Education Office for Civil Rights Annual Report, 2005; Gentry et al., 2014). This problem exists not because Indigenous students do not possess incredible gifts and talents, but because of structural racism, including the fact that some gifted programs are funded at the local level, leading to more access and opportunity for white students who live in wealthier communities with more well-resourced public schools.

More specifically, unlike special education programs that are regulated under the Individuals With Disabilities Education Improvement Act (IDEIA), gifted education programs do not have federal mandates and oversight. This results in funding, policies, and laws related to the implementation of gifted programs being left to the discretion of state and local governments (Ford et al., 2008). Resultantly, the administration of gifted education programs is uneven in the U.S., using a range of funding formulas and implementation procedures that do not always result in an equitable distribution of funds. For instance, 28 states have formal requirements for both identification and provision of gifted education programs, while four states have them related to identification only (National Association for Gifted Children, 2015). Even in states where gifted education programs are common, Black, Latinx, and Indigenous students are often denied access and participation. Though government agencies have publicly acknowledged that talent undeniably exists in Indigenous communities (United States Department of Education [U.S. DOE]; 1993), Indigenous students remain underrepresented in gifted education programs and opportunity gaps persist (Gentry et al., 2014).

Relevance of Critical Race Theory to Gifted Education and Indigenous Students

CRT is a useful tool for analysis of disproportionality (i.e., underrepresentation or overrepresentation of specific student demographics) in gifted education because it allows us to examine the societal factors that are responsible for barriers to gifted education access and participation. Next, we illustrate the utility of CRT for understanding issues related to Indigenous students and gifted education, particularly their access to and participation in gifted programs. We specifically connect the four commonly agreed-upon tenets of CRT described earlier in this chapter to this discussion: (1) Race is a social construction, (2) Racism is a normal part of U.S. society, (3) Dismantling racist systems requires counter-narratives of marginalized populations, and (4) White people will only advance anti-racism if it advances their own self-interest to maintain their privilege and white supremacy.

Race as Social Construction and Racism as Normalcy

The problem of access to gifted education for Indigenous students is linked to educators' deficit views of Black, Latinx, and Indigenous students. These deficit views are not ahistorical, which Sabnis and Martinez described in Chapter 3 as a tendency to present sanitized versions of history that minimize the responsibility of dominant groups in perpetuating oppression. Instead, deficit views are often connected to socially constructed perceptions of who a student is in relation to being viewed as part of a racialized group. In the social construction of race in the U.S., whiteness—along with behavioral norms associated with whiteness—is valued. Those whose physical characteristics and "ways of being" deviate furthest away from whiteness are "racialized," "othered," and receive the least benefits associated with whiteness. "Othering" is a key feature of white supremacy and shows up in both how educators view students in terms of who should get gifted education referrals and how gifted education processes work in determining who, ultimately, is eligible. As described earlier in this chapter, racism in gifted education is normalized through the use of culturally loaded measures with proven potential for racism, such as IQ tests; educators' unchallenged deficit views of Black, Latinx, and Indigenous students as possessing less "intelligence" compared to White peers; and marginalization of Black, Latinx, and Indigenous students who do participate in gifted programs. Using the CRT tenets of "race as a social construction" and "racism as normalcy" helps us see the problem of lack of access to and participation in gifted education as a systemic problem related to structural racism versus individual student-focused deficits.

Interest Convergence

Barriers to gifted education for Indigenous students may be related to *interest convergence*, or lack thereof, with white parents' desires. Interest convergence is the CRT tenet that asserts white people will only advance anti-racism if it advances their own self-interest to maintain their privilege and white supremacy. For instance, it is less likely that white parents would advocate for gifted education programs at reservation schools Indigenous students may attend, given their own children are less likely to attend these schools. In this example, there is a *lack of interest convergence*. On the other hand, white parents might advocate for gifted programs at reservation schools where their children attend magnet programs, which would open up the opportunity for Indigenous students on reservations to have more access and opportunity. While not directly related to Indigenous student populations, we have seen instances in the research where white parents would only send their white children to less well-resourced schools in racially minoritized communities when opportunities for participation in gifted and magnet programs were available (Chapman & Donnor, 2015; Staiger, 2004). This represents interest convergence—that is, white parents will support the establishment of gifted programs because of their desire for their own children to participate in and receive the benefits of gifted education. Because gifted education is funded at the state and, sometimes, local level where white parents have a much stronger say in allocation of resources than if funded at the national level, interest convergence is a factor that *prevents* Indigenous students from receiving equitable allocation of funds for gifted education. This is complicated by the fact that

Black, Latinx, and Indigenous communities in the U.S. have less financial capital than white ones, a pattern that exists due to systemic and historic disenfranchisement of Black, Latinx, and Indigenous people. Thus, along with lack of interest convergence from white parents, Indigenous communities also have less capital to fund gifted education programs at the local/community level.

Counter-Narratives

In CRT, counter-narratives speak to the importance of centering the voices of marginalized people to dismantle racist systems. Yet, it is clear from the research related to Indigenous students and gifted education that their voices are missing. When research is conducted with Indigenous students, they are essentialized and discussed as a monolithic group without care given to understanding the rich diversity that exists between and within their communities. Counter-narratives call for us to center Indigenous student voices to understand how they experience both exclusion from and, for a few, inclusion in gifted education programs in the U.S. When we do not make space for hearing, listening, and documenting the voices of Indigenous students and those within their families and communities, we miss important culturally rich counter-narratives that decenter whiteness. Counter-narratives help us better understand the ways in which whiteness works to exclude, harm, and continuously disenfranchise Black, Latinx, and Indigenous students. Niibwin's narrative offers an opportunity to listen to the experiences of an Indigenous student and his family regarding gifted education. Experiential activities follow that push us to connect Niibwin' experience to CRT to help us think about ways to dismantle whiteness, white supremacy, and racism in gifted education processes and practices.

Case Narrative

Niibwin (pronounced Knee-bwin) Spotted Bear is a 5th-grade boy from a small town called Twin Buttes located on the Fort Berthold Reservation in North Dakota. Niibwin comes from the Mandan, Hidatsa, and Sahnish people, who are known for their agricultural competence and expertise. Historically, the Mandan, Hidatsa, and Sahnish (Arikara; MHA) people were three separate bands before a series of smallpox epidemics nearly destroyed them. To ensure their survival, protection, and economic health, the Mandan, Hidatsa, and Sahnish banded together into what is now known as Three Affiliated Tribes (TAT). In the present day, Niibwin and his family have carried on the tradition of growing and keeping seeds and take great pride in their corn and squash. These were traditional vegetables that their ancestors would harvest and transform into dry squash and dry corn during the winter months. Because Niibwin grew up on the reservation, his family had access to a plot of land on which to create and grow their crops. Niibwin knows the stories of how his ancestors would rotate their crops to let the land heal between seasons and how they meticulously engineered the best seeds to survive the four seasons of North Dakota. Niibwin has an immense foundation of plant knowledge. The holding, carrying, and passing of knowledge is important for the MHA people as their tribe continues to grow in population and expand in their territory. Children are especially sacred and important to protect. Oral histories and knowledge are given to the younger generation to ensure the continued existence of the MHA people. Knowing this, Niibwin takes great pride in the land and honors it every day by taking care of his garden and teaching his little sister, Willow, how to care for their plants. On any given day Niibwin would often be found talking and singing to his plants. Unfortunately for Niibwin, his parents recently told him that they would be moving to the larger town of Bismarck, which is about two hours from his hometown. This was a devastating blow to Niibwin, but important for the family so that his parents could secure more stable employment and have access to better and closer schools for Niibwin and his sister. This big change also meant that they would be living in an apartment with no access to land in which Niibwin could plant and tend a garden. As is tradition, Niibwin secured his seeds in a pouch made of deer hide that he would hang around his neck. On the first day of school, he wore this medicine pouch to give him the courage to face the first day in his new school. This school reflected the community in that it was majority white and affluent. Niibwin and his sister were two of a handful of students who identified as Indigenous, and they were not met with open arms by their white peers. Regardless, Niibwin thrived academically. In his former school, he was referred for the Talented and Gifted (TAG) program; the referral never came to fruition because of the move. In his new school, teachers did not appear to recognize his academic skills as extraordinary, which made Niibwin think that he was not as smart as the other students. To make matters worse, he began to experience bullying behaviors from his peers. One day in gym class, the teacher was showing the students how to shoot archery and when it was Niibwin's turn, he could see students motioning their flat hands up and down over their mouths indicating the gesture for a stereotypical Indigenous person. Niibwin did not tell anyone about the incident or any of the other things his white peers said and did to him throughout the following months. Instead, he kept to himself throughout the school day, went home, did his homework, and remained close with his family until their weekend visits back to Twin Buttes. The weekends became his refuge as he got to see family, engage in ceremony, and reconnect with the land. As time passed, Niibwin's parents became more involved in the PTA at Niibwin and Willow's school. One day, Niibwin's parents were attending a PTA meeting where there was continued discussion from the previous meeting about gifted testing. Reminded of Niibwin's missed opportunity at his last school, they decided to request that Niibwin be tested for the TAG program. The first time, the request was denied because there was no "evidence" to support that Niibwin should be considered for testing despite his perfect grades and attendance. The current school requires at least two data points to be above the 95th percentile across two benchmark timepoints on AIMSweb, a teacher referral, and scores at or above the 95th percentile on a standardized achievement test and a cognitive score of 130 or higher. Niibwin's parents decided to contact his previous teachers, who urged them to make another formal written request for testing, citing his grades and previous performance and consideration for TAG in his previous school. The second request was accepted. Testing took place nearly two months later. Another two weeks passed before the results meeting was scheduled with the disappointing result of "Not Eligible." Niibwin's parents were informed that he did not have the two AIMSweb data points required, no teacher had referred him, and he did not meet the cutoff criteria for the cognitive portion of the test—a score of 130. Niibwin's score was 128, no teacher had referred him because no teacher bothered to get to know him, and he had not been at the school long enough to participate in two benchmark screeners. However Niibwin did ace the academic achievement portion of the testing to no surprise to his parents. Yet, Niibwin's parents still left feeling upset knowing that their child was dismissed without consideration given to his many talents that could not possibly be measured by a two-hour testing session.

Experiential Activities

Normalization of Racism in Gifted Education Processes

- Review your school's or a local district's gifted education policies; specifically identify how referrals occur and what assessments are conducted to determine whether a student qualifies for gifted education. How is access for Black, Latinx, and Indigenous students limited based on the current policies? What standards of whiteness are being upheld in the policies? Identify one aspect of the policy that perpetuates systems of oppression and what would need to replace it to be more equitable. How would you go about bringing this to the attention of your school administration?
- Review stories on blogs and social media by parents and students of color who discuss their experiences trying to navigate the gifted education system. Do some self-reflection: What assumptions do you and others in your school make about Indigenous students' intelligence and academic abilities? What about Black students? Asian students? Latinx students? White students?
- Consider the assessments used to determine Niibwin's narrative of intelligence. What should have been done to ensure anti-racist and culturally responsive assessment practices, and what factors should have been considered in the analysis of the data collected? What school professionals comprise the team to determine whether a student receives assessment for gifted education? What prerequisites are required to start an evaluation process, and how are these tied to practices that reinforce whiteness as the standard? How are students referred to the process, and how seriously does the school administration take parental requests?

Counter-Narrative

- As mentioned earlier in the chapter and stated in Chapter 3 by Sabnis and Martinez, "Counter-narratives are readings of the world emerging from historically oppressed people that challenge or disrupt dominant narratives about the social world" (p. 39). Whose voices have been traditionally ignored or overlooked in your school? How can you amplify these voices to be heard so that counter-narratives can be documented, written, and heard?

Whiteness as Property

- Gifted education can fast-track a student to better opportunities as they progress through school. How do white students benefit from opportunities provided in gifted education? How are Indigenous, Black, and Latinx students purposely excluded from access to social mobility?
- What do schools gain from maintaining the status quo of white supremacist practices that may prevent school staff's willingness to disrupt systems that disproportionately negatively impact Black and Brown students?

Anti-Essentialism

- How do the assumptions we make about groups of Indigenous, Black, and Latinx students ignore the realities of their individual, lived experiences? How does essentialism shape views of the gifts and talents Black and Brown students possess?
- How might the educators involved in the gifted education process at Niibwin's school learn to look beyond stereotypes and recognize his talents and abilities?
- Review common practices for disrupting microaggressions and stereotypes so that you have the skills in place to be a disruptor when a peer or colleague is microaggressive:
    - "A Guide to Responding to Microaggressions" by Kevin L. Nadal https://advancingjustice-la.org/sites/default/files/ELAMICRO%20A_Guide_to_Responding_to_Microaggressions.pdf
    - "Disarming racial microaggressions: Microintervention strategies for targets, White allies, and bystanders" (Sue et al., 2019).
    - Identify your own hesitations that interfere with being a disruptor to the gifted education systems that reinforce white supremacy.

Conclusion

CRT has utility to aid in the interrogation of the ways white supremacy and racism manifest in our schools, including racial inequities in gifted education programs. Through use of CRT, we conceptualized several specific barriers to gifted education programs for students of color, with an emphasis on Indigenous students. We detailed how giftedness is a white supremacist construct from its inception and described the ways racism makes it more difficult for Black and Brown students to gain access and benefit from gifted education today. Using the case narrative of Niibwin, we highlighted how Indigenous students are shut out of gifted education. Our use of narrative is consistent with a key CRT tenet of counter-narratives. Through Niibwin's narrative, we aimed to illustrate the impact when school professionals fail to counteract inherently racist school policy with intentional anti-racist actions. Finally, experiential activities presented offer the reader the opportunity to connect CRT tenets to the case narrative, engage in self-reflection, and consider some actions educators can take to disrupt racism in gifted education.

References

Anyon, Y., Lechuga, C., Ortega, D., Downing, B., Greer, E., & Simmons, J. (2018). An exploration of the relationships between student racial background and the school sub-contexts of office discipline referrals: A critical race theory analysis. *Race Ethnicity and Education*, *21*(3), 390–406. https://doi.org/10.1080/13613324.2017.1328594

Aston, C., & Brown, D. L. (2020). Progress or setback: Revisiting the current state of assessment practices of Black children. *Contemporary School Psychology*. https://doi.org/10.1007/s40688-020-00308-7

Barlow, K., & Dunbar, E. (2010). Race, class, and whiteness in gifted and talented identification: A case study. *Berkeley Review of Education*, *1*(1), 63–85. https://doi.org/10.5070/B81110014

Brayboy, B. M. J. (2005). Toward a tribal critical race theory in education. *The Urban Review*, *37*(5), 425–446. https://doi.org/10.1007/s11256-005-0018-y

Chapman, T. K., & Donnor, J. K. (2015). Critical race theory and the proliferation of U.S. charter schools. *Equity & Excellence in Education*, *48*(1), 137–157. https://doi.org/10.1080/10665684.2015.991670

Connery, C. E., Green III, P. C., & Kaufman, J. C. (2019). The underrepresentation of CLD students in gifted and talented programs: Implications for law and practice. *University of Maryland Law Journal of Race, Religion, Gender, & Class*, *19*, 81–101. https://digitalcommons.law.umaryland.edu/rrgc/vol19/iss1/5

Connor, D., Cavendish, W., Gonzalez, T., & Jean-Pierre, P. (2019). Is a bridge even possible over troubled waters? The field of special education negates the overrepresentation of minority students: A DisCrit analysis. *Race and Ethnicity in Education*, *22*(6), 723–745. https://doi.org/10.1080/13613324.2019.1599343

Cumings Mansfield, K. (2016). The color of giftedness: A policy genealogy implicating educators past, present, and future. *Educational Studies*, *52*, 289–312. https://doi.org/10.1080/00131946.2016.1190364

DeMonte, J., & Hanna, R. (2014). Looking at the best teachers and who they teach: Poor students are less likely to get highly effective teaching. *Center for American Progress*. https://cdn.americanprogress.org/wpcontent/uploads/2014/04/TeacherDistribution-Brief1.pdf

Dismantling Racism Works. (2020). *Racism defined*. Dismantling Racism Works (dRworks) Web Workbook. www.dismantlingracism.org/racism-defined.html

Elhoweris, H., Mutua, K., Alsheikh, N., & Holloway, P. (2005). Effect of children's ethnicity on teachers' referral and recommendation decisions in gifted and talented programs. *Remedial and Special Education*, *26*, 25–31. https://doi.org/10.1177/07419325050260010401

Fisher, A. E., Fisher, B. W., & Railey, K. S. (2019). Disciplinary disparities by race and disability: Using DisCrit theory to examine the manifestation determination review process in special education in the United States. *Race Ethnicity and Education, pre-print*, https://doi.org/10.1080/13613324.2020.1753671

Ford, D. Y. (1998). The underrepresentation of minority students in gifted education. *The Journal of Special Education*, *32*, 4–14. https://doi.org/10.1177/002246699803200102

Ford, D. Y., Grantham, T. C., & Whiting, G. W. (2008). Culturally and linguistically diverse students in gifted education: Recruitment and retention issues. *Exceptional Children*, *74*(3), 289–306. https://doi.org/10.1177/001440290807400302

Ford, D. Y., & Harmon, D. A. (2001). Equity and excellence: Providing access to gifted education for culturally diverse students. *The Journal of Secondary Gifted Education*, *12*, 141–147. https://doi.org/10.4219/jsge-2001-663

Ford, D. Y., & King Jr., R. A. (2014). No Blacks allowed: Segregated gifted education in the context of Brown vs Board of Education. *The Journal of Negro Education*, *83*, 300–426. https://doi.org/10.7709/jnegroeducation.83.3.0300

Ford, D. Y., Wright, B. L., Washington, A., & Henfield., M. S. (2016). Access and equity denied: Key theories for school psychologists to consider when assessing Black and Hispanic students for gifted education. *School Psychology Forum*, *10*, 265–277.

Gentry, M., & Fugate, C. M. (2012). Gifted Native American students: Underperforming, under-identified, and overlooked. *Psychology in the Schools*, *49*, 631–646. https://doi.org/10.1002/pits.21624

Gentry, M., Fugate, C. M., Wu, J., & Castellano, J. A. (2014). Gifted Native American students: Literature, lessons, and future directions. *Gifted Child Quarterly*, *58*(2), 98–110. https://doi.org/10.1177/0016986214521660

Goodwin, C. J. (2015). *A history of modern psychology* (5th ed.). John Wiley & Sons, Inc.

Grissom, J. A., & Redding, C. (2016). Discretion and disproportionality: Explaining the underrepresentation of high-achieving students of color in gifted programs. *AREA Open*, *2*, 1–25. https://doi.org/10.1177/2332858415622175

Henfield, M. S., Owens, D., & Moore III, J. L. (2008). Influences on young gifted African Americans' school success: Implications for elementary school counselors. *The Elementary School Journal*, *108*, 392–406. https://doi.org/10.1086/589469

Hines-Datiri, D., & Carter Andrews, D. J. (2020). The effects of zero tolerance policies on Black girls: Using critical race feminism and figured worlds to examine school discipline. *Urban Education*, *55*(10), 1419–1440. https://doi.org/10.1177/0042085917690204

Howard, J. (2018). The White kid can do whatever he wants: The racial socialization of a gifted education program. *Educational Studies*, *54*, 553–568. https://doi.org/10.1080/00131946.2018.1453512

Ladson-Billings, G., & Donnor, J. (2005). The moral activist role of critical race theory scholarship. In N. Denzin & Y. Lincoln (Eds.), *The SAGE handbook of qualitative research*. (3rd ed., pp. 279–301). Sage Publications.

Montoya, R., Matias, C. E., Nishi, N. W. M., & Sarcedo, G. L. (2016). Words are wind: Using Du Bois and Bourdieu to "unveil" the capricious nature of gifted and talented programs. *Journal for Critical Education Policy Studies*, *14*, 127–143. www.researchgate.net/publication/301918116_Words_are_wind_Using_du_bois_and_bourdieu_to_'unveil'_the_capricious_nature_of_gifted_and_talented_programs

Nadal, K. (2014). A guide to responding to microaggressions. *City University of New York (CUNY) Forum*, *2*(1), 71–76. https://advancingjustice-la.org/sites/default/files/ELAMICRO%20A_Guide_to_Responding_to_Microaggressions.pdf

National Association for Gifted Children. (2010). *Redefining giftedness for a new century: Shifting the paradigm.* www.nagc.org/sites/default/files/Position%20Statement/Redefining%20Giftedness%20for%20a%20New%20Century.pdf

National Association for Gifted Children. (2015). *2014–2015 State of the states in gifted education: Policy and practice data.* www.nagc.org/sites/default/files/key%20reports/2014-2015%20State%20of%20the%20States%20(final).pdf

National Center for Educational Statistics. (2019). *Number of public school students enrolled in gifted and talented programs, by sex, race/ethnicity, and state: Selected years, 2004 through 2013–14.* https://nces.ed.gov/programs/digest/d19/tables/dt19_204.80.asp

National Congress of American Indians. (2020). *Tribal Nations of the United States: An introduction* (Updated February 2020 Edition). National Congress of American Indians. www.ncai.org/tribalnations/introduction/Indian_Country_101_Updated_February_2019.pdf

Norris, T., Vines, P. L., & Hoeffel, E. M. (2012). *The American Indian and Alaska native population: 2010.* United States Census Bureau. www.census.gov/history/pdf/c2010br-10.pdf

Silverman, L. K., & Gilman, B. J. (2020). Best practices in gifted identification and assessment: Lessons from the WISC-V. *Psychology in the Schools, 57*(10), 1569–1581. https://doi.org/10.1002/pits.22361

Staiger, A. (2004). Whiteness as giftedness: Racial formation at an urban high school. *Social Problems, 51*, 161–181. https://doi.org/10.1525/sp.2004.51.2.161

Sue, D. W., Alsaidi, S., Awad, M. N., Glaeser, E., Calle, C. Z., & Mendez, N. (2019). Disarming racial microaggressions: Microintervention strategies for targets, White allies, and bystanders. *American Psychologist, 74*(1), 128–142. https://doi-org.proxy1.cl.msu.edu/10.1037/amp0000296

Title 20. Education, 20 U.S.C. § 7801 *et seq.* (2011). www.govinfo.gov/content/pkg/USCODE-2011-title20/pdf/USCODE-2011-title20-chap70-subchapIX-partA-sec7801.pdf

Tomlinson, C. A., & Jarvis, J. M. (2014). Case studies of success: Supporting academic success for students with high potential from ethnic minority and economically disadvantaged backgrounds. *Journal for the Education of the Gifted, 37*, 191–219. https://doi.org/10.1177/0162353214540826

Tonemah, S. (1991). *Gifted and talented American Indian and Alaska Native students.* Department of Education. https://eric.ed.gov/?id=ED343769

United States Department of Education. (1993). *National excellence: A case for developing America's talent.* Author. https://files.eric.ed.gov/fulltext/ED359743.pdf

U.S. Department of Education Office for Civil Rights. (2005). *Annual report to congress FY 2005.* https://www2.ed.gov/about/reports/annual/ocr/annrpt2005/report_pg6.html

Wu, J. (2011). *Gifted Native American students: A review of the extant literature.* Unpublished manuscript, Purdue University.

Yoon, S. Y., & Gentry, M. (2009). Racial and ethnic representation in gifted programs: Current status of and implications for gifted Asian American students. *The Gifted Child Quarterly, 53*, 121–136. https://doi.org/10.1177/0016986208330564

8

DISCRIT THEORY

Emotional and Behavioral Disturbance Assessment and Identification

Amanda L. Sullivan, Rose Vukovic, Thuy Nguyen, Tara Kulkarni, Jiwon Kim, and Sydney Carlson

The assessment and identification of emotional and behavioral disturbance (hereafter, ED) remain a practice domain persistently beset with concern for inequity, amplified by the stark outcomes of identified students (Sullivan, 2017). Indeed, students with ED have some of the poorest outcomes of various subgroups in schools and, on average, seem to have benefited little from advancements in special education despite gains observed for other groups of students with disabilities (Bradley et al., 2008). Outcomes are especially dire for students from racially minoritized backgrounds, and special education is considered by many to be a means of de facto marginalization and segregation (e.g., Beratan, 2006; Blanchett, 2006). DisCrit offers a lens through which to conceptualize the identification of ED in schools such that profession-wide aspirations related to social justice, equity, and cultural competence can be advanced. In this chapter, we provide a brief introduction to DisCrit, research on ED assessment and identification, and the intersections thereof, followed by a case study and experiential activities.

Brief Introduction to DisCrit Theory

DisCrit provides a framework for exploring the intersections of race and dis/ability[1] to understand historic and contemporary responses to normal human variation, including perceptions of typical and acceptable behavior. Importantly, DisCrit emphasizes that "racism and ableism inform and rely on each other in interdependent ways" (Annamma et al., 2013, p. 5). In articulating DisCrit Theory, Annamma et al. (2013) emphasized the social construction of race and dis/ability, categories of which "are *not* 'given' or 'real' *on their own*" but "are largely determined by relatively arbitrary distinctions" (p. 3, emphasis in original) in which "normative cultural standards such as whiteness and ability lead to viewing

DOI: 10.4324/9780367815325-10

differences among certain individuals as deficits" (p. 12). This construction has material (i.e., observable) consequences for educational systems, which both implicitly and explicitly reify these arbitrary distinctions through policies, procedures, and practices. As such, the experiences of students from racially minoritized backgrounds are qualitatively different from those of white students, including in special education. Consistent with the ecological orientation common in school psychology and related fields, DisCrit offers a lens through which to "recognize[e] the historical, social, political, and economic interests of limiting access to educational equity to students of color with dis/abilities" (p. 7). Whereas traditional school psychology frameworks emphasize intraindividual differences or deficits and interpersonal interactions, DisCrit pushes us to confront how macro-systemic racism operates in conjunction with ableism to influence the structuring of educational opportunity, as well individual interactions and educational decisions in ways that influence students, families, communities, and educators' lived experiences.

This dynamic is especially true in special education, where the earliest special schools and classes emerged, at least in part, as a means for segregation and assimilation of increasingly racially and ethnically diverse populations in cities, and as a means for *pushing out* students from minoritized backgrounds when policy and case law for compulsory education and desegregation reduced other modes of exclusion (Dunn, 1968). Thus, as Annamma and colleagues (2013) noted, the "construction of dis/ability depends heavily on race and can result in marginalization, particularly for people of color and those from non-dominant communities" (p. 6) and has been used to rationalize unequal and unjust treatment.

Notably, DisCrit also calls attention to how students' multidimensional identities and associated identity markers (e.g., race, language, class, gender, nationality) shape the ways they experience educational environments and the ways educational professionals respond to perceived differences that position certain students as deficient or problematic. At the micro- and meso-systemic levels most proximally related to practice, this means not just considering the intersections of racism and ableism in practice, but also actively dismantling them via social activism and resistance to normative (e.g., white, middle- and upper- class) cultural standards, be it through pedagogy, scholarship, or activism. For instance, educators, school leaders, and other service providers might consider the following questions: How do identity markers shape how you interpret the behaviors of some students or families compared to others? How do those markers influence how you engage with some students and families compared to others? How do those markers influence how you advocate for some students, groups, or communities compared to others? Annamma et al. (2013) noted that "those with admirable equity-based goals can inadvertently maintain and perpetuate inequity for other groups" (p. 18) if they ignore the needs and realities of those they claim to serve (e.g., perceiving behavioral differences as attributable to poor parenting, poverty, moral failings, or social maladjustment; applying individual skill-building interventions rather than addressing systemic inequities).

As a field, school psychology must acknowledge its (perhaps unwitting) complicity in the preservation of racism and ableism and, through individual and collective action, reject deficit perspectives of dis/ability and "question the very norms that create difference" while elevating counter-narratives and voices of individuals with dis/abilities (Annamma et al., 2013, p. 18). Adopting the DisCrit framework provides a pathway for school psychologists and others to broaden our understanding of how race and dis/ability are intertwined within the educational system by using methods that do not further marginalize dis/abled students of color, a crucial step in creating schools that are equitable and just for all students.

ED Assessment and Identification

The education of students identified with ED has long been fraught with controversy and concern for discrimination (for discussion, see Sullivan, 2017). Herein, we discuss issues related to ED as a category of special education eligibility while recognizing that the terminology of emotional and behavioral disability or disturbance has been used in professional and scholarly communities to refer to students broadly perceived to have or be at-risk for emotional or behavioral functioning considered non-normative. Importantly, there is *no consensus* in operationalizing ED, be it within the context of special education or use of the term in other contexts. Even the definition of ED in special education law (see Table 8.1) is imprecise and includes language subject to ongoing professional debate and conflicting interpretation in policy, case law, and resulting assessment practices (Sadeh & Sullivan, 2017; Sullivan & Sadeh, 2014). This conflict originated with the federal definition that excludes social maladjustment from eligibility despite the scholarly definition on which it was based, defining ED *as* social maladjustment (Sullivan & Sadeh, 2014). Perhaps unsurprisingly then, states' ED criteria vary, and the courts have offered a range of divergent interpretations in disputes between families and schools on students' eligibility and needs (e.g., Sadeh & Sullivan, 2017; Sullivan & Sadeh, 2014). These controversies notwithstanding, reliance on subjective interpretation of deviation from norms for school behavior—indeed, racially and culturally based perceptions of behavior 'troubling' to school professionals (Hart et al., 2010)—is common across conceptualizations.

Of the more than 6 million school-age children served through special education, approximately 5.5% of those, or 0.5% of all students, are identified as ED (Office of Special Education and Rehabilitative Services & New Editions Consulting, 2020), with substantial variability in states' identification and placement (Villarreal, 2015). Although concern for over-identification of students from racially and culturally minoritized backgrounds predates the formalization of the current special education system (Dunn, 1968), there has also long been

TABLE 8.1 Definition of Emotional Disturbance in the Individuals With Disabilities Education Act

(i) **Emotional disturbance** means a condition exhibiting one or more of the following characteristics over a long period of time and to a marked degree that adversely affects a child's educational performance:
(A) An inability to learn that cannot be explained by intellectual, sensory, or health factors.
(B) An inability to build or maintain satisfactory interpersonal relationships with peers and teachers.
(C) Inappropriate types of behavior or feelings under normal circumstances.
(D) A general pervasive mood of unhappiness or depression
(E) A tendency to develop physical symptoms or fears associated with personal or school problems.
(ii) Emotional disturbance includes schizophrenia. The term does not apply to children who are socially maladjusted, unless it is determined that they have an emotional disturbance under paragraph (c)(4)(i) of this section (34 C.F.R. § 300.8(c)(4)).

the supposition that schools *under*-identify ED given the much higher prevalence of mental health disorders diagnosed via criteria used by health service providers (e.g., Kauffman, 2001). Identification of ED in schools remains an area of practice characterized by unreliability and where atheoretical and unvalidated practices predominate (e.g., screeners or other rating forms or decision trees that purport to differentiate ED from social maladjustment; Sullivan, 2017). Critically, because the concept of ED is so vague and inconsistent across states and within the scholarly community, there can be no consensus on best practices to identify it, though general recommendations on legally and ethically defensible decision-making are offered elsewhere (Sadeh & Sullivan, 2017; Sullivan & Sadeh, 2014). Although experimental evidence of racial bias in ED identification is inconclusive, detection is likely impeded by the general inconsistency in professionals' linking of legal criteria to observed data (Sullivan et al., 2019). That is, pervasive unreliability might mask racial bias in experimental contexts even when bias is a facet in educational decision-making, including teacher referrals (e.g., Fish, 2017). Conversely, qualitative research highlights how bias shapes these educational processes (e.g., Harry & Klingner, 2014).

Relevance of DisCrit Theory to ED Assessment and Identification

As Sabnis and Martinez noted in Chapter 3, the seven core tenets of DisCrit guide the application of the theory to specific issues or questions. Herein, we consider how DisCrit can be leveraged to understand and disrupt the complexities and inequities involved in ED assessment and identification. These are summarized in Table 8.2.

Special education scholars have called attention to ED identification as being highly subjective—i.e., in the "eye of the beholder" (Algozzine, 2017, p. 138)—but DisCrit necessitates moving beyond a focus on individual perceptions of troubling behavior to consider how racism and ableism are intertwined in the identification of ED. Special education legislation was and continues to be used as a tool to marginalize students from racially and ethnically minoritized

TABLE 8.2 Relevance of DisCrit Tenets to ED Assessment and Identification

1. Racism and ableism are mutually constitutive: Racialized notions of behavior influence conceptualizations of normal and abnormal school behavior, including culpability and deservingness of support versus punishment. Disabled students of color are disproportionately subjected to sanctions for behavior considered non-normative because of overlapping negative perceptions and discrimination.
2. Identities as multidimensional: Intersecting identity markers (race, dis/ability, class, gender, etc.) are perceived relative to normative cultural standards such that particular students are differentially viewed as disturbed and are consequently stigmatized and segregated. Assessment and identification procedures and related research do not account for multidimensional identities.
3. Materiality: Material and psychological consequences of being labeled ED differ by race. The ED label is used to deny some students educational opportunities. The ED label influences how students perceive themselves and how others perceive them, and these perceptions are differentially affected by race. The uncritical assumption that ED justifies restrictive placements or discipline must be challenged.
4. Voice: The perspectives, values, and needs of marginalized groups are often silenced in research, policy, and practice related to ED. Engagement or silencing varies depending on race, dis/ability, or other identities and the intersections thereof. Perspectives and experiences of students with ED should be solicited to create counter-narratives.
5. Historicity: ED has been used to deny opportunity and rights historically and currently. The use of ED to deny opportunity intersects with other legal-historic processes (e.g., compulsory education, desegregation, residential composition, school funding, teacher preparation). Pseudoscientific knowledge related to causes of behavioral differences and culpability (e.g., assumptions of causality, biological differences in criminality) and subjective assessment procedures and tools treated as objective and culture-free are used to justify disparate treatment and outcomes.
6. Whiteness and ability as property: Whiteness and normative ability confer privilege relative to ED assessment and identification. White students and families are treated differently in processes related to potential ED assessment and identification. Disabled people of color were denied the privileges supposedly conferred via student and family rights under special education law.
7. Activism: Individuals, families, communities, and professionals can engage in diverse forms of resistance to oppose interlocking systems of oppression affecting the treatment of ED.

backgrounds, regardless of individual intent (Beratan, 2006). This is evidenced in the wording of IDEA itself, laden with language that defines disability as a failure of an individual to assimilate and adapt to standards of normalcy (Alur, 2009), without consideration of how social contexts influence the development and perceptions of certain behaviors or impairments that are identified as disabilities. Such a focus at the individual level ignores the "historical and structural influences . . . of people's actions and decisions or fram[es] them as static factors with linear relations" (Artiles, 2013, p. 330).

Perceptions of what constitutes ED are derived from what school professionals expect is "normal" behavior, often involving pathologization of certain behaviors as impairments that arise from prevailing racialized norms for how students should speak and act (Mahon-Reynolds & Parker, 2016). These norms have sociohistorical roots. In particular, anti-Black biases affect educators' behavior and engagement with students of color from early childhood education onward—not because of actual differences in behavior but rather due to stereotypes and resultant attention to children's actions perceived as problematic (e.g., Gilliam et al., 2016; Skiba, 2015; Todd et al., 2016). Consequently, Black students are more likely to be perceived as engaging in inappropriate or illicit behaviors, identified as ED, and subjected to exclusionary disciplinary action. Yet, as Skiba (2015) summarized, "Research has not found that students of color engage in more seriously disruptive behavior warranting higher rates of school punishment. . . . Second, race persists as a determinant of school punishment, regardless of the characteristics or seriousness of student behavior" (p. 110). In addition, teachers hold more positive expectations and speak more positively or neutrally to white students than students from racially minoritized backgrounds (Tenenbaum & Ruck, 2007). These differential behaviors and perceptions are all too often ignored or minimized in the identification of students' learning needs and disabilities.

Returning to the basic notion of ED as a special education category, a DisCrit orientation prompts several considerations of the federal criteria (see Table 8.1) and related state criteria and regulations. Under the spirit of special education law, services are meant to be needs-driven as opposed to label-based, but labels can drive how students are perceived and treated (Arishi et al., 2017). The ambiguity of key elements of the criteria regarding chronicity and severity invite racist, ableist bias into interpretation of student behaviors and resulting responses. In particular, "oppressive notions of normalcy" (see p. 38 of Chapter 3, this volume) disproportionately affect students from minoritized backgrounds when we problematize contextually or culturally appropriate behaviors based on centering of white values and norms, and ignore the influence of educational systems and adults within them in creating the very behaviors deemed 'disturbed' through differences in interactions and relationships that in turn influence students' learning and other behaviors. Further, the interplay between racism and dis/ability is relevant across minoritized groups. For instance, the role of anti-Black bias and opposition to the Civil Rights Movement in the creation and perpetuation of the model minority myth for Asian students helps us to understand present-day patterns of their underrepresentation in special education and why patterns of educational inequity vary by race or ethnicity (Sullivan et al., 2020). Thus, in the context of assessment and identification of ED, DisCrit forces us to interrogate assumptions of normality and ask critical questions such as:

1. How have normative behavioral, emotional, and social functioning been conceptualized? How have these influenced what is considered non-normative, and indicative of ED (i.e., as defined in federal law, see Table 8.1)? Who has been involved in determining these conceptualizations? Who has been left out?
2. In considering ED eligibility, what is the evidence that this suspicion of ED is not based on stereotypes or biased assumptions? How might biases and actions of adults in the school or peers shape the observed behaviors? What is the evidence that the student's behaviors are not the result of contextual, cultural, or economic differences relative to the school staff? How have assessment procedures accounted for such differences?
3. How have we ruled out adults' treatment of the student as a determinant of the focal behaviors? How have we ruled out opportunities to learn and practice desired behaviors?
4. What is the school-level evidence that biased or ineffective policies, procedures, or practices have not had an adverse effect on students of a particular race to create the observed behaviors?
5. How do family and community members regard students' behavior generally and in cases where ED is specifically considered? How have family members been involved in educational decisions, including identification?
6. What is the evidence that the student needs special education services due to a disability?

These questions are salient at all levels of discourse surrounding ED, from building level interaction and decisions to national debates on disproportionality in special education, particularly where, based on a very constrained number of teacher ratings of behavior, some scholars have argued that many more students of color need to be identified as disabled based on implicit assumptions of racial and socioeconomic deficits and pathologization of behavior without consideration of contextual determinants or racialized dynamics (for discussion, see Cohen et al., 2015; Skiba et al., 2016; Sullivan & Proctor, 2016).

The subjectivity and unreliability of traditional assessment approaches are one justification for use of multitier systems of support (MTSS), including response to intervention, to identify disabilities. Yet color-evasive or race-neutral implementation will not eliminate the detrimental effects of racial bias—or ableism—in the assessment, eligibility determination, and intervention processes (Newell & Kratochwill, 2007). For this reason, it is unsurprising that evidence for the efficacy of these frameworks in reducing disproportionality is mixed at best (e.g., Kramarczuk Voulgarides et al., 2017). Furthermore, even where policy includes safeguards to curb disproportionality in special education identification, recent data show little substantive change as states have used the latitude within the law to avoid substantive changes in practice while engaging in technical compliance with the law (for discussion, see Sullivan & Osher, 2019). Thus, DisCrit pushes us to consider how policy is enacted at all levels (federal, state, district, school, classroom) to reify racist and ableist norms that may, in turn, be reflected in differential treatment of students from minoritized backgrounds and resulting inequitable and disparate outcomes. Accordingly, data collected in MTSS processes can be used to consider differential opportunity, participation, and outcomes.

The material consequences DisCrit calls attention to are apparent in the treatment of students identified with ED. Among students with disabilities, outcomes are often poorest for students with ED, especially those from racially minoritized backgrounds (e.g., Losen et al., 2014). DisCrit also facilitates consideration of how ED is constructed in such a manner that the disability is "inherently negative or shameful," leading students, families, and professionals to avoid, as opposed to being claimed, and consequently reject those to whom is it applied (Annamma et al., 2013, p. 8). Educators regard students with ED as the most unwelcomed members of general education environments (Wagner et al., 2006). The implications for such attitudes are largely unexplored empirically, yet we can infer implications from the treatment and outcomes of labeled students. They are among the least likely to be taught by highly qualified, appropriately trained teachers; are typically served by educators who lack any knowledge of evidence-based interventions or services (Stormont et al., 2011); are often subject to ineffective practices and segregation from typically functioning youth; and experience some of the poorest educational and long-term outcomes of any group studied in schools when considering retention, suspension, expulsion, failure, and graduation rates; employment outcomes; incarceration; health status; quality of social engagement and relationships; or life satisfaction (Katsiyannis et al., 2005; Wagner et al., 2006). Taken together, DisCrit offers a valuable framework for conceptualizing and addressing inequities in the educational treatment of students with ED.

Case Study

Part 1: *Mia, a newly graduated school psychologist, is getting ready for her first round of evaluations at one of her schools, a Title I school in a mid-sized city that serves students from diverse backgrounds: 35% of students are Black/African American, 25% are Latinx, 20% are Asian American, and 20% are white American. Mia is excited about working here, as they have a reputation as a "progressive" school, teachers and other school professionals report a supportive work environment, and Mia has heard that the parent association is very active. A review of the school's website revealed what Mia could see as a clear commitment to diversity: The principal identified diversity as one of the school's core values, the school improvement plan includes an equity goal, and the school website shows pictures of students from diverse backgrounds and dis/abilities. In reviewing the school documents, Mia learned that last year, the school had been identified as a school in need of targeted support and improvement in the area of special education; apparently, students who receive special education services had been falling behind compared to other students receiving special education services in the state. Mia also found some concerning information about the school's record on academics and equity on an external school-rating website. Although she had no reason to distrust the positive reviews from her colleagues, she was glad to know this information. Arriving at the school for the first time, Mia observed that the school exterior seemed well kept, the children on the playground—who were as diverse as the website suggested—seemed to be having fun, and the security guard eagerly welcomed Mia. On the short walk to the office, Mia noticed the student work displayed on the walls focused on embracing diversity; she saw African artwork and a saying in Spanish was painted on the wall. "They don't just pay lip service to diversity; they live it," she thought to herself happily. In meeting with one of the teachers on the Multidisciplinary Evaluation Team Mia will be joining, her colleague noted that Mia's predecessor told them research shows students of color are actually under-identified for special education and thus, the teams have been careful to make sure their Black and Latinx students get the services they need.*

Mia's first few ED cases included those presented in Table 8.3. Consider how each of the six sets of questions presented in the previous section might be applied in this scenario and cases.

These scenarios invite consideration of how systemic inequity and bias can influence decision-making, and how over-representation in special education categories like emotional disturbance can have cascading negative long-term impacts on students (Wagner et al., 2006). Both cases had students who were struggling with academics and behavior; however, the process of special education and indeed, the pre-evaluation process was markedly different. In Eve's case, her parents' knowledge about the special education system, their financial resources, the school's intervention, and special education resources, along with the collaborative nature of the school-home relationship allowed Eve to receive services without the ED label, and service providers worked toward protecting Eve with the primary goal being integration. Umar had a very different experience from the same education professionals in the same system concerned about the same behaviors as Eve, which exemplifies the need for a DisCrit lens. The differences between Eve's and Umar's family background, home–school relationship, parent advocacy, and the school's willingness to problem-solve with the family resulted in a strength-based outcome for Eve but an ED identification and removal from general education for Umar.

Part 2. *Toward the end of the school year, Ms. Cristal, a newly hired special education teacher and one of only two people of color at the school, shared privately with Mia her concerns about discriminatory practices in the evaluation process, using Eve and Umar as specific examples. "I'm not saying we made the right or wrong decision for either student. What I am saying is that for the same behaviors, we treated the students differently. And*

TABLE 8.3 Student Scenarios

Scenario A: Eve	*Scenario B: Umar*
Eve is a 10-year-old white student from a middle-class family. Her parents are divorced and share equal custody. Her mother is a member of the parent-teacher association, and her employment allows her flexible work hours that she spends volunteering at the school for various activities. Teachers noted Eve has had several behavioral challenges following the divorce in 2nd grade, including physical aggression toward peers, verbal aggression toward teachers, inattention, disruptive behaviors during class, and limited engagement in class or with peers. As a result, Eve participated in group social skills and math interventions. Following limited improvement, her parents requested an evaluation of special education eligibility in 3rd grade. Eve's evaluation included cognitive assessment, academic testing, and teacher and parent rating scales, resulting in a recommendation for identification as ED. Eve's mother asked for alternatives to the ED label that would still allow services. Though other members of the team didn't see data supporting eligibility in other disability categories, they noted she may have ADHD given her rating scale scores. The team counseled the parents on how to gather data from Eve's pediatrician to facilitate identification for a health impairment and recommended therapy from an outside provider. Eve's parents postponed signing consent for services and had her privately assessed for ADHD. After providing Eve's medical diagnosis, she was identified for special education under Other Health Impairments, with the services recommended remaining the same as originally proposed in the initial meeting. The parents and school agree that the aim is to exit Eve from special education before she moves to middle school.	Umar is a 10-year-old Black boy whose parents emigrated as refugees before his birth. His parents work full-time to support their family of five; Umar frequently cares for the younger siblings. Most of the teachers in the grade level have fewer than five years of experience and are women from the surrounding predominantly white suburbs. Umar recently started to fail multiple subjects and does not complete homework. Attempts to get him to return homework have resulted in outbursts in class, with the teacher using planned ignoring throughout the day. His parents cannot help him as they are not fluent in English, and they do not have the time to attend frequently requested meetings. Teachers noted Umar has escalating behavioral challenges including physical aggression toward peers, verbal aggression toward teachers, inattention, and disruptive behaviors during class. After his second fight, he is suspended for several days. By winter break, his teacher says his symptoms have worsened and (unable to manage his behavior) refers him to the child find team, which, in turn, suggests a special education evaluation. Umar's evaluation included cognitive assessment, academic testing, and teacher and parent rating scales resulting in a recommendation for ED eligibility, with secondary eligibility of specific learning disability in reading. Umar's father signs the consent and IEP forms without any question, trusting the school to do what they can to help Umar. Umar is initially pulled out for behavioral and academic services three days per week, and at the end of the year, his teacher suggests placement in a self-contained classroom for students with behavioral challenges so he can get all-day services.

the student who is not in ED is the white student. I just don't see how we're being systematic about who is getting identified and how we use that information. We have been written up for discriminatory practices in special ed, yet I don't see how we're working to address it." Mia's heart sank. Although she had earnestly tried to conduct a fair and culturally competent evaluation of both children, she realized she missed the larger school context. She went back to review the school website and documents; this time she saw what she didn't see the first time. The school did include a diversity goal in their school improvement plan, but the goal was written about improving performance for all *students; there was no specific mention of students of color or other marginalized groups. In a school newsletter describing the school as in need of targeted support, the principal obscured the problems within special education. Instead, the newsletter articulated the importance of working with* all *kids. Nowhere in the documents or website was there a clear and explicit commitment to actively combating discriminatory practices within special education or the school as a whole. Mia sat down and began sketching a plan for how to systemically combat the issues at her school through a DisCrit lens.* Does this new information change your responses to the questions you considered for Part 1? What acts of resistance could Mia pursue to address the issues identified?

Experiential Activities

As described in Chapter 3, theorists have articulated seven tenets of DisCrit. As such, we encourage readers to consider the following activities aligned with each of the tenets.

1. **Racism and ableism as mutually constitutive:** How would you and teachers in your school answer this question: What is required to be successful in my classroom? Consider the extent to which the requirements reflect white, ableist, American cultural norms. What does it mean to teachers if their expectations are not met? Do teachers ascribe a discrepancy between desired and undesired behaviors as residing within the child or the environment? Can a student be successful in a teacher's classroom if they display behaviors that are unfamiliar to the teacher? Alternately, if you are not in a school, take an implicit bias test. Tests are available for many identities, including dis/ability and race. Reflect honestly on your results. What are your assumptions about persons with dis/abilities? How do these assumptions differ for non-white students?
2. **Identities as multidimensional:** Review your school/district ED policy, practice, and procedures. Consider how students with multiple identities may not have equal access to fair and unbiased processes. For example, how might the policy interpretation differ for students based on different combinations of race, gender, class, or other dimensions of identity?
3. **Materiality:** Review the placement patterns for students with ED in your school/district. Consider whether students with ED are segregated from

their peers. Is there evidence that these programs and placements are effective? For whom? Can programming be provided in general education settings? Are there better, more effective ways to educate students with ED that do not require segregation? If segregation is determined to be in the best interest of the student, has the student been consulted? Has the segregated setting resulted in improved outcomes? What does this say about how students with ED are valued?

4. **Voice:** Review three blogs, videos, or social media accounts of advocates who represent multiple identities, among them dis/ability. Consider also how students and families with disabilities are engaged in school processes. How are their voices and contributions sought and elevated?
5. **Historicity:** How has ED, and social maladjustment if included in your state law, been operationalized by your state and district? How have these operationalizations influenced professional learning, practices, and educational decisions for students? How have associated policies, procedures, and practices been used to deny educational opportunity based on race and ability?
6. **Whiteness and ability as property:** Consider how white students with social, emotional, or behavioral challenges are treated differently in educational systems than students from racially minoritized backgrounds. How, for instance, does this affect special education eligibility, placement, and other service receipt? How does potential ED identification intersect with other federal categories of disability (e.g., developmental delay, learning disability, autism, other health impairment) when white privilege is or is not an influencer in student-level decisions? In policy and procedure specification? In professional learning?
7. **Activism:** Read about stories of activism and resistance. Identify two acts of activism you will do in the next month and two acts of activism you will do this year to disrupt the dominant narratives related to ED identification in schools in research, policy, or practice.

Conclusion

Annamma et al. (2018) articulated DisCrit "as an analytic tool to articulate how ideologies of normal(cy) reflect and reinforce mutually constitutive forms of racism and ableism . . . positioning individuals that do not fit taken-for-granted race and ability norms as problematic, labeling them as disabled, and relegating them to the margins of society" (p. 232). Most fundamentally, DisCrit necessitates a reconsideration of the entire enterprise of ED identification and treatment. If nothing else, we must ask why we consider it necessary to apply an ED label and how it helps and harms the student. We cannot shy away from critical reflection on how racism and ableism shape these processes at all levels of educational systems and their intersections with other systems of care (e.g., health, social services, juvenile justice). Notably, DisCrit "renounces imposed segregation and promotes an ethic of unqualified belonging and full inclusion in schools and society" (Annamma et al., 2013, p. 15), "encourage[ing] society to become more encompassing of diversity and perceived difference" (p. 18). This will necessitate ongoing interrogation and disruption of the ways we, as school professionals, perceive and respond to behavioral, social, and emotional differences in ways that create inequitable opportunity, participation, and outcomes with corresponding activism. We must keep in mind that "either you're committed to disrupting status quo policies and practices that marginalize particular students, or you're complicit in those practices. There is no neutral" (Great Lakes Equity/MAP Center, 2020).

References

Algozzine, B. (2017). Toward an acceptable definition of emotional disturbance: Waiting for change. *Behavioral Disorders, 42*, 136–144. https://doi.org/10.1177%2F0198742917702117

Alur, M. (2009). Empowerment and political social action: The policy process. In M. Alur & V. Timmons (Eds.), *Inclusive education across cultures: Crossing boundaries, sharing ideas*. SAGE Publications India.

Annamma, S. A., Connor, D., & Ferri, B. (2013). Dis/ability critical race studies (DisCrit): Theorizing at the intersections of race and dis/ability. *Race Ethnicity and Education, 16*(1), 1–31. https://doi.org/10.1080/13613324.2012.730511

Annamma, S. A., Ferri, B. A., & Connor, D. J. (2018). Cultivating and expanding disability critical race theory (DisCrit). In K. Ellis, R. Garland-Thomson, M. Kent, & R. Robertson (Eds.), *Manifestos for the future of critical disability studies: Volume 1* (pp. 230–238). Routledge.

Arishi, L., Boyle, C., & Lauchlan, F. (2017). Inclusive education and the politics of difference: Considering the effectiveness of labeling in special education. *Educational & Child Psychology, 34*(4), 9–19.

Artiles, A. J. (2013). Untangling the racialization of disabilities: An intersectionality critique across disability models. *Du Bois Review: Social Science Research on Race, 10*(2), 329–347. https://doi.org/10.1017/S1742058X13000271

Beratan, G. D. (2006). Institutionalizing inequity: Ableism, racism and IDEA 2004. *Disability Studies Quarterly, 26*(2). https://doi.org/10.18061/dsq.v26i2.682

Blanchett, W. (2006). Disproportionate representation of African American students in special education: Acknowledging the role of White privilege and racism. *Educational Researcher, 35*(6), 24–28. https://doi.org/10.3102/0013189X035006024

Bradley, R., Doolittle, J., & Bartolotta, R. (2008). Building on the data and adding to the discussion: The experiences and outcomes of students with emotional disturbance. *Journal of Behavioral Education, 17*, 4–23. https://doi.org/10.1007/s10864-007-9058-6

Cohen, D. R., Burns, M. K., Riley-Tillman, C., & Hosp, J. L. (2015). Are minority students under- or overrepresented in special education? *Communique, 44*(2), 1, 22–23.

Dunn, L. M. (1968). Special education for the mildly retarded: Is much of it justifiable? *Exceptional Children, 35*, 5–22. https://doi.org/10.1177/001440296803500101

Fish, R. E. (2017). The racialized construction of exceptionality: Experimental evidence of race/ethnicity effects on teachers' interventions. *Social Science Research, 62*, 317–334. https://doi.org/10.1016/j.ssresearch.2016.08.007

Gilliam, W. S., Maupin, A., N., Reyes, C. R., Accavitti, M., & Shic, F. (2016). *Do early educators' implicit biases regarding sex and race relate to behavior expectations and recommendations of preschool expulsions and suspensions?* Yale University Child Study Center. https://medicine.yale.edu/childstudy/zigler/publications/Preschool%20Implicit%20Bias%20Policy%20Brief_final_9_26_276766_5379.pdf

Great Lakes Equity/MAP Center [GreatLakesEAC]. (2020, March 5). *Either you're committed to disrupting status quo policies and practices that marginalize particular students, or you're complicit in those practices* [Tweet]. Twitter. https://twitter.com/GreatLakesEAC/status/1235589856790753280

Harry, B., & Klingner, J. K. (2014). *Why are so many minority students in special education? Understanding race & disability in schools* (2nd ed.). Teachers College Press.

Hart, J. E., Cramer, E. D., Harry, B., Klingner, J. K., & Sturges, K. M. (2010). The continuum of "troubling" to "troubled" behavior: Exploratory case studies of African American students in programs for emotional disturbance. *Remedial and Special Education, 31*(3), 148–162. https://doi.org/10.1177/0741932508327468

Katsiyannis, A., Zhang, D., Woodruff, N., & Dixon, A. (2005). Transition supports to students with mental retardation: An examination of data from the National Longitudinal Transition Study 2. *Education and Training in Developmental Disabilities, 40*(2), 109–116.

Kauffman, J. M. (2001). *Characteristics of emotional and behavioral disorders of children and youths* (7th ed.). Merrill/Prentice Hall.

Kramarczuk Voulgarides, C., Fergus, E., & King Thorius, K. A. (2017). Pursuing equity: Disproportionality in special education and the reframing of technical solutions to address systemic inequities. *Review of Research in Education, 41*(1), 61–87. https://doi.org/10.3102/0091732X16686947

Losen, D., Hodson, C., Ee, J., & Martinez, T. (2014). Disturbing inequities: Exploring the relationship between racial disparities in special education identification and discipline. *Journal of Applied Research on Children, 5*(2), 88–103.

Mahon-Reynolds, C., & Parker, L. (2016). The overrepresentation of students of color with learning disabilities. In D. J. Connor, B. A. Ferri, & S. A. Annamma, *DisCrit: Disability studies and critical race theory in education* (pp. 145–154). Teachers College Press.

Newell, M., & Kratochwill, T. R. (2007). The integration of response to intervention and critical race theory-disability studies: A robust approach to reducing racial discrimination in evaluation decisions. In S. Jimerson, M. Burns, & A. VanDerHayden (Eds.), *Handbook of response to intervention* (pp. 65–79). Springer. https://doi.org/10.1007/978-0-387-49053-3_5

Office of Special Education and Rehabilitative Services (ED), & New Editions Consulting, I. (2020). 41st annual report to Congress on the implementation of the Individuals with Disabilities Education Act, 2019. In *Office of special education and rehabilitative services, US Department of Education*. Office of Special Education and Rehabilitative Services, US Department of Education. https://www2.ed.gov/about/reports/annual/osep/index.html

Sadeh, S., & Sullivan, A. L. (2017). Ethical and legal landmines: Causal inference in special education decisions. *Psychology in the Schools, 54*(9), 1134–1147. https://doi.org/10.1002/pits.22046

Skiba, R. J. (2015). Interventions to address racial/ethnic disparities in school discipline: Can systems reform be race-neutral? In R. Bangs & L. E. Davis (Eds.), *Race and social problems* (pp. 107–124). Springer. https://doi.org/10.1007/978-1-4939-0863-9_7

Skiba, R. J., Artiles, A. J., Kozleski, E. B., Losen, D. J., & Harry, E. G. (2016). Risks and consequences of oversimplifying educational inequities: A response to

Morgan et al. (2015). *Educational Researcher, 45*(3), 221–225. https://doi.org/10.3102/0013189X16644606

Stormont, M., Reinke, W., & Herman, K. (2011). Teachers' knowledge of evidence-based interventions and available school resources for children with emotional and behavioral problems. *Journal of Behavioral Education, 20*(2), 138–147. https://doi.org/10.1007/s10864-011-9122-0

Sullivan, A. L. (2017). Wading through quicksand: Making sense of minority disproportionality in identification of emotional disturbance. *Behavioral Disorders, 43*(1), 244–252. https://doi.org/10.1177/0198742917732360

Sullivan, A. L., Kulkarni, T., & Chhuon, V. (2020). Making visible the invisible: Multi-study investigation of disproportionate special education identification of U.S. Asian American and Pacific Islander students. *Exceptional Children*, OnlineFirst. https://doi.org/10.1177/0014402920905548

Sullivan, A. L., & Osher, D. (2019). IDEA's double bind: A synthesis of disproportionality policy interpretations. *Exceptional Children, 85*(4), 395–412. https://doi.org/10.1177/0014402918818047

Sullivan, A. L., & Proctor, S. (2016). The shield or the sword? Revisiting the debate on racial disproportionality in special education and implications for school psychologists. *School Psychology Forum, 10*, 278–288.

Sullivan, A. L., & Sadeh, S. S. (2014). Differentiating social maladjustment from emotional disturbance: An analysis of case law. *School Psychology Review, 43*(4), 450–471. https://doi.org/10.1080/02796015.2014.12087415

Sullivan, A. L., Sadeh, S., & Houri, A. (2019). Are school psychologists' decisions reliable and unbiased? A multi-study experimental investigation. *Journal of School Psychology, 77*, 90–109. https://doi.org/10.1016/j.jsp.2019.10.006

Tenenbaum, H. R., & Ruck, M. D. (2007). Are teachers' expectations different for racial minority than for European American students? A meta-analysis. *Journal of Educational Psychology, 99*(2), 253. https://doi.org/10.1037/0022-0663.99.2.253

Todd, A. R., Thiem, K. C., & Neel, R. (2016). Does seeing faces of young black boys facilitate the identification of threatening stimuli? *Psychological Science, 27*(3), 384–393. https://doi.org/10.1177/0956797615624492

Villarreal, V. (2015). State-level variability of educational outcomes of students with emotional disturbance. *Exceptionality, 23*(1), 1–13. https://doi.org/10.1080/09362835.2014.986610

Wagner, M., Friend, M., Bursuck, W. D., Kutash, K., Duchnowski, A. J., Sumi, W. C., & Epstein, M. H. (2006). Educating students with emotional disturbances: A national perspective on school programs and services. *Journal of Emotional and Behavioral Disorders, 14*(1), 12–30. https://doi.org/10.1177/10634266060140010

Note

1. Following Annamma et al. (2013, p. 24), we "deliberately use 'dis/ability' instead of 'disability' throughout this article to call attention to ways in which the latter overwhelmingly signals a specific inability to perform culturally-defined expected tasks (such as learning or walking) that come to define the individual as primarily and generally 'unable' to navigate society. We believe the '/' in disability disrupts misleading understandings of disability, as it simultaneously conveys the mixture of ability and disability. We have maintained the use of 'disability' when referring to its official use within classification structures" (e.g., research reporting special education identification).

9

QUEER THEORY AND SCHOOL-BASED COUNSELING FOR LGBTQ STUDENTS

David P. Rivera, Sherrie L. Proctor, Cliff Yung-Chi Chen, and Pam W. Gershon

According to the 2019 Youth Risk Behavior Survey (YRBS; Centers for Disease Control (CDC), 2020), 11.2% of high school students identified as LGB (lesbian, gay, bisexual), and 4.5 % of youth ages 13–18 were unsure of their sexual orientation. Although most United States (U.S.) national population-based surveys have rarely included questions to identify transgender individuals, the Williams Institute estimated that 0.7% of youth ages 13–17 identify as transgender based on state-level population-based data (Herman et al., 2017). Another report, based on available data from selected states and districts, estimated that 1.8% of U.S. high school students identify as transgender (Johns et al., 2019). Altogether, the data suggest that 12–15% of high school students identify as LGBTQ. The percentage of LGBTQ elementary and middle school students is much harder to estimate due to lack of population-based data and students' age and developmental stage. However, research has indicated that LGBTQ middle school students and young children whose gender expression is not consistent with stereotypical gender roles are often subjected to harassment and violence in schools due to pervasive heteronormativity (i.e., a worldview or perspective that promotes heterosexuality as normal or default sexual orientation) and cisnormativity (i.e., the belief that everyone is cisgender, or has a gender identity that matches society's gender norms associated with assigned sex at birth).

The Centers for Disease Control's Youth Risk Behavior Surveillance System (YRBSS) monitors health-related behaviors and experiences (e.g., sexual behavior, high-risk substance use, exposure to violence, mental health issues, and suicide) among students across the U.S. Since YRBS started collecting data about LGB high school students in 2015, large disparities in risk factors that put LGB youth at higher risk for death and disability than their heterosexual peers have been observed. Transgender youth are particularly at higher risk for violence,

DOI: 10.4324/9780367815325-11

victimization, substance use, and suicide than cisgender youth (Johns et al., 2019; Meyers et al., 2020).

LGBTQ youth often face disparities in mental health and suicide risk compared to their non-LGBTQ peers. The Trevor Project, which is the world's largest suicide prevention and crisis intervention organization for LGBTQ youth, estimates that more than 1.2 million LGBTQ youth aged 13–18 in the U.S. seriously consider suicide each year. According to their 2019 National Survey on LGBTQ Mental Health, 45.3% of LGBTQ youth aged 13–18 seriously considered suicide in the past 12 months (Green et al., 2019). These disparities are primarily due to stressors and discrimination associated with a socially stigmatized position, rather than being LGBTQ. The school-to-coffin pipeline framework (Wozolek et al., 2017) depicts school as a system that (un)intentionally positions LGBTQ in the epidemic of LGBTQ youth suicide through institutional homophobia and transphobia manifested or hidden in school rhetoric and school policy. Educators and school staff, including teachers, administrators, counselors, and school psychologists need to acknowledge and examine their (un)knowing participation in the pipeline and contribution to structural LGBTQ oppression in order to interrupt the cycle of LGBTQ youth suicide.

This chapter will provide an overview of Queer Theory and discussion about some of the salient issues that impact the schooling experiences of LGBTQ youth created by heteronormativity. We will contextualize these heteronormative problems with a case narrative and offer exercises to help synthesize the case narrative with Queer Theory fundamentals. While we use the term *LGBTQ* to include individuals with diverse sexual orientation and gender identities in this chapter, we recognize the categorization and use of *LGBTQ* inherently represents a power structure and inevitably imposes oppression to free and authentic expression and identity of self.

Brief Introduction to Queer Theory

As articulated by Rivera in Chapter 4, there are no agreed-upon standard, key tenets of Queer Theory given its intent not to replicate heteronormative society's attempts to restrain and limit human expressions of human sexuality and gender. Thus, the following discussion briefly reviews the six "fundamentals of Queer Theory" put forth by Rivera.

The first is the *Problem of Heteronormativity*. This fundamental relates to how the dominance of heterosexual ways of being, thinking, and feeling pervades every aspect of societal institutions. Heteronormativity is a problem because it privileges those who are heterosexual and cisgender, while penalizing those who are not. Queer Theory centers heteronormativity as a main lens to view, understand, and critique the world.

The second is *Genealogical Approach to Interrogating Discourses*. This fundamental includes two key concepts. The first is the genealogical approach to historicizing ideas and events. The second is discourses, which are the ways we communicate that shape how we think about and understand these ideas and events. The genealogical approach to historicizing sexualities and genders and the resulting discourses is a common methodology used by queer theorists to understand and critique the manifestation of heteronormativity across the human experience.

The third is *Deconstruction of Finite Categorization*. This fundamental challenges us to interrogate and deconstruct binaries and finite categories related to sexuality (heterosexual-homosexual) and gender (man-woman) that are limiting and often static. It is important to deconstruct finite categorization because it creates hierarchies that are often the basis for the creation of rules, laws, procedures, and practices that govern how sexuality and gender are to be understood and expressed.

The fourth is *Resistance to Essentialism and Essential States of Being*. Essentialism refers to the classifications people use to make sense of the world by assigning "essential" characteristics, both observable and unobservable, to create finite categories. For instance, often people's essentialism of gender is underdeveloped, and many believe that there are underlying realities that are common for all women and for all men. Such essentialism is the foundation for stereotypes that can be harmful because they are based on incomplete understanding of people's reality and lived experiences.

The fifth is *Realities Are Socially Constructed/Constricted*. This fundamental acknowledges that gender and sexuality categorizations are socially created and maintained. Gender, for example, is not inherently innate but is learned and maintained through gender social norms that dictate gendered-behaviors, thinkings, and feelings from the moment one is born until their death.

Finally, the sixth is *Challenges to Empiricism*. Empiricism mandates the use of observable data to support understanding of the phenomenon in question. An example is the use of positivist methods in psychology. Queer Theory challenges the notion that positivist methods capture the experiences of the socially marginalized. Queer Theory supports the interrogation of the entire process of scientific inquiry, including the hierarchy that often exists between the "researcher" and the "researched."

In the next section, we review research related to the experiences of LGBTQ youth in middle schools. Understanding the research related to this specific student group will help contextualize the case narrative of James, whom we present after connecting the fundamentals of Queer Theory to LGBTQ youths' experiences in schools.

Experiences of LGBTQ Youth in Middle School

Although there is a robust body of research that explores the experiences of LGBTQ students, most studies do not focus exclusively on the middle school population and their schooling context. Yet, middle school students report more hostile school environments and experiences and less access to school-based support than LGBTQ high school students (Kosciw et al., 2020). Further, many LGBTQ youth are rejected by family and friends and, given their young age, lack resources to be independent and to access needed support (Holmes & Cahill, 2004). When LGBTQ youth do attempt to access health and human services, lack of acceptance and discomfort disclosing sexuality have been significant barriers to them (Graybill & Proctor, 2016). Although research documents that LGBTQ youth miss school and avoid school functions because they feel unsafe (Kosciw et al., 2020), these youth still spend a significant amount of their time in schools. This makes them vulnerable to systems of oppression like homophobia or biophobia (i.e., bias and discrimination toward lesbian, gay, or bisexual people) and transphobia (i.e., bias and discrimination toward transgender and gender nonbinary people) that are at work in school settings. Given we know that LGBTQ students in middle school report lower levels of school support, it is important to understand the experiences of this specific student group to facilitate socially just, safe, supportive, and affirming school environments for them that will lead to more positive outcomes (Dinkins & Englert, 2015).

A recent survey conducted by the Gay, Lesbian, and Straight Education Network (GLSEN) investigated the experiences of middle and high school students who identify as members of the LGBTQ community (Kosciw et al., 2020). The survey's findings reveal that schools are hostile and oppressive environments for middle and high school LGBTQ students, but even more so for LGBTQ middle school students. Eighty-seven percent of middle school students reported that they heard anti-LGBTQ language (e.g., "That's so gay"); 80% experienced victimization and discrimination at school (e.g., bullying, verbal harassment, sexual harassment, physical assault) based on their sexual orientation, 64% based on gender expression, and 61% based on gender. Regrettably, most students did not report victimization to school staff because they doubted effective intervention would take place or, if they did report, school staff did not respond or told them to ignore the harassment or assault.

Most (69%) LGBTQ middle schoolers reported that they personally experienced LGBTQ-related discriminatory policies and practices at school. These discriminatory practices included being prevented from using the restroom aligned with their gender identity, being banned from using their chosen names or pronouns, being stopped from discussing or writing about LGBTQ topics in school work, being disciplined for public displays of affection, and being stopped from forming Gay-Straight Alliances or Gender and Sexuality Alliances (GSA), among other punitive and oppressive actions. Discriminatory practices and victimization led to many LGBTQ middle schoolers' avoidance of school and school-related activities (Kosciw et al., 2020).

In terms of support, 10.7% of LGBTQ middle schoolers in the GLSEN survey indicated that their school had a comprehensive anti-bullying or harassment policy, while 7% noted the presence of a transgender/nonbinary student policy. Thirty-two percent indicated having 11 or more supportive staff present in their school, while 35% believed their school administration was "somewhat" or "very supportive." Fifteen percent of LGBTQ middle schoolers reported that their school curriculum had positive inclusion of LGBTQ issues, while 15% reported negative inclusion of LGBTQ curriculum. Findings revealed that several school-based factors relate to a safer and more inclusive school climate, including the presence of supportive educators, curricula that is LGBTQ inclusive, policies that are inclusive and supportive of LGBTQ students, and affinity clubs such as GSAs (Kosciw et al., 2020). Next, we describe the dynamics of systems of oppression and marginalization that necessitate the need to build safer and more inclusive school structures to better support the experiences of LGBTQ students.

Systems of Oppression and Marginalization of LGBTQ Middle Schoolers

As noted in the introduction, the school-to-coffin pipeline framework describes school as a system that positions LGBTQ students in the epidemic of LGBTQ youth suicide through institutional homophobia and transphobia manifested or hidden in school rhetoric and school policy (Wozolek et al., 2017). Because what happens in schools can have devastating effects on the educational outcomes and physical and mental health and well-being of LGBTQ students, it is important to understand, interrogate, and dismantle the systems of oppression that marginalize LGBTQ students in middle schools. To be clear, systems of oppression relate to the systemic use of institutional power and ideological and cultural hegemony, which results in one group benefiting at the expense of another. Systems of oppression can operate at an intentional or unintentional level, can be conscious or unconscious, and can be visible or invisible (GLSEN, 2014). Oppression can manifest in schools for LGBTQ middle school students based on their identities and can create both challenges and opportunities for strength-building and advocacy (GLSEN, 2014; Holmes & Cahill, 2004).

Systems of oppression in schools show up in the practices, policies, and also curricula schools engage. Next, we use the research to provide two examples that illustrate how systems of oppression are at play in middle school environments. Whether overtly visible or invisible, systems of oppression impact all aspects of schooling and contribute to schools being oppressive and marginalizing spaces and places for LGBTQ middle schoolers.

Transphobia and Gender Policing. We now illustrate how systems of oppression like transphobia underlie gender policing in schools and how these contribute to LGBTQ students' negative school experiences. There is a significant research base that explores bullying and its outcomes on LGBTQ students in schools (Meyers et al., 2020). This research typically frames bullying as peer-to-peer aggression, labeling LGBTQ students as victims and bullies as anti-socials displaying pathological behavior (Payne & Smith, 2013). Payne and Smith (2013) challenged this framing of bullying by educators and researchers. Instead, they contended that "cultural systems of power" such as heteronormativity in schools privilege some youth, while marginalizing others in relation to gender and sexuality (Payne & Smith, 2013, p. 3). They proposed gender policing as an alternative conceptualization of bullying targeting LGBTQ students. Gender policing "draws attention to how normative gender expectations function as tools for targeting peers, as well as the role schools and other cultural institutions play in reproducing strict rules for 'normal' gender expression" (p. 3). Their conceptualization identifies bullying of LGBTQ students as being rooted in a "heteronormative and heterosexist culture that is reinforced through the institution and practices of schooling—not in individual aggressive children" (p. 3).

In relation to bullying of LGBTQ students in schools, the "cultural systems of power" Payne and Smith (2013) identified are directly related to systems of oppression LGBTQ students experience in schools, namely transphobia. While LGBTQ students experience interpersonal oppressions such as bullying in schools, educators' focus on individual-level explanations for LGBTQ students' marginalizing school experiences is short-sighted and harmful because those explanations do not acknowledge, account for, or address, for instance, the transphobia that underlies gender policing in schools. Effective intervention and advocacy for LGBTQ middle school students *must* eliminate systemic oppressions along with the resulting interpersonal ones.

Heteronormativity and Anti-LGBTQ Curricula. Heteronormativity—the privileging of heterosexual practices and assumption that everyone is heterosexual—is a system of oppression that often influences an overall school culture, including what curricula students are taught and how pedagogy is engaged (Batchelor et al., 2018; Dinkins & Englert, 2015). More specifically, heteronormativity often shows up in gender binaries in the curriculum and the exclusion of LGBTQ-related content from the curriculum (Batchelor et al., 208). Yet, research conducted in middle schools has found that reading and discussing literature focused on LGBTQ characters can challenge myths students have about sexuality; help them build acceptance; foster their ability to understand multiple perspectives; and combat homophobia, transphobia, and heterosexism in schools (Dinkins & Englert, 2015).

Dinkins and Englert (2015) studied how the heteronormative nature of one middle school classroom environment shaped the climate of safety, support, and learning for LGBTQ students engaged in studying a novel with a gay character. Despite the school introducing students to LGBTQ-focused literature, Dinkins and Englert (2015) found that by assuming all students were heterosexual, the overwhelming heteronormativity of the school did not make space for LGBTQ students. For instance, while reading one LGBTQ-focused text, a teacher asked students to consider their social world while reading the text, but she assumed their social worlds involved heterosexual relationships. Furthermore, while reading LGBTQ-focused literature, both students and teachers "othered" non-heteronormative sexual identity and gender performance. This made the school an unsafe place for LGBTQ students to express their identities.

While research supports that schools having curricula that is LGBTQ-inclusive creates safer and more inclusive school climates (Kosciw et al., 2020), Dinkins and Englert's (2015) findings illustrated the power of systems of oppression like heteronormativity. They noted that "merely including LGBT text in the curriculum does not systematically address the pervading heteronormative environment in the classroom" and that "it is imperative that classroom contexts represent spaces free of heterosexual dominance and rigid binaries" (Dinkins & Englert, 2015, p. 403). Thus, educators must receive training on how to integrate LGBTQ-related content into the curriculum in ways that disrupt heteronormativity, not perpetuate it.

Relevance of Queer Theory to the Experiences of LGBTQ Youth in Middle School

The fundamentals of Queer Theory articulated earlier in this chapter and by Rivera (this volume) in Chapter 4 are relevant to the experiences of LGBTQ youth in middle school. The *Problem of Heteronormativity* appears to be particularly applicable to LGBTQ youth given the pervasiveness of heteronormativity in school settings. As detailed earlier, heteronormativity overlays and undergirds school structures, policies, and behavioral norms. One of the most explicit examples of heteronormativity's influence on the regulation of gender and sexuality is that of sexuality education curricula and related policies that often contain specific, rigid, and limited messages about gender and sexuality expectations (Mayo, 2004). Middle schoolers are often in their pre-teen and early-teen years of life, which corresponds to early experiences of puberty. The power inherent in schooling should not be overlooked or dismissed, as schools are afforded great power and responsibility for shaping and regulating the young people in their care. As such, the messaging conveyed via compulsory sexuality education in schools carries significant weight in terms of the influence these curricula and related policies have on student development, including the ways young people conceptualize and understand their gender and sexuality.

McNeill (2013) revealed heteronormativity's prevalence in sexuality education and contended that the state-sanctioned laws and policies that dictate sexuality education curricula serve to regulate, reinforce, and promote heterosexuality and cisgender ways of being. Using Virginia's Family Life Education (Commonwealth of Virginia Department of Education, 2020) guidelines and standards as a case study, McNeill (2013) found extensive proof of the curricula regulating specific gendered and sexual ways of being that hinge on heteronormativity. Upon reviewing the most recent edition of Virginia's Family Life Education guidelines for the middle school years the following examples of heteronormativity were found: the use of binaried gender (boys and girls); a focus on the nuclear family as a "basic unit" of society; a focus on marriage as the point when sexual behavior can commence; a focus on childrearing and the need for a mother and father for optimal development; and a focus on the negative experiences related to sexuality such as incestuous behavior, human trafficking, and sexual harassment. These foci of sexual education curricula all serve to rigidly regulate sexuality with an absolute favoring of heterosexuality. Consider the messaging this sends to students who do not identify as heterosexual or who live in non-nuclear-family homes. The resulting message only serves to invalidate and pathologize their experiences.

Case Narrative

James is a 13-year-old middle school student who identifies as a boy, multiracial (Black, Korean, and white) and lives in a multigenerational home with his mother, maternal grandmother, and 17-year-old brother. His father lives in the same city, and they see each other on a regular basis. James attends a middle school of 700 students in his middle-class neighborhood located in a Midwestern city with a population of 200,000. James has a well-developed social network, as he's attended school with many of the same peers since kindergarten. He enjoys reading, cooking, and playing tennis. He has a strong academic record and often performs near the top of his class. His teachers consistently report that James displays positive interpersonal behaviors, and he has never been disciplined at school.

Recently, some students in the school have started calling James gay. Some of his close friends also think he is gay because of his gender expression and mannerisms. He feels confused and pressured to clarify his sexual orientation. He thinks he might be bisexual or queer, but people keep telling him that he is gay and pressuring him to "choose" his identity. As a result, James approaches Dr. Ford, the school psychologist, to ask if he can make an appointment to discuss some personal issues. James felt comfortable approaching Dr. Ford because during one of their previous meetings, which was about testing for the gifted and talented program, James saw a small rainbow flag on Dr. Ford's desk. During their meeting, James shows Dr. Ford a book he checked out from the public library in his neighborhood. The book, titled That's So Gay, *is about bullying in schools, and James uses the book as means to start their conversation about his sexuality and the experiences with his peers. During their conversation, James conveys that his experiences at the school have mostly been positive up to recently. In addition to his peers calling him gay, James also told Dr. Ford about his experiences in sex ed class. James conveyed that the teacher made some statements that made him feel uneasy. For example, there is an emphasis in class on abstaining from sex until marriage, an assertion that marriage and starting a family is a primary life goal, and that heterosexual sex is the only kind of sex that is natural. Dr. Ford conveys empathy to James and informs James that the curriculum is set by the state's department of education and cannot be altered. They have a conversation about James' sexuality, and Dr. Ford emphasizes that James doesn't have to make a decision regarding his sexual orientation at this time. They discuss ways that James can negotiate these conversations with his peers, and they make an appointment to meet in two weeks. When James returns back to class with the book, his teacher notices the book, confiscates it, tells James the book is inappropriate for school, and sends James to the vice principal's office to discuss the "inappropriate behavior." James is on the brink of tears, as he's never been disciplined at school, and he is confused to hear that the book is inappropriate given that he has just met with Dr. Ford, who actually praised James for learning more about bullying.*

Experiential Activities

The following experiential activities can be used to unpack the case narrative utilizing Queer Theory's fundamentals.

Reveal Heteronormativity's Impact on the Student and School Climate

- The concept of heteronormativity will likely be new for your students. Given the normalcy of heterosexuality and how pervasive it is throughout the school system, embedded in structures and policies, and apparent in interpersonal interactions, these discussions must be deliberate. A focus on the prevalence of heteronormativity can be used to help the student make sense of experiences with bullying, microaggressions (i.e., interpersonal and environmental forms of subtle, covert bias), and macroaggressions (i.e., the aggressions that result from heterosexist structures, policies, rules, and curricula). If school staff engage in behaviors that perpetuate gender norms and heteronormativity and pathologize and harm the student, the counselor may advocate for the student by challenging these ideas. Conjoint consultation with counseling may be necessary.
- What are the implicit and explicit messages embedded in sexuality education? What are the discourses regarding sexuality and gender in the school? What rules and policies enforce gender and sexuality norms? Does the school have student organizations or support groups for LGBTQ students? What types of literature are available to students regarding sexuality and gender?
- You can promote self-advocacy by helping the student learn about and access resources in the school and community that will support the student as they negotiate an invalidating environment. If the student needs specific help speaking with peers, teachers, or family about these issues in order to self-advocate or to deal with microaggressions, role-playing may be used to practice various approaches.

Take a Genealogical Approach to Understanding School-Based Issues

- One way of increasing awareness regarding issues that negatively impact the academic and personal development of LGBTQ identified students is to understand how school structures, policies, rules, and curricula came to be.

For example, when interrogating the heteronormative nature of sexuality education, it can be helpful to understand what purpose the curriculum serves and how the curriculum came to exist. This can help unearth the original intentions that may serve to control how young people develop their understandings of sexuality and gender or may be based in religious doctrine. Knowledge of this history can be helpful in developing advocacy efforts geared toward changing the curriculum. Discussions of this history can also be included in counseling sessions to provide students with information they can use to resist the heteronormative messaging that is often included in sexuality education.

Deconstruct Finite Categorization and Resist Essentialism

- In addition to helping the student deconstruct finite categorizations often attributed to gender (boy or girl) and sexuality (gay or straight), there often exists a similar binaried categorization in relation to roles in schools, such as that of teacher or student, school psychologist or student, etc. These binaried categorizations create rigid roles that include elements of power and control. This can translate into the quality of how referrals to the school psychologist are made, with the adult (school personnel) deciding the reason for the referral and controlling the process of counseling/service provision, while the student is a passive participant. Addressing this role binary can allow the student to lead the process, since they are the expert in their experiences.
- Let the student define the concerns addressed in counseling, and allow them to lead the direction of the discussion during the sessions. The counselor should engage in active listening and make reflective paraphrases that capture the student's point of view, concerns, and experiences. The counselor should demonstrate a nonjudgmental stance and unconditional positive regard toward the student.
- The overreliance on finite and binaried categories for gender and sexuality, as well as school-based roles, only serves to essentialize these identity and role categories. One way to address essentialism is to have critical conversations about the supposed "nature" of gender and sexuality. How do we know gender is a natural state of being? How do we know what it means to be of a certain gender, such as a girl or a boy? How come there is pressure to identify and remain faithful to a specific sexuality? In processing the case of James, these types of questions can help James develop more comfort with not knowing how to specifically identify his sexual orientation.

Emphasize How Realities Are Socially Constructed (and Often Constricted)

- The social pressures that result from heteronormativity can create constrictions in how young people understand and actualize their gender and sexuality. This is likely a pressure that is creating some of the confusion that James is experiencing regarding his sexuality. He's being told that he has to be gay, when he feels his sexuality is something other than gay or straight. Providing James with information about how identities are socially constructed might help relieve some of the pressure to identify with a specific, static identity.

- Utilize a storytelling technique where the student is presented with a story about a child or adolescent facing a struggle related to rigid gender and sexuality norms (such as the case narrative of James). The student is encouraged to explore the character's experience, identify and challenge untrue rules that cause the character harm, and help the character problem-solve in developmentally appropriate ways. This allows the student to explore the issues with some distance, which might feel safer for a student who is at the beginning stages of understanding gender and sexuality dynamics.

Conclusion

LGBTQ students are likely to experience a range of threats during their schooling experiences that emanate from the pervasiveness of heteronormativity embedded throughout the structures and processes of education. These threats present themselves via the curricular policies that serve to limit and control gender and sexuality development, as well as experiences with bullying and microaggressions. These experiences can inhibit and constrict their ability to actualize their fullest academic potentials. We offer Queer Theory as an antidote to the ills of heteronormativity and the resulting harms on LGBTQ students. Applying fundamentals of Queer Theory to counseling can assist young people in developing a greater awareness of the impact of heteronormativity on their lived experiences, as well as in deconstructing and resisting the essentialized and limiting categories and discourses regarding gender and sexuality that can be a source of much of the tension experienced by LGBTQ youth. While we work to support LGBTQ youth in coping with the experiences of learning and living in heteronormative school contexts, we can also use Queer Theory as a guide to direct our advocacy efforts in schools to help break down heteronormative structures and policies in order to build a schooling environment that is affirming and validating of LGBTQ youth. Our LGBTQ youth need and deserve better.

References

Batchelor, K. E., Ramos, M., & Neiswander, S. (2018). Opening doors: Teaching LGBTQ-themed young adult literature for an inclusive curriculum. *The Clearing House: A Journal of Educational Strategies, Issues and Ideas*, *91*(1), 29–36. https://doi.org/10.1080/00098655.2017.1366183

Centers for Disease Control and Prevention (CDC). (2020). *Youth risk behavior survey (YRBS)*. Retrieved from https://www.cdc.gov/healthyyouth/data/yrbs/2019_tables/students_by_sexual_identity.htm

Commonwealth of Virginia Department of Education. (2020). *Family life education board of education guidelines and standards of learning for Virginia public schools.* Retrieved April 1, 2021, from www.doe.virginia.gov/testing/sol/standards_docs/family_life/index.shtml

Dinkins, E. G., & Englert, P. (2015). LGBTQ literature in middle school classrooms: Possibilities for challenging heteronormative environments. *Sex Education, 15*(4), 392–405. https://doi.org/10.1080/14681811.2015.1030012

Gay, Lesbian, & Straight Network. (2014). *Key concepts and terms.* www.glsen.org/sites/default/files/2020-04/GLSEN%20Terms%20and%20Concepts%20Thematic.pdf

Graybill, E., & Proctor, S. L. (2016). Lesbian, gay, bisexual, and transgender youth: Limited representation in school support personnel journals. *Journal of School Psychology, 54,* 9–16. https://doi.org/10.1016/j.jsp.2015.11.001

Green, A. E., Price-Feeney, M., & Dorison, S. H. (2019). *National estimate of LGBTQ youth seriously considering suicide.* The Trevor Project.

Herman, J. L., Flores, A. R., Brown, T. N. T., Wilson, B. D. M., & Conron, K. J. (2017). *Age of individuals who identify as transgender in the United States.* The Williams Institute.

Holmes, S. E., & Cahill, S. (2004). School experiences of gay, lesbian, bisexual, and transgender youth. *Journal of Gay and Lesbian Issues in Education, 1*(3), 53–66. https://doi.org/10.1300/J367v01n03_06

Johns, M. M., Lowry, R., Andrzejewski, J., Barrios, L. C., Zewditu, D., McManus, T., Rasberry, C. N., Robin, L., & Underwood, J. M. (2019). Transgender identity and experiences of violence victimization, substance use, suicide risk, and sexual risk behaviors among high school students—19 states and large urban school districts, 2017. *Morbidity and Mortality Weekly Report, 68*(3), 65–71. https://doi.org/10.15585/mmwr.mm6803a3

Kosciw, J. G., Clark, C. M., Truong, T. L., & Zongrone, A. D. (2020). *The 2020 national school climate survey: The experiences of lesbian, gay, bisexual, transgender, and queer youth in our nation's schools.* GLSEN. www.glsen.org/research/2019-national-school-climate-survey

Mayo, C. (2004). *Disputing the Subject of Sex: Sexuality and public school controversies.* Rowman & Littlefield Publishers.

McNeill, T. (2013). Sex education and the promotion of heteronormativity. *Sexualities, 16*(7), 826–846. https://doi.org/10.1177/1363460713497216

Meyers, W., Turanovic, J. J., Lloyd, K. M., & Pratt, T. C. (2020). The victimization of LGBTQ students at school: A meta-analysis. *Journal of School Violence, 19*(4), 421–432. https://doi.org/10.1080/15388220.2020.1725530

Payne, E., & Smith, M. (2013). LGBTQ kids, school safety, and missing the big picture: How the dominant bullying discourse prevents school professionals from thinking about systemic marginalization or . . . why we need to rethink GLBTQ bullying. *A Journal in LGBTQ Worldmaking, Fall 2013,* 1–36. https://doi.org/10.14321/qed.0001

Wozolek, B., Wootton, L., & Demlow, A. (2017). The school-to-coffin pipeline: Queer youth, suicide, and living the in-between. *Cultural Studies ↔ Critical Methodologies, 17*(5), 392–398. https://doi.org/10.1177/1532708616673659

10

INTERROGATING COGNITIVE ASSESSMENT USING A CRITICAL STUDY OF WHITENESS LENS

Tyler A. Womack, Jessica Mercado Anazagasty, Desireé Vega, and Austin H. Johnson

For at least the last 40 years, school psychologists have reported spending more than 50% of their professional time engaged in assessment in service of the special education process (Benson et al., 2019), with cognitive tests being commonly employed in order to evaluate students for specific learning disabilities (SLD), intellectual disabilities (ID), and giftedness (Kranzler et al., 2016). Although some have considered the data derived from intelligence testing to assist in the special education identification process and aid intervention design, such data have served as a means to label and segregate students (Wasserman, 2018). When viewed through the lens of Critical Study of Whiteness (CSW), intelligence testing is visible as a tool through which white supremacy is enshrined, reproduced, and enforced.

The history of cognitive assessment has long been entrenched in white supremacy; indeed, from its origins, intelligence testing has deliberately excluded children of color in normative samples in favor of white middle-class children (Valencia & Suzuki, 2001). Intelligence testing remains the core feature of assessment for SLD in many schools and districts through an IQ-achievement discrepancy model or one of the many methods used in cognitive profile analysis (Maki et al., 2015). However, there is strong evidence to suggest that both of these IQ-dependent methods for identifying a student with SLD are without merit. This has understandably raised concerns about the misuse, or use altogether, of cognitive assessment as it continues to perpetuate racist myths regarding intelligence levels, those abilities' ties to genetics, and the subsequent judgment of students' innate capabilities to thrive in school. Cognitive assessment has contributed to the overrepresentation of minoritized children in special education and underrepresentation in gifted programs (based on IQ testing; Blanchett et al., 2009). Negative long-lasting effects tied to overrepresentation and underrepresentation include lowered teacher expectations and concordant biases, the limiting of

DOI: 10.4324/9780367815325-12

student opportunities, the application of prejudicial labels, and challenges toward succeeding in school (Brown et al., 2019). These effects reinforce and perpetuate assumptions about the nature of intelligence and a subsequent belief by some in the cognitive inferiority of minoritized students, which benefits (and indeed is necessary for) a white supremacist society.

In addition to highlighting the inherent whiteness in intelligence testing in this chapter, we use a critical perspective that acknowledges structural racism and its effects on students of color, specifically Black and emergent bilingual (EB) students, many of whom also identify as students of color; in 2014–2015, 78% of students classified as English learners (ELs) by the Department of Education were identified as Hispanic or Latino (U.S. Department of Education [USDOE], 2018). We offer an overview of the history of cognitive assessment with minoritized populations and its misuse for student educational placement, and we apply concepts rooted within CSW to assess the impact of white supremacy and racism on these "data"-based decisions.

In light of the racism entrenched in intelligence testing, research contradicting its use and appropriateness in supporting students, and evidence challenging the validity of popular IQ tests when used with students of color (e.g., Graves et al., 2020), we critically question the purpose of cognitive testing in educational systems, particularly when used with minoritized students. We argue that these tests should not only be used with caution but that their use is largely unnecessary for all students and especially for students of color.

Brief Introduction to the Critical Study of Whiteness

Like neighboring theories of Dis/Crit and that theory's foundational model of Critical Race Theory, CSW understands whiteness as a social construct with enduring powers and effects. Whiteness is not dependent upon a "real" property but rather a division of groups based on priorities for power and consequent exclusions. Whiteness is an ideology designed to perpetuate race relations through stratification and domination over people of color (Leonardo & Broderick, 2011). Sustaining these relationships of social domination requires institutionalism and ideological control, which means that whiteness is dependent on the preservation and immortalization of white myths and knowledge (Croizet, 2013). As such, discerning the effects of whiteness necessitates debunking elements of society that seem natural or "common sense," a term defined by Gramsci as an "uncritical and largely unconscious way of perceiving and understanding the world that has become 'common' in any given epoch" (Hoare & Nowell-Smith, 2005, p. 322). Critically, CSW calls for a careful examination of how common sense promotes socially constructed beliefs about race and ability by normalizing unexamined historical ideals, philosophical opinions, and scientific notions (Leonardo & Broderick, 2011).

Within education, systemic inequity is perpetuated by 'common sense' beliefs about intelligence, which shape normative practices of creating intellectual hierarchies based on race (Mendoza et al., 2016). Given that whiteness is dependent on stratification, an 'intelligent' person in a white supremacist society will not exist without someone who is subsequently made intellectually inferior. Those who are labeled 'intelligent' are taught that they are entitled to more social and material wealth compared to their 'intellectually inferior' peers. This ideology is deeply entrenched in schooling systems when cognitive assessments are used to measure the intelligence of children and justify educational segregation. Intelligence testing carries important ideological functions within education systems, as it can control students' social mobility as well as which groups have access to quality education (Croizet, 2013).

Intelligence tests have been used to promote ideologies of *scientific racism* and *eugenics*, in which the intellectual inferiority of whole racial-ethnic populations has been asserted through the naming and assignment of fixed genetic factors. These concepts continue to permeate education through what Gillborn (2016) labeled a "*softly, softly*" approach, in which intelligence categories are prevalent but carefully constructed to avoid explicit references to race (p. 366). Education thereby takes a 'color-blind' approach in which tools that were historically employed as a scientific basis for Black intellectual inferiority and segregation continue to be used to limit educational opportunities for Black children and other vulnerable populations without explicitly acknowledging ties to racism (Gillborn, 2016). These practices are subsequently reflected in the low representation of students of color in 'gifted' placements and the overrepresentation of students of color in special education (Mendoza et al., 2016).

Within education and school psychology, there are misconceptions, perceptions, and beliefs on the usefulness of cognitive testing and the factors that contribute to testing bias. Critiques surrounding cognitive assessment emphasize that such tests: (a) unfairly divide examinees by race, culture, language, gender, income, and educational level, (b) lack acknowledgment of creativity and practical knowledge, and (c) perpetuate misconceptions of intelligence as a predictor of success and achievement (Ford et al., 2016). It is difficult to eliminate cultural and learning experiences from IQ tests as these aspects are embedded in content, the phrasing of questions, directions, and scoring criteria (Ford et al., 2016). As argued by Blanchett et al. (2009), students of color typically present deficiencies in cognitive tests not because they are incapable of success but rather because these tests are a reflection of cultural, social, and linguistic knowledge that is bound within whiteness.

IQ Testing With Students of Color and Emergent Bilingual Students

Historical Context of IQ Testing

The use of intelligence tests with historically minoritized populations remains polemical due to both its fraught history as well as its contemporary use in perpetuating injustices such as the disproportionate placement of minoritized students in special education (Graves & Aston, 2016; Sullivan & Proctor, 2016). In 1904, the French government sought the expertise of Alfred Binet, known as the founding father of the psychometrics movement, in the development of intelligence tests because they wanted to use these tests to determine the best way to educate students (Bennett, 1970). More specifically, they hoped that these tests would be used to identify which students would experience difficulty learning in schools following the implementation of a compulsory attendance law (Graves & Aston, 2016). An important and neglected point made by Binet was that the test could not measure innate characteristics of a person (White & Hall, 1980); nonetheless, his tests would be later used to justify the eugenics movement and supposed inherent intellectual differences between racial groups (Graves & Aston, 2016). In the U.S., Lewis Terman adapted Binet's instrument into the Stanford-Binet Intelligence Scale in 1916, further contributing to scientific racism by facilitating the rationalization of intellectual differences between white and non-white people (Graves & Aston, 2016). For decades, the normative sample of the Stanford-Binet scale did not include children of color (Terman & Merrill, 1973); nevertheless, and predictably within a frame of the perpetuation of white supremacy, the test was used to exclude kids of color from educational opportunities.

During World War I, the military used group intelligence testing with the Army Alpha and Beta tests to determine one's suitability for military service (White & Hall, 1980; Guthrie, 2004). Despite validity issues and the use of these tests to prevent Black men from serving in non-manual-labor positions, the tests were also used to screen immigrants at Ellis Island for intellectual disabilities (or "mental defects"), which contributed to inaccurate generalizations about racial differences in intelligence (Graves & Aston, 2016; Guthrie, 2004).

The importance of intelligence testing to the historical foundation of psychology in part explains why major psychological organizations consistently defend its utility and importance (Croizet, 2013). In 1968, the Association of Black Psychologists presented a moratorium on intelligence testing to the American Psychological Association (APA; Williams, 1974). Their six-point statement argued that parents are fully within their rights to refuse intelligence testing due to their use in order to: "(1) Label [B]lack children as uneducable; (2) Place [B]lack children in special classes; (3) Potentiate inferior education; (4) Assign [B]lack children to lower educational tracks than whites; (5) Deny [B]lack children higher educational opportunities; and (6) Destroy positive intellectual growth and development of [B]lack children" (Williams, 1974, p. 17). The APA dismissed the moratorium by countering with a statement that intelligence tests were psychometrically fair and valid and that intellectual deficits amongst Black children could not be ignored (Croizet, 2013). Eight years later, the *Clinical Psychology Division* within APA asked for warning labels to be placed on IQ tests explaining that the use of the test on populations not included in norming samples (typically ethnically/racially minoritized children) may be harmful to that population. However, this resolution was postponed indefinitely by the APA's Evaluation and Measurement Division (Croizet, 2013).

Relevance of Critical Study of Whiteness to IQ Testing With Students of Color and Emergent Bilingual Students

As viewed through the lens of CSW, the APA's continued resistance to critiques of intelligence testing reflects a defense of whiteness ideologies of intelligence grounded in deficit-driven concepts of ability and dis/ability. These concepts are effectively used as a weapon against students of color to enforce stratification based on supposed scientific merit (Leonardo & Broderick, 2011) and are reflected in issues such as underrepresentation in gifted education (USDOE Office for Civil Rights, 2016) and the disproportionality in special education (Artiles et al., 2010; Sullivan & Proctor, 2016). These outcomes have anchors in the use of IQ tests in American education as well as actions by judicial and legislative systems in understanding and regulating their use.

Contemporary Issues in IQ Testing—Use and Interpretation

In an educational context, IQ tests are chiefly used for the identification of three special education eligibility categories: SLD, ID, and giftedness. For each of these categories, the validity of decisions made based upon the scores derived from intelligence tests is questionable, not only for students of color but also the educational community writ large. Of the three central models for determining eligibility for special education services under SLD, two are dependent upon IQ scores: the ability-achievement discrepancy model and those methods that exist under the larger umbrella of cognitive profile analysis (with the third non-IQ-based model being response to intervention; Maki et al., 2015; McGill et al., 2018). Put simply, the ability-achievement discrepancy model is unsupported in the literature and has been known to be for over 20 years (e.g., Dombrowski et al., 2004). The reasons for this have been widely described in the literature and include a lack of validity toward identifying students with academic difficulties (Stuebing et al., 2002) and the codification of a "wait to fail" model, which requires substantial academic difficulty before identification can occur. Cognitive profile analysis is fraught with its own controversies, and compelling evidence exists to suggest that there's little to be gained from its use (McGill et al., 2018).

While there are global criticisms to be leveled against cognitive assessment's role in SLD, the disproportionate representation of certain groups in this eligibility category provides further fuel for critical examination. In Fall 2018, students who were identified as American Indian or Alaskan Native were 1.9 times as likely to be labeled as SLD compared to all other racial/ethnic groups combined; Black students were 1.5 times as likely, and Hispanic/Latino students were 1.4 times as likely. Emergent bilingual (EB) students are also overrepresented in the

SLD eligibility category, particularly once they reach secondary school (Clark-Gareca et al., 2020). Garcia (2015) argued for the elimination of the use of cognitive tests with EB students as these tests are culturally and linguistically biased against EB students and do not accurately reflect their abilities. Furthermore, the technical properties of scores derived from a popular cognitive assessment may not be consistent when applied to Black students (Graves et al., 2020).

While SLD does not necessarily "require" the results of a cognitive assessment in federal law, the two other labels that drive the use of IQ testing in schools do. ID is defined in federal special education law as "significantly subaverage general intellectual functioning" alongside adaptive deficits, essentially guaranteeing the use of an IQ test in its evaluation procedures (Individuals with Disabilities Education Act 34 C.F.R. § 300.8(c)(6)). Similarly, 90% of states use "intelligence" as a domain in their definition of giftedness, and 16 states mandate the use of an IQ test when assessing for giftedness (McClain & Pfeiffer, 2012). As a result of pronounced historical issues with cognitive assessments, minoritized students—particularly Black, Indigenous, Latinx, and EB learners—are far more likely to qualify for special education under ID. In Fall 2018, Black students were 2.2 times more likely to be identified as ID compared to all other racial/ethnic groups combined in this disability category. Native Hawaiian or Other Pacific Islander students were 1.8 times as likely to be labeled as ID, and American Indian or Alaskan Native students were 1.6 times as likely (USDOE, 2021). Although this may be unsurprising given the considerable evidence suggesting racial bias (and particularly anti-Black bias) in cognitive assessments, it becomes even more alarming due to Black students' concordant placement in more restrictive settings (Graves & Ye, 2017; Skiba et al., 2006), as well as the increased risk for dropout and push into the school-to-prison pipeline for Black students (Annamma et al., 2014; Artiles et al., 2010).

Regarding gifted placements, the total percentage of students in gifted programs in the U.S. is 6.7%; however, when disaggregating these data by race and ethnicity, disparities are evident: 13.3% of Asian, 7.7% of white, 5.3% of American Indian/Alaska Native, 4.9% of Latinx, and 4.3% of African American students are placed in gifted programs (National Center for Education Statistics, 2018). Given the prominent role played by IQ testing in gifted assessment, often identified by meeting an IQ cut-off score (e.g., 130 or above), as well as the lack of national consensus on how to identify giftedness (McClain & Pfeiffer, 2012), the cultural and linguistic bias within cognitive instruments (Ford et al., 2008) is strongly positioned to contribute to the disproportionate exclusion of Black, American Indian/Alaskan Native, EB, and Latinx students from gifted programming.

Contemporary Issues in IQ Testing—Judicial and Legislative

These differences in placement by race/ethnicity foreground evidence suggesting the subjective and biased nature of intelligence tests and special education-related decisions as well as the resulting harm on Black students due to lost educational opportunities. Concerning evidence regarding flaws in the interpretation and use of IQ tests has led to civil rights issues regarding the appropriateness and utility of such tests; in 1970, *Diana v. California State Board of Education* foregrounded such problems with Spanish-speaking Latinx populations. In this case, the use of English cognitive instruments with Spanish-speaking Mexican American students had led to their identification as 'educable mentally retarded' or intellectually disabled and to their subsequent placement in restrictive settings. Because of (a) a cultural bias in these tests, which were not designed for use with non-white populations, and (b) many students' inability to understand the test items due to English language proficiency, the court ruled that students must be assessed in their primary language or using a nonverbal cognitive test. This ruling informed later provisions in IDEA (2004; Section 300.304.c) and California state law (Cal. Ed. Code Sec. 56320), perhaps most notably in the case of *Larry P. v. Riles* (1979), which emerged as a function of the placement of Black students in restrictive classes designed for students with ID. The court in *Larry P. v. Riles* (1979) ruled that IQ tests were in fact racially and culturally biased, emphasizing the history of the use of IQ tests to segregate students and the assumption present within such applications of IQ tests that Black children are more likely to be intellectually disabled. The California State Department of Education (SDE) and the plaintiffs reached a settlement in 1986 in which the court ordered the SDE to notify all school districts of a prohibition on the administration of IQ tests with Black students (Dent et al., 1987). To this day, IQ tests cannot be used with Black children in California.

Should We Continue Using IQ Tests?

Given the historical roots of IQ testing in eugenics, racism, and white supremacy, as well as evidence that its current use continues to negatively impact the educational opportunities of students of color, a question arises as to whether these tests should be continued to be used at all in placement decisions. Although California is the only state to legally ban the use of IQ tests with Black children, there is debate as to whether this ruling should extend to other states and other minoritized groups (Aston & Brown, 2020). For instance, although *Diana v. State Board of Education* mandated testing in a student's native language, Garcia (2015) argued that this mandate does not adequately address the cultural elements required to perform well on these tests that EB students may not be exposed to. As such, Garcia (2015) called for a similar ban to be applied to EB students given their substantial risk of being misidentified for special education placement.

When examining this issue from a CSW perspective, it can be argued that IQ tests are a socially evolved, cultural tool that reflects institutionalized rules for social stratification and control (Richardson, 2002). Specifically, IQ tests are a cultural tool designed to test a very particular set of skills based on a definition of intelligence that benefits whiteness. Often, IQ tests contain items that narrowly rely on a student's exposure to certain experiences or deliberate teachings at school that are more likely to occur in white, middle-class families than those of working-class or minoritized families (Martinez, 2014). This issue is especially relevant on IQ measures that emphasize culturally specific forms of language and semantic subtleties that may disadvantage non-English speakers and minoritized student populations (e.g., verbal comprehension, word problem solving). These particular patterns of language are more likely to occur in white middle-class homes, which can better prepare children for IQ testing simply because of their cultural background (Martinez, 2014). In addition to issues with language on IQ tests, the skills needed to solve problems on 'non-verbal items' also rely on culturally dominant and white structures of thought. Often non-verbal items involve the manipulation of symbols and the employment of problem-solving skills already commonly used and communicated within white middle-class homes (Richardson, 2002). As such, it may not be possible for IQ tests to be a non-biased measure given that these measures are inherently bound by cultural and societal norms (Cole, 1992). Richardson (2002) went so far as to argue that IQ tests are not a measure of intelligence, but rather a measure of cultural background, social class, and opportunity to learn that ultimately benefits the hierarchical positioning of the white middle class (Richardson, 2002).

The detrimental effects of IQ testing on students of color warrant a serious decision for the field of school psychology: whether to continue to facilitate and employ the use of cognitive testing in educational settings, or whether to advocate for its abandonment altogether. A shift away from IQ testing would also require a departure from dominant, 'common sense' understandings of intelligence, race, ability, and the structure of schools. Current understandings of intelligence are embedded in a whiteness ideology of stratification and hierarchical divisions of labor that benefit those deemed 'intelligent.' Schools reflect this stratification in their placement of students in gifted and special education programming on the basis of those who meet a certain cut-off score measured by intelligence tests. This stratification within schools ultimately serves to benefit white children, while limiting educational opportunities for students of color. As such, not only must we consider removing the tool that enables this stratification, but we must also reconsider the ways in which schools are currently structured.

One of school psychology's central missions is to support students with dis/abilities who will benefit from specialized instruction and programming. However, being considered for and then receiving these types of specialized programming should not result in worse outcomes for children, and it is fundamentally unclear whether cognitive testing can meaningfully contribute to our collective mission toward supporting the academic, behavioral, and social/emotional success of all students. Evidence suggests that Black students who are placed in special education are exposed to poor instruction, lower teacher expectations, and inequitable opportunities to learn (Harry & Klingner, 2014). Improving special education programming and services requires a shift in the way education settings are structured to explicitly center social justice and equity for minoritized students. Such a focus will allow schools to realize their vision of being inclusive and supportive of the long-term outcomes of all students.

Case Narratives

To facilitate conversation on the use of cognitive assessment in school psychology and its relationship to systemic racism, we provide two case narratives: Donovan's evaluation for ID and Sergio's evaluation for SLD. Donovan's case narrative is based on research conducted by Sullivan et al. (2019), in which the authors assessed, in part, whether school psychologists could make accurate eligibility decisions of ID and whether racial bias was present in such determinations. Sergio's case narrative is rooted within an article by Clark-Gareca et al. (2020), which explored the long-term designation and diagnosis of bilingual learners.

Donovan's Case Narrative: Intellectual Disability

Donovan is a 6-year-old Black student who enrolled in elementary school with no prior history of schooling. He attends a school in a low-income and economically marginalized community with poor staff retention and generally poor academic outcomes. His kindergarten class is taught by a white teacher, Ms. Green, who is in her second year of teaching. A few months into the school year, Ms. Green has become increasingly concerned that Donovan has difficulty maintaining attention in her class; she notes that he is struggling across academic areas, including his writing and beginning reading performance. She also notices he has some fine-motor difficulties, particularly the way he grips his pencil and opens containers. Ms. Green makes a referral for a special education evaluation for Donovan. As a part of his initial evaluation, the school psychologist administers the WISC-V and obtains an IQ score of 68 for Donovan. His scores on the WJ IV Tests of Achievement are inconsistent, with him scoring within the average range on some of the subtests and in the below-average range on others. In order to assess for adaptive functioning, the school psychologist interviews Donovan's mother using the Vineland-3 Comprehensive Interview form. Donovan obtains an overall score of 83, which is just above one standard deviation below the mean of 100; the 95% confidence interval for this score ranges from 80 to 86. Based on the school psychologist's interview, it appears that Donovan met all of his developmental milestones but still has some trouble using the toilet by himself and sometimes wears training underwear in case of accidents. Ms. Green says that some of Donovan's strengths are that he is sociable and likes making friends, which is borne out within the Vineland with above-average scores for the Socialization domain and all associated subdomains. During the eligibility meeting, Ms. Green notes that Donovan's behavior and academic performance continue to worsen, and she repeats her belief that Donovan should receive special education services. The special education team agrees that, in light of Donovan's low IQ score, his trouble with toileting, and his difficulties in class, he can qualify for special education services under ID. Donovan's mother is unfamiliar with special education processes, does not say much during the meeting, and consents to the IEP. The team agrees to move Donovan to a special day class.

Sergio's Case Narrative: Specific Learning Disability

Sergio is an 8-year-old Latinx elementary school student who attends an economically marginalized elementary school with predominantly white monolingual staff. His parents completed a home language survey upon enrollment and indicated that Spanish was the primary language spoken at home. Sergio was then evaluated and identified as an English language learner/emergent bilingual student who qualified to receive English as a Second Language services. Although he has good conversational skills in English, he was placed in small-group Tier 2 intervention due to teacher concerns about his academic ability compared to his monolingual English-speaking peers. However, there were no evidence-based interventions in place, and progress monitoring was inconsistent. Despite these factors, Sergio's teacher referred him to the Student Support Team for a special education evaluation. The school psychologist and the rest of the team are monolingual English speakers with little training on administering bilingual assessments. Since Sergio has strong oral English skills, the school psychologist administers assessments in English even though scores on his diagnostic English language proficiency test suggest he falls within the beginning stages of developing English skills in the areas of listening, reading, and writing. As part of the evaluation, the school psychologist sends Sergio's mother an interview form where she reports that he met all of his developmental milestones and can understand both Spanish and English. The school psychologist then administers the WISC-V to Sergio, resulting in an IQ score of 91. On the WJ IV Tests of Achievement, Sergio scores within the extremely low range (65–69 standard score) on basic reading skills, reading comprehension, and reading fluency. Sergio's scores demonstrate an IQ-achievement discrepancy, so the team agrees that he qualifies for services under SLD. Sergio's teacher advocates for identification under this eligibility category, stating that Sergio is far behind all of his peers and has not demonstrated improvement or capability of completing grade-level work due to his poor reading skills. The team generally ignores the possibility of Sergio's difficulties being attributable to his developing English language proficiency. Since the interview form was completed in English by Sergio's mom, the IEP team assumes an interpreter is not needed. At the IEP team meeting, although she understands English, Sergio's mom brought a friend for support and to help interpret any special education terms in Spanish. From what she understands, the eligibility would offer access to services, and she agrees to the determination.

Experiential Activities

When dissecting these case narratives, readers are encouraged to consider and discuss them within a CSW framework as structured in the following points.

Challenging White Myths and Knowledge. 'Common sense' notions abound within schools regarding intelligence and IQ tests. Counter-storytelling is one technique to expose and critique commonsense beliefs about intelligence that perpetuate racism. Based on this concept, consider the following: What are the purposes of IQ tests? What types of decisions are being made with IQ testing? Who is more likely to perform well on IQ tests, and who is not? Are there clear distinctions on performance based on race, class, gender, or language? In both case narratives, Donovan's and Sergio's mothers agreed to their children's eligibility for special education. What are ways in which systemic racism affects parents' ability to advocate for their children and make informed decisions? Consider power structures within IEP meetings; how would you advocate for the student when all other team members agree on eligibility?

Racial Contract. Racism in schools can be carried out in both conscious and unconscious ways. These methods serve to privilege white people and the subsequent othering of children and families of color. Based on this concept, review your school district's policy on IQ assessment procedures. Are there student identities more likely to be subjected to biased and unequal testing procedures based on dimensions of race, gender, class, language, and other identities? Are the assessments used within the school normed and validated with culturally and linguistically diverse students? Are assessments being used at appropriate times? Are there other methods that may better capture the needs of students and are culturally aligned with their family's values? How do we assess the appropriateness of the test being used to evaluate students of color? How do the use of IQ tests and beliefs on intelligence influence student access to quality intervention?

Whiteness as Property. Within schools, tracking, gifted programs, and special education placements are a myriad of ways in which schools continue to be segregated. As such, whiteness as property is seen in schools through the numerous ways in which the rights to possess, use, enjoy, and benefit from schooling have been exclusive to whites (Ladson-Billings & Tate, 1995).

Based on this concept, consider the following: Are there placement patterns for students in your school/district in special education, gifted, and other programs dependent on IQ tests? Are the selection and eligibility for these programs based on empirically validated selection criteria? Are IQ tests being used with methodologies that have been discredited? Are there quality general education programming and evidence-based interventions in place to adequately meet the needs of students? Other than the use of biased IQ tests, the assessment process and assessor can be influenced by considerations exclusive to white students. What non-discriminatory practices should be in place when evaluating these students?

Challenging the Belief of Post-Racism. Civil rights gains within communities of color should be examined through a critical eye, as opportunities for communities of color often converge with the self-interest of white people. For example, earlier the chapter mentioned the civil rights case of *Larry P. v. Riles* (1979), which was intended to combat racism in IQ tests, yet the gains of this law have not impacted issues in special education placement for Black children. Based on this concept consider the following: How have placement decisions regarding ID, SLD, and gifted programs been defined in your state and district? Would you expect these policies and practices to continue patterns of excluding students of color in gifted placements and continue overrepresentation in ID and SLD?

Color Evasiveness. The notion of color blindness has permeated contemporary debates on IQ testing, which justifies ignoring the racism inherent in IQ tests that continue to be used as means to segregate children of color. Based on this concept, consider the following: What are the long-lasting consequences of gifted or special-education placement decisions based on IQ tests? Who is more likely to benefit from this type of decision-making?

Conclusion

The disproportionate placement of students of color in special education and underrepresentation in gifted placements has been an issue for over 50 years. Education has attempted to ameliorate the impact IQ testing has had on disproportionality with students of color by advocating for alternative methods of assessment and non-discriminatory cognitive assessment practices. Reauthorizations of IDEA have sought to safeguard minoritized students by mandating non-discriminatory assessment practices such as assessing a child in their native language, selecting and administering assessment instruments that are not racially or culturally biased, and utilizing instruments most likely to yield the most accurate information about a child's skill level (IDEA, 2004). Nonetheless, disproportionality persists, particularly as inequities are observed in more subjective special education dis/ability categories that often employ the use of IQ tests such as SLD and ID when compared to dis/abilities such as blindness and autism (Artiles et al., 2010). It is therefore worth considering whether the core issue is actually rooted in perpetuated systemic racism within education disproportionality rather than test bias alone. Given the history and continuous flaws of cognitive assessment as used in our education systems, we should look toward abolishing its use. It is important for educators and school psychologists to reevaluate their professional judgment, beliefs, and practices by adopting a critical approach to cognitive assessment. Awareness of the structural racism embedded in our education system and its effects on students of color is one step in the right direction. Thus, our most critical act as a field is to move toward assessment and practices that inform intervention that in turn will lead to positive and equitable outcomes for students of color.

References

Annamma, S., Morrison, D., & Jackson, D. (2014). Disproportionality fills in the gaps: Connections between achievement, discipline and special education in the school-to-prison pipeline. *Berkeley Review of Education, 5*(1), 53–87.

Artiles, A. J., Kozleski, E. B., Trent, S. C., Osher, D., & Ortiz, A. (2010). Justifying and explaining disproportionality, 1968–2008: A critique of underlying views of culture. *Exceptional Children, 76*(3), 279–299. https://doi.org/10.1177/001440291007600303

Aston, C., & Brown, D. L. (2020). Progress or setback: Revisiting the current state of assessment practices of Black children. *Contemporary School Psychology*. https://doi.org/10.1007/s40688-020-00308-7

Bennett, V. D. (1970). Who is a school psychologist? (and what does he do?). *Journal of School Psychology*, *8*(3), 166–171.

Benson, N. F., Floyd, R. G., Kranzler, J. H., Eckert, T. L., Fefer, S. A., & Morgan, G. B. (2019). Test use and assessment practices of school psychologists in the United States: Findings from the 2017 National Survey. *Journal of School Psychology*, *72*, 29–48. https://doi.org/10.1016/j.jsp.2018.12.004

Blanchett, W. J., Klingner, J. K., & Harry, B. (2009). The intersection of race, culture, language, and disability: Implications for urban education. *Urban Education*, *44*(4), 389–409. https://doi.org/10.1177/0042085909338686

Brown, M. R., Dennis, J. P., & Matute-Chavarria, M. (2019). Cultural relevance in special education: Current status and future directions. *Intervention in School and Clinic*, *54*(5), 304–310. http://doi.org/10.1177/1053451218819252

Clark-Gareca, B., Short, D., Lukes, M., & Sharp-Ross, M. (2020). Long-term English learners: Current research, policy, and practice. *TESOL Journal*, *11*(1), 1–15. https://doi.org/10.1002/tesj.452

Cole, M. (1992). Cognitive development and formal schooling: The evidence from cross-cultural studies. In L. C. Moll (Ed.), *Vygotsky and education: Instructional implications and applications of sociohistorical psychology* (pp. 89–110). Cambridge University Press.

Croizet, J. C. (2013). On the fatal attractiveness of psychology: Racism of intelligence in education. In P. Smeyers & M. Depaepe (Eds.), *Educational research: The attraction of psychology* (pp. 33–51). Springer. https://doi.org/10.1007/978-94-007-5038-8_3

Dent, H. E., Mendocal, A., & Pierce, W. (1987). Court bans use of IQ tests for Blacks for any purpose in California state schools. *The Negro Educational Review*, *38*(2), 190–199.

Diana v. State Board of Education (1970) CA 70 RFT (USA).

Dombrowski, S. C., Kamphaus, R. W., & Reynolds, C. R. (2004). After the demise of the discrepancy: Proposed learning disabilities diagnostic criteria. *Professional Psychology: Research and Practice*, *35*(4), 364–372. https://doi.org/10.1037/0735-7028.35.4.364

Ford, D. Y., Grantham, T. C., & Whiting, G. W. (2008). Culturally and linguistically diverse students in gifted education: Recruitment and retention issues. *Exceptional Children*, *74*(3), 289–306. https://doi.org/10.1177/001440290807400302

Ford, D. Y., Wright, B. L., Washington, A., & Henfield, M. S. (2016). Access and equity denied: Key theories for school psychologists to consider when assessing Black and Hispanic students for gifted education. *School Psychology Forum*, *10*(3), 265–277.

Garcia, E. (2015). Lorenzo P. v. Riles? Should the "Larry P." prohibitions be extended to English language learners? Considering public policy & IQ testing in schools. *Multicultural Education*, *22*(2), 2–7.

Gillborn, D. (2016). Softly, softly: Genetics, intelligence and the hidden racism of the new geneism. *Journal of Education Policy*, *31*(4), 365–388. https://doi.org/10.1080/02680939.2016.1139189

Graves, S. L., Jr., & Aston, C. (2016). History of psychological assessment and intervention with minority populations. In S. L. Graves & J. J. Blake (Eds.), *Applying psychology in the schools book series. Psychoeducational assessment and intervention for ethnic minority children: Evidence-based approaches* (pp. 9–21). American Psychological Association. https://doi.org/10.1037/14855-002

Graves, S. L., Smith, L. V., & Nichols, K. D. (2020). Is the WISC-V a fair test for Black children? Factor structure in an urban public school sample. *Contemporary School*. https://doi.org/10.1007/s40688-020-00306-9

Graves, S. L., & Ye, F. F. (2017). Are special education labels accurate for Black children? Racial differences in academic trajectories of youth diagnosed with specific learning and intellectual disabilities. *Journal of Black Psychology*, *43*(2), 192–213. https://doi.org/10.1177/0095798416636280

Guthrie, R. V. (2004). *Even the rat was white: A historical view of psychology*. Pearson Education.

Harry, B., & Klingner, J. (2014). *Why are so many minority students in special education? Understanding race and disability in schools* (2nd ed.). Teachers College.

Hoare, Q., & Nowell-Smith, G. (2005). *Selections from prison notebooks*. Lawrence & Wishart.

Individuals with Disabilities Education Act of 2004, 20 U.S.C. § 1400 et seq.

Kranzler, J. H., Benson, N., & Floyd, R. G. (2016). Intellectual assessment of children and youth in the United States of America: Past, present, and future. *International Journal of School & Educational Psychology*, *4*(4), 276–282. https://doi.org/10.1080/21683603.2016.1166759

Ladson-Billings, G., & Tate, W. (1995). Toward a critical race theory of education. *Teachers College Record*, *97*(1), 47–68.

Larry P. v. Riles. (1979). 495 F. Supp. 926.

Leonardo, Z., & Broderick, A. A. (2011). Smartness as property: A critical exploration of intersections between Whiteness and Disability Studies. *Teachers College Record*, *113*(10), 2206–2232.

Maki, K. E., Floyd, R. G., & Roberson, T. (2015). State learning disability eligibility criteria: A comprehensive review. *School Psychology Quarterly*, *30*(4), 457. http://doi.org/10.1037/spq0000109

Martinez, M. E. (2014). *Education as the cultivation of intelligence*. Routledge.

McClain, M. C., & Pfeiffer, S. (2012). Identification of gifted students in the United States today: A look at state definitions, policies, and practices. *Journal of Applied School Psychology*, *28*(1), 59–88. http://doi.org/10.1080/15377903.2012.643757

McGill, R. J., Dombrowski, S. C., & Canivez, G. L. (2018). Cognitive profile analysis in school psychology: History, issues, and continued concerns. *Journal of School Psychology*, *71*, 108–121. https://doi.org/10.1016/j.jsp.2018.10.007

Mendoza, E., Paguyo, C., & Gutiérrez, K. (2016). Understanding the intersection of race and dis/ability. In D. J. Conner, B. A. Ferri, & S. A. Annamma (Eds.), *DisCrit: Disability studies and critical race theory in education* (pp. 71–86). Teachers College Press.

National Center for Education Statistics. (2018). *Digest of Statistics. Percentage of public school students enrolled in gifted and talented programs by sex, race/ethnicity, and state: Selected years, 2004 through 2013–14*. https://nces.ed.gov/programs/digest/d18/tables/dt18_204.90.asp

Richardson, K. (2002). What IQ tests test. *Theory & Psychology*, *12*(3), 283–314. https://doi.org/10.1177/0959354302012003012

Skiba, R. J., Poloni-Staudinger, L., Gallini, S., Simmons, A. B., & Feggins-Azziz, R. (2006). Disparate access: The disproportionality of African American students with disabilities across educational environments. *Exceptional Children*, *72*(4), 411–424. https://doi.org/10.1177%2F001440290607200402

Stuebing, K. K., Fletcher, J. M., LeDoux, J. M., Lyon, G. R., Shaywitz, S. E., & Shaywitz, B. A. (2002). Validity of IQ-discrepancy classifications of reading disabilities: A meta-analysis. *American Educational Research Journal*, *39*(2), 469–518. https://doi.org/10.3102%2F00028312039002469

Sullivan, A. L., & Proctor, S. L. (2016). The shield or the sword? Revisiting the debate on racial disproportionality in special education and implications for school psychologists. *School Psychology Forum*, *10*(3), 278–288.

Sullivan, A. L., Sadeh, S., & Houri, A. K. (2019). Are school psychologists' special education eligibility decisions reliable and unbiased? A multi-study experimental investigation. *Journal of School Psychology*, 77, 90–109. https://doi.org/10.1016/j.jsp.2019.10.006

Terman, L. M., & Merrill, M. A. (1973). *Stanford-Binet intelligence scale: 1972 norms edition*. Houghton Mifflin.

U. S. Department of Education. (2018). *Our nation's English learners: What are their characteristics?* https://www2.ed.gov/datastory/el-characteristics/

U. S. Department of Education. (2021). *42nd annual report to congress on the implementation of the individuals with disabilities education act, 2020*. https://sites.ed.gov/idea/files/42nd-arc-for-idea.pdf

U. S. Department of Education Office of Civil Rights. (2016). *2013–2014 civil rights data collection: A first look*. https://www2.ed.gov/about/offices/list/ocr/docs/2013-14-first-look.pdf

Valencia, R. R., & Suzuki, L. A. (2001). *Intelligence testing and minority students: Foundations, performance factors, and assessment issues. Racial and ethnic minority psychology series*. http://doi.org/10.4135/9781452231860

Wasserman, J. D. (2018). A history of intelligence assessment: The unfinished tapestry. In D. P. Flanagan & E. M. McDonough (Eds.), *Contemporary intellectual assessment: Theories, tests, and issues* (pp. 3–55). The Guilford Press.

White, M. B., & Hall, A. E. (1980). An overview of intelligence testing. *Educational Horizons*, *58*(4), 210–216.

Williams, R. (1974). A history of the Association of Black Psychologists: Early formation and development. *Journal of Black Psychology*, *1*(1), 9–24. https://doi.org/10.1177/009579847400100102

SECTION 3

Theory to Supervision

11

INFUSING INTERSECTIONALITY THEORY INTO MULTICULTURAL SUPERVISION PRACTICES

A Case Narrative Centering Latinx, LGBT-QIA+, and Undocumented Structural Identities

Meaghan Guiney and Sherrie L. Proctor

> *"There is no such thing as a single-issue struggle, because we do not live single-issue lives."*
>
> ~ *Audre Lorde*

Students who attend schools in the United States (U.S.) represent a diversity of culturally rich and beautiful backgrounds related to their race, ethnicity, socioeconomic status, language use, sexual orientation, gender, and other identity dimensions (Hussar et al., 2020). Given that an individual student has multiple, intersecting identities that interface with existing societal and educational structures, we should not view students through a singular lens (e.g., a sole focus on race or gender when supporting an Asian American transgender student). This is because, based on their intersecting identities, students can have a myriad of experiences ranging from liberating to oppressive, depending on the context and circumstances at play. For students who need school-based support from school psychologists and other school professionals, intersectionality is a useful theory in which to ground service delivery. As we describe in more detail later, intersectionality offers a lens for helping us see how, through no fault of their own, a student's structural intersecting identities compound risk for being discriminated against and oppressed within systems (Proctor, 2020).

One group of students who are marginalized—meaning they experience systematic disempowerment by denial of access to necessary resources, silencing of their voices, and prejudicial treatment—in U.S. schools are those who identify as lesbian, gay, bisexual, transgender, questioning, intersex, asexual, and gender non-conforming and non-binary (LGBT-QIA+) (Kosciw et al., 2020). Because

DOI: 10.4324/9780367815325-14

of homophobia and biphobia (i.e., bias and discrimination toward lesbian, gay, and bisexual people), transphobia (i.e., bias and discrimination toward transgender people), and heterosexism (i.e., discrimination or prejudice against lesbian, gay, and bisexual people on the assumption that heterosexuality is the normal sexual orientation), and other systems of oppression, these students are subjected to hostile environments both in and outside of schools. According to the 2019 National School Climate Survey conducted by the Gay Lesbian Straight Education Network (GLSEN), over 69% of LGBT-QIA+ students experienced verbal harassment based on sexual orientation, 69% based on gender expression, and 54% based on gender (Kosciw et al., 2020). Forty-five percent dealt with cyber-bullying via text messages or postings on social media. Furthermore, 26% were physically harassed based on their sexual orientation and 22% based on gender expression and gender. Eleven percent reported being physically assaulted at school based on sexual orientation, 9.5% based on gender expression, and 9.3% based on gender (Kosciw et al., 2020).

Sadly, 56% of LGBT-QIA+ students in the GLSEN study did not report their assault to school staff because they did not believe any effective intervention would take place, while 61% of those who did report to school staff said that nothing was done or they were told to ignore the assault (Kosciw et al., 2020). This may be a reason why LGBT-QIA+ students are more likely to avoid school compared to their non-LGBT-QIA+ peers, and they are also more likely to experience depression, have suicidal thoughts, attempt suicide, feel socially isolated, and use and abuse alcohol and other substances (Johns et al., 2019; Kosciw et al., 2020; Raifman et al., 2020). Research suggests that many of the negative mental health outcomes LGBT-QIA+ youth have are related to their experiences of victimization associated with school (Huebner et al., 2015).

LGBT-QIA+ students of color are subjected to discriminatory experiences based on race, sexual orientation, gender identity, or all of these simultaneously—highlighting the interplay of their intersectional identities with systems of oppression such as racism, heterosexism, and cisgenderism (i.e., systemic ideology that denies, denigrates, or pathologizes self-identified gender identities that do not align with assigned gender at birth as well as their behavior, expression, and community) (Kosciw et al., 2020). LGBT-QIA+ students of color across races reported experiencing victimization based on their race *and* LGBT-QIA+ identities, but Indigenous LGBT-QIA+ students were more likely than other racial groups to experience anti-LGBT-QIA+ victimization and discrimination (Kosciw et al., 2020). Across all racial groups, Black LGBT-QIA+ students were more likely to feel unsafe about their race (Kosciw et al., 2020). It is important to acknowledge that LGBT-QIA+ youth of color often have additional identities (e.g., English Learner, undocumented immigrant or refugee, low-income, etc.) that are marginalized in schools.

Fortunately, support (i.e., how respected, recognized, and cared about youth feel by parents, peers, and school staff as well as the extent to which youth feel these people are there when needed) and accepting school climates moderate negative outcomes for LGBT-QIA+ youth, including those with multiply marginalized identities (Eisenberg et al., 2020). For instance, research documents that there are beneficial outcomes associated with the establishment of Gay Straight Alliance (GSA) clubs in schools. More specifically, LGBT-QIA+ youth who attend schools with GSAs report less substance use, fewer depressive symptoms, lower suicidal ideation, and less general psychological distress than their LGBT-QIA+ counterparts in schools without GSAs (Hackimer & Proctor, 2015). Furthermore, LGBT-QIA+ youth report higher academic achievement, more postsecondary educational aspirations, and lower school dropout rates compared with peers in schools that lack a GSA (Hackimer & Proctor, 2015). Still, without using Intersectionality Theory as a practice lens, school professionals might overlook the multitude of ways in which schools, including their practices and policies, oppress LGBT-QIA+ students who have identities that are multiply marginalized, resulting in less effective intervention and advocacy for those who are the most marginalized and may need them most.

The purpose of this chapter, therefore, is to describe how Intersectionality Theory can be used in practice by school psychologists who supervise graduate students in field-based placements, particularly K-12 schools. We begin with a brief introduction to Intersectionality Theory. To connect Intersectionality Theory to a practice issue that school psychologists and other school professionals could face in real life, we present a case narrative that highlights the experiences of Elena, a 16-year old undocumented gay student from Honduras who attends high school in the Northeastern U.S. To build knowledge regarding LGBT-QIA+, undocumented Latinx students, we offer a brief review of the research in this area. Then, we describe the relevance of Intersectionality Theory to understanding the triumphs and challenges undocumented LGBT-QIA+ Latinx youth experience. We next present Elena's case narrative. Finally, we close out the chapter illustrating how intersectionality can be used as a tool in multicultural supervision to provide Elena with culturally responsive support and services, and also how Intersectionality Theory can be integrated into multicultural supervision practices to encourage social justice for Elena and other students with identities that are marginalized in schools and society at large.

Brief Introduction to Intersectionality Theory

Intersectionality is a theory that explains how the simultaneous experience of identities such as race, gender, socioeconomic status, and sexual orientation overlap and intersect to create interdependent systems of power (e.g., white supremacy, patriarchy, heteronormativity) and oppression (e.g., racism, classism, sexism, heterosexism; Cooper, 2016). While Kimberlé Crenshaw, a Black feminist legal scholar and critical race theorist, is credited with coining the term *intersectionality*, influential Black women feminist scholars and activists such as Sojourner Truth,

Patricia Hill Collins, Angela Davis, bell hooks, Audre Lorde, members of the Combahee River Collective, and others laid the foundation for intersectionality by naming the unique challenges and types of marginalization Black women faced when their race, class, sexual orientation, and other identities intersected and interfaced with systems of oppression (Combahee River Collective [CRC], 1979; Cooper, 2016; Lewis et al., 2018).

Importantly, to use Intersectionality Theory effectively one must understand its truest intent. A common misuse of intersectionality is using it to essentialize (see Chapter 4 for more detailed discussion of essentialism of human characteristics) personal identities, which intersectionality was never meant to focus on (Cooper, 2016). Intersectionality was intended to highlight *structural identities* of gender, race, sexual orientation, or national origin—identities that were consistent with how the law conceptualized people (Cooper, 2016). To clarify, when Crenshaw (1989) initially presented Intersectionality Theory she was concerned that the legal system did not account for the multiple ways in which Black women experienced employment discrimination. At the time, Black women were invisible in the law because a single-axis framework (i.e., one that considers single, rather than multiple categories of identity) was used in rendering legal decisions in employment cases involving Black women. Cooper (2016) noted that "intersectionality was a first, formative step that allowed for recognition of the black female subject within juridical power structures" (p. 3904). Therefore, effective use of intersectionality must involve understanding how students' multiple and intersecting identities *interact with* structures and systems of power and oppression. Viewing students' identities in this way moves us from essentializing students' personal identities to focusing on students' structural identities.

A main intent of intersectionality is to bring about social justice for those who are the most marginalized by demonstrating how one's intersecting structural identities combine to create unique modes of discrimination. So, while intersectionality can certainly be used to uncover how the intersection of identities can privilege and provide one with power when interacting with structures and systems (Cole, 2009), "focusing on the most privileged group members further marginalizes those who are multiply burdened and obscures claims that cannot be understood as resulting from discreet sources of discrimination" (Crenshaw, 1989, p. 140). The *most critical* use of intersectionality is its use to center those who experience the most marginalization so that we have a way of making sense of how oppressions manifest at the intersection of a person's multiple identities and how those identities interact with structural forces, resulting in multi-layered dimensions of social inequality and injustice (Crenshaw, 1991; Proctor, 2020). Using intersectionality in this critical way can be transformative for students in schools, leading to fairer and more just educational processes and systems for all (Proctor, 2020).

In the next section, we review several of the few studies available on the experiences of undocumented LGBT-QIA+ Latinx young people. The review centers an additional identity some LGBT-QIA+ Latinx youth have—*undocuqueer*. A deeper understanding of the *undocuqueer* population will develop readers' knowledge about this specific population of Latinx people, while also offering some contextualization for Elena's forthcoming narrative.

Experiences of Undocumented LGBT-QIA+ Latinx Students

> *"For many Latino UndocuQueer individuals, the experiences of coming out not only once, but twice, as LGBTQ and being undocumented in relation to their cultural background, is an even greater feat."*
>
> *~Duarte (2016)*

Much of the research on undocumented LGBT-QIA+ students is focused on college-age populations and offers retrospective accounts of their years during K-12th grade. This is not uncommon in research related to LGBT-QIA+ K-12 populations, generally because of difficulty accessing this population for research given many are not out yet and also issues of parent consent (Flores et al., 2018). There is also relatively little research available about the undocumented LGBT-QIA+ population in the U.S., possibly because they represent a small, geographically dispersed group (there are approximately 267,000 LGBT-QIA+ undocumented adults living in the U.S., and 70% are Latinx), and they may be doubly hidden, meaning they do not share their LGBT-QIA+ identities nor their undocumented status with others (Cisneros, 2015; Duarte, 2016). While not all LGBT-QIA+ students who are Latinx will have an identified political identity, we wanted to center those who identify as *undocuqueer*, given that their adoption of this identity adds a powerful counter-narrative to commonly deficit-framed descriptions of LGBT-QIA+ and Latinx student populations. Further, *undocuqueer* identity adds a dimension of power to LGBT-QIA+ Latinx students' intersectional identities that many are not familiar with, and their involvement in the *undocuqueer* activist community offers empowering counterspaces from which these youth can explore intersections of their identities and advocate for others like them. Next, we share two studies that offer insight into this often hidden population.

Cisneros (2015) explored the experiences of 31 (21 were Deferred Action for Childhood Arrivals [DACA] recipients) *undocuqueer* (devised by the National Immigrant Youth Alliance as a political identity) *activists* between the ages of 19 and 41 regarding how they made sense of being queer and undocumented. Findings revealed three major themes related to *vulnerability*, *complexity*, and *resilience*. Cisneros (2015) wrote:

> Recognizing their vulnerability within a state of illegibility, participants described a sense of exclusion within spaces of belonging, and

> wariness managing relationships with others; opting for more complex self-definitions, they resisted simplistic conceptions of identity that rendered their social locations invisible (e.g., homonormativity, heteronormativity, DREAMer); and describing themselves as resilient, they described surviving societal as well as familial rejection even when surviving seemed impossible to do so. Interacting and working within the intersection of gender, sexuality and immigration status, participants described identity negotiation and coming out as a form of resistance to institutionalized oppression, and resilience amidst simultaneous anti-immigrant, xenophobic and heterosexist power structures. Participants learned to live in multiple worlds at the same time, and embrace the multiplicity of their undocuqueer identity while seeking to bridge their communities through stories, activism and peer education.
>
> *(p. 3)*

While the participants were adults at the time of the study, all had attended secondary educational institutions in the U.S. These findings highlighted the importance of recognizing how important it is to acknowledge all aspects of undocumented, immigrant Latinx LGBT-QIA+ students' experiences and full humanity, including the complexity of their identities. Importantly, the participants reminded us of the strength, resiliency, and power of undocumented Latinx LGBT-QIA+ students and how, often, they use those qualities in service, power, and advocacy to create more liberatory spaces for those who come behind them and also face oppressive forces in this country.

Another informative study was conducted by Duarte (2016), who studied the experiences of seven undocumented LGBTQ Latinx people (average age of 22) who politically identified as *undocuqueer* to understand better the experiences and struggles of a multiply minoritized group in the U.S. All participants immigrated to the U.S. at an early age (youngest at time of arrival was 6 months, and oldest was 11 years) and attended U.S. schools as young people. The study revealed major themes related to participants' *conflicting values*, *onset of internalized homophobia*, *feelings of identity-based pride*, and *stressors behind the impact of policies such as the DACA* and the *Marriage Equality Act*.

Specifically, Duarte's (2016) participants perceived receiving more support from the Latinx community for being an undocumented immigrant than for being LGBTQ. They perceived the lack of support for LGBTQ people as stemming from Latinx people's religion (many associated with Catholicism) and traditional cultural values such as machismo (i.e., strong or exaggerated sense of manliness). It was noted that "Latino immigrant parents tend to be more closed off about the LGBTQ community than U.S. born Latinos who were acculturated to the ever-changing mainstream American society at a younger age" (Duarte, 2016, p. 29). For many participants, stigma around being LGBTQ that stemmed from religion and cultural values resulted in their own internalized homophobia that negatively impacted or delayed their coming-out process. Although participants believed

DACA was a protective factor for them that opened up opportunities (e.g., to obtain higher education), many experienced stressors associated with DACA such as outing themselves to the government and the reality that the government would know who and where they are at all times. Finally, similar to participants in Cisneros (2015), Duarte's (2016) participants viewed their intersecting identities from a strength-based perspective that helped them build character and coping skills. Like those in Cisneros (2015), these participants were also civically and politically engaged around LGBTQ, immigrant, and Latinx issues to help make a better world for themselves and others who hold *undocuqueer identities*.

Relevance of Intersectionality Theory to the Experiences of Undocumented LGBT-QIA+ Latinx Students

Intersectionality Theory is an excellent theoretical tool to use to help uncover the multiple ways undocumented, LGBT-QIA+ Latinx students can experience schools and communities as oppressive spaces and places because it forces us to consider how multiple categories of identity intersect with existing societal structures to increase risk for discriminatory and marginalizing experiences. For undocumented LGBT-QIA+ Latinx students, an intersectional lens is critically important because they have many vulnerable identities that can lead to negative mental health outcomes, but if an intersectional approach to understanding their specific issues isn't used, important factors could be overlooked that are necessary for socially just intervention, advocacy, and support efforts. Importantly, in using Intersectionality Theory to support undocumented, LGBT-QIA+ Latinx students it is critical to understand their strengths as well as challenges these students experience.

As can be seen from the research reviewed, there are challenges related to systems of oppression like racism, heterosexism, and cisgenderism, but strengths are often present within the advocacy communities students build for themselves (the school-based support personnel who reach out to, support, and love them and work to build liberatory school spaces for them); strength is also found within their own power, autonomy, and survival despite the forces that work against them. In essence, while Intersectionality Theory helps us to see how these students are multiply marginalized so that we can intervene and fix the systems that contribute to this current reality for many, the full story of undocumented, LGBT-QIA+ Latinx students must include the story of their triumphs and resiliency and power. When we listen to their narratives, we can use Intersectionality Theory to shed light on their challenges as well as their power.

Case Narrative

Elena is a 16-year-old student at a high school of about 1,500 students in a Northeastern suburb where the district enrollment includes more than 50% Latinx students. A number are immigrants from Central America; many are undocumented. Elena was born in

Honduras but left with her older sister and parents when she was 6 years old. They settled in this particular town because one of Elena's uncles moved there a few years prior; his two children attend the same school as Elena. They are all part of a small but supportive Honduran community in the town. The school district has publicly professed a commitment to promoting educational access to all children, regardless of immigration status.

Elena has always been a good student, but her English teacher noticed that her typically strong grades had started to slip and that she seemed increasingly distracted and withdrawn. Concerned, she approached the school psychologist, Dr. Sullivan, about whether Elena might be depressed. Dr. Sullivan thought the case seemed like an appropriate learning opportunity for her intern, Victoria, and asked her to schedule an initial meeting with Elena to explore the teacher's concerns. Victoria began the session as she always did, by assuring Elena that she was there to listen and support her and by explaining that, other than sharing information with her supervisor, what they talked about—including any discussions regarding immigration status—would remain confidential unless she learned that Elena or someone else was at risk of harm.

Though Elena was initially quiet and responded to Victoria's questions with only brief answers, after a few minutes she burst into tears. "I don't even know where to start, I feel so overwhelmed." Elena disclosed that she and her parents were undocumented. "Every single day I feel sick to my stomach, worrying that we are going to be found out and deported." She explained that these fears had intensified in recent weeks, after a family member of a student in the senior class had been arrested by Immigration and Customs Enforcement (ICE) agents at his home one morning before school. Despite the fact that thousands of community members signed an online petition supporting the student's family member and opposing his deportation, Elena felt deeply afraid that more such ICE enforcement actions were likely to come and that no amount of outcry from her neighbors would be enough to protect her family. Victoria validated Elena's feelings and continued to listen supportively, "That sounds like so much to be worried about and is already a lot to have on your mind. Are there any other things going on for you that are adding to your stress level?"

After a brief pause, Elena sighed, "I recently came out to a classmate who I thought I could trust, but it turns out I was wrong." She explained that soon after she told her classmate she was gay, a few boys in her class started harassing her. It started with name-calling in the hallways and cafeteria, but it escalated when several boys started texting her graphic pictures and posting sexually suggestive things about her on social media. One of the primary perpetrators cornered her after school one day and threatened Elena that if she told anyone he'd "call ICE" and report her as an "illegal." Despite this, Elena managed to work up the courage to talk to the assistant principal about it. She was somewhat vague about the nature of the slurs and posts because she felt humiliated talking about the things the boys were sending and saying. He listened, but in the end said it sounded like "boys being boys" and told her to just ignore them and eventually they'd stop. Victoria asked Elena whether she had talked to her parents about the situation. "Oh, no way! They're super Catholic and would freak out if they knew I'm gay. Even if they did know they'd never tell the school to do anything—they're terrified about ever speaking up because of our immigration status. I dread coming to school now, but I do it because otherwise, my parents would know something was wrong and just be more stressed than they already are." Victoria felt slightly panicked about all there was to consider for this client. She couldn't wait to speak to Dr. Sullivan about what to do.

Case Narrative Supervision Process Discussion Using Intersectionality Lens

The Developmental Ecological Problem-Solving (DEP) model (Simon & Swerdlik, 2017) is the only model of supervision designed specifically for school psychology training and practice. As such, it provides a framework for examining ways in which intersectionality can be applied to the supervision of school-based services.[1] Practicing from a DEP approach, there is a range of ways in which Dr. Sullivan could integrate Intersectionality Theory into supervising Victoria's work with Elena, a client whose lived experiences reflect a diversity of identities related to gender, immigration status, sexual orientation, and religion. To comprehensively address Elena's needs and model cultural responsiveness for Victoria, supervision must address how the intersection of identities with existing educational and/or societal structures can increase experiences of marginalization or discrimination.

Development and Intersectional Supervision

The *developmental* component of the DEP model emphasizes ongoing assessment and collaborative goal-setting to organize the training experience, along with the provision of frequent feedback to guide learning. Techniques and modalities of supervision are selected to match the supervisee's level of development and individual needs, recognizing that growth may occur unevenly across the varied domains of school psychology practice. Working from an intersectional perspective, Dr. Sullivan's initial assessment of Victoria's level of development would consider her knowledge of Intersectionality Theory, which would guide her subsequent approach to integrating intersectionality into supervision. Assuming that Victoria is at a relatively early stage of development, Dr. Sullivan would likely begin with some direct, didactic instruction and readings on what Intersectionality Theory is and how it can be used to promote social justice (e.g., Proctor, 2020). Dr. Sullivan also remains cognizant of the fact that supervisees at this level may be anxious, skills-focused, and eager to know the "right" way to do things, as well as highly dependent on their supervisors, who serve as some of their most powerful and influential role models (Rønnestad & Skovholt, 2012; Stoltenberg & McNeill, 2011). For example, she may find that Victoria is nervous about integrating a new and relatively unfamiliar theoretical approach into her work with Elena or has many questions about what to do, so she is mindful of providing sufficient time and space for Victoria to process her concerns during supervision.

Contracting is a key component of the developmental aspect of the DEP model. Like many models of supervision, DEP recognizes that a strong working relationship is essential and emphasizes starting with a thoughtful and intentional process that clarifies roles, responsibilities, and expectations for the supervision experience. While developing a contract with Victoria at the start of the internship year, Dr. Sullivan made it clear that considerations related to culture, diversity, and social justice were always going to be "on the table" and a routine aspect of supervision discussions. Given the disproportionate power held by supervisors who evaluate supervisee performance and often act as gatekeepers to future training or practice opportunities, it is the supervisor's responsibility to introduce this discussion. As Porter (2014) observed, "An honest and sensitive discussion of power in the relationship lays the foundation for a meaningful supervisor-supervisee relationship" (p. 76). Although supervisors are always, by virtue of their evaluative responsibilities, in a position of greater power than supervisees, steps can be taken to reduce that power differential (Greene & Flasch, 2019). For example, Dr. Sullivan actively engaged Victoria in co-constructing the supervision contract, emphasizing that both parties play key roles and have important, if different, responsibilities in the supervision relationship. She also introduced discussions of power more broadly, including how societal structures and systems, such as schools, contribute to experiences of oppression for those whose identities yield less power. By openly and transparently addressing supervision expectations and the nature of power, Dr. Sullivan worked to "demystify the process" and provided an avenue for an introduction to Intersectionality Theory (Degges-White et al., 2013; Greene & Flasch, 2019).

Porter (2014) emphasized the importance of openly addressing that multicultural supervision is likely to involve feelings of vulnerability, exposure, and uncertainty on the part of both supervisor and supervisee and requires a willingness to explore difficult issues in order to foster growth and learning. A supervisor who makes explicit an expectation that "all supervision is multicultural supervision" (Bernard & Goodyear, 2019, p. 118) helps to normalize discussions of topics that supervisees might otherwise be hesitant to raise with supervisors who have not made clear a commitment to considering issues of culture, diversity, and identity. Such culturally responsive approaches to supervision have been shown to foster more positive supervision relationships, increased satisfaction with supervision, and less fear about discussing cultural issues for white supervisees as well as feelings of validation for supervisees of color (Burkard et al., 2006). This type of supervisor behavior also provides an outlet for addressing how school psychologists can incorporate social justice action into their efforts to address clients' needs.

After engaging in a comprehensive contracting process, Dr. Sullivan introduces an examination of both her own and Victoria's identities and consideration of how they could affect their perspectives on and approaches to Elena's case. For example, she is aware that her identity and worldview can affect the kinds of issues she might raise or emphasize in supervision (Porter, 2014). As a white, cisgender, heterosexual, English-speaking woman in her mid-40s who was raised Catholic and has lived most of her life in upper-middle-class suburbs, Dr. Sullivan is quick to acknowledge multiple bases of power and privilege that have resulted in relatively few lived experiences of oppression or marginalization. Following Dr. Sullivan's modeling, Victoria reflects that she identifies as a cisgender, heterosexual, bilingual (Spanish-speaking), first-generation American child of parents who immigrated to the U.S. from Ecuador before she was born and who are legal permanent residents. She is in her mid-20s and lives with her parents in a middle-class community just outside the city. Like Dr. Sullivan, Victoria identifies as Catholic, though she is more actively involved in the church and attends Mass weekly with her parents. She recognizes that her status as a native speaker of English as well as her gender identity and sexual orientation have afforded her some privilege relative to otherwise minoritized groups, but she described experiences of discrimination based on her race as well as marginalization due to her parents' limited English language proficiency and lack of economic opportunities during her childhood. Still, neither Dr. Sullivan nor Victoria has much direct knowledge of the LGBT-QIA+ Latinx experience. With these realities in mind, Dr. Sullivan and Victoria can begin to approach Elena's case with an awareness of how intersecting identities affect the experiences of all three members of the supervisory triad.

An Ecological Approach to Systems of Power

DEP emphasizes an *ecological* approach to the supervision of school psychology services that considers the influence of the various social systems outlined in Bronfenbrenner's (1979) ecological systems theory. This component of Simon and Swerdlik's (2017) supervision model emphasizes the need for supervisors and supervisees to develop multicultural competence and the advocacy skills needed to promote change and social justice. It incorporates Bernard and Goodyear's (2019) four-dimensional approach to multicultural supervision. This approach suggests that supervisors must attend to: (1) the intrapersonal dimensions of identity that affect a person's sense of self in relationship to others, (2) interpersonal dimensions related to biases and prejudices, (3) interpersonal influences on expectations regarding cultural identity and behavior, and (4) sociopolitical factors, including the level of oppression someone experiences based on race, gender, sexual orientation, or other aspects of their identity.

With these dimensions and an ecological perspective in mind, Dr. Sullivan engages Victoria in a discussion of Elena's case. Beginning with the intrapersonal dimension, she prompts Victoria to consider how the identities she noted previously might influence how she sees the world and Elena. For example, Victoria has lived experience as a child of immigrants: How might that affect how she conceptualizes Elena's circumstances? Victoria is a practicing Catholic: What beliefs or assumptions might come with such a background? Next, considering Bernard and Goodyear's (2019) two interpersonal dimensions, Dr. Sullivan encourages Victoria to reflect on how racism, classism, sexism, or heterosexism might affect her perceptions of Elena and prompts a discussion about cultural expectations, stereotypes of Latinx clients, and the acculturation process of immigrant families. Modeling her thought process for Victoria using a think-aloud approach, Dr. Sullivan ponders whether Elena might have a supportive group of friends who are LGBT-QIA+ and whether that may have created any possible conflict with her parents or other members of the community whose Catholic identity may be to some degree at odds with embracing LGBT-QIA+ individuals. "Elena may feel she is not able to express her true self to some of the closest and most important people in her life. Ironically, it's possible that the very community that serves as a support system for Elena and her family and a protective factor for their undocumented status also acts as an oppressive force, given her gay identity."

Both supervisor and supervisee also agree to do some exploration and readings regarding the experiences of undocumented LGBT-QIA+ youth. Together they educate themselves on the *undocuqueer* community (Cisneros, 2015; Duarte, 2016) and develop a better-informed sense of the needs of students with these intersecting identities. They also make an intentional effort to investigate the many strengths of individuals with these identities, including resilience and identity-based pride. Finally, building on what she introduced to Victoria previously regarding intersectionality, Dr. Sullivan leads Victoria through an exploration of how Elena is experiencing the effects of institutionalized oppression based on her gender, sexual orientation, ethnicity, and immigration status. There is much to discuss; these conversations likely unfold over several supervision sessions and recur throughout the supervision process as Victoria works to develop her skills as a culturally responsive school psychologist.

In addition to attending to multicultural considerations, the ecological component of the DEP supervision model emphasizes training in systems change. Simon and Swerdlik (2017) outlined an approach for training supervisees in program development that begins with need identification based on observations and assessment. The process includes an analysis of school culture, procedures, organizational structure, and barriers to change, as well as identification of faculty and staff who are supportive, and it outlines steps for designing plans for change and ensuring sustainability. Seeing a potentially valuable learning opportunity, Dr. Sullivan shares these steps with Victoria and discusses how they might work together to analyze the extent to which the high school has a culture that tolerates bullying and homophobia and take steps to implement changes that would promote an affirming climate for LGBT-QIA+ students. For example, Victoria might research the district's written policies on bullying to ensure that they specifically protect students based on actual or perceived sexual orientation and gender expression. She could also assess the extent to which the school curriculum is inclusive and helps all students learn about LGBT-QIA+ history and individuals' experiences (National Association of School Psychologists [NASP],

2017). Additionally, with Dr. Sullivan's support, Victoria could work to establish a gender and sexuality alliance (GSA) and provide professional development to educate faculty about the needs of LGBT-QIA+ students, including the increased risks of these adolescents being marginalized and targeted and how to intervene when bullying occurs (NASP, 2017).

Problem Solving: Intersectional Case Conceptualization and Treatment Planning

The type of systems-change work Victoria and Dr. Sullivan consider is also a feature of the third and final component of the DEP model, which focuses on *problem solving*. This component emphasizes data-based decision-making, application of evidence-based interventions, multidisciplinary collaboration, and multi-tiered systems of support. It also incorporates structured case conceptualization. Thus, Dr. Sullivan works with Victoria to examine the various factors that are impacting Elena's well-being, both at the individual level and systemically. For example, Elena is clearly experiencing anxiety related to immigration status. Dr. Sullivan directs Victoria to research federal, state, and local regulations regarding disclosures of citizenship status so that she can confidently and accurately reassure Elena about the protections to which she is entitled. Notably, as a result of the 1982 Supreme Court decision in *Plyler v. Doe*, public schools cannot deny any child access to an education based on immigration status (American Immigration Council, 2016). Students may also be eligible for protections under the McKinney-Vento Act of 1987, which was designed to ensure that highly mobile or unaccompanied youth have access to education (Sulkowski, 2017). Victoria should also remain cognizant of the school's obligation to uphold the Family Educational Rights and Privacy Act (FERPA), which prohibits schools from disclosing student information—including immigration status—and can assure Elena that ICE and U.S. Customs and Border Protection maintain a policy of refraining from enforcement actions on school grounds (American Civil Liberties Union, n.d.). Finally, it would be important for Victoria to understand the Deferred Action for Childhood Arrivals (DACA) program and be prepared to discuss with Elena how this might be a potential protection against deportation.

Additionally, Victoria spends time exploring community organizations that might be able to provide support to Elena and her family. Armed with this knowledge, Victoria and Dr. Sullivan role-play a conversation with Elena's parents in which Victoria seeks their consent to work with Elena in individual school-based counseling. Beginning with this conversation, Victoria can work to build a positive, trusting family-school connection with Elena's parents. However, Dr. Sullivan reminds Victoria that, as Simon and Swerdlik (2017) explained, "histories and consequences of oppression and power differences may impact relationships with clients and the character of family relationships with school personnel" (p. 146) and encourages her to work patiently and empathically to build an alliance with Elena's family. Meanwhile, from an intersectional lens at the systems level, Victoria and Dr. Sullivan also explore strategies for fostering stronger partnerships with parents from throughout the school community, as research has shown that such efforts serve to empower disenfranchised families and increase social capital (Henderson & Mapp, 2002; Sulkowski, 2017). To start, Victoria uses her Spanish language skills to translate a recent issue of the school newsletter and includes a summary of available school-based mental health resources for distribution to parents.

In addition to building Elena's coping strategies for managing the very real and valid stress that comes with being an undocumented immigrant in the U.S., Victoria must address what she is experiencing as an LGBT-QIA+ student, albeit within the context of Elena's intersectional identities. Once again considering Victoria's level of development, Dr. Sullivan assesses her knowledge of best practices for working with LGBT-QIA+ youth. Victoria acknowledges that this is an area in which she has learning to do, so the supervisor and supervisee discuss resources and readings that will help to empower Victoria with the knowledge she needs to work effectively with Elena, such as the NASP position statement, *Safe and Supportive Schools for LGBTQ Youth*.

First and foremost, Victoria recognizes the importance of providing Elena with affirmation and validation as an LGBT-QIA+ student (APA & NASP, 2015) and the increased risks of negative outcomes such as school dropout and suicide for this population (NASP, 2017). Dr. Sullivan and Victoria also consider how these rates might be exacerbated for students experiencing additional forms of oppression and discrimination due to their structural identities. They make a plan for Victoria's next meeting with Elena, during which she will begin by assessing symptoms of depression while continuing to build rapport. Because being gay is not a universal experience, Victoria will ask what being gay means to Elena, as well as explore who she is "out" to, whether she has friends who are gay, and what kinds of supports she has access to as a gay student at this school and in this community. They also consider what it is like to "come out twice" as both an LGBT-QIA+ individual and an undocumented immigrant. As Duarte (2016) noted, "As a member of a culture that is centered on the traditional values and gender roles, Latino individuals who come out as LGBT-QIA+ to their families are oftentimes more at a disadvantage in the U.S. society being undocumented" (p. 2). Elena may continue to experience difficulty related to coming out to her parents, and Dr. Sullivan should ensure Victoria is prepared to navigate that.

Throughout their work together, Victoria and Elena focus on the pride associated with being gay, as well as the strength and resilience that comes with being an immigrant. Victoria might look to connect Elena to local advocacy groups or online communities for *undocuqueer* youth. For example, engaging with United We Dream (UWD, n.d.), the largest youth-led immigrant group in the country, could connect Elena to a nation-wide network of peer advocates and advocacy opportunities. Their LGBTQ Justice program is designed to organize and empower LGBTQ immigrants and allies and includes the UWD

Queer Undocumented Immigrant Project, or QUIP. QUIP seeks to "empower immigrants and allies to address social and systemic barriers that affect themselves and the broader LGBTQ and immigrant community" (UWD, n.d.). If Elena is already involved with such organizations, they might set goals for remaining connected and engaging in additional advocacy and activism, as research has found that this work can empower undocumented youth with respect to both their legal status and sexual orientation (Terriquez, 2015).

As an additional feature of the problem-solving component of DEP supervision, Victoria and Dr. Sullivan have a legal and ethical responsibility to address the bullying and harassment that Elena reported in her initial meeting. This presents an opportunity for Dr. Sullivan to walk Victoria through any state laws or district policies regarding reporting incidents of bullying. Given the sensitive nature of Elena's situation, as well as the need to address the assistant principal's lack of responsiveness to Elena's report, Dr. Sullivan takes the lead on navigating the process, providing Victoria with a valuable opportunity to observe the considerations, communications, and processes involved. Given that Elena has shown some willingness to disclose the harassment, Dr. Sullivan joins Victoria in meeting with her to explain her obligation to report and discuss how to do so in a way that best respects Elena's feelings and concerns. As part of making her report, Dr. Sullivan meets with the assistant principal, with whom she has a positive working relationship, to explain how what Elena's classmates are doing is more than "boys being boys" and in fact constitutes discrimination based on her identity as an LGBT-QIA+ student. Victoria was able to observe this meeting and learn advocacy and communication skills from her supervisor's example.

Conclusion

The APA's (2015) *Guidelines for Supervision in Health Service Psychology* describe diversity competence as "an inseparable and essential component of supervision" (p. 15). Dr. Sullivan demonstrated well-developed skills in this domain in working with Victoria on Elena's case. By applying Intersectionality Theory to the DEP model she was able to build Victoria's knowledge of this approach to understanding the role of power and structural identities, both within the supervision relationship and in Victoria's work with her client, Elena. Taking development into account across the various considerations the case presented, Dr. Sullivan worked thoughtfully and intentionally with Victoria to foster examinations of both individual and systemic variables. This case provided a range of valuable learning opportunities for Victoria, from understanding strategies for collaborating with parents to increasing her knowledge of best practices for working with LGBT-QIA+ students to building awareness of the needs, rights, and strengths of unauthorized immigrant students and families. By working from an intersectional perspective, Dr. Sullivan served to significantly foster Victoria's development while also ensuring effective services to meet Elena's social and emotional needs.

Note

1. For an additional illustrative example applying Intersectionality Theory to a developmental approach to counseling supervision, readers are referred to Greene and Flasch (2019).

References

American Civil Liberties Union. (n.d.). *FAQ for educators on immigrant students in public schools*. Author. www.aclu.org/other/faq-educators-immigrant-students-public-schools

American Immigration Council. (2016). *Public education for immigrant students: Understanding Plyler v. Doe*. www.americanimmigrationcouncil.org/research/plyler-v-doe-public-education-immigrant-students

American Psychological Association. (2015). Guidelines for clinical supervision in health service psychology. *American Psychologist*, *70*(1), 33–46. https//doi.org/10.1037/a0038112

American Psychological Association & National Association of School Psychologists. (2015). *Resolution on gender and sexual orientation diversity in children and adolescents in schools*. www.nasponline.org/about_nasp/resolution/gender_sexual_orientation_diversity.pdf

Bernard, J. M., & Goodyear, R. K. (2019). *Fundamentals of clinical supervision* (6th ed.). Pearson.

Bronfenbrenner, U. (1979). *The ecology of human development: Experiments by nature and design*. Harvard University Press.

Burkard, A. W., Johnson, A. J., Madson, M. B., Pruitt, N. T., Contreras-Tadych, D. A., Kozlowski, J. M., . . . Knox, S. (2006). Supervisor cultural responsiveness and unresponsiveness in cross-cultural supervision. *Journal of Counseling Psychology*, *53*(3), 288.

Cisneros, J. (2015). *Undocuqueer: Interacting and working within the intersection of LGBTQ and undocumented* [Unpublished doctoral dissertation]. Arizona State University.

Cole, E. R. (2009). Intersectionality and research in psychology. *American Psychologist*, *64*, 170–180. https://doi.org/10.1037/a0014564

Combahee River Collective: A Black feminist statement. (1979). *Off Our Backs*, *9*(6), 6–8. www.jstor.org/stable/25792966

Cooper, B. (2016). Intersectionality. In L. Disch & M. Hawkesworth (Eds.), *The Oxford handbook of feminist theory* (pp. 385–406). Oxford University Press.

Crenshaw, K. (1989). Demarginalizing the intersection of race and sex: A Black feminist critique of antidiscrimination doctrine, feminist theory, and antiracist politics. *University of Chicago Legal Forum*, *1989*(1), 139–167.

Crenshaw, K. (1991). Mapping the margins: Intersectionality, identity politics, and violence against women of color. *Stanford Law Review*, *43*(6), 1241–1299.

Degges-White, S. E., Colon, B. R., & Borzumato-Gainey, C. (2013). Counseling supervision within a feminist framework: Guidelines for intervention. *The Journal of Humanistic Counseling*, *52*(1), 92–105. https://doi.org/10.1002/j.2161-1939.2013.00035.x

Duarte, C. C. (2016). *Exploring the intersectionality of undocumented LGBTQ Latino persons aka undocuqueer Latinos: A qualitative study* [Unpublished master's thesis]. California State University, Long Beach.

Eisenberg, M. E., Erickson, D. J., Gower, A. L., Kne, L., Watson, R. J., Corliss, H. L., & Saewyc, E. M. (2020). Supportive community resources are associated with lower risk of substance use among lesbian, gay, bisexual, and questioning adolescents in

Minnesota. *Journal of Youth and Adolescence, 49*(4), 836–848. https://doi.org/10.1007/s10964-019-01100-4

Flores, D., McKinney, Jr., R., Arscott, J., & Barroso, J. (2018). Obtaining waivers of parental consent: A strategy endorsed by gay, bisexual, and queer adolescent males for health prevention research. *Nursing Outlook, 66*(2), 138–148. https//doi.org/10.1016/j.outlook.2017.09.001

Greene, J. H., & Flasch, P. S. (2019). Integrating intersectionality into clinical supervision: A developmental model addressing broader definitions of multicultural competence. *The Journal of Counselor Preparation and Supervision, 12*(4). https://repository.wcsu.edu/jcps/vol12/iss4/14

Hackimer, L., & Proctor, S. L. (2015). Considering the community influence for lesbian, gay, bisexual, and transgender youth. *Journal of Youth Studies, 18*(3), 277–290. https://doi.org/10.1080/13676261.2014.944114

Henderson, A. T., & Mapp, K. L. (2002). *A new wave of evidence: The impact of school, family, and community connections on student achievement. Annual synthesis 2002.* National Center for Family and Community Connections with Schools.

Huebner, D. M., Thoma, B. C., & Neilands, T. B. (2015). School victimization and substance abuse use among lesbian, gay, bisexual, and transgender adolescents. *Prevention Science, 16*(5), 734–743. https://doi.org/10.1007/s11121-014-0507-x

Hussar, B., Zhang, J., Hein, S., Wang, K., Roberts, A., Cui, J., Smith, M., Bullock Mann, F., Barmer, A., & Dilig, R. (2020). *The condition of education 2020 (NCES 2020–144).* U.S. Department of Education. National Center for Education Statistics. Retrieved March 13, 2021, from https://nces.ed.gov/pubsearch/pubsinfo.asp?pubid=2020144

Johns, M. M., Lowry, R., Andrzejewski, J., Barrios, L. C., Zewditu, D., McManus, T., Rasberry, C. N., Robin, L., & Underwood, J. M. (2019). Transgender identity and experiences of violence victimization, substance use, suicide risk, and sexual risk behaviors among high school students—19 states and large urban school districts, 2017. *Morbidity and Mortality Weekly Report, 68*(3), 65–71. http://doi.org/10.15585/mmwr.mm6803a3

Kosciw, J. G., Clark, C. M., Truong, T. L., & Zongrone, A. D. (2020). *The 2020 national school climate survey: The experiences of lesbian, gay, bisexual, transgender, and queer youth in our nation's schools.* GLSEN. www.glsen.org/research/2019-national-school-climate-survey

Lewis, J. A., Williams, M. G., Moody, A. T., Peppers, E. J., & Gadson, C. A. (2018). Intersectionality theory and microaggressions: Implications for research, training, and practice. In G. C. Torino, D. P. Rivera, C. M. Capodilupo, K. L. Nadal, & D. W. Sue (Eds.), *Microaggression theory: Influence and implications* (pp. 48–64). Wiley.

National Association of School Psychologists. (2017). *Safe and supportive schools for LGBTQIA+ youth* (Position statement).

Porter, N. (2014). Women, culture, and social justice: Supervision across the intersections. In C. A. Falender, E. P. Shafranske, & C. J. Falicov (Eds.), *Multiculturalism and Diversity in Clinical supervision: A competency-based approach.* The American Psychological Association.

Proctor, S. L. (2020). Intersectionality as a prism for situating social justice at the intersection of marginalization and discrimination. *Communique, 49*(1), 1, 30–32.

Raifman, J., Charlton, B. M., Arrington-Sanders, R., Chan, P. A., Rusley, J., Mayer, K. H., Stein, M. D., Austin, S. B., & McConnell, M. (2020). Sexual orientation and suicide attempt disparities among U.S. adolescents: 2009–2017. *Pediatrics, 145*(3). https://doi.org/10.1542/peds.2019-1658

Rønnestad, M. H., & Skovholt, T. (2012). *The developing practitioner: Growth and stagnation of therapists and counselors*. Routledge.

Simon, D. J., & Swerdlik, M. E. (2017). *Supervision in school psychology: The developmental, ecological, problem-solving model*. Routledge.

Stoltenberg, C. D., & McNeill, B. W. (2011). *IDM supervision: An integrative developmental model for supervising counselors & therapists* (3rd ed.). Routledge.

Sulkowski, M. L. (2017). Unauthorized immigrant students in the United States: Educational policies, practices, and the role of school psychology. *Communiqué*, *46*(1), 1.

Terriquez, V. (2015). Intersectional mobilization, social movement spillover, and queer youth leadership in the immigrant rights movement. *Social Problems*, *62*, 343–362. https://doi.org/10.1093/socpro/spv010

United We Dream. (n.d.). *LGBT-QIA+ justice*. https://unitedwedream.org/our-work/LGBT-QIA+-justice/

12

PREPARING SUPERVISEES TO SUPPORT STUDENTS EXPERIENCING MICROAGGRESSIONS

Application of Critical Race Theory to Clinical Supervision

Celeste M. Malone

This chapter focuses on creating culturally affirming environments for racially and ethnically minoritized (REM) students in response to school-based microaggressions. This chapter begins with a brief introduction to Critical Race Theory (CRT). The next section of the chapter examines racial/ethnic microaggression experiences in school with a focus on microaggressions directed toward Latinx individuals. This is followed by a discussion of how racial/ethnic microaggressions at school replicate and mirror societal oppression and are a manifestation of racism leading to segregated schools. The chapter shares a narrative based on the experiences of Latinx middle school students following the 2016 election. Using this narrative, supervision practices framed in a CRT lens, as well as strategies for affirming REM youth, are shared to promote inclusive school climates.

Brief Introduction to Critical Race Theory

Critical Race Theory (CRT) has its origins in legal scholarship and is a response to critical legal studies. Specifically, CRT critiques liberalist notions of color blindness, neutrality of the law, and incremental change because these ignore the impact of racism and focus on racial equality as opposed to racial equity (DeCuir & Dixson, 2004). CRT scholars highlight that there is no biological basis for race and argue that race is a product of racism, a system of structuring opportunity and assigning value based on phenotypic properties (e.g., skin color and hair texture) and assumptions about ancestry (Brown, this volume; Jones, 2000). The social construction of race leads to the inequitable distribution of goods, services, and resources. Thus, race-based differences show the impact of racism as opposed to being characteristics of any racial group.

DOI: 10.4324/9780367815325-15

As described in Chapter 2, the key tenets of CRT are: (1) Race is a social construction, (2) Racism is ordinary, pervasive, and endemic to American society, (3) Counter-stories that center the voices and highlight the racialized experiences of marginalized groups are necessary to disrupt racism, and (4) White allies are only interested in disrupting racism when doing so advances their own self-interests. The pervasive nature of racism extends to school settings as REM students regularly experience overt and covert racism that create aversive experiences in schools.

Racial Microaggressions and Students' Perceptions of School Climate

School climate refers to the quality and character of school life. It is based on the patterns of experience of students, parents, and school personnel, and it reflects norms, goals, values, interpersonal relationships, teaching and learning practices, and organizational structures (Cohen et al., 2009). School climate is of interest to educators, school personnel and administrators, and policy makers because of its relationship with student outcomes, such as improved academic outcomes, reduced dropout rate, better student-teacher and peer relationships, and improved school attendance (Cohen et al., 2009; Mattison & Aber, 2007). In assessing school climate, some elements (e.g., environment, quality of instruction) are observable and/or easily operationalized and measurable; however, other elements, such as relationships, connectedness, and safety, are subjective and may vary based on an individual student's experience. Because of this, differing perceptions of school climate across groups in a school may be equally valid. Several studies that examined multiple aspects of school climate have found that REM students are more likely to report negative perceptions of school climate, especially in the areas of relationship and racial climate, compared to white peers (Mattison & Aber, 2007; Watkins & Aber, 2009). Additionally, Voight and colleagues (2015) suggested that this racial, school-climate gap impacts academic performance. Middle schools with larger Black-white and Latinx-white school-climate gaps in perceived safety and connectedness had larger Black-white and Latinx-white differences on academic achievement measures. Opportunities for participation and adult-student climate gaps were also associated in lowered academic achievement for Black and Latinx students, respectively (Voight et al., 2015). Given the relationship between positive perceptions of school climate and school outcomes, it is important to investigate potential causes of REM students' negative school-climate perceptions to develop appropriate interventions to improve the school climate and to increase REM students' sense of belonging and connectedness to the school environment.

The negative perceptions that REM students have of the school climate may be partially attributed to their experiences of microaggressions. The term *microaggressions* was coined by psychiatrist Chester Pierce in 1970 to describe the insults and dismissals he regularly saw inflicted on Black people (Sue et al., 2007). Microaggressions are brief interpersonal exchanges or environmental conditions that violently attack cultural identity (i.e., microassault), convey rudeness or insensitivity to a person's cultural identity (i.e., microinsult), or dismiss a person's cultural reality and lived experiences (i.e., microinvalidation) that are directed toward members of socially marginalized groups (Sue et al., 2007). While most microaggressions research focuses on adult populations, there is evidence that REM students in PK-12 schools experience microaggressions from other students, from adults in the school, and through the school environment, which make them feel unwelcome or devalued (Kohli & Solórzano, 2012; Wintner et al., 2017). Black, Asian, and Latinx students report receiving significantly more microaggressions from both peers and teachers than do white students (Forrest-Bank & Jenson, 2015; Huynh & Fuligni, 2010). Moreover, these microaggression experiences are associated with more negative perceptions of school climate and a decreased sense of belonging.

Racial microaggressions are enacted based on factors associated with race which, for Latinx students, includes language, culture, and immigration status. Immigrant and non-immigrant Latinx youth report experiencing discrimination based on accents, physical appearance, native language, country of origin, and immigration status. Additionally, non-immigrant Latinx students may be assumed to be foreign immigrants or stereotyped as gang members (Espinola et al., 2019). Sue and colleagues (2007) described these microaggressions as "alien in own land" and "pathologizing cultural styles"; they send the message that Latinx cultural values, norms, and traditions are abnormal and that Latinx individuals will never fully be embraced as American. These microaggressions reflect stereotypes associated with high numbers of recent immigrants whose primary language may not be English and whose cultural practices are considered less westernized (Forrest-Bank & Jenson, 2015; Sue et al., 2007). As Latinx youth are exposed to anti-immigrant bias, they start to internalize these deficit beliefs as non-immigrant Latinx youth direct microaggressions toward their immigrant peers (Espinola et al., 2019). In addition to microaggressions exoticizing their culture, Latinx youth also report that teachers make negative assumptions about them based on their race and dismiss their reports of experiencing bias at school (Forrest-Bank & Jenson, 2015; Huynh, 2012). These microaggressions reflect teachers' low expectations for Latinx students based on their race, ethnicity, or language (Huber & Cueva, 2012; Huynh, 2012). From both peers and from teachers, Latinx students receive messages that they do not belong and are not valued at school.

Experiencing microaggressions and discrimination can have a deleterious impact on emotional health, including depressive symptoms, negative affect, and lowered self-esteem (Nadal et al., 2014; Sue et al., 2008). Microaggressive experiences are also associated with elevated anxiety, anger, and stress, which may further exacerbate emotional health concerns and physical problems (Huynh, 2012). This is particularly concerning since children experiencing internalizing distress (e.g., depression, anxiety) and externalizing problems (e.g., disruptive behavior) are at greater risk for a wide range of school difficulties such as learning problems, poor achievement, social rejection, aggressive behavior, and school dropout. For example, in a sample of Black adolescents, Wong and colleagues (2003) found that perceived discrimination by peers and teachers was positively related to anger, depressive symptoms, and problem behavior, as well as diminished motivation to do well in school. Similarly, discrimination from peers is associated with psychological maladjustment, and discrimination from school personnel is associated with poorer academic performance among Asian, Black, and Latinx youth (Benner & Graham, 2013). Huynh and Fuligni (2010) also found that reports of discrimination significantly predicted lower GPAs, higher levels of depression, higher levels of distress, lower self-esteem, and more physical complaints.

Microaggressions also negatively affect relationships between REM students and their peers and teachers. Students targeted by microaggressions often withdraw socially and lose interest in school. They also may also retaliate in ways that get them labeled as "troublemakers," which further disrupts relationships with teachers and contributes to ongoing cycles of microaggressions and relational or physical aggression with peers (Wintner et al., 2017). In a qualitative study of adolescent Latinx students identified as at-risk for behavioral disorders, Balagna and colleagues (2013) found that most of the students reported being the target of overt racism and microaggressions from peers and engaging in maladaptive behaviors (e.g., aggression, school avoidance) in response to the anger and other negative emotions evoked by these discriminatory experiences. When teachers responded to their acts of aggression without also attending to the microaggressions that precipitated those acts, Latinx students felt unsupported (Balagna et al., 2013). This further distanced Latinx students from the teachers and reinforced negative perceptions of the school climate.

Understanding Microaggressions Within the Context of CRT

The primary notion of CRT is that racism, both overt and covert, is an embedded and permanent fixture of American life. As such, it is important to examine race and racism as social constructs and the extent to which they lead to societal and institutional inequities that impact marginalized groups (DeCuir & Dixson, 2004; Ladson-Billings, 1998). The microaggressions that REM students experience in school create invalidating and hostile environments that limit their success. As a form of interpersonal racism, they reflect stereotypes that people from REM groups are less intelligent, more dangerous, and are inferior to white people and thereby lead to REM students' differential treatment by school staff and peers (Sue et al., 2007). Moreover, they reflect pro-white biases held by teachers and reflected more broadly in society (Starck et al., 2020). Microaggressions and other forms of interpersonal racism maintain institutional racism as individuals' biases are replicated through collective decision-making and actions leading to policies and practices that limit REM students' potential for school success.

Both interpersonal and institutional racism lead to education disparities. Vague and ambiguous school policies around special education placement, referral to gifted education programs, and school discipline lead to educators relying on stereotypes formed by their implicit biases to guide their decision-making. This then leads to disparities that emerge as restricted access to educational opportunities or different staff reactions to student misbehavior (Carter et al., 2017). Compared to white students, Black, Latinx, and Indigenous students are more likely to be identified as having a disability requiring special education (United States Department of Education, 2017). Moreover, they are overrepresented in the categories of emotional disturbance, intellectual disability, and specific learning disability, categories that have more subjectivity in their eligibility criteria (Skiba et al., 2008). This stands in marked contrast to these students' underrepresentation in gifted education programs (Grissom & Redding, 2015). Differential treatment is also evident in disciplinary practices. Black and Latinx students are more likely to be disciplined for subjective behavior infractions such as disruptive behavior, disrespect, and defiance compared to white peers and to be punished more harshly through exclusionary discipline (Girvan et al., 2017). The excessive use of exclusionary discipline with Black and Latinx youth erodes their connection to school and removes them from the instructional environment, placing them at greater risk for academic failure. Eventually, these students are pushed out of school and often pushed into the carceral system (Hughes et al., 2020).

Racial hierarchies are further maintained when educators deny the existence of racism. Teachers and other school staff tend to equate racism with overtly aggressive acts and may ignore more subtle forms of racism (Call-Cummings & Martinez, 2017). This invalidates REM students' racial identity and their experiential reality (Sue et al., 2007). By not acknowledging students' experiences and by demanding that students prove that microaggression experiences are racist, white teachers claim the power to define racism and justify their non-response to microaggressions (Call-Cummings & Martinez, 2017). For example, if microaggressions are not recognized as a form of racism, REM students calling out microaggressions may be disciplined for being disrespectful or disruptive instead of being supported. Schools' inaction further reinforces the message that REM students are not valued in schools, which contributes to negative perceptions of school climate as well as feelings of self-doubt, isolation, and frustration (Yosso et al., 2009). Thus, while *Brown v. Board of Education* (1954) ended legal segregation in schools, REM students still experience de facto segregation through a bifurcated education system that denies them access to educational opportunities and creates intolerable environments that prevent them from thriving.

CRT highlights the importance of storytelling to help REM individuals give voice to their realities and lived experiences. One way of doing so is through microaffirmations. These are small acts that foster inclusion, comfort, and support for individuals who may feel isolated or invisible in an environment (Rowe, 2008). When directed toward REM individuals, microaffirmations provide counter-stories that affirm their lived experiences when they experience microaggressions. In contrast to the insults and dismissals of microaggressions, microaffirmations are subtle acknowledgements of a person's worth. When examined from a CRT lens, microaffirmations provide insight on how REM individuals affirm their racial identities, validate their racialized identities, transform their academic or social lives, and provide protective measures against racism (Rolón-Dow & Davison, 2021). The use of personal narratives and stories are valid forms of evidence for REM individuals to document inequity and discrimination when their experiences are invalidated. For those who experience microaggressions, healing comes from the creation of affirming spaces in which they can share their personal testimonies and build community through collective meaning making and empowerment (French et al., 2020; Yosso et al., 2009).

The Experiences of Latinx Students During the 2016 Presidential Election

The 2016 presidential election was notable among recent U.S. elections with the persistent themes of racist and anti-immigrant rhetoric. The Republican presidential candidate regularly portrayed Latinx immigrants as dangerous criminals and campaigned on the promise of increased deportations of non-white immigrants and building a wall at the Mexican border to keep out migrants from Latin American countries. The vitriol he and other public figures regularly spewed toward non-white immigrants and communities of color emboldened some Americans to engage in public displays of racist and dehumanizing language and acts. Not surprisingly, the increase in hate and bias-related crimes leading up to and following the election has been termed the "Trump effect" by many media outlets.

Schools reported growing tension among students of different racial/ethnic groups and general increases in bullying based on race, language, and immigration status. In a post-election survey of K-12 educators, the Southern Poverty Law Center received over 10,000 responses with the vast majority reporting that the school climate was negatively impacted (90%) and that students from marginalized groups had heightened anxiety (80%) following the election with 40% reporting students' use of derogatory language based on race, ethnicity, immigration status, and sexual orientation (Southern Poverty Law Center, 2016). Similarly, Huang and Cornell (2019) found that schools located in districts that voted for the Republican candidate reported increased bullying and students being teased due to their race or ethnicity. This was an increase from the data collected by these researchers in 2013 and 2015, and it was the first time in their data collection that school reports of bullying differed between Republican and Democratic communities (Huang & Cornell, 2019). Other studies found that Latinx students reported experiencing language discrimination, racism, and discrimination in school and online and feelings of exclusion due to racism (Vos et al., 2021; Wray-Lake et al., 2018). Because of the adverse impact of microaggressions and racism, it is critical that school personnel have the skills to intervene appropriately and support students targeted by bias-based bullying.

Case Narrative

This case narrative describes the experiences of Latinx students at River Park Middle School during and following the 2016 presidential election. The school is in a large suburban school district in the mid-Atlantic region. The surrounding county is predominantly white; however, there has been a growing Latinx immigrant population from Central America and Mexico. The county has a history of racial tension and bias incidents, with most hate crimes reported in the state occurring in this particular county. Moreover, most bias incidents are related to race or ethnicity. This has also spilled into the school setting with Latinx students disproportionately impacted by bullying. Notably, 29.4% of middle school bullying incidents targeted Latinx students; however, Latinx students only comprise 11.2% of middle school students. Since the beginning of the school year, Latinx students reported receiving comments from peers questioning their or their parents' legal status in the United States (e.g., "You're going to get deported," "I can't wait to throw you over the wall") and mocking them for speaking Spanish (e.g., "This is the United States; speak English!"). There have also been incidents of vandalism and social media posts targeting Latinx students. Some of these incidents have led to altercations between students at school or arguments on social media. The day after the election, many Latinx families opted to keep their children home from school due to these racist and anti-immigrant incidents. While the school has an anti-bullying program in place, the principal and school leaders are at a loss on how to specifically respond to this bias-based bullying and have sought the assistance of the school psychologist.

River Park Middle School's school psychologist, Ms. Thomas, is a white female who has worked in the district for the past 15 years. Her intern Emily is also a white female who relocated to the state from the Midwest. Because of Emily's interest in bullying interventions, Ms. Thomas has asked her to provide counseling support to two students who experienced bullying in the school: Juan, a 7th-grade Salvadorean American male student, and Rosalia, a 6th-grade female student originally from Mexico. Although these two students were specifically identified for intervention, they both shared that other Latinx students in the school are also being bullied but are reluctant to seek help because they feel that teachers and other adults have been unhelpful in the past.

Case Narrative Supervision Process Discussion Using Critical Race Theory Lens

Through this case conceptualization, I describe how a CRT lens can be integrated in the clinical supervision process and in the development of an intervention plan to support Latinx students who are the targets of microaggressions. Using feminist multicultural supervision (FMS) techniques, I will demonstrate how supervisees develop cultural humility and how the supervisory relationship serves as a model for supervisees to learn how power dynamics will impact their therapeutic work with clients. Additionally, I describe strategies at the student- and school-wide levels to affirm and support REM students.

Supervision Process

The supervisory relationship has a significant influence on supervisees' learning. It provides the foundation for supervisees' clinical skill development, as well as personal growth and self-awareness. As such, supervision is an effective vehicle to help supervisees develop cultural humility. Cultural humility is the "ability to maintain an interpersonal stance that is other-oriented (or open to the other) in relation to aspects of cultural identity that are most important to the [person]" (Hook et al., 2013, p. 2). It goes beyond cultural competence to include a lifelong commitment to self-evaluation and self-critique, the desire to fix power imbalances, partnerships with people and groups who advocate for others, and institutional accountability (Tervalon & Murray-Garcia, 1998). Culturally humble clinicians are less likely to avoid discussions about race or minimize the importance of racial-cultural issues when working with REM students (Hook et al., 2016). Supervisors model cultural humility by demonstrating their cultural self-awareness and modeling the use of cultural skills to create a supervisory relationship in which supervisees feel safe to address multicultural issues related to clients and the supervision process itself (Chopra, 2013). Through process discussions, Ms. Thomas will teach Emily how to apply these skills to her work with Juan, Rosalia, and other Latinx students at River Park Middle School. It will be important for Emily to demonstrate her comfort discussing topics related to race, ethnicity, and culture so students feel safe sharing microaggressions they have received and know that Emily will not dismiss their experiences. Accordingly, Ms. Thomas's supervision goals for Emily are for her to: (1) develop cultural self-awareness to understand her experiences of privilege and marginalization, (2) develop her critical consciousness to recognize the influence of systems on individual clients, and (3) empower her to engage in systems-level advocacy work.

FMS provides a useful theoretical framework to create supervisory relationships that are collaborative, mutual, and reflective and that will promote supervisees' cultural humility (Porter & Vasquez, 1997). A central component of FMS is a focus on power and power dynamics within the supervisory relationship and, by extension, supervisees' therapeutic relationships with clients. Supervisors working from an FMS orientation recognize that the power differentials inherent to the supervisor-supervisee and supervisee-client relationships are further complicated due to power associated with the supervisor's, supervisee's, and client's social positions (Arczynski & Morrow, 2017). To manage power and create a more egalitarian relationship, supervisors use strategies to promote trust, empower supervisees, and engage in critical reflexivity (Arczynski & Morrow, 2017). Specifically, supervisors share power through collaboration and transparency and empower supervisees by highlighting their existing areas of competence. They engage in ongoing reflection on the influence of social locations, structural power, bias, and history on their supervision strategies and encourage their supervisees to engage in advocacy to challenge institutional power imbalances. By modeling this cultural humility in the supervision process, supervisees learn to take a similar approach when working with clients.

Developing Cultural Humility

Cultural self-awareness is the first component of cultural humility. Because of the power differential, it is the responsibility of supervisors to initiate conversations about cultural issues in supervision. Supervisors can prompt self-awareness by initiating focused discussions to examine cultural group memberships and explore issues of power, culture, and privilege (Chopra, 2013; Glosoff & Durham, 2010). This can lead to a discussion of the cultural similarities and differences in the supervisory relationship and how individual social identities will affect power dynamics within the relationship. To further build cultural self-awareness, supervisors also initiate discussions on how supervisees' identity and lived experiences will affect how they work with clients. To guide these discussions, Ms. Thomas uses the ADDRESSING model. It provides a framework to reflect on sociocultural diversity along 10 cultural identifiers: age, disability status (developmental and acquired), religion, ethnic identity, socioeconomic status, sexual orientation, Indigenous group membership, national origin, and gender (Hays, 2016). This model highlights the complexity of individual identity. For example, both Ms. Thomas and Emily are white and female; however, they experience the world differently based on their other cultural group memberships. The personal work of introspection and self-reflection will help Emily better understand how her culture influences her worldview. Additionally, the model provides a framework for her to learn from Juan and Rosalia about their cultural identities and consider how the differences and similarities in their cultural experiences will influence development of the therapeutic relationship.

Cultural humility also requires critical consciousness, the ability to recognize and analyze systems of inequity and the commitment to act against these systems. It comprises three components: critical reflection, political efficacy, and critical action (Watts et al., 2011). Through critical reflection, social problems and inequalities are viewed in terms of systemic oppression. This reflection is a prerequisite for political efficacy, or the confidence in one's ability to facilitate social change through individual and/or collective activism. *Critical action* refers to individual or collective action taken to change unjust institutional policies and practices (Watts et al., 2011). To facilitate the development of Emily's critical consciousness, Ms. Thomas can engage in reflective questioning to help her understand the power dynamics operating in her life and her student-clients' lives and consider how these dynamics impact the therapeutic and supervisory relationships (Glosoff & Durham, 2010). Such questions may include: What cultural variables construct your cultural identity? or What cultural or sociopolitical factors may influence how your clients interact with the educational system? This questioning can also be embedded in case conceptualization discussions. Specifically, Ms. Thomas can ask Emily about the historical, cultural, and sociopolitical factors that may influence her impressions of and experiences with Latinx students (Glosoff & Durham, 2010). Subsequent discussions would focus on how these impressions are formed based on deficit narratives of Latinx students perpetuated by individual, institutional, and structural racism.

As supervisees develop their critical consciousness and become more aware of social justice issues, the hope is that they will recognize that systems-level change is needed to disrupt the oppressive systems contributing to their clients' challenges. While advocacy has long been part of school psychologists' professional role, the focus has been advocating on others' behalf. This creates a power imbalance in which the school psychologists are viewed as the "experts" who know what marginalized communities need. In contrast to traditional professional advocacy models, social justice advocacy focuses on empowering communities and working both for and with marginalized groups (Malone & Proctor, 2019). Using power-sharing strategies modeled in FMS, culturally humble school psychologists position themselves to learn from and work alongside marginalized communities (Arczynski & Morrow, 2017; Tervalon & Murray-Garcia, 1998). The advocacy competencies endorsed by the American Counseling Association (ACA) provide a model for this work on three levels: client/student, school/community, and public arena (Ratts et al., 2007; Toporek & Daniels, 2018). These levels are further distinguished by the level of client involvement (i.e., advocacy in collaboration with the client vs. advocacy on behalf of the client). Ms. Thomas can introduce Emily to this model to highlight the multiple ways she can work within her spheres of influence to enact change and empower the students with whom she is working. In addition to teaching the model, Ms. Thomas can support Emily in identifying and working through personal and professional barriers to engaging in social justice advocacy. These barriers may include limited exposure to social justice content in her graduate program, lack of awareness of school psychologists' advocacy role, or fear of disrupting the status quo. Due to Emily's intern status at the school, Ms. Thomas will also use her power and influence to create opportunities for Emily to engage in advocacy and legitimize Emily's work in this area.

Developing a Plan to Support Latinx Students

Porter (2009) described a four-stage model of FMS. In the first stage, the supervisee takes a didactic approach to exploring all aspects, including sociocultural aspects, of a client's problem to gain fundamental information. This is followed by an exploration of larger social and cultural issues of power, privilege, and oppression as they pertain to the client's problems. Supervisees explore their own misconceptions, biases, and privilege, and consider how their lived experience will impact their approach to the client's treatment. Finally, the focus of supervision expands beyond an individual client's treatment to explore broader areas of systems change and community engagement to empower clients and promote their well-being.

Applying the FMS model to the case narrative, one of Ms. Thomas's first tasks would be to teach Emily about microaggressions. Emily's knowledge in this area is likely limited because the topic of microaggressions has received little attention in school psychology. Through readings and discussion, Ms. Thomas would assist Emily in developing the knowledge to recognize microaggressions and the skills to appropriately address them. Part of the supervisee's education is learning the explicit connection between microaggressions and racism—specifically, that microaggressions are a form of interpersonal racism that can lead to internalized racism (i.e., minoritized students internalizing negative beliefs about themselves) and that maintain institutional racism by leading to differential treatment of students. Ms. Thomas would guide Emily through self-reflection exercises for her to consider any biases and misconceptions she may have about Latinx students and previous experiences working with that population. Additionally, Emily is encouraged to consider her own experiences with microaggressions and how they affected her emotional well-being, sense of belonging, and access to opportunities. These focused and reflective discussions provide a foundation for Emily to recognize that direct intervention is needed to support Juan, Rosalia, and other Latinx students, but that systems-level intervention is also warranted so that school personnel are better equipped to intervene with microaggressions. Both approaches are needed to protect Latinx students' well-being and ensure that their identities are affirmed in school.

Students need support navigating the complex emotions evoked by microaggressions and advocates empowered to address microaggressions and the systemic forces that sustain them. The ACA advocacy competencies provide a framework for intervention at both the student and school-wide levels. On the client/student level, Emily will advocate on behalf of Latinx students and provide intervention to develop self-advocacy skills. In collaboration with school personnel, she will work on the school/community level to address issues of school climate.

Intervention at the Client/Student Level

The goal of intervention at this level is to mitigate the negative psychological outcomes of racism and discrimination. An additional goal is to empower students with self-advocacy skills to help them navigate challenging environments (Goodman et al., 2004). Cultural affinity groups are one way to meet both goals. These groups provide a counterspace in schools for REM students to celebrate their culture and feel affirmed. Cultural affinity groups can also promote positive racial/ethnic identity development and provide educational/peer support in navigating microaggressions. For example, these programs are associated with increased resilience, greater levels of cultural identity, as well as positive outcomes related to reduced disciplinary referrals, increased attendance, and increased sense of safety and empowerment (Aston & Graves, 2016; Gbolo & Grier-Reed, 2019). Additionally, participating in these groups can promote students' critical consciousness as they learn how their individual experiences of microaggressions are connected to systemic oppressive systems and how to use civic engagement for institutional change (Wray-Lake et al., 2018).

Intervention at the School/Community Level

Systems advocacy entails advocating on behalf of a group of students in the school and working with community partners to address systemic factors that are barriers to students' development (Ratts et al., 2007). The goal of intervention at this level is to create caring schools with educators who affirm students' cultural identities, have high expectations for all students, and are committed to creating learning environments free from race-based discrimination (Nganga et al., 2019). Through professional development and consultative support, educators can learn how to create culturally affirming school environments and build positive relationships with all students (Malone et al., in press). Professional development would improve educators' ability to recognize microaggressions, understand how microaggressions impact recipients, and engage in corrective action when microaggressions occur (Sue et al., 2009). Emily can work in partnership with her supervisor Ms. Thomas to create and deliver in-service training to school staff. As a follow-up to these trainings, the intern and supervisor can provide consultative support to school leaders as they review the school's existing bullying prevention program and incorporate modules that address microaggressions (Wintner et al., 2017). Not only would this approach build educators' capacity, but it will help to create a more supportive school climate as other students who are either the targets of or witnesses to microaggressions learn how to confront those who perpetrate microaggressions.

Conclusion

Racism is present in every facet of American life; schools are no exception. If schools are committed to creating safe, supportive, and affirming environments for all students, educators must recognize and acknowledge microaggressions and, more importantly, label microaggressions as racism. Until this occurs, they will continue to approach school climate and bullying interventions with a colorblind lens that ignores the experiences of REM students. Consistent with a CRT lens, educators have to assume a stance of cultural humility, listen to the voices of those who experience racism, and validate their experiences if they are truly committed to creating anti-racist schools.

References

Arczynski, A. V., & Morrow, S. L. (2017). The complexities of power in feminist multicultural psychotherapy supervision. *Journal of Counseling Psychology*, *64*, 192–205. https://doi.org/10.1037/cou0000179

Aston, C. & Graves, S. L., Jr. (2016). Challenges and barriers to implementing a school-based Afrocentric intervention in urban schools: A pilot study of the Sisters of Nia cultural program. *School Psychology Forum*, *10*, 165–176.

Balagna, R. M., Young, E. L., & Smith, T. B. (2013). School experiences of early adolescent Latinos/as at risk for emotional and behavioral disorders. *School Psychology Quarterly*, *28*, 101–121. https://doi.org/10.1037/spq0000018

Benner, A. D., & Graham, S. (2013). The antecedents and consequences of racial/ethnic discrimination during adolescence: Does the source of discrimination matter? *Developmental Psychology*, *49*, 1602–1613. https://doi.org/10.1037/a0030557

Brown v. Board of Education, 347 U.S. 483 (1954). https://oyez.org/cases/1940-1955/347us483

Call-Cummings, M., & Martinez, S. (2017). "It wasn't racism; it was more misunderstanding." White teachers, Latino/a students, and racial battle fatigue. *Race, Ethnicity, and Education*, *20*, 561–574. https://doi.org/10.1080/13613324.2016.1150830

Carter, P. L., Skiba, R., Arredondo, M. I., & Pollock, M. (2017). You can't fix what you don't look at: Acknowledging race in addressing racial discipline disparities. *Urban Education*, *52*, 207–235. https://doi.org/10.1177%2F0042085916660350

Chopra, T. (2013). All supervision is multicultural: A review of literature on the need for multicultural supervision in counseling. *Psychological Studies*, *58*, 335–338. https://psycnet.apa.org/doi/10.1007/s12646-013-0206-x

Cohen, J., McCabe, L., Michelli, N. M., & Pickeral, T. (2009). School climate: Research, policy, practice, and teacher education. *Teachers College Record*, *111*(1), 180–213.

DeCuir, J. T., & Dixson, A. D. (2004). "So when it comes out, they aren't that surprised that it is there": Using critical race theory as a tool of analysis of race and racism in education. *Educational Researcher*, *33*, 26–31. https://doi.org/10.3102%2F0013189X033005026

Espinola, M., Zhen-Duan, J., Suarez-Cano, G., Mowry-Mora, I., & Shultz, J. M. (2019). The impact of US sociopolitical issues on the prejudicial treatment of Latino children and youth. In *Handbook of children and prejudice* (pp. 161–180). Springer.

Forrest-Bank, S., & Jenson, J. M. (2015). Differences in experiences of racial and ethnic microaggression among Asian, Latino/Hispanic, Black, and White young adults. *Journal of Sociology and Social Welfare*, *42*, 141–161.

French, B. H., Lewis, J. A., Mosley, D. V., Adames, H. Y., Chavez-Dueñas, N. Y., Chen, G. A., & Neville, H. A. (2020). Toward a psychological framework of radical healing in communities of color. *The Counseling Psychologist*, *48*, 14–46. https://doi.org/10.1177%2F0011000019843506

Gbolo, S., & Grier-Reed, T. L. (2019). An African American student networking group in an urban high school: Experiences and outcomes. *Urban Education*, *54*(9), 1210–1232. https://doi.org/10.1177%2F0042085916641170

Girvan, E. J., Gion, C., McIntosh, K., & Smolkowski, K. (2017). The relative contribution of subjective office referrals to racial disproportionality in school discipline. *School Psychology Quarterly*, *32*, 392–404. https://doi.org/10.1037/spq0000178

Glosoff, H. L., & Durham, J. C. (2010). Using supervision to prepare social justice counseling advocates. *Counselor Education and Supervision*, *50*, 116–129. https://doi.org/10.1002/j.1556-6978.2010.tb00113.x

Goodman, L. A., Liang, B., Helms, J. E., Latta, R. E., Sparks, E., & Weintraub, S. R. (2004). Training counseling psychologists as social justice agents: Feminist and multicultural principles in action. *The Counseling Psychologist*, *32*, 793–836. https://doi.org/10.1177%2F0011000004268802

Grissom, J. A., & Redding, C. (2015). Discretion and disproportionality: Explaining the underrepresentation of high-achieving students of color in gifted programs. *AERA Open*, *2*(1), 2332858415622175.

Hays, P. A. (2016). *Addressing cultural complexities in practice: Assessment, Diagnosis, and therapy* (3rd ed.). American Psychological Association. https://doi.org/10.1037/14801-000

Hook, J. N., Davis, D. E., Owen, J., Worthington Jr., E. L., & Utsey, S. O. (2013). Cultural humility: Measuring openness to culturally diverse clients. *Journal of Counseling Psychology*, *60*, 353–366. https://doi.org/10.1037/a0032595

Hook, J. N., Farrell, J. E., Davis, D. E., DeBlaere, C., Van Tongeren, D. R., & Utsey, S. O. (2016). Cultural humility and racial microaggressions in counseling. *Journal of Counseling Psychology*, *63*, 269–277. https://doi.org/10.1037/cou0000114

Huang, F. L., & Cornell, D. G. (2019). School teasing and bullying after the presidential election. *Educational Researcher*, *48*, 69–83. https://doi.org/10.3102%2F0013189X18820291

Huber, L. P., & Cueva, B. M. (2012). Chicana/Latina testimonios on effects and responses to microaggressions. *Equity and Excellence in Education*, *45*, 392–410. https://doi.org/10.1080/10665684.2012.698193

Hughes, T., Raines, T., & Malone, C. (2020). School pathways to the juvenile justice system. *Policy Insights from the Behavioral and Brain Sciences*, 7, 72–79. https://doi.org/10.1177%2F2372732219897093

Huynh, V. W. (2012). Ethnic microaggressions and the depressive and somatic symptoms of Latino and Asian American adolescents. *Journal of Youth and Adolescence*, *41*, 831–846. https://doi.org/10.1007/s10964-012-9756-9

Huynh, V. W., & Fuligni, A. J. (2010). Discrimination hurts: The academic, psychological, and physical well-being of adolescents. *Journal of Research on Adolescence*, *20*, 916–941. https://doi.org/10.1111/j.1532-7795.2010.00670.x

Jones, C. P. (2000). Levels of racism: A theoretic framework and a gardener's tale. *American Journal of Public Health*, *90*, 1212–1215. https://doi.org/10.2105/AJPH.90.8.1212

Kohli, R., & Solórzano, D. G. (2012). Teachers, please learn our names! Racial microaggressions and the K-12 classroom. *Race, Ethnicity, and Education*, *15*, 441–462. https://doi.org/10.1080/13613324.2012.674026

Ladson-Billings, G. (1998). Just what is critical race theory and what's it doing in a nice field like education? *International Journal of Qualitative Studies in Education*, *11*, 7–24. https://doi.org/10.1080/095183998236863

Malone, C. M., & Proctor, S. L. (2019). Demystifying Social Justice for School Psychology Practice. *Communiqué*, *48*(1), 1–21.

Malone, C. M., Wycoff, K., & Turner, E. A. (in press). Applying a MTSS framework to address racism and promote mental health for racial/ethnic minoritized youth. *Psychology in the Schools*.

Mattison, E., & Aber, M. S. (2007). Closing the achievement gap: The association of racial climate with achievement and behavioral outcomes. *American Journal of Community Psychology, 40*, 1–12. https://doi.org/10.1007/s10464-007-9128-x

Nadal, K. L., Griffin, K. E., Wong, Y., Hamit, S., & Rasmus, M. (2014). The impact of racial microaggressions on mental health: Counseling implications for clients of color. *Journal of Counseling and Development, 92*, 57–66. https://doi.org/10.1002/j.1556-6676.2014.00130.x

Nganga, L., Kambutu, J., & Han, K. T. (2019). Caring schools and educators a solution to disparities in academic performance: Learners of colors speak. *SAGE Open, 9*(2), 2158244019841923.

Porter, N. (2009). Feminist and multicultural underpinnings to supervision: An overview. *Women and Therapy, 33*, 1–6. https://doi.org/10.1080/02703140903404622

Porter, N., & Vasquez, M. (1997). *Covision: Feminist supervision, process, and collaboration.* In J. Worell & N. G. Johnson (Eds.), *Psychology of women book series. Shaping the future of feminist psychology: Education, research, and practice* (p. 155–171). American Psychological Association. https://doi.org/10.1037/10245-007

Ratts, M. J., DeKruyf, L., & Chen-Hayes, S. F. (2007). The ACA advocacy competencies: A social justice advocacy framework for professional school counselors. *Professional School Counseling, 11*, 90–96. https://doi.org/10.1177%2F2156759X0701100203

Rolón-Dow, R., & Davison, A. (2021). Theorizing racial microaffirmations: A Critical Race/LatCrit approach. *Race, Ethnicity, and Education, 24*, 245–261. https://doi.org/10.1080/13613324.2020.1798381

Rowe, M. (2008). Micro-affirmations and micro-inequities. *Journal of the International Ombudsman Association, 1*(1), 45–48.

Skiba, R. J., Simmons, A. B., Ritter, S., Gibb, A. C., Rausch, M. K., Cuadrado, J., & Chung, C. G. (2008). Achieving equity in special education: History, status, and current challenges. *Exceptional Children, 74*, 264–288. https://doi.org/10.1177%2F001440290807400301

Southern Poverty Law Center. (2016). *The Trump effect: The impact of the 2016 presidential election on our nation's schools.* www.splcenter.org/20161128/trump-effect-impact-2016-presidential-election-our-nations-schools

Starck, J. G., Riddle, T., Sinclair, S., & Warikoo, N. (2020). Teachers are people too: Examining the racial bias of teachers compared to other American adults. *Educational Researcher, 49*, 273–284. https://doi.org/10.3102%2F0013189X20912758

Sue, D. W., Capodilupo, C. M., & Holder, A. (2008). Racial microaggressions in the life experience of Black Americans. *Professional Psychology: Research and Practice, 39*, 329. https://doi.org/10.1037/0735-7028.39.3.329

Sue, D. W., Capodilupo, C. M., Torino, G. C., Bucceri, J. M., Holdreder, A., Nadal, K. L., & Esquilin, M. (2007). Racial microaggressions in everyday life: Implications for clinical practice. *American Psychologist, 62*(4), 271–286. https://doi.org/10.1037/0003-066X.62.4.271

Sue, D. W., Lin, A. I., Torino, G. C., Capodilupo, C. M., & Rivera, D. P. (2009). Racial microaggressions and difficult dialogues on race in the classroom. *Cultural Diversity and Ethnic Minority Psychology, 15*, 183–190. https://doi.org/10.1037/a0014191

Tervalon, M., & Murray-Garcia, J. (1998). Cultural humility versus cultural competence: A critical distinction in defining physician training outcomes in multicultural education. *Journal of Health Care for the Poor and Underserved, 9*, 117–125. https://doi.org/10.1353/hpu.2010.0233

Toporek, R. L., & Daniels, J. (2018). *ACA advocacy competencies*. www.counseling.org/docs/default-source/competencies/aca-advocacy-competencies-updated-may-2020.pdf?sfvrsn=f410212c_4

United States Department of Education. (2017). *Digest of education statistics. Indicator 9: Students with disabilities*. https://nces.ed.gov/programs/raceindicators/indicator_RBD.asp

Voight, A., Hanson, T., O'Malley, M., & Adekanye, L. (2015). The racial school climate gap: Within-school disparities in students' experiences of safety, support, and connectedness. *American Journal of Community Psychology*, *56*, 252–267. https://doi.org/10.1007/s10464-015-9751-x

Vos, S. R., Shrader, C. H., Alvarez, V. C., Meca, A., Unger, J. B., Brown, E. C., . . . Schwartz, S. J. (2021). Cultural stress in the age of mass xenophobia: Perspectives from Latin/o adolescents. *International Journal of Intercultural Relations*, *80*, 217–230. https://doi.org/10.1016/j.ijintrel.2020.11.011

Watkins, N. D., & Aber, M. S. (2009). Exploring the relationships among race, class, gender, and middle school students' perceptions of school racial climate. *Equity and Excellence in Education*, *42*, 395–411. https://doi.org/10.1080/10665680903260218

Watts, R. J., Diemer, M. A., & Voight, A. M. (2011). Critical consciousness: Current status and future directions. *New Directions for Child and Adolescent Development*, *2011*, 43–57. https://doi.org/10.1002/cd.310

Wintner, S., Almeida, J., & Hamilton-Mason, J. (2017). Perceptions of microaggression in K-8 school settings: An exploratory study. *Children and Youth Services Review*, *79*, 594–601. https://doi.org/10.1016/j.childyouth.2017.07.020

Wong, C. A., Eccles, J. S., & Sameroff, A. (2003). The influence of ethnic discrimination and ethnic identification on African American adolescents' school and socioemotional adjustment. *Journal of Personality*, *71*, 1197–1232. https://doi.org/10.1111/1467-6494.7106012

Wray-Lake, L., Wells, R., Alvis, L., Delgado, S., Syvertsen, A. K., & Metzger, A. (2018). Being a Latinx adolescent under a Trump presidency: Analysis of Latinx youth's reactions to immigration politics. *Children and Youth Services Review*, *87*, 192–204. https://doi.org/10.1016/j.childyouth.2018.02.032

Yosso, T., Smith, W., Ceja, M., & Solórzano, D. (2009). Critical race theory, racial microaggressions, and campus racial climate for Latina/o undergraduates. *Harvard Educational Review*, *79*, 659–691. https://doi.org/10.17763/haer.79.4.m6867014157m707l

13

DISCRIT THEORY APPLIED TO CLINICAL SUPERVISION FOR MINORITIZED STUDENTS WITH SOCIAL, EMOTIONAL, AND BEHAVIORAL CONCERNS

Shereen C. Naser, Sally L. Grapin, Charity Brown Griffin, and Jeffrey M. Brown

In this chapter, we will use DisCrit Theory as a lens through which to examine the process of identifying students struggling socially, behaviorally, and emotionally; school responses to student social, emotional, and behavioral struggles; and ultimately special education referrals for emotional disturbance (ED). Specifically, we will review the research that addresses these issues in relation to racially minoritized student populations. We will use DisCrit Theory to provide concrete suggestions for guiding clinical supervision practices in school psychology when working with students whose primary referral is for social, emotional, and behavioral concerns.

Teachers report that student behavioral struggles are the most burdensome barriers to teaching and learning (Moon et al., 2017; Wei et al., 2009). Classroom management and response to student behavior is an area in which teachers receive little to no training, and a gap exists between knowledge of best practices in classroom management strategies and teacher training in best practices (Freeman et al., 2014; Stormont et al., 2011). Teachers who struggle to support student behavior in the classroom might rely on external systems such as special education referrals for ED and school discipline practices such as office discipline referrals, suspensions, and expulsions to address behaviors that they feel unable to address in the classroom. However, a robust body of literature has identified racial disproportionality in who is referred to school disciplinary systems (i.e., office discipline referrals, suspensions, and expulsions) for behavioral problems (Skiba et al., 2011; U.S. Department of Education OCR, 2014) as well as identification for ED (Bal et al., 2019). While schools have come to rely heavily on data-based decision-making regarding monitoring student academic progress, they still largely rely on subjective practices when it comes to student behavior (Bruhn et al., 2014).

DOI: 10.4324/9780367815325-16

As school practitioners who often are asked to help teachers and schools better understand and respond to student behavior, it is important to think critically about how behavior is viewed, monitored, measured, and treated in the school setting. This is particularly true in key training practices such as supervision for school psychologists, as supervision experiences lay the foundation for future independent practice.

Brief Introduction to DisCrit Theory

DisCrit is an emerging theoretical paradigm that explores the inextricable linkages between race and dis/ability. It acknowledges the many ways racism and ableism converge to create and reinforce interlocking systems of oppression. Because the foundations of DisCrit were described extensively in Chapter 3, this section reviews each tenet only briefly. The section also highlights the implications of DisCrit tenets for delivering supervision in school psychology.

The first two tenets of DisCrit Theory highlight the many ways race and dis/ability interact. Specifically, DisCrit's first tenet acknowledges the ways racism and ableism converge to cultivate oppressive social conditions and systems. In other words, although these phenomena are distinct, they are also mutually reinforcing. The second tenet of DisCrit acknowledges race and dis/ability as intersecting identities, which in turn shape individuals' experiences with prejudice and discrimination. As noted by Annamma et al. (2013), the simultaneous experience of multiple marginalized identities may add further complexity and nuance to an individual's experiences with stigma and discrimination.

The third tenet of DisCrit Theory acknowledges that both race and dis/ability are socially constructed (rather than biologically based). Annamma et al. (2013) further noted that while racism and ableism are products of social construction, their consequences are felt at a material, economic, and physical (e.g., bodily) level. The fourth tenet focuses on privileging the voices of those who have been marginalized. DisCrit does not aim to "give" voice to those who have been marginalized (as these individuals already have a voice); rather, it urges others to listen attentively to counter-narratives that challenge mainstream discourse around dis/ability and race.

DisCrit's fifth tenet acknowledges the legal and historical underpinnings of racism and ableism. In particular, it rejects the notion of "ahistoricism," or a lack of regard for the ways racism and ableism were (re)produced in the past. For example, DisCrit scholars would contend that a sound understanding of the historical forces that have perpetuated oppression in schools (e.g., *the historical* legacy of segregation) is essential for engaging in sound case conceptualization, decision-making, and advocacy.

The sixth and seventh tenets of DisCrit focus on the nature of social change and advocacy, respectively. DisCrit's sixth tenet acknowledges whiteness and ability as forms of property; in other words, those who successfully claim these identity markers enjoy access to numerous social and economic privileges that are systematically denied to marginalized groups (Annamma et al., 2013). The seventh and final tenet of DisCrit contends that activism is essential for interrupting misguided assumptions of "normality" and for deconstructing systems of oppression. At the same time, Annamma et al. (2013) noted that an excessive emphasis on traditional forms of resistance (e.g., sit-ins and marches) can disenfranchise those with disabilities. In light of this consideration, they encourage scholars, practitioners, and community members to embrace an expanded spectrum of advocacy behaviors, including both scholarly and pedagogical activities (e.g., mentoring and curriculum reform; Sabnis and Bueno Martinez, this volume).

This chapter uses DisCrit Theory as a lens to examine the school-based process of identifying and responding to students struggling socially, behaviorally, and emotionally. Before applying DisCrit in this way, the next section proposes a definition for behavioral and emotional risk and outlines traditional school models of identifying and responding to behavioral and emotional risk.

Behavioral and Emotional Risk From a School Perspective

Behavioral and emotional risk is the presence of social, emotional, and behavioral (SEB) patterns that might qualify a student in the future for more intensive behavioral and emotional services such as special education or therapeutic services (Kamphaus et al., 2014). *Risk* as a term used clinically is distinct from the phrase "at-risk," which has become synonymous with a deficit perspective rooted in stereotypes of Black youth living in poverty. The term "at-risk" is vague, prescribes blame to marginalized communities rather than systemic barriers to access and equity, and upholds a discourse of white supremacy and colonialism providing little meaning for understanding and addressing the SEB functioning of marginalized youth (Pica-Smith & Veloria, 2012). However, in a clinical context, *SEB risk* refers to the potential need for more supportive services due to measured social, emotional, and behavioral patterns empirically linked to higher rates of clinical psychopathology should those patterns persist without intervention and is not inherently associated with class, race, or dis/ability status. The presence of risk also does not preclude the presence of resilience. As will be discussed later in this chapter, the measures traditionally used to assess SEB risk in the school setting may themselves be influenced by implicit racial biases and deficit, resulting in the over- or under-identification of youth of color for SEB supports. The development and implementation of more equitable, holistic, and accurate assessment and measurement practices, however, can increase early identification and therefore early intervention and support for those youth who need them most.

SEB risk can be categorized as either internalizing or externalizing risk, with internalizing risk representing more internal struggles such as anxiety or depression, and externalizing struggles representing externally expressed symptoms such as difficulty concentrating and aggressive interactions with others. Externalizing risk is most common in childhood, and internalizing risk increases as children move into adolescence (Naser & Dever, 2019), though the two symptom categories are interrelated. While there are broad patterns for understanding the development of behavioral and emotional risk over time, patterns of risk can be impacted by factors both internal and external to the child. Factors internal to the child can include gender (Naser & Dever, 2019), while factors external to the child can include exposure to stressful or traumatic life events such as acts of violence at home or in the community, transience, poverty, exposure to discrimination, or school-level events (Costello et al., 2003; Li et al., 2007; Prelow et al., 2004). The presence of behavioral and emotional risk is often associated with poor school and relational functioning, including for students of color (Bulotsky-Shearer & Fantuzzo, 2011; Darney et al., 2013; Reinke et al., 2008). While the presence of these factors may negatively impact youth mental health, there are also a number of factors that build youth resilience including strong self-esteem and family connectedness (Li et al., 2007).

As already noted, the presence of behavioral and emotional risk speaks to the potential of clinically significant symptoms of mental illness, not the immediate presence of clinically significant symptoms. School environments can play a role in identifying risk and intervening to help build student resilience and promote positive youth development. Systematic, early, and equitable identification of student behavioral and emotional risk can help support students of color who might otherwise be missed when relying on subjective and reactive discipline referrals (Raines et al., 2012). While schools have the potential to support youth positive development, they also have the potential to create stressful events that might exacerbate social, emotional, and behavioral struggles. Unique school systems and structures that might negatively impact youth of color include school tolerance for acts of discrimination from teachers and peers, school curriculum choices that are exclusionary or provide misinformation regarding students' cultural or racial heritage, and the willingness of schools to provide space for youth to positively explore their own and their peers' identities (Griffin et al., 2017; Najjar & Naser, 2019).

Ultimately, school responses to student behavior play a role in students' ability to thrive. Okonofua et al. (2016) outlined a process through which teacher bias and student behavior interact in what they call a vicious cycle. Teachers' implicit biases create a cycle by which students of color, particularly Black students, are seen as more troublesome while students of color worry about whether teachers and school administrators will treat them fairly. These psychological processes inform student behavioral responses where students feel less motivated to build positive relationships with teachers and school administrators. Teacher stereotypes about behavior for Black, Latinx, and Indigenous students result in these students carrying a disproportionate burden of poor school discipline practices.

In the following section, we explore ways that DisCrit Theory provides a framework for understanding behavioral and emotional risk and the role of school systems and structures in who is identified as struggling behaviorally and emotionally. While DisCrit Theory is built to explore the link between race and dis/ability, there are unique considerations for how behavioral and emotional risk, as well as behavioral and emotional disorders, are assessed, categorized, and treated in youth of color. Using a DisCrit lens in exploring behavioral and emotional risk and disorders requires a critical examination of the referral and diagnostic process to better understand how we can mitigate the role of stereotyping and implicit bias in referral practices to accurately identify students with true behavioral, emotional, and social struggles and connect them to needed resources.

Relevance of DisCrit to Behavioral and Emotional Concerns in Schools

A core purpose of DisCrit is "to investigate how patterns of oppression uniquely intersect to target students at the margins of whiteness and ability" (Annamma et al., 2018, p. 46). A clear impact of racial oppression in schools is how school personnel define and identify who is "good" or who displays acceptable behavior and who does not. Broderick and Leonardo (2016) argued that "goodness" is socially constructed and that whiteness is a central part of what is considered good. Some aspects of "goodness" constitute moral values that allow for peaceful coexistence in society, such as sharing, taking turns, and refraining from physically harming others. However, Broderick and Leonardo (2016) argued that other aspects of goodness are oppressive and are used to distribute authority in schools irrespective of a student's actual behavior. They go on to define "goodness" in the school setting as a "performative, cultural, and ideological system that operates in the service of constructing the normative center of schools" (Broderick & Leonardo, 2016, p. 57).

If the definition of "goodness" inherently includes whiteness, then the distribution of discipline practices such as office discipline referrals (ODR) would disproportionately impact students of color, a pattern robustly supported in the literature. Although teachers play a valuable role in identifying students struggling with behavioral, emotional, and social concerns (Stiffman et al., 2004), including through tracking behavioral concerns through ODRs, their ability to accurately identify student need is impacted by their own personal biases, expertise, knowledge, and the school culture (Vanlommel et al., 2018). Their concepts of which students are displaying disruptive behaviors reflect patterns of bias observed in society as a whole (Starck et al., 2020). Implicit bias is one mechanism through which dysfunctional educational ecologies are maintained (Annamma & Morrison, 2018).

The impact of implicit bias on the evaluation of unacceptable student behaviors can be seen when evaluating the use of ODR and other school disciplinary referrals such as suspensions and expulsions. For example, Skiba et al. (2011) found that African American elementary school students were more than twice as likely to receive an ODR as their white peers. The higher incidence of discipline referrals is more likely to occur with subjective behaviors (e.g., disrespect, defiance; Girvan et al., 2017) and is not attributed to a difference in actual student behavior (American Psychological Association Zero Tolerance Task Force, 2008; Fish, 2017; Skiba et al., 2011). The racial disproportionality seen in ODR is mirrored in other exclusionary discipline practices such as suspensions and expulsions. A 2014 report by the United States (U.S.) Department of Education Office for Civil Rights highlighted considerable racial disproportionality in suspension and expulsion rates in the U.S. For example, while Black male students make up 8% of enrolled K-12 students, they made up 25% of suspended and 23% of expelled students. Thus, traditional school referral methods disproportionately impact racially and ethnically minoritized youth.

Research regarding teacher decision-making around student behavior elucidates potential bias in these systems as one mechanism for racial disproportionality in discipline referrals (Kunesh & Noltemeyer, 2019). In a study by Fish (2017), teachers were given vignettes regarding student behavior and asked to determine whether student behavior warranted a special education referral. The behaviors described in the vignettes remained the same; however, name and other potential indicators of the student's race varied. For example, the student name may have been changed from Jacob, representing the white student, or Carlos, representing the Latino student. Results of the study indicated that teachers were more likely to refer students of color to special education assessments for behavior problems than white students (Fish, 2017). Another study utilizing similar methodology asked pre-service teachers to rate vignettes depicting disruptive behaviors by Black students and white students (Kunesh & Noltemeyer, 2019). Study participants were asked to rate whether they thought the described behavior was likely to occur again, indicating beliefs about behavior stability. Results indicated that participants were more likely to attribute the behavior of Black students to stable causes than white students, though they did not rate the behaviors of Black students as more inappropriate than white students (Kunesh & Noltemeyer, 2019). The bias evidence in vignette ratings likely impacts how students are referred for ODR.

The dual-process model helps explain how bias might show up in inequitable disciplinary practices in schools. The dual-process model describes two types of cognitive processes that occur around decision-making—System I and System II processes. System I processes are automatic, happen quickly, and are effortless. System II thinking is deliberate, considers context, and is rational and slow. The automatic nature of System I thinking means that it relies on information we have the quickest access to, including our implicit bias. The speed at which System I decisions can be made also means that it is more likely to be utilized in situations where the person making the decision is stressed or overwhelmed. School-based research indicates that System I thinking is more likely to be used when a teacher is making decisions in the classroom around student behavior, and therefore these decisions are more likely to be influenced by implicit bias (Girvan et al., 2017).

The dual-process model also provides some guidance on intervention and training strategies. For example, incorporating objective data into the decision-making process to cue more deliberate thinking about student behavior is one way to negate bias in the discipline referral system by complementing intuitive and experiential judgments with less-subjective data. Data-based decision-making has been cited as a key ingredient to any equitable school decision-making protocol (Gregory et al., 2017) and is especially important when the subject of referral requires a judgment of more ambiguous and subjective constructs such as behavior (Girvan et al., 2017). Applying the dual-process model to decision-making around student behavior includes implementing processes around the time of decision-making that might cue more rational decision-making that is less vulnerable to bias (McIntosh et al., 2014). However, this process is still reactive and while it may reduce disproportionality in discipline referrals, it does not aid in pushing schools to also consider proactive data-based decisions that can help to increase access to behavioral and emotional supports. School referral strategies for connecting students to needed social, emotional, and behavioral supports would still require an accumulation of teacher-initiated discipline referrals. As schools are one of the most important gateway providers for mental health support, increasing access to mental health care for racially minoritized youth requires early and effective identification of behavioral and emotional risk. Therefore, discussion of student behavior should include an analysis of the way behavioral data is being collected and the potential for bias in that process, attention to the skills the student may be missing and ways those skills might be remediated and not simply punished, how the use of new skills might be reinforced, and a review of system-level school processes that can facilitate learning and reinforcing new behaviors.

Disproportionality in ODR is not in and of itself problematic if it represents true student need and connects students to services that result in better student outcomes (Sullivan & Proctor, 2016). Research indicates, however, that the over-representation of racially and ethnically minoritized students in discipline referrals has a high likelihood of resulting reactions that perpetuate educational disparities (Darensbourg et al., 2010; Skiba et al., 2002; Sullivan & Proctor, 2016). For example, students who receive out-of-school suspensions continue to experience higher rates of behavioral referrals, lower academic achievement, and lower school attendance (Iselin, 2010). These students also experience increased risk for school drop-out (Noltemeyer et al., 2015), opportunities for delinquency (The Advancement Project, 2005), and restricted access to school services such as school-based mental health supports (Townsend, 2000). Increased suspension and expulsion for students of color have been implicated as a foundation to the school-to-prison pipeline, engaging students in a cycle of continued poor academic performance and exclusion (Nelson & Lind, 2015). Therefore, the current behavioral referral system perpetuates a harmful cycle for racially minoritized youth while the gap in mental health supports limits access to intervention services that might interrupt such harmful practices.

The implications of racial disproportionality in teacher referrals go far beyond simply reacting to student behavior punitively. While this is the immediate repercussion, the repeated use of reactive and punitive referrals launches students into cycles of exclusion, which themselves escalate and serve as the foundation for the school-to-prison pipeline. Students who are labeled as "good" are given more latitude and freedoms, while those who are labeled as "bad" are often given this label as a part of their character, are continuously targeted, and are therefore more restricted (Broderick & Leonardo, 2016). In a study by Okonofua and Eberhardt (2015), teachers were asked not only to rate student behaviors in a vignette but to identify patterns of student behavior. Results indicated that teachers were more likely to label Black students as "troublemakers," or students with consistent patterns of disruptive behaviors despite the described behavior in the vignette being identical for the white and Black student. Okonofua et al. (2016) dubbed this process a "vicious cycle" in which bias and apprehension about bias build on one another in the school setting, negatively impacting the relationship between teachers and students and further solidifying this process of withholding the privileges afforded to those students perceived as good students.

Studies evaluating racial disproportionality across special education categories consistently find that simply being Black—and especially being poor, Black, and male—increases the chances of being identified for ED as a special-education qualification (Sullivan & Bal, 2013). ED as a qualification category is one of the most contested definitions within special education. Recent estimates indicate that 20% of children experience some psychopathology (Whitney & Peterson, 2019), and 10.6% of youth experience psychiatric disorders with severe impairment (Williams et al., 2018). However, only 5% of students in the school setting from ages 3 to 21 are served under the ED category of special education (National Center for Education Statistics, 2019).

Like subjective ODR categories, the subjective feature of ED as a qualification lends itself to a greater impact of bias in the process of referral to ED (Fish, 2017). There is some debate as to whether the process for qualification for ED categories is biased or rather reflects true student need; however, research regarding decision-making practices inherent in ED qualification processes themselves are biased (Sullivan, 2017). Algozzine (2017) noted that "in special education, a definition creates a condition and identification practices bring it to life" (p. 136). Algozzine (2017) went on to note that the definition for ED used for special education qualification includes characteristics that can be attributed universally to all youth as opposed to specific characteristics unique to students with ED. Other scholars have noted that the definition of ED is "nebulous and highly subjective" (Gresham, 2005, p. 330) and that ED as a category "remains indistinct—some would say even unintelligible—in both scholarship and practice" (Sullivan, 2017,

p. 246). Following Algozzine's (2017) logic then, an unclear condition has left a wide berth for subjective identification and assessment practices.

Finally, the construction of "goodness" in schools has unique implications for those who are stereotyped as "model minorities" in the U.S. context or "good minorities." Asian American youth are often stereotyped as hard-working, smart, and compliant. This construction of both compliance and smartness serves as the lens through which school personnel judge Asian youth, which can render the struggles of Asian youth invisible. Asian American students are largely underrepresented in school behavioral referral programs and are less likely to use school-based mental health services than their peers (Anyon et al., 2014). This persists despite higher rates of depression among Asian youth and higher rates of suicide among Asian youth compared to their white peers (Abright & Chung, 2002; Wyatt et al., 2015).

DisCrit provides a theoretical framework through which we can better understand how systems of power and privilege determine which students are identified as having a dis/ability in the school context, which students are disciplined, and the services that are ultimately shared with students in need. As noted previously, current school patterns of discipline and special education qualification mirror the biases seen in society, with Black, Latinx, and Indigenous youth experiencing higher rates of discipline and referral to special education for ED. The presence of racial bias in the decision-making process around student social, emotional, and behavioral functioning means that students who need support aren't getting it and, in many cases, are experiencing harm at the hands of racially biased school responses to student behavior. While sweeping system-level change is needed to address these inequalities and injustices, supervision is one way to influence the training of future school psychologists who regularly act as gatekeepers to special education through responding to school referrals for special education for ED.

How Can We Use DisCrit Theory in Supervision for Cases With Social, Emotional, and Behavioral Referral Questions?

Supervision is a critical practice in the training of school psychologists. Definitions of supervision within the school psychology literature emphasize the importance of supervision in supporting the development of professional competencies for the supervisee (McIntosh & Phelps, 2000). DisCrit's underlying theory and assumptions have clear implications for school psychology training and practice. While a number of authors have discussed multicultural supervision in school psychology (Proctor & Rogers, 2013; Eklund et al., 2014), scholarship in this area is only beginning to uncover the many ways supervisors can challenge systems of oppression through their work with supervisees and clients. DisCrit has the potential to expand these discussions in several ways. First, it reminds supervisors of the inextricable linkages among race, dis/ability, and other facets of identity (e.g., gender, socioeconomic status). As highlighted by Annamma et al.

(2018), practitioners must acknowledge the myriad ways in which supervisees' and clients' intersecting identities contribute to their social experiences. Attempting to separate these identities would be not only challenging (if not impossible altogether) but also egregiously misguided.

DisCrit also reminds supervisors that the experiences of youth of color and youth with disabilities are steeped in a complex history of oppression and resilience. While it is not uncommon for school psychology scholars to emphasize an ecological approach to case conceptualization (e.g., Sheridan & Gutkin, 2000), it is less common for them to incorporate an explicitly historical one. DisCrit reminds school psychology supervisors of the need to openly and critically consider historical trends and ideologies that have shaped school-based policy and practice. These historical trends and ideologies are important at all levels including global, national, state, as well as community, and school level. For example, the community may have experienced a mass exodus of white affluent populations. It is also possible the community may be experiencing gentrification. Both instances change the student population, the expectations of the school from the community, and the political and cultural dynamics around the school. By assuming a historical perspective, practitioners can: (1) more readily and accurately identify institutional barriers to their clients' well-being, and (2) better position themselves to challenge pseudoscientific practices and mainstream narratives that perpetuate oppression.

Finally, Annamma et al.'s (2018) expanded conceptualization of resistance highlights supervision itself as a potentially powerful and meaningful form of advocacy. By its very nature, supervision carves out a designated space for supervisors and supervisees to reflect on a variety of individual and contextual issues that impact service delivery. Ultimately, supervision may serve as an essential form of advocacy in several ways. In particular, it provides a forum for supervisors to model self-reflection and effective forms of resistance for their supervisees. It also creates opportunities for supervisors and supervisees to share knowledge and to form alliances dedicated to the dismantling of oppressive institutional norms and practices and develop critical consciousness. *Critical consciousness* refers to a pedagogical approach rooted in liberation, justice, and equity. Critical consciousness was developed by Brazilian educator Paulo Freire, who noted that there is no such thing as a neutral educational process and that through critical consciousness we can create an educational system that promotes liberty, equity, and justice. Broadly, being critically conscious means being aware of inequity in systems and the mechanisms that perpetuate them as well as the means for changing them.

A DisCrit Model for Supervision Practice for Cases With Social, Emotional, and Behavioral Referral Questions

The process of becoming critically conscious requires cognitive, behavioral, and emotional work. Green et al. (2009) described a process for developing multicultural competence that they title "getting it" and that can be expanded to apply not only to multicultural competence but to critical consciousness as well. Green et al. (2009) noted that moving beyond your comfort zone and personal experiences requires conceptual understanding, acknowledging and utilizing emotional responses to grow, and allowing conceptual and emotional understanding to change behavior. None of these pathways alone is enough to fully develop multicultural competence, and all three must be experienced and enacted. Green et al. (2009) provided examples of ways that training is central to guiding supervisees onto the path of multicultural competence, including pushing them to explore conceptual content about the differences and commonalities of groups of people; ecosystemic theories and perspectives; issues of educational equity; study of people and groups who are underserved, misrepresented, and marginalized; and content about the impact of oppression, power, privilege, racism, social justice, social location, and colonization. After exposure to content, supervisors should be prepared to guide supervisees through emotional reaction and reflection in response to new content knowledge to foster openness, flexibility, and understanding. The model also pushes supervisors to ultimately move beyond a framework of emotional empathy to action and developing commitments that allow supervisees to act on their knowledge and experience.

The model of *getting it* provides a framework to support a process of internal change in the understanding of cultures other than one's own. Also important is an explicit understanding of the mechanisms of power and privilege at play in the supervision relationship, and between the supervisee and the students they serve. The power and privilege inherent in institutional systems sustains itself through often-invisible processes that confer benefits to white individuals and those considered able while creating unwelcoming and unsafe environments for people of color, those of other marginalized identities such as those with dis/abilities, and those with intersecting marginalized identities. Proctor and Rogers (2013) named five implicit processes that occur in the supervision relationship that are critical points of reflection to uncover these invisible processes. By uncovering them and naming them, they can be addressed.

The invisible processes named in Proctor and Rogers (2013) are power, racial microaggressions, relational safety, supervisory working alliance, and empowerment. *Power* refers to the impact of the power dynamic between the supervisor and the supervisee that might inhibit the supervisee's learning experience. There is a layer of power inherent in the role of supervisor over supervisee, and an added layer if the supervisor is white as they benefit from white privilege. *Racial microaggressions* refer to intentional and unintentional actions that communicate hostile, derogatory, and negative racial attitudes. Racial microaggressions can make an environment unwelcome and unsafe for people of color and can inhibit honest and open communication. *Relational safety* is an intentional creation of a supervisor and supervisee relationship where the supervisee feels safe to express themselves and their ideas, facilitating a learning environment where they can be challenged, raise questions, and engage fully in the learning experience. Creation of relational safety allows for an authentic and positive *supervisory working alliance* where there is mutual respect, positive regard, and an emotional bond between the supervisor and supervisee. Discussions about race support both relational safety and a positive supervisory working alliance. Finally, *empowerment* refers to the fostering of student self-confidence and self-efficacy. Supervisors empower supervisees of color when they respect and value the student's personal experiences and diversity-specific knowledge. No assumptions should ever be made regarding a supervisee's expertise, but through conversations regarding race supervisors can learn more regarding the experiences and expertise students bring to the table. While Proctor and Rogers (2013) focused on cross-racial supervision, the first two tenets of DisCrit highlight the many ways that race and dis/ability interact, and more specifically the way racism and ableism converge to cultivate oppressive social conditions and systems.

Table 13.1 presents a model for guiding supervisory practices that extends the concepts presented to not only the supervisor and supervisee but also to the referred student and that includes a discussion of the interaction of race and dis/ability. The model outlines the process of making the invisible visible across the pathways of *getting it*. By integrating these two frameworks (the process of *getting it* and making the invisible visible) supervisors can guide a supervision and case-consultation process that fits within a DisCrit framework. This model can be used in a learning setting to guide the conversation between the supervisor and supervisee as they work through a case.

Case Narrative

The following case narrative is intended to guide the application of the model presented in Table 13.1. As you read this case narrative, note important information about Sanaa, her family, and her community as well as her school interactions and relationships. Once you have completed the case narrative, there are two activities that will guide you through organizing what you have learned about Sanaa and applying the model in Table 13.1 to this case.

Sanaa is a 7-year-old 2nd-grade Afro Colombian student attending a mostly white public school located in a medium-sized, rural city in the southeastern U.S. Sanaa's family immigrated to the U.S. from Colombia when Sanaa was 5. Sanaa lives at home with her biological mother and father, three siblings (ages 3, 10, and 14), and maternal grandmother. Sanaa's biological parents and grandmother predominantly speak Spanish at home; however, her older siblings speak both English and Spanish across home and community settings. Sanaa and her siblings are eligible for the school district's free lunch program based on the family's household income.

Sanaa was born full-term after a typical pregnancy and met all developmental milestones, such as sitting independently, walking, crawling, talking, and toileting training, within typical limits. From birth through age 4, Sanaa was cared for in the home by her

TABLE 13.1 A Process for Using DisCrit to Guide Supervision Practice for Cases With Social, Emotional, and Behavioral Referral Questions

	Power	**Race and Ableist Microaggressions**	**Relational Safety**	**Working Alliances**	**Empowerment**
Knowledge	Understanding power and privilege as it pertains to racism and ableism.	Learning to identify racial microaggressions and microaggressions that enable ableism.	Understanding the mechanisms that might make a relationship feel unsafe or unwelcoming to those with diverse racial identities and diverse abilities.	Identifying the key aspects of a strong working alliance between key case stakeholders (supervisor, supervisee, student, family, teachers).	Learning about the processes that occur that mute the power and voice of marginalized communities.
Emotional Change	Understanding your own role in systems of power and privilege and ways you may inherit or perpetuate racism and ableism.	Contend with how you either perpetuate or experience racial and ableist microaggressions.	Contending with how you either create unsafe or are in unsafe professional relationships.	Letting go of defensiveness and embarrassment that might be experienced with conversations about race, ethnicity, and ableism.	Contending with how trainees, students, and families of diverse identities and abilities are marginalized, and how their power and voice is muted.
Behavioral Commitment	Use access to power and privilege to upend systems of oppression.	Commit to naming and combating racial and ableist microaggressions as they occur in the supervision relationship and school environment as a whole.	Committing to intentionally creating relationships that honor and respect differences.	Having conversations with supervisees about race, ethnicity, and ableism.	Committing to and intentionally fostering power in supervisees, students, and families whose power and voice are muted by systems of oppression.

biological mother and maternal grandmother. During this period of development, Sanaa is described by her mother to have been a "quiet" child who often "watched TV" and "played with toys" by herself. Her parents report that, though infrequently, Sanaa often cried loudly and for an extensive period any time she was separated from her mother or grandmother. At age 6, Sanaa experienced a difficult transition into kindergarten and cried every day when dropped off at school by her mother. On some days at drop-off, Sanaa refused to enter her kindergarten classroom and instead, would run down the hallway away from her teacher. Over several months, Sanaa gradually began to adapt to kindergarten; however, Sanaa's 1st-grade teacher describes similar challenges regarding Sanaa's emotional regulation and ability to engage with her and her peers at school.

Currently, Sanaa is described by her 2nd-grade teacher, Mrs. Fraizer, as a moody student who cares little for her peers or the authority of her teachers, the majority of whom are white and middle-class. Mrs. Frazier perceives Sanaa to be a student who is often unhappy and notes that Sanaa frequently complains of body aches and pains. Mrs. Fraizer also reports that Sanaa frequently cries in class with no apparent trigger, and when she is not crying, she lays her head down on her desk with minimal engagement in academic activities. When asked to complete assignments or when called on during class, Sanaa sometimes talks back to her teacher. On the occasion Sanaa engages with academic activities, Sanaa has significant difficulty attending. She works at an incredibly slow pace and appears to be very anxious about the correctness of her work products and typically does not finish completing a task before becoming visibly frustrated and stopping. At this point, Sanaa often refuses to complete the assignment. Overall, Sanaa's academic skills across all subjects are below grade-level. Sanaa's parents share similar concerns about Sanaa's behavior across home and community settings. Sanaa's parents observe her to be withdrawn from siblings and same-age peers living in her neighborhood, have a sad disposition at most times along with random outbursts of crying, and often complain of stomach pains with no apparent medical origin. All of Sanaa's teachers have been white women.

Case Narrative Supervision Process Discussion Using DisCrit Lens

Supervisor Positionality

The following exercises are meant to guide conversation regarding the presented case narrative. These exercises are conceptualized as questions to ask in a supervisor/supervisee discussion and an activity to use in a larger group discussion of the case narrative. In reading the case narrative, the supervisor will want to evaluate their positionality and potential reaction to Sanaa's behaviors. The supervisor will also want to identify gaps in knowledge regarding Sanaa's experiences and ways to learn more about Sanaa specifically, and her background broadly, that infuse both interactions with Sanaa and her parents while balancing knowledge-building that can be done outside of speaking to Sanaa and her parents. The supervisor will then want to share these techniques with the supervisee and develop questions utilizing the model presented previously. Examples can be found in Table 13.2.

TABLE 13.2 Case Narrative Guiding Questions

	Guiding Questions
Power	1. **Knowledge:** What is our own, and Sanaa's, access to power and privilege? 2. **Emotional change:** How do I feel about my own positionality, and my positionality in relation to yours and Sanaa's? 3. **Behavioral commitment:** In what ways can we incorporate the knowledge of power and privilege into our response to this referral?
Racist and Ableist Microaggressions	1. **Knowledge:** What are racist and ableist microaggressions? What are some that Sanaa might experience? How might they show up in our supervision discussions? How might they show up in assessment, intervention, and consultation practice? 2. **Emotional change:** How do I respond emotionally when I identify a microaggression that I am perpetuating? How do I respond emotionally when I identify a microaggression in the referral and assessment process? 3. **Behavioral commitment:** In what ways can we name and interrupt microaggressions?
Relational Safety	1. **Knowledge:** What do I need to experience relational safety? What does Sanaa need to experience relational safety? How might my experiences align with or be different from Sanaa's? 2. **Emotional change:** When I think about Sanaa's needs for relational safety, how do I respond cognitively and emotionally? 3. **Behavioral commitment:** How can we promote relational safety for Sanaa and model relational safety in supervision practice?
Working Alliance	1. **Knowledge:** What are key relationships in this case, and why are they important? 2. **Emotional change:** What is the temperature of the relationships around this case? 3. **Behavioral commitment:** What actions can be put into place to ensure positive and affirming interactions between stakeholders that encourage open and honest communication?
Empowerment	1. **Knowledge:** Whose power and voices are marginalized and muted when considering the supervision setting and the student? How do our intervention and assessment strategies interact with student empowerment? 2. **Emotional change:** Am I experiencing resistance or defensiveness when answering these questions? How do I feel when I imagine what it would feel like to be empowered? How do I feel when I imagine what it would mean to empower others' voices? 3. **Behavioral commitment:** How will I use my access to power and privilege to support the voice and power of stakeholders in this case who might be muted by systems of oppression? What intervention and assessment considerations can I make that enable empowerment as opposed to labeling or othering of the student?

Again, it is key that supervisors also examine their own positionality so the supervisees are not left in a position where they are primarily guiding supervision and supporting the supervisor in navigating questions of multicultural competence.

Timeline Development

Another useful activity to help guide the discussion of this case narrative would be the creation of a timeline. Parsing apart this student's experiences and the presence or absence of behaviors over time could help identify critical timepoints where students' needs and environmental factors were in sync or clashed. For example, when did the student's trouble with peers begin? How about with teachers? What changed in the student's environment?

Eco-Map and Guiding Questions

Two activities are provided in this section to guide the case narrative. The first is the use of an eco-map and the second a list of questions that will guide participants in applying a DisCrit lens to this case. We ask that you complete the eco-map first, as the use of an eco-map can help students gain a bird's eye view of the case and the systems impacting Sanaa. An eco-map is a tool that school psychologists and other educators can use to better understand how youth, including young children, see and experience the world. Eco-maps also allow us to understand support systems in a child's life and their interactions across ecological systems including home, school, and community. Eco-maps have been used globally to apply an ecological-systems approach to understanding students' environments and whether they feel that certain relationships are stressful, supportive, or whether the student might be ambivalent about the interaction. To complete an eco-map, students draw themselves at the center of the eco-map and then draw significant people, places, and things around them. Traditional eco-maps focus on people and pets; however, we have expanded eco-maps here to include systems and environments. The student then draws a solid line to those depictions that feel supportive and a dashed line to those that feel stressful. If students feel like certain depictions are both stressful and supportive, they can draw both a solid and a dashed line. For this activity, ask your school psychology supervisee to draw an eco-map for Sanaa. Though eco-maps are usually drawn by the child themselves, this exercise will help supervisees step back from a focus simply on behavior to better understand what interactions in the student's life might be feeding behavior. An example is provided in Figure 13.1. If Sanaa feels like her teacher and peers are not supportive relationships, why might this be? How might Sanaa's interactions in different systems impact how she feels about those systems and her behavior in those environments? Ask supervisees to get creative in thinking across both Sanaa's immediate environment but also including things like

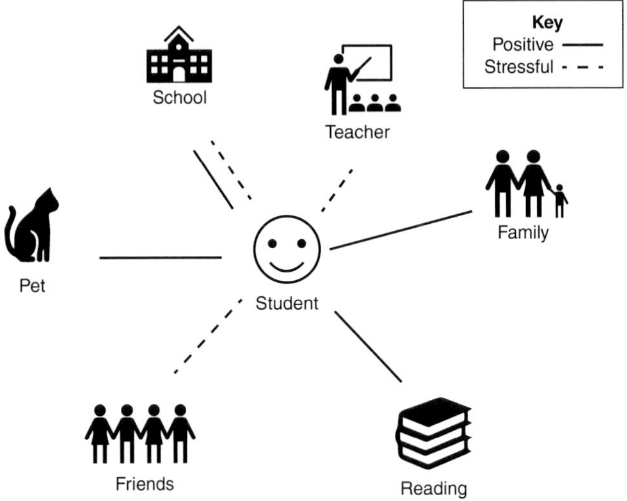

FIGURE 13.1 Example Eco-Map

government structures around Sanaa. How might Sanaa's status as an immigrant student impact her interactions in these environments?

Once the student has completed the eco-map, work through the questions in Table 13.2. It is best to complete the questions in order, as each section builds on the one before, and each question within a section walks through the three stages of *getting it*.

Conclusion

Student behavioral concerns present significant barriers to teaching and learning in the classroom. While student behavioral and emotional concerns can indicate an underlying support need for a child, our systems for identifying and tracking student behavioral and emotional concerns are fraught with problems that make these systems vulnerable to implicit and explicit racial biases. Using a DisCrit lens when thinking about student behavioral and emotional concerns at the student and systems-level provides school-based personnel with guidance on collecting and interpreting student behavioral data in a way that includes consideration of racial bias. While this chapter provides an outline for guiding supervision practices utilizing DisCrit in considering student behavioral and emotional concerns, the processes and procedures presented here and elsewhere in this book provide an important framework that can be used widely in school-based practice to reduce the impact of implicit and explicit bias.

References

Abright, A. R., & Chung, H. (2002). Depression in Asian American children. *Western Journal of Medicine, 176*(4), 244–248.

Advancement Project. (2005). *Education on lockdown: The schoolhouse to jailhouse track.* https://b.3cdn.net/advancement/5351180e24cb166d02_mlbrqgxlh.pdf

Algozzine, B. (2017). Toward an acceptable definition of emotional disturbance: Waiting for the change. *Behavioral Disorders, 42*(3), 136–144. https://doi.org/10.1177/0198742917702117

American Psychological Association Zero Tolerance Task Force. (2008). Are zero tolerance policies effective in the schools? An evidentiary review and recommendations. *The American Psychologist, 63*(9), 852–862.

Annamma, S. A., Connor, D., & Ferri, B. (2013). Dis/ability critical race studies (DisCrit): Theorizing at the intersections of race and dis/ability. *Race Ethnicity and Education, 16*(1), 1–31. https://doi.org/10.1080/13613324.2012.730511

Annamma, S. A., Ferri, B. A., & Connor, D. J. (2018). Disability critical race theory: Exploring the intersectional lineage, emergence, and potential futures of DisCrit in education. *Review of Research in Education, 42*(1), 46–71. https://doi.org/10.3102/0091732X18759041

Annamma, S., & Morrison, D. (2018). Identifying dysfunctional education ecologies: A DisCrit analysis of bias in the classroom. *Equity & Excellence in Education, 51*(2), 114–131. https://doi.org/10.1080/10665684.2018.1496047

Anyon, Y., Ong, S. L., & Whitaker, K. (2014). School-based mental health prevention for Asian American adolescents: Risk behaviors, protective factors, and service use. *Asian American Journal of Psychology, 5*(2), 134–144. https://doi.org/10.1037/a0035300

Bal, A., Betters-Bubon, J., & Fish, R. E. (2019). A multilevel analysis of statewide disproportionality in exclusionary discipline and the identification of emotional disturbance. *Education and Urban Society, 51*(2), 247–268. https://doi.org/10.1177/0013124517716260

Broderick, A., & Leonardo, Z. (2016). What is a good boy: The deployment and distribution of "goodness" as ideological property in schools. In D. Connor, B. Ferri, & S. A. Annamma (Eds.), *DisCrit: Critical conversations across race, class, & dis/ability* (pp. 55–69). Teachers College Press.

Bruhn, A. L., Woods-Groves, S., & Huddle, S. (2014). A preliminary investigation of emotional and behavioral screening practices in K–12 schools. *Education and Treatment of Children, 37*(4), 611–634. https://doi.org/10.1353/etc.2014.0039

Bulotsky-Shearer, R. J., & Fantuzzo, J. W. (2011). Preschool behavior problems in classroom learning situations and literacy outcomes in kindergarten and first grade. *Early Childhood Research Quarterly, 26*(1), 61–73. https://doi.org/10.1016/j.ecresq.2010.04.004

Costello, E. J., Compton, S. N., Keeler, G., & Angold, A. (2003). Relationships between poverty and psychopathology: A natural experiment. *JAMA: Journal of the American Medical Association, 290*(15), 2023–2029. https://doi.org/10.1001/jama.290.15.2023

Darensbourg, A., Perez, E., & Blake, J. J. (2010). Overrepresentation of African American males in exclusionary discipline: The role of school-based mental health professionals in dismantling the school to prison pipeline. *Journal of African American Males in Education, 1*(3), 196–211.

Darney, D., Reinke, W. M., Herman, K. C., Stormont, M., & Ialongo, N. S. (2013). Children with co-occurring academic and behavior problems in first grade: Distal outcomes in twelfth grade. *Journal of School Psychology, 51*(1), 117–128. https://doi.org/10.1016/j.jsp.2012.09.005

Department of Education, E.O. for C.R. (OCR). (2014). Civil rights data collection. Data snapshot: School discipline. Issue Brief No. 1. In *Office for Civil Rights, US Department of Education*. Office for Civil Rights, US Department of Education.

Eklund, K., Aros-O'Malley, M., & Murrieta, I. (2014). Multicultural supervision: What difference does difference make? *Contemporary School Psychology, 18*(3), 195–204. https://doi.org/10.1007/s40688-014-0024-8

Fish, R. E. (2017). The racialized construction of exceptionality: Experimental evidence of race/ethnicity effects on teachers' interventions. *Social Science Research, 62*, 317–334. https://doi.org/10.1016/j.ssresearch.2016.08.007

Freeman, J., Simonsen, B., Briere, D. E., & MacSuga-Gage, A. S. (2014). Pre-service teacher training in classroom management: A review of state accreditation policy and teacher preparation programs. *Teacher Education and Special Education, 37*(2), 106–120. https://doi.org/10.1177/0888406413507002

Girvan, E. J., Gion, C., McIntosh, K., & Smolkowski, K. (2017). The relative contribution of subjective office referrals to racial disproportionality in school discipline. *School Psychology Quarterly, 32*(3), 392. https://doi.org/10.1037/spq0000178

Green, T., Cook-Morales, V., Robinson-Zanartu, C., & Ingraham, C. (2009). Pathways on a journey of getting it: Multicultural competence training and continuing professional development. In J. M. Jones (Ed.), *The psychology of multiculturalism in the schools: A primer for practice, training, and research* (pp. 83–113). National Association of School Psychologists.

Gregory, A., Skiba, R. J., & Mediratta, K. (2017). Eliminating disparities in school discipline: A framework for intervention. *Review of Research in Education, 41*(1), 253–278. https://doi.org/10.3102/0091732X17690499

Gresham, F. (2005). Response to intervention: An alternative means of identifying students as emotionally disturbed. *Education and Treatment of Children, 28*(4), 328–344.

Griffin, C. B., Cooper, S. M., Metzger, I. W., Golden, A. R., & White, C. N. (2017). School racial climate and the academic achievement of African American high school students: The mediating role of school engagement. *Psychology in the Schools, 54*(7), 673–688. https://doi.org/10.1002/pits.22026

Iselin, A. M. (2010). Research on school suspension. In *Center for child and family policy, Duke University*. Center for Child and Family Policy, Duke University.

Kamphaus, R. W., Reynolds, C. R., & Dever, B. V. (2014). Behavioral and mental health screening. In R. J. Kettler, T. A. Glover, C. A. Albers, & K. A. Feeney-Kettler (Eds.), *School psychology book series. Universal screening in educational settings: Evidence-based decision making for schools* (pp. 249–273). American Psychological Association. https://doi.org/10.1037/14316-010

Kunesh, C. E., & Noltemeyer, A. (2019). Understanding disciplinary disproportionality: Stereotypes shape pre-service teachers' beliefs about black boys' behavior. *Urban Education, 54*(4), 471–498. https://doi.org/10.1177/0042085915623337

Li, S. T., Nussbaum, K. M., & Richards, M. H. (2007). Risk and protective factors for urban African-American youth. *American Journal of Community Psychology, 39*(1–2), 21–35. https://doi.org/10.1007/s10464-007-9088-1

McIntosh, D. E., & Phelps, L. (2000). Supervision in school psychology: Where will the future take us? *Psychology in the Schools, 37*(1), 33–38. https://doi.org/10.1002/(SICI)15206807(200001)37:1%3C33::AID-PITS4%3E3.0.CO;2F

McIntosh, K., Predy, L. K., Upreti, G., Hume, A. E., Turri, M. G., & Mathews, S. (2014). Perceptions of contextual features related to implementation and sustainability of school-wide positive behavior support. *Journal of Positive Behavior Interventions, 16*(1), 31–43. https://doi.org/10.1177/1098300712470723

Moon, J., Williford, A., & Mendenhall, A. (2017). Educators' perceptions of youth mental health: Implications for training and the promotion of mental health services in schools. *Children and Youth Services Review, 73*, 384–391. https://doi.org/10.1016/j.childyouth.2017.01.006

Najjar, K., & Naser, S. C. (2019). Experiences of Arab heritage youth in US schools and impact on identity development. *School Psychology International, 40*(3), 251–274. https://doi.org/10.1177/0143034319831057

Naser, S., & Dever, B. V. (2019). Mapping trajectories of behavioral and emotional risk among predominantly African American youth across the middle school transition. *School Psychology Review, 48*(4), 362–376. https://doi.org/10.17105/SPR-2018-0054.V48-4

National Center for Education Statistics. (2019). *Students with disabilities*. https://nces.ed.gov/programs/coe/indicator_cgg.asp

Nelson, L., & Lind, D. (2015). *The school to prison pipeline, explained*. Justice Policy Institute. www.justicepolicy.org/news/8775.

Noltemeyer, A. L., Ward, R. M., & Mcloughlin, C. (2015). Relationship between school suspension and student outcomes: A meta-analysis. *School Psychology Review, 44*(2), 224–240.

Okonofua, J. A., & Eberhardt, J. L. (2015). Two strikes: Race and the disciplining of young students. *Psychological Science, 26*(5), 617–624. https://doi.org/10.1177/0956797615570365

Okonofua, J. A., Walton, G. M., & Eberhardt, J. L. (2016). A vicious cycle: A social—psychological account of extreme racial disparities in school discipline. *Perspectives on Psychological Science, 11*(3), 381–398. https://doi.org/10.1177/1745691616635592

Pica-Smith, C., & Veloria, C. (2012). "At risk means a minority kid:" Deconstructing deficit discourses in the study of risk in education and human services. *Pedagogy and the Human Sciences, 2*(1), 33–48.

Prelow, H. M., Danoff-Burg, S., Swenson, R. R., & Pulgiano, D. (2004). The impact of ecological risk and perceived discrimination on the psychological adjustment of African American and European American youth. *Journal of Community Psychology, 32*(4), 375–389. https://doi.org/10.1002/jcop.20007

Proctor, S. L., & Rogers, M. R. (2013). Making the invisible visible: Understanding social processes within multicultural internship supervision. *School Psychology Forum: Research in Practice*, 7(1), 1–12.

Raines, T. C., Dever, B. V., Kamphaus, R. W., & Roach, A. T. (2012). Universal screening for behavioral and emotional risk: A promising method for reducing disproportionate placement in special education. *Journal of Negro Education, 81*(3), 283–296. https://doi.org/10.7709/jnegroeducation.81.3.0283

Reinke, W. M., Herman, K. C., Petras, H., & Ialongo, N. S. (2008). Empirically derived subtypes of child academic and behavior problems: Co-occurrence and distal outcomes. *Journal of Abnormal Child Psychology, 36*(5), 759–770. https://doi.org/10.1007/s10802-007-9208-2

Sabnis, S. & Bueno Martinez, C., this volume.

Sheridan, S. M., & Gutkin, T. B. (2000). The ecology of school psychology: Examining and changing our paradigm for the 21st century. *School Psychology Review, 29*(4), 485–502. https://doi.org/10.1080/02796015.2000.12086032

Skiba, R. J., Horner, R. H., Chung, C. G., Rausch, M. K., May, S. L., & Tobin, T. (2011). Race is not neutral: A national investigation of African American and Latino disproportionality in school discipline. *School Psychology Review, 40*(1), 85–107. https://doi.org/10.1080/02796015.2011.12087730

Skiba, R. J., Michael, R. S., Nardo, A. C., & Peterson, R. L. (2002). The color of discipline: Sources of racial and gender disproportionality in school punishment. *The Urban Review, 34*(4), 317–342. https://doi.org/10.1023/A:1021320817372

Starck, J. G., Riddle, T., Sinclair, S., & Warikoo, N. (2020). Teachers are people too: Examining the racial bias of teachers compared to other American adults. *Educational Researcher, 49*(4), 273–284. https://doi.org/10.3102/0013189X20912758

Stiffman, A. R., Pescosolido, B., & Cabassa, L. J. (2004). Building a model to understand youth service access: The gateway provider model. *Mental Health Services Research, 6*(4), 189–198.

Stormont, M., Reinke, W., & Herman, K. (2011). Teachers' knowledge of evidence-based interventions and available school resources for children with emotional and behavioral problems. *Journal of Behavioral Education, 20*(2), 138–147. https://doi.org/10.1007/s10864-011-9122-0

Sullivan, A. L. (2017). Wading through quicksand: Making sense of minority disproportionality in identification of emotional disturbance. *Behavioral Disorders, 43*(1), 244–252. https://doi.org/10.1177/0198742917732360

Sullivan, A. L., & Bal, A. (2013). Disproportionality in special education: Effects of individual and school variables on disability risk. *Exceptional Children, 79*(4), 475–494. https://doi.org/10.1177/001440291307900406

Sullivan, A. L., & Proctor, S. L. (2016). The shield or the sword? Revisiting the debate on racial disproportionality in special education and implications for school psychologists. *School Psychology Forum: Research in Practice, 10*, 278–288.

Townsend, B. L. (2000). The disproportionate discipline of African American learners: Reducing school suspensions and expulsions. *Exceptional Children, 66*(3), 381–391.

Vanlommel, K., Van Gasse, R., Vanhoof, J., & Van Petegem, P. (2018). Teachers high-stakes decision making. How teaching approaches affect rational and intuitive data collection. *Teaching and Teacher Education, 71*, 108–119. https://doi.org/10.1016/j.tate.2017.12.011

Wei, R. C., Darling-Hammond, L., Andree, A., Richardson, N., Orphanos, S., & National Staff Development Council. (2009). Professional learning in the learning profession: A status report on teacher development in the U.S. and abroad. Technical report. *National Staff Development Council.*

Whitney, D. G., & Peterson, M. D. (2019). US national and state-level prevalence of mental health disorders and disparities of mental health care use in children. *JAMA Pediatrics, 173*(4), 389–391. https://doi.org/10.1001/jamapediatrics.2018.5399

Williams, N. J., Scott, L., & Aarons, G. A. (2018). Prevalence of serious emotional disturbance among US children: A meta-analysis. *Psychiatric Services, 69*(1), 32–40. https://doi.org/10.1176/appi.ps.201700145

Wyatt, L. C., Ung, T., Park, R., Kwon, S. C., & Trinh-Shevrin, C. (2015). Risk factors of suicide and depression among Asian American, Native Hawaiian, and Pacific Islander youth: A systematic literature review. *Journal of Health Care for the Poor and Underserved, 26*(2), 191–237. https://doi.org/10.1353/hpu.2015.0059

14

QUEER THEORY AND INTERN SUPERVISION

The Harm of Heteronormative Supervision

Amy R. Cannava and David P. Rivera

Author Note

The authors wish to acknowledge the contributions and support of Bret Morrison in the writing of this chapter.

The application of Queer Theory to the supervision of interns has not been the focus of much empirical literature, but the intersection of gender and sexuality with professional roles, such as in school psychology, has become more prolific in recent years. At the surface level, how one identifies (e.g., woman, man, transgender woman, transgender man, nonbinary, cisgender, etc.) and who they are attracted to (sexuality) may seem to have very little to do with how one would perform one's job; but that presumption is likely based on cissexist and heterosexist norms (i.e., social norms that favor cisgender and heterosexual identities as "normal").The pervasiveness of heteronormativity (see Chapter 4) creates and maintains the misguided presumption that one's gender identity and sexuality have no impact on professional roles.

Intern school psychologists who are LGBTQIA+ (this acronym, while not perfect, will be used throughout the chapter to refer to people who do not identify as cisgender or heterosexual) do not have the privilege to NOT think about how their sexuality or gender identity might impact their professional roles. They are also at the beginning of their careers, still learning, and hoping to land full-time employment at the end of internship. As a result, some may want to stand out professionally while blending in personally. Others may not be able to blend in even if they desire to. How do the intern's gender identity and expression affect them at work and in the communities in which they work? Similarly, how does the intern's sexual orientation impact them at work and in the surrounding

DOI: 10.4324/9780367815325-17

community? How do these aspects of identity impact their work with students, parents, and supervisors?

This chapter seeks to answer these questions while posing others that should be considered in the important role of supervision from a queer theoretical perspective. More specifically, we will explore how the interpersonal and systemic dynamics related to sexual orientation and gender identity impact the school psychology intern's professional development. These issues will be contextualized via a case narrative discussion with recommendations for how Queer Theory can be used to inform the supervision process to create a validating and affirming learning experience for school psychology interns.

Brief Introduction to Queer Theory

Queer Theory can be an elusive field of study to define, as there is not a common set of tenets or guiding principles agreed upon by queer theorists. As such, Rivera (Chapter 4, this volume) synthesized Queer Theory literature to develop the six following fundamentals of Queer Theory that can be used as lenses to analyze and understand the dynamics and manifestation of sexuality and gender: (1) the Problem of Heteronormativity, (2) Genealogical Approach to Interrogating Discourses, (3) Deconstruction of Finite Categorization, (4) Resistance to Essentialism, (5) Realities Are Socially Constructed/Constricted, and (6) Challenges to Empiricism. This section briefly reviews these fundamentals of Queer Theory.

While articulating a cohesive and commonly accepted narrative of Queer Theory is challenging and even counter to the origination and persistence of the theory (Jagose, 1996; McCann & Monaghan, 2020), issues stemming from heteronormativity's pervasiveness in society (Fundamental 1; Warner, 1991) tend to be of concern to those who utilize and advance Queer Theory. Society is full of "heteronormative problems" (e.g., proclaiming the gender of a newborn, gendered clothing, gendered bathrooms, gendered social activities and sports) that restrict the ways sexuality and gender are conceptualized, experienced, and expressed. An implicit quality of heteronormativity is control and the facets of control that emanate from a heteronormative society. This upholds gender hierarchies that position men as stronger, more intelligent, and sexually "freer" than women, for example, and it erases the existence of anyone who doesn't identify as a cisgender woman or man and those with same-sex attractions. Taking a genealogical approach (Fundamental 2; Foucault, 1972) is a helpful tool for understanding how heteronormativity was designed and is maintained, which is necessary for deconstructing the finite categories of gender and sexuality (Fundamental 3; Dilley, 1999).

Gender and sexual orientation are commonly conceptualized as binaried identity constructs and are only a couple examples of the many binaried concepts found in society. Psychological essentialism explains the way humans make sense of concepts and phenomena by deeming them as natural, stable, and necessary to the human condition, such as binaried gender (man-woman) and sexuality (heterosexual-homosexual) (Prentice & Miller, 2007). Queer Theory resists essential states of being (Fundamental 4), since essentialism leads to an oversimplification of gender and sexuality that encourages people to adopt and believe that binaried gender and sexuality are "natural" states of being. A resistance of essentialism along with historicizing the development of gender and sexuality discourses reveals that our realities are socially constructed and constricted (Fundamental 5) by the dominant heteronormative paradigm. For example, Butler's (2011) theory of gender performativity elucidates how gender is constructed through repetitive and ritualized actions related to gender norms that create the internal sense of gender that translates to the way people identify their gender.

The final fundamental concerns a reliance on empiricism as an overarching paradigm for scientific inquiry. Empirical methods and philosophies mandate that evidence for any given phenomena must be observable and measurable, often in large quantities. Queer Theory challenges empiricism (Fundamental 6) in that many lived realities are rendered invisible, especially those who are socially marginalized, such as queer and trans people, and suggests other ways of conceptualizing research methodologies and concepts (Muñoz, 1996; Rivera & Nadal, 2019). This chapter will use Queer Theory as a framework to analyze heteronormative and cissexist issues embedded in schools and the supervisory relationship and process.

Supervision Practices and LGBTQIA+ Interns

The National Association of School Psychologists (NASP) *Standards for Graduate Preparation of School Psychologists* (2010) stated that psychologists "contribute to the development of effective school psychology services by identifying critical graduate education experiences and competencies needed by candidates preparing for careers as school psychologists" (p. 2). While the NASP allows for accreditation at the specialist and doctoral levels and there are differences in the amount of coursework for each degree, both require a one-year supervised internship during the last year of the program. Most programs also require a supervised practicum. School psychology students will generally maintain university supervisors and site-based supervisors, reporting to both during internship, but the focus of this chapter is on the site-based supervision. The *Professional Standards of the National Association of School Psychologists* (2020, p. 13) Organizational Principle 5: Supervision, Peer Consultation, and Mentoring states that:

> The school system ensures that all personnel have opportunities for supervision, peer consultation, and mentoring adequate to ensure the provision of effective and accountable services. Supervision and mentoring are provided through an ongoing, career-long, positive, systematic, collaborative process between the school psychologist and a school psychology

> supervisor or other school psychology colleagues. This process focuses on promoting professional growth and exemplary professional practice leading to improved performance among all participants, including the school psychologist, supervisor, students, and the entire school community.

While public schools fall under the authority of the Department of Education (DOE) and not NASP, these guiding principles of school psychologists emphasize the importance of continuing professional development and supervision. The DOE in most states provides certification for school psychologists, and credentialing usually requires the successful completion of a supervised internship. There is great variation at state and local levels in terms of qualifications for supervisors, if any exist. Requirements often include years of practice post-degree and specific coursework, but the focus of such is generally on theoretical models of supervision and evaluation of staff (e.g., administrative supervision) rather than clinical competencies or the interpersonal relationship between supervisor and supervisee.

Gibbs et al. (2016) recognized that the most comprehensive overviews of supervisory literature within the field are found in the works of McIntosh and Phelps (2000) and Smith Harvey and Stuzziero (2008). Gibbs et al. (2016) found that supervision entails supervision practices within the field, the congruence of supervision with professional standards, the role of supervision within training programs, the provision of effective supervision, and the evaluation of models of supervision. In 2014, following a task-force report, the American Psychological Association (APA) recognized that supervision is a distinct area of practice that requires specific and ongoing skills training and development. The NASP concurs with this finding, and the 2020 professional standards now include supervision as a distinct area of practice in the practice model. It is well known that while few school psychologists receive pre-service training in providing supervision, most students will eventually go on to supervise others during the course of their careers. Anyone who has suffered through poor supervision will tell you that being a competent practitioner does not automatically equate to being an effective supervisor (Simon et al., 2014). In fact, Gibbs et al. (2016) found support for theoretical supervision models that suggested the importance of an "emotionally supportive functioning of supervision" (p. 422). Their findings provide support for supervisory 'values' defined by Dunsmuir and Leadbetter (2010), who recommended creating "safe and trusting" spaces where interns can discuss freely despite the inherent power imbalance and be able to "expose vulnerabilities, discuss mistakes, and take risks" (p. 15). Effective supervision generally shows progression from dependence to interdependence to independence as the intern grows in skills and competence. For this progression to take place there must be comfort, trust, and security between the supervisor and supervisee.

When one considers that few school psychologists are adequately prepared to work with LGBTQIA+ youth in general, supervision of queer and/or trans supervisees may add even more complexity to a crucial role. For example, a national study conducted by the Gay Lesbian Straight Education Network (2019) found that 70% of school psychologists and other school-based mental health professionals received minimal to no preparation in working with queer youth, and 81% received little to no training in working with transgender populations. Furthermore, over one-third did not receive any additional formal education or training on LGBTQIA+ specific student issues during their professional careers. Researchers have consistently found that trainees in mental health training programs do not feel prepared by their programs to address lesbian, gay, and bisexual concerns in their therapeutic practice, much less those of transgender and gender-diverse clients (e.g., Craig et al., 2014). Furthermore, LGBTQIA+ topics are often lacking or inadequately covered in graduate psychology curricula in general (Johnson & Federman, 2014).

Psychology has made significant progress developing affirmative/affirming frameworks and guidelines for work with LGBTQIA+ people (APA, 2015, 2021). One investigation of supervision experiences of lesbian, gay, and bisexual (LGB) practicum students revealed that they benefited from LGB affirmative supervision and that this experience had a positive impact on the supervision relationship, clinical outcomes, and their own professional development (Burkard et al., 2009). In LGB non-affirming supervision, supervisees perceived supervisors to be biased or oppressive toward supervisees' clients or themselves on the basis of LGB concerns or identity. From the supervisees' perspectives, the non-affirming supervision qualities negatively affected the supervision relationship, clinical outcomes, and the supervisees' professional development.

Psychologists have reported that internship was the period when they worked directly with LGBTQIA+ students/clients, but only half of interns received supervision regarding LGB concerns, and only 25% reported that their supervisors were knowledgeable about LGB topics in client treatment (Murphy et al., 2002). Gatmon et al. (2001) found that only 12.5% of supervisees reported discussing sexual orientation issues during supervision, and more than half of the discussions that did take place were initiated by supervisees. Older research (Pilkington & Cantor, 1996) found that trainees were actually exposed to heterosexual bias during supervision. Fifty percent of their survey respondents experienced supervisors who pathologized queer orientations, made derogatory comments, inappropriately stressed the client's sexual orientation, and even discussed "curing" homosexuality.

There is great discussion and controversy over whether or not psychologists and other mental health professionals should be out. Some people feel that queer and trans persons have a duty to be out so as to signal that the clients' story and experience will be safe to share with them. This would sometimes be in keeping with professional ethics that suggests a clinician's sexual orientation and/or gender identity should only be disclosed when in the best interest of the client if doing so supports the therapeutic alliance (Herlihy & Corey, 2015). School psychologists in Sowden et al.'s (2015) study varied in terms of the choice of doing so and resulting impact. Some school psychologists did not want to be known as "the gay psychologist" or the one who only addressed LGBT issues. Others were out and enjoyed being the go-to person about anything gay. Almost all reported covert and overt examples of heterosexism that impacted their coming-out decisions and their school-based behaviors such as feeling like they could not talk about their personal lives. Participants reported that professional and personal relationships were stronger when they were able to come out and be out. One expressed professional insecurity given her heterosexual colleagues were able to build rapport with parents by sharing information about their own personal experiences (e.g., relationship and children) and her own uncertainty that she could share something to which parents could relate. Not being out subsequently impacted her ability to share personal anecdotes with students and families and get to know colleagues personally.

The school psychologists' experiences shared here reveal another heterocentric expectation for marriage and child-bearing often experienced by LGBTQIA+ persons. The LGBTQIA+ community includes more diversity within relationships outside of monogamy and long-term commitments that are often judged more openly and publicly than queer and trans existence itself. Furthermore, while many LGBTQIA+ couples desire to have children and do so, for those involved in non-cisgender/heterosexual relationships, having children is often an expensive, emotionally draining, extensive, lengthy, and arduous process involving fertility treatments, surrogacy, adoption, or fostering. While some people may desire to share their experiences, for others, having to explain to cisgender and heterosexual couples can be discouraging and requires sharing intimate details about their life.

Relevance of Queer Theory to School Psychology Intern Supervision

Historically, it was suggested that 'outness,' or the degree to which an individual makes their sexuality and/or gender identity known, correlated with mental wellness (Legate et al., 2012). Today we recognize that being out and affirmed is a protective factor, and being unsupported and out is not. Why is one's sexuality and gender relevant to their work professionally and as an intern? One might falsely presume that it's not, unless the school psychologist or intern is working with a queer or transgender youth; but this presumption is based in heterosexist and cissexist norms. For example, gender and sexuality may not directly affect the standardized administration of the *WISC-V*, but rather it can impact the way the intern is perceived and treated by the school administration, parents, students, and staff if stereotypes or preconceived notions are made about the intern's gender identity and sexual orientation. Biased notions of the intern based on their true or presumed sexual orientation or gender identity can impact appraisals of their work, including their administration of an assessment.

Revealing the harms that stem from heteronormativity is in line with Queer Theory's fundamental of using heteronormativity as a lens to analyze structures and concepts. Heteronormativity and cissexism's pervasiveness in society, including in schools, supports the maintenance of rigid gender norms that translate into stereotypes. Gender stereotypes affect the way we perceive and treat others, including in biased ways when gender norms and role expectations are not met (Ellemers, 2018). Implicit and explicit biases (e.g., ignoring, verbal assault, physical harm) can be directed toward people whose gender expression via hairstyle, dress, mannerism, or speech qualities do not align with social norms and related expectations based on gender.

Examples of breaking gender norms that can be met with judgment and presumptions about gender identity and sexual orientation include short/shaved hair on a woman; a man who crosses his leg at the knee when sitting; an AFAB (Assigned Female at Birth) person wearing a basketball jersey, shorts, and a sweatband; and an AMAB (Assigned Male at Birth) person carrying a purse or wearing makeup. Presumptions made about one's gender identity, gender presentation, gender expression, and/or sexuality can result in variations in how they are treated, interacted with, respected, and included. Whether these 'othering' behaviors are through microaggressions (interpersonal forms of covert bias) or macroaggressions (institutional and policy-level forms of bias), the intern is likely to feel unwelcome, excluded, judged, invalidated, or insulted, which can lead to compromises in their satisfaction and performance (Rivera et al., 2012).

Many indications exist of heteronormativity and cissexism's wide reach in schools, which directly impacts students and school personnel alike (Garcia, 2009; Wilkinson & Pearson, 2009). School environments perpetuate heteronormativity via the presence of gendered bathrooms/locker rooms and gendered sports (e.g., boys play football, girls play volleyball, etc.), for example. The mere presence of these gendered dynamics regarding where one uses the bathroom, where one can change their clothing for gym class, and which sports they are allowed to play sends strong messages about gender role expectations. The presence of these heteronormative structures and practices has been shown to compromise the well-being of youth with same-sex attractions (Wilkinson & Pearson, 2009). This research also suggests that the school and community context matters in that same-sex attracted youth were at highest risk in nonurban settings and in schools with a larger emphasis on football and religion. While this research focused on the impact of heteronormativity on students, the presence of these heteronormative structures and practices signals the same expectations to interns and other school personnel, which can influence "coming-out" decisions.

Similarly, the nature and quality of sex education in schools can provide an additional layer of heteronormative threats for young people, as this curriculum is often created and delivered within a heterosexual framework (Garcia, 2009). This heterosexually framed sex education is not helpful for anyone, in that it explicitly promotes heterosexuality as the prized norm. However, Garcia (2009) found that there is also gendered racism experienced in sex education that promotes the "good girl/bad girl" dichotomy that overemphasizes a "need" for girls to act like "young ladies" in order to achieve the respect of boys and racialized stereotypes for girls of color being sexually promiscuous and teenage mothers. These examples illustrate the pervasiveness of heteronormativity in schools and their damaging impacts. The sexuality education curricula, often dictated by departments of education, is expected to be upheld by school personnel, including the intern who may be required to frame the inclusion of gender and sexuality in their practice by the standards dictated by the department.

We know through an abundance of research that in order for students to be ready to learn, they have to feel physically and psychologically safe. The same is true for interns—they come to us with minimal privilege when viewed through Pamela Hays' (1996, 2008) ADDRESSING Model, which provides a framework for understanding the social construct of power. At a minimum, supervisors are generally older and have more experience and education than their interns, which affords the supervisors more privilege, even though only the education is earned. The queer or trans intern may also presume they have less privilege than the supervisor without knowing the supervisor's sexual orientation and/or gender identity, leading them to assume the supervisor is heterosexual and/or cisgender. Regardless of the supervisor's identity, it will become part of their role to ensure that the supervisee feels physically and psychologically safe at work and therefore "supported."

As discussed in Chapter 4 (Rivera, this volume), a foundational element of Queer Theory is "questioning of dominant conceptualizations of sexualities, genders, and other phenomena" (p. 49). While sexuality, and to a greater extent gender, has historically (and even recently) been policed due to social and political motivations to control and regulate human interaction, greater social acceptance of diversity in attraction and gender has led to an increase in the number of queer (sexuality and gender) persons being able to present openly and authentically. This is in keeping with Queer Theory, which postulates that "'natural' and 'essential' states of being, developed and supported by discourses and regulated by social institutions, are challenged and resisted by queer theorists" (p. 50). Some queer and trans people take great pride in openly asserting that they are challenging heteronormativity and corresponding ciscentric expectations of gender. Others, even when openly out, do not consider their mere existence to be a challenge to anything. Nevertheless, while LGBTQIA+ people continue to represent a numerical minority (though growing), we must recognize the harm inherent in heteronormativity. Professionally, we are ethically obliged to recognize that the gender and sexuality of our students exists in a dynamic matrix, and the same applies to our co-workers and our graduate students and interns. Neglecting the dynamic quality of gender and sexuality leads to a gross misunderstanding of these concepts that leads to heterosexual and cisgender identities being prized as normal and valued, while all other sexual and gender identities and expressions are deemed strange and unworthy (Dragowski et al., 2014).

Case Narrative

Hudson is a 26-year-old school psychology intern at a high school of about 600 students located in a rural school district in the Mid-Atlantic region. The town sits adjacent to an active coal mine that employs a large percentage of the town's population. Most residents of the town are working- to lower-middle class, identify as Christian, and are multigenerational to the town. Hudson is not from this region of the country originally, but he attends a graduate school psychology program at a nearby university. Hudson identifies as a non-religious, biracial, bisexual, cisgender man and was born and raised in an urban, liberal city in the Northwest United States. Hudson purposefully chose to study in a rural context as to expand his worldview in terms of geography.

Hudson considers himself a social justice activist, and he regularly engages in activism geared toward racial, queer, and trans liberation. Hudson engages in some racial advocacy within the middle school through existing efforts started by a small group of teachers. However, there are no previously existing advocacy efforts focused on queer and trans students, not even a Gay-Straight Alliance. When Hudson first interviewed for the intern position, he noticed that the school psychologist, Dr. Smith, was wearing a golden cross. When meeting with other school personnel, he noticed many of them wearing crosses too and heard the phrase "God bless" many times. These religious cues discourage Hudson from revealing his bisexual identity, and he avoids any conversation about his personal life. During his time at the school, Hudson regularly hears microaggressive statements from students and school personnel, such as "That's so gay," "Act like a man," "Boys will be boys," and the term queer *used in a derogatory way. None of these are directed toward Hudson, but he feels vicarious harm from merely bearing witness to these comments.*

While evaluating a student, Jake, for a specific learning disability, the student asks to be referred to by "they/them" pronouns. Hudson is pleasantly surprised to hear Jake's request, and he inquires about the student's gender identity. Jake adamantly asserts that they are a boy, but as a feminist they prefer to use non-gendered pronouns that do not inherently equate to unearned privilege. Hudson has no hesitation in doing so and feels a sense of connection to the student. Hudson continues with the evaluation and finds preliminary evidence of a learning disability, so he schedules another appointment to meet with Jake to take place after Hudson has supervision with Dr. Smith. When Dr. Smith is reading his report, she crosses out the "their" pronouns and writes in "he," "him," or "his" instead. Dr. Smith doesn't verbally comment on the pronouns during their supervision session. Hudson, curious about the pronoun change, nervously asks Dr. Smith why she changed the pronouns, explaining that Jake prefers "they/them" pronouns. Dr. Smith forthrightly tells Hudson that the county will not allow for changes to a student's demographic information within a psychological report or in any school documents without a court order. This causes more confusion and concern for Hudson, as he wasn't changing the student's gender in the report, and he feels compelled to be accepting and affirming of Jake's pronouns. This experience leads Hudson to consider how Jake is treated by others in the school when Jake uses "they/them" pronouns, and it also serves to reinforce his decision to remain closeted about his bisexual identity. Hudson finds himself in the bind of wanting to support and advocate for Jake as much as possible and not believing he'll have the support of Dr. Smith or other school personnel who have evaluative power over Hudson.

Case Narrative Supervision Process Discussion Using Queer Theory Lens

Taking an affirmative stance toward sexual orientation and gender identity in the supervision process has been shown to positively support the intern's experience and professional development (Burkard et al., 2009). Having a clear and practical understanding of what is meant by "affirmative supervision" is necessary for the successful application of this supervisory style. Burkard et al. (2009) suggested borrowing from Tozer and McClanahan's (1999) definition of LGB-affirming counseling and using such to define affirming supervision. The following definition of affirmative supervision is proposed in keeping with Van Den Bergh and Crisp's (2004) Affirmative Practices model: Affirmative supervision recognizes the complexity and beauty in the diversity of sexual orientations and gender identities. Affirmative supervision recognizes the inherent harm to the intern, the supervisor/supervisee relationship, and the students and families served, in operating from a heteronormative lens. Affirmative supervision recognizes the inherent bias and unearned privilege afforded to members of majority groups and the responsibility to make proactive, conscientious, and systematic steps to ensure that microaggressions are avoided, confronted when witnessed, and healed when endured. Affirmative supervisors recognize it is their duty to self-educate in the requisite knowledge and skills of working with LGBTQIA+ persons so that the attitude reflects needed understanding, awareness, validation, and support.

Dr. Smith can benefit from learning about affirmative supervision models and can ground her work in this definition of affirmative supervision. This can serve as a helpful paradigm for work with all supervisees and would create a supervisory relationship quality that would invite Hudson to share more openly about his personal experiences as they relate to his school-based experiences and his role as a school psychology intern.

In addition to Dr. Smith grounding herself in a clear and dynamic definition of affirmative supervision, she can also benefit from Pett's (2000) five general tenets that are imperative to LGB-affirmative supervision and will be used as another frame for this case's narrative-process discussion:

1. Supervisors' acceptance of LGB identification and the belief that heterosexism is pathological;

2. Supervisors' awareness of their own attitudes, beliefs, and feelings regarding LGB identification;
3. Supervisors' respect for LGB supervisees;
4. Supervisors' knowledge about heterosexism, coming out, and related aspects of LGB peoples' lives;
5. Supervisors' use of supervision to educate trainees about LGB issues and challenge supervisees' negative stereotypes.

Supervisors may self-identify as affirming, but that label should actually be bestowed upon them by the ones they are allegedly affirming; in this case, Hudson's appraisal of Dr. Smith is of utmost importance in making this determination. A person may not realize their outwardly heteronormative projections conveyed in *not* discussing sexuality and gender. The exclusion of sexuality and gender from supervision discussions sends the implicit message that these are meaningless to the supervisor. Therefore, a supervisor's reluctance to even inquire about or discuss a supervisee's sexual orientation and/or gender identity could be seen as presumptive heteronormativity that can impede the optimal development of the supervisor/supervisee relationship. Similarly, given the social and political forefront of all things LGBTQIA+ in recent years (e.g., mainstream media about conversion therapy, anti-LGBTQIA legislation, bathroom bills in the news, celebrities coming out, etc.), a supervisor's failure to mention school policies that protect LGBTQIA+ youth from bullying at school, the school's Gender Sexuality Alliance (GSA), or antiquated but existent gender-specific dress codes could inadvertently perpetuate the supervisee's perception that the supervisor is unaware and not affirming. Hudson would benefit from Dr. Smith introducing sexuality and gender into their supervision discussions, especially regarding heterosexism problems embedded in the school climate. This might signal to Hudson that gender and sexuality matter and that Dr. Smith expects discussion of these concepts in their supervision meetings and how they will conceptualize student issues.

Supervisors may have a desire to understand, incorporate, and alter their practices from a queer theory lens. According to Pett's (2000) second tenet, Dr. Smith would benefit from increasing self-awareness regarding sexuality and gender identity, especially as they relate to LGBTQI+ people. One way this can be accomplished is by using Van Den Bergh and Crisp's (2004) Affirmative Practices Model as well as the ALGBTIC's 21 Competencies for Counseling LGBQQIA Individuals as a guide for identifying necessary components of affirmative supervision (Harper et al., 2013). The following are suggested competencies for supervising LGBTQIA+ interns, adapted from the ALGBTIC's 21 Competencies for Counseling LGBQQIA (see Table 14.1). These competency areas can serve as a guide for Dr. Smith's development of more self-awareness, as well as practical ways to guide supervisees.

TABLE 14.1 Competencies for LGBTQIA+ Affirming Supervision

Knowledge Competencies
1. Educate yourself on queer/trans identities and experiences. Do not expect the LGBTQIA+ person to educate you on 'all things queer and trans.' Remember that while they may be knowledgeable about the greater Community, it is not their job to educate you, nor does their personal experience necessarily correlate with that of others.
2. Continue to seek awareness, knowledge, and skills through professional development, which is necessary due to rapid development of research and growing knowledge related to the LGBTQIA+ diverse experiences.
3. Understand the ADDRESSING Model (Hays, 1996) and the impact of such on supervisor/supervisee relationships.
Skills Competencies
4. Acknowledge the challenges and opportunities related to voluntary disclosure of affectional orientation. Be aware of not just the school/district policy and union protections, but also the experiences of staff members you work with who have come out. Remember that 'the law protects you retroactively; it does not protect you in the moment.' In other words, while there may be written protections on the books, that doesn't always equate with everyone in the district being affirming. Nor does policy ensure behavior.
5. Communicate and create a nonjudgmental, LGBTQ+-affirming environment. Do you use non-gendered language? Have LGBTQIA+ artwork and literature in your office? Do you address and correct micro- and macroaggressions you hear or are made aware of?
6. Utilize consultation and supervision with other mental health professionals who are competent and experienced in working with LGBTQIA+ individuals and especially those who may have already practiced affirming supervision.
7. Be mindful of stereotypes of LGBTQIA+ persons, and work to keep from perpetuating them.
8. Seek to understand by asking questions in a non-judgmental manner. Admit when you are unfamiliar with terminology used or topics discussed, but do not expect the supervisee to provide you with all of the information. The supervisee's 'job' ends with answering your question; it then becomes your obligation to seek out further information and knowledge related to the discussion to address your areas of newly learned shortcomings.
9. Remember that in regard to identity, orientation, and/or relationship status, it is the individual's story to tell. An intern may desire you to help introduce them to others and in so doing mention their identity, but they may also want to be able to do so independently on their own terms and timeline.
10. If the rapport, trust, or feeling of safety has been compromised, work with the intern to restore such. If the intern does not feel comfortable doing so, or is unaware of how to improve upon such, offer suggestions and allow the intern to determine whether your recommendations will help (which may or may not

(*Continued*)

TABLE 14.1 (Continued)

involve including additional parties). If the relationship has been damaged beyond repair, assist the intern in finding someone they can work with to complete their internship so as not to compromise their graduation and/or career. If this occurs, recognize that your work is not done, and ethically and morally you must now take steps to address your shortcomings and build your competence.
11. When you evaluate the intern's performance and experience, provide a forum through which they can in turn evaluate your supervision. Be sure to include questions related to Queer Theory and the intern's experience and perception of you as affirming. Use this feedback to further develop your professional competencies.
Attitude Competencies
12. Do not assume or presume sexual orientation, gender identity, or relationship status. It is okay to introduce yourself by extending your arm and offering your pronouns, but it is the intern's choice if they want to do the same. If they choose not to do so, explain your reasoning for designating your pronouns, but also recognize that the intern may have reasons for not doing so (such as not wanting to broadcast that they use 'they/them' until they feel comfortable doing so). If this is the case, remember such when co-leading groups or in introductions to colleagues. Similarly, do not presume that because an intern has mentioned a date/outing or living with a person that they are in a relationship with them, as there are greater ranges and diversity with regard to queer relationships, especially among younger generations.
13. Understand that supervisees have the resiliency to live fully functioning, healthy lives despite experiences with prejudice, discrimination, and oppression. Ensure that your supervision does not perpetuate the minoritization the supervisee experiences or may have experienced, and help him/her/them to address negative experiences within the school building, school faculty, and community.
14. Recognize that there are differences in privilege within the LGBTQIA+ community and that, as a result, the experience of a lesbian/gay individual may be very different from that of a pansexual/bisexual individual or transgender/nonbinary individual.
15. Demonstrate an awareness of one's own affectional orientation, the fluidity of sexuality and gender, and how your own life experience can contribute to or blind you from the experiences of others.
16. Acknowledge that past negative experiences may have resulted in an individual's fear of voluntary self-disclosure. Create a supportive environment that helps to counteract that negative experience.
17. Understand how intersecting identities and oppressions may have affected a supervisees' lived experiences.
18. Be open to expanding your consciousness and allowing the supervisee to teach you while also not expecting them to do so, both with you and with others.

Note: Adapted from ALGBTIC's Competencies for Counseling LGBTQQIA Individuals (Harper et al., 2013)

Conclusion

The use of affirmative supervision in school-based practices can help to interrogate, challenge, dismantle, reimagine, and rebuild structures, policies, and procedures that are harmful to interns and all students, school personnel, and families. In order for students to feel safe, valued, included, welcomed, affirmed, and valuable within the school setting, the adults charged with their care must feel so as well, including school psychology interns. The supervisory relationship has the power to support and encourage interns to have the confidence to overtly support LGBTQIA+ students and work toward dismantling oppressive structures within the school system and beyond. As supervisors, it is our obligation to help develop interns' professional competence while being mindful and conscientious about continuing to expand our own.

References

American Psychological Association. (2014). *Guidelines for clinical supervision in health service psychology*. http://apa.org/about/policy/guidelines-supervision.pdf

American Psychological Association. (2015). Guidelines for psychological practice with transgender and gender nonconforming people. *American Psychologist, 70*(9), 832–864. https://doi.org/10.1037/a0039906h

American Psychological Association, APA Task Force on Psychological Practice with Sexual Minority Persons. (2021). *Guidelines for psychological practice with sexual minority persons*. www.apa.org/about/policy/psychological-practice-sexual-minority-persons.pdf

Burkard, A. W., Knox, S., Hess, S. A., & Schultz, J. (2009). Lesbian, gay, and bisexual supervisees' experiences of LGB-affirmative and nonaffirmative supervision. *Journal of Counseling Psychology, 56*(1), 176–188. https://doi.org/10.1037/0022-0167.56.1.176

Butler, J. (2011). *Gender trouble: Feminism and the subversion of identity*. Routledge.

Craig, S. L., Dentato, M. P., Messinger, L., & McInroy, L. B. (2014). Educational determinants of readiness to practise with LGBTQ clients: Social work students speak out. *The British Journal of Social Work, 46*(1), 115–134. https:/doi.org/10/1093/bjsw/bcu107

Dilley, P. (1999). Queer theory: Under construction. *International Journal of Qualitative Studies in Education, 12*(5), 457–472. https://doi.org/10.1080/095183999235890

Dragowski, E., McCabe, P., Rubinson, F., & Scharron-del Rio, M. (2014, February 18). *Damaging assumptions: Avoiding your LGBTQ, gender, and cultural blindspots* [Paper Presentation]. National Association of School Psychologists Annual Convention, Washington, DC.

Dunsmuir, S., & Leadbetter, J. (2010, November). *Professional supervision: Guidelines for practice for educational psychologists*. British Psychological Society.

Ellemers, N. (2018). Gender stereotypes. *Annual Review of Psychology, 69*, 275–298. https://doi.org/10.1146/annurev-psych-1222216-011719

Foucault, M. (1972). *The archaeology of knowledge and the discourse on language*. Translated from the French by A. M. Sheridan Smith. Pantheon Books.

Garcia, L. (2009). "Now why do you want to know about that?" Heteronormativity, sexism, and racism in the sexual (mis) education of Latina youth. *Gender & Society, 23*(4), 520–541. https://doi.org/10.1177/0891243209339498

Gatmon, D., Jackson, D., Koshkarian, L., Martos-Perry, N., Molina, A., Patel, N., & Rodolfa, E. (2001). Exploring ethnic, gender, and sexual orientation variables in supervision: Do they really matter? *Journal of Multicultural Counseling and Development*, *29*, 102–113. https://doi.org/10.1002/j.2161-1912.2001.tb00508.x.

Gibbs, S., Atkinson, C., Woods, K., Bond, C., Hill, V., Howe, J., & Morris, S. (2016). Supervision for school psychologists in training: Developing a framework from empirical findings. *School Psychology International*, *37*(4), 410–431. https://doi.org/10.1177/0143034316653443

GLSEN, ASCA, ACSSW, & SSWAA. (2019). *Supporting safe and healthy schools for lesbian, gay, bisexual, transgender, and queer students: A national survey of school counselors, social workers, and psychologists*. GLSEN.

Harper, A., Finnerty, P., Martinez, M., Brace, A., Crethar, H. C., Loos, B., Harper, B., Graham, S., Singh, A., Kocet, M., Travis, L., & Hammer, T. R. (2013). Association for Lesbian, Gay, Bisexual, and Transgender Issues in Counseling Competencies for counseling with lesbian, gay, bisexual, queer, questioning, intersex, and ally individuals. *Journal of LGBT Issues in Counseling*, 7(1), 2–43. https:// 10.1080/15538605.2013.755444

Hays, P. A. (1996). Addressing the complexities of culture and gender in counseling. *Journal of Counseling & Development*, *74*, 332–338. https://doi.org/10.1002/j.1556-6676.1996.tb01876.x

Hays, P. A. (2008). *Addressing cultural complexities in practice: Assessment, diagnosis, and therapy* (2nd ed.). American Psychological Association.

Herlihy, B., & Corey, G. (2015). *ACA ethical standards casebook* (7th ed.). American Counseling Association.

Jagose, A. (1996). *Queer theory: An introduction*. New York University Press.

Johnson, L., & Federman, E. J. (2014). Training, experience, and attitudes of VA psychologists regarding LGBT issues: Relation to practice and competence. *Psychology of Sexual Orientation and Gender Diversity*, *1*(1), 10–18. https://doi.org/10.1037/sgd0000019

Legate, N., Ryan, R. M., & Weinstein, N. (2012). Is coming out always a "good thing"? Exploring the relations of autonomy support, outness, and wellness for lesbian, gay, and bisexual individuals. *Social Psychological and Personality Science*, *3*(2), 145–152. https://doi.org/10.1177/1948550611411929

McCann, H., & Monaghan, W. (2020). *Queer theory now: From foundations to futures*. Red Globe Press.

McIntosh, D. E., & Phelps, L. (2000). Supervision in school psychology: Where will the future take us? *Psychology in the Schools*, *37*(1), 33–38. https://doi.org/10.1002/(SICI)1520-6807(200001)37:1<33::AID-PITS4.3.0.CO;2-F

Muñoz, J. E. (1996). Ephemera as evidence: Introductory notes to queer acts. *Women & Performance*, *8*(2), 5–16. https://doi.org/10.1080/07407709608571228

Murphy, J. A., Rawlings, E. I., & Howe, S. R. (2002). A survey of clinical psychologists on treating lesbian, gay, and bisexual clients. *Professional Psychology: Research and Practice*, *33*(2), 183–189. https://doi.org/10.1037/0735-7028.33.2.183

National Association of School Psychologists. (2010). *Standards for graduate preparation of school psychologists*. www.nasponline.org/assets/Documents/Standards%20and%20Certification/Standards/1_Graduate_Preparation.pdf

National Association of School Psychologists. (2020). *The professional standards of the National Association of School Psychologists*. www.nasponline.org/standards-and-certification/nasp-2020-professional-standards-adopted

Pett, J. (2000). *Gay, lesbian and bisexual therapy and its supervision*. In D. Davies & C. Neal (Eds.), *Therapeutic perspectives on working with lesbian, gay and bisexual clients* (pp. 54–72). Open University Press.

Pilkington, N. W., & Cantor, J. M. (1996). Perceptions of heterosexual bias in professional psychology programs: A survey of graduate students. *Professional Psychology: Research and Practice*, *27*(6), 604–612. https://doi.org/10.1037/0735-7028.27.6.604

Prentice, D. A., & Miller, D. T. (2007). Psychological essentialism of human categories. *Current Directions in Psychological Science*, *16*(4), 202–206. https://doi.org/10.1111/j.1467-8721.2007.00504.xh

Rivera, D. P. & Nadal, K. L. (2019). The intersection of queer theory and empirical methods. In M. Brim & A. Ghaziani (Eds.), *Queer methods* (pp. 191–206). New York University Press.

Rivera, D. P., Nadal, K. L., Fisher, L. D., & Skolnik, A. A. (2012). Sexual orientation and gender identity microaggressions in the workplace. In M. Paludi (Ed.), *Managing diversity in today's workplace* (pp. 71–95). Praeger.

Simon, D. J., Cruise, T. K., Huber, B. J., Swerdlik, M. E., & Newman, D. S. (2014). Supervision in school psychology: The developmental/ecological/problem-solving model. *Psychology in the Schools*, *51*(6), 636–646. https://doi.org/10.1002/pits.21772

Smith Harvey, V., & Stuzziero, J. A. (2008). *Professional development and supervision of school psychologists: From intern to expert*. National Association of School Psychologists.

Sowden, B., Fleming, J., Savage, T. A., & Woitaszewski, S. A. (2015). Lesbian, gay, bisexual, and transgender-identified school psychologists: A qualitative study of their professional experiences. *Contemporary School Psychology*, *20*, 1–9. https://doi.org/10.1007/s40688-015-0050-1

Tozer, E. E., & McClanahan, M. K. (1999). Treating the purple menace: Ethical considerations of conversion therapy and affirmative alternatives. *The Counseling Psychologist*, *27*(5), 722–742. https://doi.org/10.1177/0011000099275006

Van Den Bergh, N., & Crisp, C. (2004). Defining culturally competent practice with sexual minorities: Implications for social work education and practice. *Journal of Social Work Education*, *40*(2), 221–238. https://doi.org/10.1080/10437797.2004.10778491

Warner, M. (1991). Introduction: Fear of a queer planet. *Social Text*, *29*, 3–17. www.jstor.org/stable/pdf/466295

Wilkinson, L., & Pearson, J. (2009). School culture and the well-being of same-sex-attracted youth. *Gender & Society*, *23*(4), 542–568. https://doi.org/10.1177/0891243209339913

15

CRITICAL STUDY OF WHITENESS TO DISMANTLE SCHOOL-TO-INCARCERATION PATHWAYS FOR RACIALLY MINORITIZED STUDENTS THROUGH SUPERVISION

Angela Mann

This chapter focuses on dismantling white supremacy, specifically surrounding anti-Blackness, by discussing a Critical Study of Whiteness (CSW) approach to supervision practices related to ending school-to-incarceration pathways. The chapter begins with a brief introduction to CSW. The next section examines school-to-incarceration pathways, also termed "the school-to-prison pipeline." This is followed by a discussion of the explicit and insidious ways anti-Black racism has permeated policy and practices in the American educational system, framed in a CSW lens. The chapter then shares a case narrative based on the experiences of Rodney,[1] a student who has been pushed through and pushed out of an educational system designed to fail him. Through this case narrative, supervision practices framed in a CSW lens, as well as advocacy and youth participatory action approaches for interrogating white supremacist policies and practices, will be shared in an effort toward ending harmful and racist policies and practices around "discipline" in schools.

Brief Introduction to the Critical Study of Whiteness

School-to-incarceration pathways are symptomatic of how—and perhaps some of the most salient ways that—white supremacy, whiteness, and racism pervade the American educational system. This section revisits Chapter 5 of this book, which describes *Critical Study of Whiteness* and the theories that underpin it. Within the chapter, Matias and Boucher (this volume) note that Critical Whiteness Studies, or what they have reconceptualized as the *Critical Study of Whiteness*, "delves directly to the root cause of racism (white supremacy) by investigating how whiteness embeds ideologically, emotionally, rhetorically, epistemologically, and behaviorally" (p. 64). More specifically, "Black whiteness studies ideologically

DOI: 10.4324/9780367815325-18

rests upon the epistemological stance that white people are not racially ignorant and thus in need of simple remedies such as anti-bias education. Instead, such an approach is more critical of race in that it does not quickly pardon those who racially benefit from hegemonic whiteness" (Matias & Boucher, this volume, p. 63). The authors break down white supremacy along two paths of impact—impacts on white people by *whiteness* (which involves elements of investment, privilege, naturalization, identity, emotionalities, racialization, property, coloniality, color blindness, wealth, entitlement, authority, Eurocentrism, determination of what is and what is not racism, and more) as well as impacts on people of color by *racism* (which involves elements of racial microaggressions, policing surveillance, marginalization, disembodiment, stereotype threat, dehumanization, job discrimination, achievement gaps, oppression, inequitable education, racial battle fatigue, racialization, racial stereotypes, Model Minority Myth, imposter phenomenon, and internalized oppression/inferiority, among others). Education is a system that is not immune to whiteness, nor is it immune to the relationship between whiteness and racism. Racism, specifically anti-Black racism, embodied within whiteness and white supremacy is baked within the policies that guide our practices, as I will outline later within the chapter. We should not only expect this, but when taking a CSW perspective, we should seek it out and act on it (Gillborn, 2005).

As Matias and Zembylas (2014) noted, many educators, and perhaps most school-based professionals, enter their respective fields often for seemingly altruistic reasons—care for students, a desire to positively impact the growing generations, and maybe even to create a more equitable world. White supremacy and the continued domination of whiteness normalizes the experiences of white people which, in turn, enables white people to "deflect, ignore, or dismiss their role, racialization, and privilege in race dynamics" (Matias et al., 2014, p. 291). The ability to be blind to race or "color-blind" to whiteness enables white educational professionals to be blind or to fail to think critically about the relational, institutional, structural, and systemic ways racism continues to marginalize and oppress Black, Indigenous, and other persons of color (BIPOC; Salter & Adams, 2013), thereby maintaining and upholding racism. Salter and Adams (2013) pointed out that whiteness even goes so far as to use civil rights and racial justice movements as support for color blindness using Dr. King's call for us to not judge others based on the color of their skin as one example. On the one hand, this "color blindness" is not without consequences for those benefiting from whiteness. In particular, pretending to not be racialized is a form of emotional distancing, producing shame and disgust that results in further defensiveness (Matias & Zembylas, 2014). So, are the ways in which educational systems and the individuals working within them creating and enacting racist policy and practice in a sense deliberate then? As Gillborn (2005) pointed out, at a minimum, "Institutional racism and race inequity are deliberate insofar as (at best) there appears to be a judgment that their eradication is simply not important enough to share the main tenets of education policy" (p. 499). He went on to note that it is also possible, at worst, that racist educational policies remain as a deliberate attempt to protect the power of whiteness (Gillborn, 2005).

Often the defensiveness or emotional distancing intertwined with whiteness is more insidious. In legal studies, where Critical Race Theory (CRT) was born, critical perspectives examined the notion of a slow process through liberalism and policy change (Ladson-Billings, 1998). We see parallels in education, especially when examining school-to-incarceration pathways, which are often suggested to be resolved by implementing positive behavior interventions and supports (that are arguably largely based on white cultural norms), examining discipline data disaggregated by race for inequities in application, and doing training for educators on implicit bias. It is clear that these remedies alone will not suffice (see Barclay, 2015; Forscher et al., 2019; McIntosh et al., 2020), and in the meantime youth of color will suffer. These remedies don't get at some of the root structural and relational contributors to school-to-incarceration pathways because they fail to specifically name them for what they are—racist. If we are to realize these collective goals of creating a more equitable and just world within and via educational systems, our work requires "unmasking and exposing racism in its various permutations" (Ladson-Billings, 1998, p. 11).

The "School-to-Prison Pipeline" and School-to-Incarceration Pathways

The "school-to-prison pipeline" is a now widely used term to describe and encompass the myriad ways in which students are set up for risk of incarceration[2] by the educational system. Scholars who study the pipeline point to exclusionary discipline policies (i.e., out-of-school suspension, expulsion, and/or the zero-tolerance policies that mandate the use of these exclusionary disciplines) that systematically push youth out of schools and increase the risk for long-term deleterious outcomes including incarceration (Skiba et al., 2014). Skiba et al. (2014) described many pathways to incarceration by school pushout through reduced engagement, greater negative attitudes toward school, reduced feelings of school connectedness, reduced instructional opportunities resulting in greater academic difficulties, and, consequently, increased risk of dropping out. Worse yet, this process is cyclical, whereby one school pushout increases the risk of likelihood to be suspended again. Further, there is evidence that this cascade of risk is initiated with that first suspension, and the risk factors are not likely to be present without this initial pushout (Skiba et al., 2014).

The existence of the school-to-prison pipeline is bad for all youth, but this process of placing youth at risk based on disciplinary responses is also discriminately applied and particularly bad for Black youth. There is evidence that school administrators are more likely to identify Black youth as "troublemakers," even though there is no reason to believe that Black youth behave any differently from white peers (Jarvis & Okonofua, 2020). In fact, research supports the "Black Escalation Effect" whereby white students and Black students can engage in the same behavior, and yet, teachers and school administrators will apply a harsher disciplinary response to the Black student (Jarvis & Okonofua, 2020; Okonofua & Eberhardt, 2015). The most recent data available from the U.S. Department of Education Office of Civil Rights (2019) found that Black students are disproportionately subject to restraint or seclusion and nearly three times as likely to be expelled or referred to law enforcement when compared to white peers. Specific to out-of-school suspensions, Black boys were three times more likely to be suspended out of school compared to white males (who were actually underrepresented), and Black girls were around five times more likely to be suspended out of school relative to white girls (who were also underrepresented in this data). It should be noted that Black students are more likely to be disciplined for subjective offenses such as "insubordination" or "willful defiance" (Skiba et al., 2011). When looking at the cost to Black students in terms of loss of instructional days, we see that Black students lost 82 more days per 100 students when compared to white students (Losen et al., 2020). Black girls were even more disproportionately instructionally marginalized relative to white girls—they lost seven times more instructional days (Losen et al., 2020). In the next section, I will further examine the links between white supremacy, the marginalization of Black students within the educational system, and school-to-incarceration pathways using a CSW lens.

Critical Study of Whiteness, Anti-Black Racism, and School-to-Incarceration Pathways

The foundation for school-to-incarceration pathways is multi-layered. One could argue that structurally, at the core, lies the extensive continued segregation of communities and schools related to discriminatory housing policies and corresponding economic marginalization (Chang, 2018; Ladson-Billings, 1998). The policies that hold up segregation serve to also perpetuate the marginalization of students of color, particularly Black students, through racist school funding formulas (Chang & Mehta, 2020; Fitzgerald, 2015; Ladson-Billings, 1998) and school voucher programs (Ford et al., 2017) that continue to benefit schools composed largely of white families. In addition, despite the fact that the literature suggests that having more diversity amongst educators might lead to more equitable approaches to responding to student behavior schoolwide (Hughes et al., 2020), diversity among school staff continues to lack across the country. Anti-Black racism and white supremacy, particularly the devaluing of Black educators, has infiltrated the hiring practices of schools (D'Amico et al., 2017), leading to what Davis (2020) called a "manufactured Black teacher shortage crisis" and making it harder to bridge that student-teacher cultural incongruence gap (p. 1). This is particularly problematic given that the predominately white teachers who work with students in marginalized settings are not immune to white supremacy.

In fact, not only does the research suggest that more than three-quarters of white teachers were found to have implicitly anti-Black racist bias, but an additional 30% demonstrated explicit anti-Black racism (Starck et al., 2020). Consequently, and likely related to racial stereotypes and cultural fear of "Black Anger," these teachers often falsely code the emotions of Black children as angry, making them more likely to also discriminatorily apply punitive disciplinary responses (Blake et al., 2016; Halberstadt et al., 2020). These relational manifestations of whiteness, as well as structural and systemic anti-Black racism, set the foundation for white power structures, enhancing pathways from school to incarceration.

Looking specifically at cultures within classrooms, the very nature of the terms *classroom management* and *discipline* denote power structures that reinforce the authority and supremacy of whiteness serving to continue the control, oppression, and marginalization of students of color. Adams (2000) outlined the history of hegemonic power structures in schools through the application of harmful, punitive disciplinary responses couched in the context of colonialism. He noted that, as far back as the 17th century, concerns about "unruly" schoolchildren and teenagers are documented and that school discipline has historically been intended to address school violence when, in fact, school discipline has often involved violence. Early in the 21st century, it was still relatively common to see corporal punishment in schools and, while less prevalent, these practices continue today. Punishment in all forms as a means of manipulating conformity, including the dramatic expansion of school pushout and suspension policies, can be its own means of violence. In the 1960s and 1970s, following a number of lawsuits and the passage of the Civil Rights Act of 1964 authorizing the federal government to file school desegregation cases (see Teaching Tolerance, 2004) and as school integration began to expand, the suspension of students increased dramatically as a means of a "quick fix" for addressing groups of students who were described as not conforming. These suspensions also served to provide school administrators with a sense of control over what was perceived as potentially "uncontrollable."

Moving into the 1980s and continuing into the 1990s, the narrative of "super predator" youth of color began to advance in media portrayals and public dialogue (Heitzeg, 2018; Bogert & Hancock, 2020). This dehumanization and adultification (see Epstein et al., 2017) of youth of color, in particular Black youth, is linked with racial profiling and occurs in tandem with mass incarceration trends, including the expansion of punitive carceral systems for youth (Heitzeg, 2018). This means increased police presence in communities of color and the advent of mandatory minimum sentencing and "three-strikes" sentencing within these communities (Heitzeg, 2018). Schools, being reflections of their communities, experience much of the same. During this period, schools began to implement similar "get tough" or zero-tolerance approaches to student behavior and substantially expanded police presence and physical security measures in schools, especially schools that are predominantly attended by youth of color *and* despite school safety data suggesting school crime was on the decline. With the passage of the Gun-Free Schools Act of 1994, zero-tolerance policies mandating expulsion and referrals to law enforcement are cemented in federal legislation. With this law and the subsequent passage of the Safe Schools Acts of 1994 and 1998 that focus on enhancing law enforcement presence in schools, we see a significant proliferation of police in schools to the present day, where nearly one-third of schools report having a law enforcement officer on campus but no school-employed mental health professionals (Whitaker et al., 2019).

This history of policing has its own deeply rooted history steeped in anti-Black racism, which makes this proliferation at the expense of equity in access to school-based mental health services especially problematic. In their extensive report documenting the use of police to intimidate and suppress social movements among youth of color, the Advancement Project (2019) outlined police involvement in criminalizing youth protesting segregation, in enforcing school segregation, in criminalizing protests for a richer educational experience for Black youth including instruction in Black history, and in stifling protests of the under-resourcing and further marginalization of predominantly Black schools. Further, the experiences of youth witnessing the murders of Black community members at the hands of police has additional serious impacts on psychological safety, among other concerns (see Proctor et al., 2020 for a review). While law enforcement was brought into schools under the guise of protecting students from "unruly youth," and a significant diversion of resources was made toward this end, there is no evidence that the presence of law enforcement in schools actually makes anyone any safer (Javdani, 2019). In fact, the presence of law enforcement seems instead to actually increase risk of the application of harmful disciplinary outcomes (Fisher & Hennessy, 2016) and risk of arrest for Black and Latinx students (Homer & Fisher, 2020). When considering the history and socialization of police toward anti-Black racism, it is perhaps not surprising to know that anti-Black racism is pervasive amongst school-based law enforcement when conducting threat assessment of youth (Fisher et al., 2020).

Despite burgeoning evidence that school-to-incarceration pathways were not only built on a foundation of colonialism and white supremacy, white refusal and the active bolstering of supremacist structures is very much alive today at the hands of the highest levels of policymakers in education. As one example, when Secretary of Education Betsy DeVos and her administration rescinded the Obama-era *Rethinking School Discipline* guidance around addressing the racist application of school discipline (Lhamon & Samuels, 2014), her office's contribution to the report from the Federal Commission on School Safety (see DeVos et al., 2018) and her testimony before the U.S. Congress (Camera, 2019) essentially used the justification that Black children simply misbehave more than their white peers and that decision-making around school discipline was not racially biased, as previous scholarship had indicated. In the words of Caldera (2020), historical views of Black culture as "deficient" and Black youth as "problematic" continue today. Looking across the educational system, we see the continued push for students to conform to white norms in dress-code policies (see Aghasaleh, 2018) and codes of conduct (see Green et al., 2020), furthering the notion of white superiority and the dehumanization of Black children.

The persistent white supremacist culture of schools and desire to control and oppress Black youth through policy, environment, force, and criminalization, combined with the imbalances of power and resources leading to continued marginalization, have serious consequences for Black youth. Specifically, Black youth experiencing anti-Black racism in their schools might, as a consequence, experience decreased self-esteem and self-worth, as well as more significant negative mental health and psychological maladjustment (Turner et al., 2020). Additionally, students who assess their schools as racially unjust are more likely to be disengaged in the classroom, and being emotionally disengaged puts these students at risk for office discipline referrals and out-of-school suspensions (Griffin, Metzger, et al., 2020), furthering the looping nature of school pushout. As mentioned previously within this chapter, disengagement and disconnectedness from school puts students at risk for dropping out and ending up incarcerated.

The white supremacist systems at play in school-to-incarceration pathways coupled with the explicitly racist musings of leaders at the highest levels of leadership in institutions of education furthers the need introduced earlier in the chapter to push past focusing primarily on understanding the data around disproportionate discipline and training our colleagues on their implicit biases. To achieve educational equity, we have to "expose racism in education *and* propose radical solutions for addressing it" (Ladson-Billings, 1998, p. 22). Through the narrative of Rodney and the illustration of a supervisory relationship with a school psychology training, strategies for beginning to dismantle white supremacist systems that maintain school-to-incarceration pathways by interrogating whiteness and challenging racist policies and practices within schools will be presented.

Case Narrative

Part of decentering whiteness involves sharing stories of BIPOC persons and, through these stories, analyzing and deconstructing the ways in which, in this case, whiteness impacts BIPOC persons through racism (Ladson-Billings, 1998). Toward this end, I share this case narrative centering the experiences of Rodney, an 8th-grade, Black middle school student who recently began attending an alternative school, in an effort to outline the relationship between white supremacy, whiteness, anti-Black racism, and school-to-incarceration pathways.

Rodney's school is located in a large urban school district in the Southeast. The city encompassing the district continues to be plagued by anti-Black racism, despite a rich civil rights history and a large Black population. During the "white flight" out of the city and into the suburbs, city officials negotiated a deal with the remaining and predominantly Black leaders of the city to annex the outlying predominantly white suburban areas and provide city services with the promise of greater political power, a greater tax base, and expanded economic development for Black communities within city limits. Decades later those promises remain unfulfilled, and Black communities within city limits continue to struggle with economic marginalization and segregation, continuing the inter-generational oppression of Black citizens. These communities have historically been plagued by violence, with some of the highest homicide rates in the country, many of which go unsolved. The majority of the city's budget is devoted to law enforcement—law enforcement who have killed multiple Black youths in the last year who were believed to be unarmed, but whose cases the sheriff's office will not release body camera footage on. Youth in the city, particularly Black youth, are also crushed by a local state attorney who was identified in national media as the "cruelest prosecutor in America" and by human rights organizations as reigning terror over youth in her jurisdiction. Specifically, the state attorney's office was known for "direct filing" the majority of youth held and awaiting trial, charging them as adults for something as simple as their attorney asking about expediting their hearings.

It is noteworthy that the city and school district are the same, and yet there are far fewer white students attending district schools than would be expected as many white parents choose to send their students to elite and expensive private schools. Perhaps ironically, the district serves white students quite well. It has some of the top (predominantly white) magnet programs in the country and is generally a top-performing large urban district. On the other hand, this same district where Rodney attends school suspends Black students out-of-school 3.5 times more often than white peers, sends Black students to alternative settings 5 times more often than they do white peers, and was 20 times more likely to expel Black students compared to white peers. The alternative setting where Rodney finds himself has been on continuous improvement plans for several years. The district-administered surveys found staff to describe their colleagues as doing less than quality work and report reduced collegiality. Parents and caregivers perceive that teachers at the school have low expectations for students, provide inadequate support and inadequate instruction to students, and that the school is not a safe place for their students to learn. Students echo these concerns about safety at school. Nearly all students have received one or more suspensions, have significantly reduced attendance, and around half of the students are not progressing as expected toward graduation and are at risk for dropping out.

Before Rodney was funneled through the system into the alternative setting, he had already encountered layers of racist systems and policies that had profound impacts on his life. Both of Rodney's parents had been incarcerated for some time as many Black people in the state, a state with one of the highest incarceration rates in the world, find themselves. Rodney was sent to the alternative setting for getting caught smoking marijuana too many times in his neighborhood school's bathroom and was himself facing charges. The school administrators referred him to the intern and the school psychology supervisor for mentoring through the Check and Connect program (see Christenson et al., 2008) that had recently started at the school. Rodney was described by school staff as being a bright, friendly kid who got along well with peers and teachers. His grandmother and primary caregiver, who consented to Rodney's participation in the program, expressed concern for Rodney. Rodney had recently witnessed violence in the community, and his older sister had "fallen in with the wrong crowd" and was no longer providing the same level of support Rodney previously had. Rodney had also recently begun to express a desire to connect with his parents, whom he had lost in the system several years back. His grandmother noted that, despite the myriad of adverse life events Rodney had experienced in his young life, he had never received any school-based mental health services or interventions that she was aware of. Within the first team meeting (Rodney, the school psychologist supervisor, and intern), Rodney spoke eloquently about the inequities he had observed within his community and his awareness of the expectation of the school community that he would likely struggle to graduate or drop out. He was eager to connect with the intern and to participate in the program.

Case Narrative Supervision Process Discussion Using Critical Study of Whiteness Lens

Through this case narrative, I will also highlight the supervision of a white school psychology intern through a CSW lens. Strategies for combating systemic white supremacy and anti-Black racism through a CSW perspective on supervision and advocacy toward ending school-to-incarceration pathways for youth will be shared.

Matias et al. (2014) identified four variations of white imagination that educational professionals often are immersed in when entering the field: (1) emotional (dis)investment in racial justice, (2) limited to only acknowledging they are white but not identifying the impact of their whiteness, (3) immersion in white guilt, or (4) an endorsement of or failure to recognize complicity in hegemonic whiteness. When engaging in the work of dismantling anti-Black racist systems, students must learn the foundations of race, including understanding whiteness and the impact of being white, before being asked to deconstruct white supremacy (Matias & Mackey, 2016). By better understanding how whiteness is at the foundation of inequities for youth, practitioners can better understand how what is needed is not "white saviorism" but rather accomplices in racial justice aimed at breaking down anti-Black racist systems and structures. Matias and Mackey (2016) outlined that this starts by explicitly preparing practitioners for the emotions that students may experience as they confront and come to terms with whiteness. This can be done by engaging students and interns in readings that may elicit these emotions. In the case of the intern seeking to develop relationships with Rodney and school staff, we began by exploring readings about civil rights leaders and liberation movements that occurred within the community, city consolidation efforts by white racist leaders to perpetuate whiteness as property and oppress Black communities while making explicit connections to present school segregation and funding inequities, as well as a review of data on educational opportunity for Black youth in the local community. The intern engaged in reflective exercises following meetings to process the emotions they experienced as they confronted whiteness, which led to debriefs with the supervisor. These emotions led to conversations of privilege—the privilege to have avoided these emotions for some time—a conversation largely guided by the National

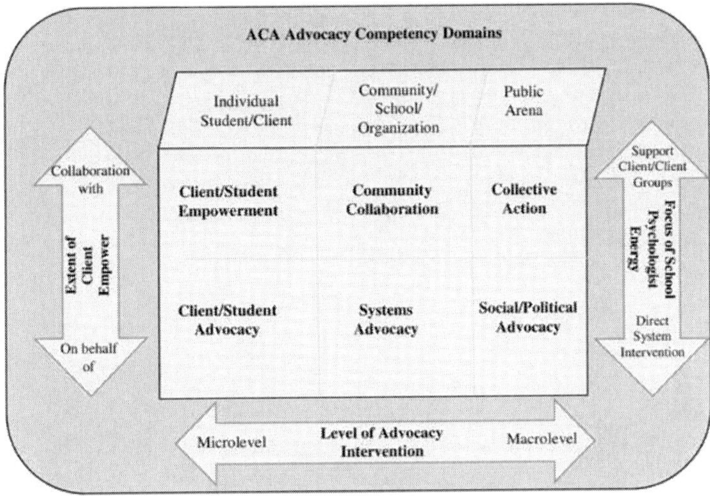

FIGURE 15.1 ACA Advocacy Competency Domains

Association of School Psychologists' (NASP; 2016) document on *Understanding Race and Privilege* with a focus on owning the emotions in a process called "sharing the burden" (Matias & Mackey, 2016).

Finally, the supervisor and intern began reviewing the levels of social justice advocacy put forth for school psychologists by Malone and Proctor (2019) as adopted by the American Counseling Association (ACA; Toporek & Daniels, 2018; Lewis et al., 2002). More specifically, the supervisor and intern collaborated in identifying organizational and local advocacy opportunities at the client/student, school/community, and public arena levels (see Figure 15.1 for the ACA Advocacy Competencies Domains) with Rodney and his family's personal goals in mind.

Advocacy on an Individual Student/Client Level

Advocacy on an individual student/client level involved *empowerment in collaboration with* Rodney and his family as well *as advocacy on behalf of* Rodney, his family, and all of the other students involved in the Check and Connect mentoring program (Christenson et al., 2008) at the school. Rodney's teachers and his grandmother cited the following as goals for Rodney: increase class attendance/decrease skipping, increase assignment completion, and serve as a leader/positive model for his peers in his classes. Rodney also expressed a desire to increase his academic success in his classes by completing his work and passing his classes. He recognized that attending classes would help him achieve this, but he also felt he could benefit from occasional breaks from class. He felt somewhat misunderstood by his teachers and identified that breaks from class allowed him time to cool off when he felt a teacher was disrespecting him. At the forefront of Rodney's mind, however, was reconnecting with his parents, who were incarcerated.

The intern used a combination of motivational interviewing and solution-focused therapy techniques to help Rodney with meeting his weekly goals. Much of the intern's work with Rodney involved enhancing coping through something similar to equity-elaborated social-emotional learning as described by Griffin, Gray, et al. (2020). They worked with the school team to allow him one break per day from his classes to visit the intern or supervisor for problem-solving if he ran into issues with school staff, and they worked with Rodney to decide what would be helpful to communicate to school staff in order to best support him. This helped the team to identify one particular teacher Rodney had a conflict with. The intern utilized an approach with this teacher similar to the Greet-Stop-Prompt and Establish-Maintain-Restore interventions described by Cook, Coco, et al. (2018) and Cook, Duong, et al. (2018) to help build a better relationship between the teacher and Rodney. The intern and school psychologist worked together to locate Rodney's parents within the prison system and assisted with processing the experience of being connected again with them. They also teamed with the school social worker, who was able to connect Rodney's grandmother with community-based family therapy support to address her concerns regarding Rodney's sister.

Advocacy on a Community/School/Organizational Level

Advocacy on a community/school/organizational level involved *collaboration with the community* as well as *systems advocacy on behalf of* Black youth within the district. As suggested by Sabnis et al. (2020), the supervisor and intern met with school leadership to discuss ways to critically interrogate practice in weekly school discipline team meetings, beginning with the evaluation of the implementation of the district's dress code policy and the school's disciplinary practices. This led to ongoing and recursive conversations about a pervasive deficit-oriented culture, as well as conversations regarding the implementation of culturally responsive positive behavioral interventions and supports in an effort to orient staff toward reducing the reliance on exclusionary discipline and pushout. The intern and supervisor also introduced the process of root cause analysis (see Osher et al., 2015) in an effort to be more explicit and direct in conversations regarding the reasons behind disproportionate discipline, including discussing broader racist structures and classroom norms that influence discipline decision-making.

In a neighboring school, a student had recently been suspended for protesting in the lunchroom for further African American studies within the district. A local community organization aimed at Black empowerment as well as a community organization centered upon the rights of youth made up of pediatricians, public defenders, psychologists, and private attorneys were both interested in this student's case, as was Rodney. Using a youth participatory action research approach (see Song et al., 2014), Rodney and his fellow students involved in the Check and Connect program partnered together with the community organizations to advocate on behalf of the student to overturn the suspension. The youth lobbied the school board for the establishment of a school board seat held by a student, highlighting the activist work of the students and the asset that this kind of passion could provide to the district. The board answered by establishing a youth advisory council to consult with district leaders. Additionally, youth chose to advocate, with the support of the community organizations, for greater Black cultural reverence acknowledging that Black students' lives matter (see Caldera, 2020) through expanding the offering of African American History courses throughout the district.

This collective group also identified a need for alternatives to suspension within the district. Joined by a local interfaith community organization that had already established a relationship with the district and that was concerned about the high rates of pushout of Black youth, it was proposed that the district receive training in the implementation of restorative practices to replace out-of-school suspensions (see Song et al., 2020 for a review of consultation and professional development around restorative justice practices). After meeting with the district, which agreed to the training and on beginning to implement restorative practices, a number of other needs were identified. The district was also interested in establishing in-school suspension centers where youth could be sent to receive academic remediation and short-term mentoring while schools received the further planned professional development. The group collaborated with the district to procure grant funding to establish these centers. The district also set up a meeting with the group and the state attorney's office to establish the criteria for a civil citation program whereby, instead of arresting youth for misdemeanor offenses (e.g., possession of alcohol, disorderly conduct, etc.), youth would be mandated to drug or alcohol counseling, assigned community service, or some other variation of a community diversion program. This program also required the officer who chose to forgo an eligible civil citation to justify why they continued with an arrest.

Additionally, after speaking with many youths at Rodney's school, the group realized that many students either weren't aware of district code of conduct policies or perceived that they were arbitrarily/discriminatorily applied. The group began to examine the district's code of conduct in an effort to create more equitable and transparent policies for students and teachers using the *Checklist for Analyzing Discipline Policies and Procedures for Equity* (CADPEE; Green et al., 2020) in collaborating with the district's director of school discipline and school safety. The group also continues to discuss district dress-code policies and areas that youth felt were problematic or discriminatory.

Advocacy on a Public Arena Level

Advocacy on a public arena level involved *collective action with* community members and *social/political advocacy on behalf of* Black youth and their families. The intern, supervisor, and the previously mentioned community organizations have engaged in a number of collective action initiatives in an effort to effect policy at a city and regional level. The youth-led community-based discussions around juvenile incarceration data included engaging the state attorney's office, which eventually led to the election of a new state attorney. The community members wrote letters to the editor and city council members regarding the city's disproportionate budget for law enforcement and the underfunding of economic development and neighborhood resources that were promised through consolidation. Finally, the group also contacted the city's coordinating agency for children's services and is collaborating on a report that would evaluate community needs and services for youth and their families (including educational services and opportunities) in an effort to better coordinate services and increase access for youth and their families living in low-income and economically marginalized, predominantly Black neighborhoods within the city.

Conclusion

With the integration of schools came well-worn pathways from school to incarceration that discriminately impact students of color, particularly Black youth. Through classroom cultural norms, codes of conduct, and dress codes that center and emphasize value on whiteness while devaluing and dehumanizing Blackness, through the criminalization of Black youth and the proliferation of policing that puts youth further at risk, Black youth are pushed out of schools at exceptional rates. At the foundation of these policies and discriminatory practices lies a white supremacist culture that values whiteness and perpetuates anti-Black racism. The proliferation of incremental liberalist practices such as examining implicit biases and discipline data disaggregated by race will not be enough and enables continued white refusal. In the meantime, generations of Black Americans continue to be marginalized and pushed out of school systems and into carceral systems. Our actions have not been enough and will not be enough until we more systematically and critically evaluate the history of racist educational systems and the contemporary influences of white supremacy and colonialism in classroom culture using a *Critical Study of Whiteness* lens. This will require us to examine our emotions around whiteness, while also de-centering whiteness and the centering of white emotions in order to explicitly name the ways in which whiteness and racism permeate our educational structures, systems, and relationships. It will also require us to ***act*** in collaboration with and on behalf of those who have been marginalized, devalued, and de-humanized by whiteness.

Notes

1. Pseudonyms are used to protect the privacy of students, staff, and educational settings.
2. I will specifically avoid using the term *juvenile justice system*, as I don't believe justice in any form is served by carceral systems.

References

Adams, A. T. (2000). The status of school discipline and violence. *The Annals of the American Academy of Political and Social Science*, *567*(1), 140–156. https://doi.org/10.1177/000271620056700101O

Advancement Project. (2019). We came to learn: A call to action for police free schools. *Advancement Project*. https://advancementproject.org/wp-content/uploads/WCTLweb/index.html#page=18

Aghasaleh, R. (2018). Oppressive curriculum: Sexist, racist, classist, and homophobic practice of dress codes in schooling. *Journal of African American Studies*, *22*(1), 94–108. https://doi.org/10.1007/s12111-018-9397-5

Barclay, C. M. (2015). Unpacking the discipline gap: Referral categories and school-wide positive behavior interventions and supports. *Graduate Theses and Dissertations*. https://scholarcommons.usf.edu/etd/5906/

Blake, J. J., Smith, D. M., Marchbanks, M. P., Seibert, A. L., Wood, S. M., & Kim, E. S. (2016). Does student–teacher racial/ethnic match impact Black students' discipline risk? A test of the cultural synchrony hypothesis. In R. Skiba, K. Mediratta, & M. Rausch (Eds.), *Inequality in school discipline* (pp. 79–98). Palgrave Macmillan. https://doi.org/10.1057/978-1-137-51257-4_5

Bogert, C., & Hancock, L. (2020). Superpredator: How media coverage affected juvenile justice. *The Marshall Project*. www.themarshallproject.org/2020/11/20/superpredator-the-media-myth-that-demonized-a-generation-of-black-youth

Caldera, A. L. (2020). Eradicating anti-Black racism in U.S. schools: A call-to-action for school leaders. *Diversity, Social Justice, and the Educational Leader*, *4*, 12–25.

Camera, L. (2019). The race research cited by DeVos. *U.S. News*. www.usnews.com/news/education-news/articles/2019-03-28/the-controversial-race-research-devos-used-to-revoke-school-discipline-guidance

Chang, A. (2018). We can draw school zones to make classrooms less segregated. This is how well your district does. Is your district drawing borders to reduce or perpetuate racial segregation? *Vox*. www.vox.com/2018/1/8/16822374/school-segregation-gerry mander-map

Chang, A., & Mehta, J. (2020). Why U.S. schools are still segregated—and one idea to help change that. *National Public Radio*. www.npr.org/sections/live-updates-protests-for-racial-justice/2020/07/07/888469809/how-funding-model-preserves-racial-segregation-in-public-schools

Christenson, S. L., Thurlow, M. L., Sinclair, M. F., Lehr, C. A., Kaibel, C. M., Reschly, A. L., Mavis, A., & Pohl, A. (2008). Check & connect: A comprehensive student engagement intervention manual. *Institute on Community Integration (NJ3)*.

Cook, C. R., Coco, S., Zhang, Y., Fiat, A. E., Duong, M. T., Renshaw, T. L., Long, A., & Frank, S. (2018). Cultivating positive teacher–student relationships: Preliminary evaluation of the establish—maintain—restore (EMR) method. *School Psychology Review*, *47*(3), 226–243. https://doi.org/10.17105/spr-2017-0025.v47-3

Cook, C. R., Duong, M. T., McIntosh, K., Fiat, A. E., Larson, M., Pullmann, M. D., & McGinnis, J. (2018). Addressing discipline disparities for Black male students: Linking malleable root causes to feasible and effective practices. *School Psychology Review, 47*(2), 135–152. https://doi.org/10.17105/spr-2017-0026.v47-2

D'amico, D., Pawlewicz, R. J., Earley, P. M., & McGeehan, A. P. (2017). Where are all the Black teachers? Discrimination in the teacher labor market. *Harvard Educational Review, 87*, 26–49. https://doi.org/10.17763/1943-5045-87.1.26

Davis, M. D. (2020). Where in the world is the Black educator? Teacher shortage as manufactured crisis. *Race and Pedagogy Journal: Teaching and Learning for Justice, 4*(3), 4.

DeVos, B., Nielsen, K. M., Azar, A. M., II, Whitaker, M., Department of Education, E. F. C. on S. S., US Department of Homeland Security, US Department of Health and Human Services, & US Department of Justice. (2018). Final report of the Federal commission on school safety. Presented to the President of the United States. In *US Department of Education*. US Department of Education.

Epstein, R., Blake, J., & González, T. (2017). *Girlhood interrupted: The erasure of black girls' childhood*. Georgetown Law Center on Poverty and Inequality. www.law.georgetown.edu/academics/centers-institutes/poverty-inequality/upload/girlhood-interrupted.pdf

Fisher, B. W., & Hennessy, E. A. (2016). School resource officers and exclusionary discipline in US high schools: A systematic review and meta-analysis. *Adolescent Research Review, 1*, 217–233. https://doi.org/10.1007/s40894-015-0006-8

Fisher, B. W., Higgins, E. M., Kupchik, A., Viano, S., Curran, F. C., Overstreet, S., Plumlee, B. & Coffey, B. (2020). Protecting the flock or policing the sheep? Differences in school resource officers' perceptions of threats by school racial composition. *Social Problems*, 1–19. https://doi.org/10.1093/socpro/spaa062

Fitzgerald, T. (2015). White racial framing related to public school financing. *Forum on Public Policy Online* (2015, 1). Oxford Round Table. 406 West Florida Avenue, Urbana, IL 61801.

Ford, C., Johnson, S., Partelow, L., & Center for American Progress. (2017). The racist origins of private school vouchers. In *Center for American progress*. Center for American Progress.

Forscher, P. S., Lai, C. K., Axt, J. R., Ebersole, C. R., Herman, M., Devine, P. G., & Nosek, B. A. (2019). A meta-analysis of procedures to change implicit measures. *Journal of Personality and Social Psychology: Attitudes and Social Cognition, 117*(3), 522–559. https://doi.org/10.1037/pspa0000160

Gillborn, D. (2005). Education policy as an act of white supremacy: Whiteness, critical race theory and education reform. *Journal of Education Policy, 20*(4), 485–505. https://doi.org/10.1080/02680930500132346

Green, A. L., Hatton, H., Stegenga, S. M., Eliason, B., & Nese, R. N. (2020). Examining commitment to prevention, equity, and meaningful engagement: A review of school district discipline policies. *Journal of Positive Behavior Interventions*, 1–12. https://doi.org/10.1177/1098300720951940

Griffin, C. B., Gray, D., Hope, E., Metzger, I. W., & Henderson, D. X. (2020). Do coping responses and racial identity promote school adjustment among black youth? Applying an equity-elaborated social–emotional learning lens. *Urban Education*, 1–26. https://doi.org/10.1177/0042085920933346

Griffin, C. B., Metzger, I. W., Halliday-Boykins, C. A., & Salazar, C. A. (2020). Racial fairness, school engagement, and discipline outcomes in African American high school students: The important role of gender. *School Psychology Review, 49*, 222–238. https://doi.org/10.1080/2372966x.2020.1726810

Halberstadt, A. G., Cooke, A. N., Garner, P. W., Hughes, S. A., Oertwig, D., & Neupert, S. D. (2020). Racialized emotion recognition accuracy and anger bias of children's faces. *Emotion*. https://doi.org/10.1037/emo0000756

Heitzeg, N. A. (2018). Criminalizing education: Zero tolerance policies, police in the hallways, and the school to prison pipeline. In A. J. Nocella II, P. Parmar, & D. Stovall (Eds.), *From education to incarceration: Dismantling the school-to-prison pipeline, counterpoints*. Peter Lang Publishing Group.

Homer, E. M., & Fisher, B. W. (2020). Police in schools and student arrest rates across the United States: Examining differences by race, ethnicity, and gender. *Journal of School Violence, 19*(2), 192–204. https://doi.org/10.1080/15388220.2019.1604377

Hughes, C., Bailey, C. M., Warren, P. Y., & Stewart, E. A. (2020). "Value in diversity": School racial and ethnic composition, teacher diversity, and school punishment. *Social Science Research, 92*, 102481. https://doi.org/10.1016/j.ssresearch.2020.102481

Jarvis, S. N., & Okonofua, J. A. (2020). School deferred: When bias affects school leaders. *Social Psychological and Personality Science, 11*(4), 492–498. https://doi.org/10.1177/1948550619875150

Javdani, S. (2019). Policing education: An empirical review of the challenges and impact of the work of school police officers. *American Journal of Community Psychology, 63*(3–4), 253–269. https://doi.org/10.1002/ajcp.12306

Ladson-Billings, G. (1998). Just what is critical race theory and what's it doing in a nice field like education? *International Journal of Qualitative Studies in Education, 11*(1), 7–24. https://doi.org/10.4324/9781003005995-2

Lewis, J. A., Arnold, M. S., House, R., & Toporek, R. L. (2002). *ACA advocacy competencies*. www.counseling.org/docs/default-source/competencies/aca-advocacy-competencies-updated-may-2020.pdf?sfvrsn=f410212c_4

Lhamon, C. E., & Samuels, J. (2014). Joint dear colleague letter. *U.S. Department of Justice & U.S. Department of Education*. https://www2.ed.gov/about/offices/list/ocr/letters/colleague-201401-title-vi.html

Losen, D. J., Martinez, P., Civil Rights Project, P. D. C. C. for C. R. R. (CCRR), & Learning Policy Institute. (2020). Lost opportunities: How disparate school discipline continues to drive differences in the opportunity to learn. In *Civil rights project—Proyecto Derechos Civiles*. Civil Rights Project—Proyecto Derechos Civiles.

Malone, C. M., & Proctor, S. L. (2019). Demystifying social justice for school psychology practice. *Communique, 48*(1), 1–21.

Matias, C. E., & Mackey, J. (2016). Breakin' down whiteness in antiracist teaching: Introducing critical whiteness pedagogy. *The Urban Review, 48*, 32–50. https://doi.org/10.1007/s11256-015-0344-7

Matias, C. E., Viesca, K. M., Garrison-Wade, D. F., Tandon, M., & Galindo, R. (2014). "What is critical whiteness doing in OUR nice field like critical race theory?" Applying CRT and CWS to understand the white imaginations of white teacher candidates. *Equity & Excellence in Education, 47*(3), 289–304. https://doi.org/10.1080/10665684.2014.933692

Matias, C. E., & Zembylas, M. (2014). "When saying you care is not really caring": Emotions of disgust, whiteness ideology, and teacher education. *Critical Studies in Education, 55*(3), 319–337. https://doi.org/10.1080/17508487.2014.922489

McIntosh, K., Smolkowski, K., Gion, C. M., Witherspoon, L., Bastable, E., & Girvan, E. J. (2020). Awareness is not enough: A double-blind randomized controlled trial of the effects of providing discipline disproportionality data reports to school administrators. *Educational Researcher, 49*(7), 533–537. https://doi.org/10.3102/0013189x20939937

National Association of School Psychologists. (2016). *Understanding race and privilege* [handout]. www.nasponline.org/resources-and-publications/resources-and-podcasts/diversity-and-social-justice/social-justice/understanding-race-and-privilege

Okonofua, J. A., & Eberhardt, J. L. (2015). Two strikes: Race and disciplining students. *Psychological Science, 26*(5), 617–624. https://doi.org/10.1177/0956797615570365

Osher, D., Fisher, D., Amos, L., Katz, J., Dwyer, K., Duffey, T., Colombi, G. D., & National Center on Safe Supportive Learning Environments (NCSSLE). (2015). Addressing the root causes of disparities in school discipline: An educator's action planning guide. In *National center on safe supportive learning environments*. National Center on Safe Supportive Learning Environments.

Proctor, S. L., Li, K., Chait, N., Owens, C., Gulfaraz, S., Sang, E., Prosper, G., & Ogundiran, D. (2020). Preparation of school psychologists to support black students exposed to police violence: Insight and guidance for critical training areas. *Contemporary School Psychology*, 1–17. https://doi.org/10.1007/s40688-020-00317-6

Sabnis, S., Castillo, J. M., & Wolgemuth, J. R. (2020). RTI, equity, and the return to the status quo: Implications for consultants. *Journal of Educational and Psychological Consultation, 30*(3), 285–313. https://doi.org/10.1080/10474412.2019.1674152

Salter, P., & Adams, G. (2013). Toward a critical race psychology. *Social and Personality Psychology Compass*, 7, 781–793. https://doi.org/10.1111/spc3.12068

Skiba, R. J., Arredondo, M. I., & Williams, N. T. (2014). More than a metaphor: The contribution of exclusionary discipline to a school-to-prison pipeline. *Equity & Excellence in Education, 47*(4), 546–564. https://doi.org/10.1080/10665684.2014.958965

Skiba, R. J., Horner, R. H., Choong-Geun, C., Rausch, M. K., May, S. L., & Tobin, T. (2011). Race is not neutral: A national investigation of African American and Latino disproportionality in school discipline. *School Psychology Review, 40*(1), 85–107. https://doi.org/10.1080/02796015.2011.12087730

Song, S., Anderson, J., & Kuvinka, A. (2014). Best practices in conducting school-based action research. *Best Practices in School Psychology: Foundations*, 257–264.

Song, S. Y., Eddy, J. M., Thompson, H. M., Adams, B., & Beskow, J. (2020). Restorative consultation in schools: A systematic review and call for restorative justice science to promote anti-racism and social justice. *Journal of Educational and Psychological Consultation, 30*(4), 462–476. https://doi.org/10.1080/10474412.2020.1819298

Starck, J. G., Riddle, T., Sinclair, S., & Warikoo, N. (2020). Teachers are people too: Examining the racial bias of teachers compared to other American adults. *Educational Researcher, 49*(4), 273–284. https://doi.org/10.3102/0013189x20912758

Teaching Tolerance. (2004). Brown v. Board: Timeline of school integration in the U.S. *Learning for Justice, 2004*(25). www.tolerance.org/magazine/spring-2004/brown-v-board-timeline-of-school-integration-in-the-us

Toporek, R. L., & Daniels, J. (2018). *2018 update and expansion of the 2003 ACA Advocacy Competencies: Honoring the work of the past and contextualizing the present*. American Counseling Association. Alexandria, VA. www.counseling.org/docs/default-source/competencies/aca-advocacy-competencies-updated-may-2020.pdf?sfvrsn=f410212c_4

Turner, E., Malone, C., & Wycoff, K. (2020). Addressing racist policies in children's mental health: The role of psychological science to promote equity in mental health care. *In Balance, 36*, 4–5.

U.S. Department of Education Office of Civil Rights. (2019). *Data highlights on school climate and safety in our nation's public schools. 2015–16 civil rights data collection.* School Climate and Safety. Revised. Office for Civil Rights, US Department of Education. https://www2.ed.gov/about/offices/list/ocr/docs/school-climate-and-safety.pdf

Whitaker, A., Torres-Guillén, S., Morton, M., Jordan, H., Coyle, S., Mann, A., & Sun, W. L. (2019). Cops and no counselors: How the lack of school mental health professionals is harming children. *American Civil Liberties Union.* www.aclu.org/issues/juvenile-justice/school-prison-pipeline/cops-and-no-counselors

INDEX

Page numbers in *italics* indicate a figure and page numbers in **bold** indicate a table on the corresponding page.

Made in United States
North Haven, CT
31 January 2023

31878471R00154